STYLISTICS

Routledge English Language Introductions cover core areas of language study and are one-stop resources for students.

Assuming no prior knowledge, books in the series offer an accessible overview of the subject, with activities, study questions, sample analyses, commentaries and key readings – all in the same volume. The innovative and flexible 'two-dimensional' structure is built around four sections – introduction, development, exploration and extension – which offer self-contained stages for study. Each topic can be read across these sections, enabling the reader to build gradually on the knowledge gained.

Written in a clear and accessible style, *Stylistics, Second Edition* is a comprehensive resource which covers all the major theories, concepts and methods required for the investigation of language in literature. From metre to metaphor, dialogue to discourse, the main topics are introduced and fully elaborated, as are the key research paradigms of this important and exciting field of study. Stylistics is richly illustrated with many examples from literary texts, including writing from the established literary canon alongside more contemporary work in poetry, prose and drama. Each of the book's twelve chapters contains clearly framed suggestions for practical work and is accompanied by an original reading on the relevant topic by a world-renowned scholar.

This exciting new second edition builds on the strengths of the first by adding many fresh exercises and worked examples. It captures the latest major developments in stylistics, such as corpus, cognitive and multimodal approaches to the study of style, and its accompanying website has also been substantially revised to feature, amongst other things, useful links, worked examples and a new web section on style and humour. In addition to the classic readings in stylistics contained in the first edition, the new edition includes a number of recent, stimulating readings by key figures in the contemporary field. Written by an experienced teacher and researcher, this accessible textbook is an essential resource for all students of English language, linguistics and literature.

Paul Simpson is Professor of English Language in the School of English at Queen's University Belfast.

The accompanying website can be found at www.routledge.com/cw/simpson

'This exciting new edition of Paul Simpson's popular *Stylistics* captures the latest developments in the field and provides a comprehensive overview of the subject in a clear, accessible, insightful and innovative way. With updated readings by key figures, abundant exercises and sample analyses, this is a one-stop resource for students interested in the theories, concepts and methods of all the major approaches of stylistics.'

Dan Shen, *Peking University, China*

'The second edition of this extremely useful and readable key textbook has been fully updated to cover all essential topics in stylistics, providing an excellent introduction to the central concepts and a valuable guide to the most significant state-of-the-art ideas in the field. This new edition offers interesting and accessible overviews of all core areas, including the most exciting recent developments in corpus, cognitive and multimodal stylistics, many additional thought-provoking activities, and a well-chosen selection of important readings from major scholars.'

Catherine Emmott, *University of Glasgow, UK*

'This is an engaging and accessible text for both beginners and established scholars in linguistics and literary studies. Simpson persuasively argues for the relevance of stylistics in the modern world and clearly lays out the key principles and analytical tools of the field using excellent illustrative examples. I know of no other book that gives such an elegant and comprehensive overview.'

Rodney Jones, *City University of Hong Kong*

'Paul Simpson's *Stylistics* is a most helpful resource from which EFL learners as well as native speakers of English will benefit. Profound yet exceptionally reader-friendly, the book is an invaluable guide for both students and teachers who are logically led from mastering basics in Introduction, through more advanced applications of the subject in Development, to "field" examples in Exploration and encouragement to read and think more in Extension sections.'

Anna Chesnokova, *Borys Grinchenko Kyiv University, Kiev, Ukraine*

ROUTLEDGE ENGLISH LANGUAGE INTRODUCTIONS

SERIES EDITOR: PETER STOCKWELL

Peter Stockwell is Professor of Literary Linguistics in the School of English Studies at the University of Nottingham, UK, where his interests include sociolinguistics, stylistics and cognitive poetics. His recent publications include *Language in Theory*, Routledge 2005 (with Mark Robson), *Cognitive Poetics: An Introduction*, Routledge 2002, *The Poetics of Science Fiction*, *Investigating English Language* (with Howard Jackson), and *Contextualized Stylistics* (edited with Tony Bex and Michael Burke).

SERIES CONSULTANT: RONALD CARTER

Ronald Carter is Professor of Modern English Language in the School of English Studies at the University of Nottingham, UK. He is the co-series editor of the Routledge Applied Linguistics Series, series editor of Interface and was co-founder of the Routledge Intertext series.

OTHER TITLES IN THE SERIES:

Introducing English Language
Louise Mullany and Peter Stockwell

Language and Power
Paul Simpson and Andrea Mayr

Language and Media
Alan Durant and Marina Lambrou

Sociolinguistics
Peter Stockwell

Pragmatics and Discourse
Joan Cutting

Grammar and Vocabulary
Howard Jackson

Psycholinguistics
John Field

World Englishes
Jennifer Jenkins

History of English
Dan McIntyre

Language in Theory
Mark Robson and Peter Stockwell

Child Language
Jean Stilwell Peccei

Researching English Language
Alison Sealey

English Grammar
Roger Berry

Discourse Analysis
Rodney Jones

Practical Phonetics and Phonology
Beverley Collins and Inger Mees

**For more information on any of these titles, or to order, go to
www.routledge.com/linguistics**

First published 2004

This edition published 2014
by Routledge
2 Park Square, Milton Park, Abingdon, Oxon OX14 4RN

Simultaneously published in the USA and Canada
by Routledge
52 Vanderbilt Avenue, New York, NY 10017

Routledge is an imprint of the Taylor & Francis Group, an informa business

© 2004, 2014 Paul Simpson

British Library Cataloguing in Publication Data
A catalogue record for this book is available from the British Library

Library of Congress Cataloging in Publication Data
Simpson, Paul, 1959–
    Stylistics: a resource book for students/Paul Simpson. – Second edition.
    pages cm. – (Routledge English Language Introductions)
    1. English language – Style – Handbooks, manuals, etc. 2. English language – Rhetoric – Handbooks, manuals, etc. 3. Creative writing – Handbooks, manuals, etc. 4. Style, Literary – Handbooks, manuals, etc. I. Title.
    PE1421.S55 2014
    808–dc23
    2013024189

ISBN: 978–0–415–64496–9 (hbk)
ISBN: 978–0–415–64497–6 (pbk)

Typeset in Minion and Helvetica Neue
by Florence Production Ltd, Stoodeigh, Devon, UK

HOW TO USE THIS BOOK

The Routledge English Language Introductions are 'flexi-texts' that you can use to suit your own style of study. The books are divided into four sections:

A: Introduction – sets out the key concepts for the area of study. The units of this section take you step-by-step through the foundational terms and ideas, carefully providing you with an initial toolkit for your own study. By the end of the section, you will have a good overview of the whole field.

B: Development – adds to your knowledge and builds on the key ideas already introduced. Units in this section might also draw together several areas of interest. By the end of this section, you will already have a good and fairly detailed grasp of the field, and will be ready to undertake your own exploration and thinking.

C: Exploration – provides examples of language data and guides you through your own investigation of the field. The units in this section will be more open-ended and exploratory, and you will be encouraged to try out your ideas and think for yourself, using your newly acquired knowledge.

D: Extension – offers you the chance to compare your expertise with key readings in the area. These are taken from the work of important writers, and are provided with guidance and questions for your further thought.

You can read this book like a traditional textbook, 'vertically' straight through from beginning to end. This will take you comprehensively through the broad field of study. However, the Routledge English Language Introductions have been carefully designed so that you can read them in another dimension, 'horizontally' across the numbered units. For example, units A1, A2, A3 and so on correspond with units B1, B2, B3, and with units C1, C2, C3 and D1, D2, D3, and so on. Reading A5, B5, C5, D5 will take you rapidly from the key concepts of a specific area, to a level of expertise in that precise area, all with a very close focus. You can match your way of reading with the best way that you work.

The glossary/index at the end, together with the suggestions in Further Reading, will help to keep you orientated. Each textbook has a supporting website with extra commentary, suggestions, additional material and support for teachers and students.

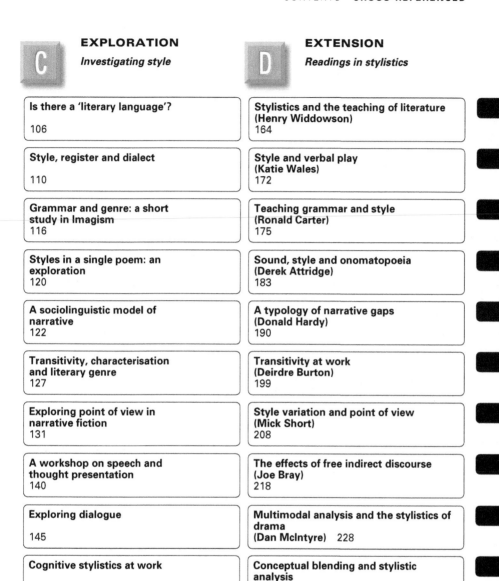

ILLUSTRATIONS

ACKNOWLEDGEMENTS

The authors and publishers would like to thank the following copyright holders for permission to reproduce the following material:

Attridge, Derek, "'Fff! Oo!': Nonlexical onomatopoeia' from *Peculiar Language: Literature as Difference from the Renaissance to James Joyce*, Routledge 2004. Reproduced by permission of Taylor and Francis.

Atwood, Margaret, three lines from an untitled poem 'you are the sun', from *Power Politics* by Margaret Atwood. Reproduced by kind permission of House of Anansi Press.

Banks, Iain, a passage from *The Crow Road*, Abacus 1993. Reproduced by permission of Little, Brown Book Group.

Berkoff, Steven. Two extracts from 'Greek' in *Decadence and Greek*, Calder 1983: 35f. Reproduced by kind permission of Steven Berkoff.

Bray, Joe, 'The Effects of Free Indirect Discourse: Empathy Revisited' from *Contemporary Stylistics* edited by Lambrou, M. and Stockwell, P. Continuum 2007. Reproduced by permission of Continuum.

Burton, Deirdre, 'Through glass darkly: through dark glasses. On stylistic and political commitment – via a study of a passage from Sylvia Plath's "The Bell Jar"' from *Language and Literature: an introductory reader in stylistics*, George Allen and Unwin 1982. Reproduced by permission of Taylor and Francis Ltd.

Carter, Ronald, 'What is stylistics and why can we teach it in different ways?' from *Reading, Analysing and Teaching Literature,* edited by Mick Short. Longman, 1989 161–77. Reproduced by kind permission of Ronald Carter.

Dancygier, Barbara, 'Blending and narrative viewpoint: Jonathan Raban's travels through mental spaces' from *Language and literature 14(2)*, 2005. Reproduced by permission of Sage.

e e cummings, 'love is more thicker than forget' from *Complete Poems, 1904–1962* edited by George J. Firmage. Copyright © 1939, 1967, 1991 by the Trustees for the e. e. Cummings Trust. Reproduced by permission of Liveright Publishing Corporation.

Hardy, Don, 'Towards a typology of narrative gaps: knowledge gapping in Flannery O'Connor's Fiction' in *Language and Literature 14(4)*, 2005. Reproduced by permission of Sage.

Hemingway, Ernest, an extract from *The Old Man and the Sea* published by Jonathan Cape. Reprinted by permission of the Random House Group Limited (UK). Reprinted with the permission of Scribner, a Division of Simon & Schuster, Inc. (US). Copyright © 1952 by Ernest Hemingway. Copyright renewed © 1980 by Mary Hemingway. All rights reserved.

Ionesco, Eugene, excerpt from 'The Bald Prima Donna' In *Plays Volume 1* [Translated by Donald Watson], London 1963 [1958]. Reproduced by kind permission of the publisher.

Jameson, Claudia, an extract from *Escape to Love,* Mills and Boon 1982. Reproduced by kind permission of the publisher.

Longley, Michael, 'The Ghost Orchid', from *The Ghost Orchid,* 1995. Reproduced by kind permission of Random House UK.

Longley, Michael, 'The Comber', from *The Weather in Japan* by Michael Longley. Reproduced by kind permission of Random House.

Lowry, Malcolm, a passage from *Under the Volcano,* Penguin 1984 [1947]. Reproduced by permission.

MacLaverty, Bernard, an extract from *Cal,* Jonathan Cape 1984. Reprinted by permission of The Random House Group Limited.

McEwan, Ian, a passage from *Amsterdam,* Anchor/Vintage Books 1998. Reproduced by permission of Anchor/ Vintage Books.

McGough, Roger, '40-Love' from *In After the Mersey Sound,* Penguin 1971. Reproduced by permission of United Agents.

McIntyre, Dan, 'Integrating multi-modal analysis and the stylistics of drama: a multimodal perspective on Ian McKellen's *Richard III*' from *Language and Literature 17(4),* 2008. Reproduced by permission of Sage.

Mahlberg, Michaela and Smith, Catherine, 'The suspended quotation and the corpus' from *Language and literature, 21(1),* 2012. Reproduced by permission of Sage.

Morgan, Edwin, 'Off Course' from *Poems of Thirty Years,* 1966. Reproduced by kind permission of Carcanet Press Ltd.

Morrison, Toni, a short fragment from *Beloved,* Knopf Publishing Group 1987. Reprinted by kind permission of The Random House Group Limited, New York, International Creative Management and Toni Morrison.

O'Connor, Flannery, extracts from *Collected works,* The Library of America 1988. Reproduced by permission.

Parker, Dorothy, 'One Perfect Rose' from *The Portable Dorothy Parker* by Dorothy Parker, edited by Marion Meade © 1926, renewed 1954. Reproduced by permission of Viking Penguin, a division of Penguin Group (USA) Inc., and Duckworth Publishers.

Passage from the television series *Monty Python's Flying Circus.* The opening of the 'Nudge Nudge' sketch, first broadcast on BBC2 in 1971. Used by kind permission of Python (Monty) Pictures

Pinter, Harold, extract from *The Dumb Waiter,* 1959, 1960 © Faber and Faber. Reproduced by kind permission of Faber and Faber and Grove Atlantic.

Poe, Edgar Allan, 'The Fall of the House of Usher' from *The Fall of the House of Usher and other Writings,* edited by D. Galloway (1986) [1839]. Reproduced by kind permission of Penguin.

Pound, Ezra, 'In a Station of the Metro' from *In A Map of Modern English Verse,* edited by J. Press. © Oxford University Press 1969 [1912].

Short, Mick, 'Graphological deviation, style variation and point of view in Marabou Stork Nightmares by Irvine Welsh' from *Journal of Literary studies/Tydskrif vir literatuurwetenskap 15*, 3/4, 1999. Reproduced by permission of Taylor and Francis Ltd.

Simpson, N. F., a scene from *One Way Pendulum,* Faber and Faber 1960. Reproduced by kind permission of Faber & Faber.

Stockwell, Peter, 'The inflexibility of invariance' by Peter Stockwell. *Language and Literature* 8(2), 1999. Reproduced by kind permission of Sage Publications.

Wales, Katie, 'Zodiac mindwarp meets the horseflies' in *English Today 50–1*, 29th January 1992. Reproduced by kind permission of Cambridge University Press.

Welsh, Irvine, a passage from *Trainspotting,* Minerva 1993. Reproduced by permission of Random House UK.

Welsh, Irvine, an extract from *Marabou Stork Nightmares*, Minerva 1995. Reproduced by kind permission of Random House.

Widdowson, Henry, an extract from *Stylistics and the Teaching of Literature*, Longman 1975.

Winterson, Jeanette, an extract from *Written on the body* © 1992 by Great Moments Ltd. Reproduced by permission of International Creative Management and Alfred A. Knopf, a division of Random House, Inc.

Wolfe, Tom, excerpt from *I am Charlotte Simmons*, Vintage 2004. Reproduced by permission.

Still 1 Shot 17 from *Richard III: Soliloquy* – change of address via change in gaze direction – Shakespeare film adapation, 1995. Reproduced with kind permission of Sage Publications and Sir Ian McKellen.

Three line drawings by Alacoque Davey, reproduced by kind permission of the artist.

While the publishers have made every effort to contact copyright holders of material used in this volume, they would be grateful to hear from any they were unable to contact.

PREFACE TO THE SECOND EDITION

Ten years is a long time in stylistics. Since the publication of the first edition of this book in 2004, the stylistic landscape has changed markedly and my challenge here has been to reflect and accommodate these changes in the discipline. In consequence, this second edition is in its scope a bit more multi-modal, a bit more cognitive and a lot more corpus-assisted. New readings and practical exercises have driven out some of the more theoretical sections that featured in the first edition. Gone – or at least shunted to the web materials that accompany this volume – are some of my 'pet' research interests that in the first edition sat less comfortably beside the more obvious and central components of modern stylistics.

I have many people to thank for the guidance and advice they have offered on this project. Too numerous to mention individually, colleagues and students the world over have provided constructive feedback and vital pointers as to what a textbook in stylistics should accomplish. This advice has extended from comments that informed the inception of the book's first edition to the more recent readers' reports which have shaped the direction of the second. I am grateful in particular to colleagues for keeping me straight on issues of stylistic theory as well as to the many students around the world who have put me right on matters of teaching, application and pedagogy (and for alerting me to more than a few lapses in the original text). I hope the second edition of *Stylistics* does justice to their invaluable support.

Section A

INTRODUCTION

KEY CONCEPTS IN STYLISTICS

WHAT IS STYLISTICS?

Some years ago, the well-known linguist Jean-Jacques Lecercle published a short but damning critique of the aims, methods and rationale of contemporary stylistics. His attack on the discipline, and by implication the entire endeavour of the present book, was uncompromising. According to Lecercle, nobody has ever really known what the term 'stylistics' means, and in any case, hardly anyone seems to care (Lecercle 1993: 14). Stylistics is 'ailing'; it is 'on the wane'; and its heyday, alongside that of structuralism, has faded to but a distant memory. More alarming again, few university students are 'eager to declare an intention to do research in stylistics'. By this account, the death knell of stylistics had been sounded and it looked as though the end of the twentieth century would be accompanied by the inevitable passing of that faltering, moribund discipline. And no one, it seemed, would lament its demise.

Modern stylistics

As it happened, Lecercle could not have been more spectacularly wrong. Stylistics in the twenty-first century is very much alive and well. It is taught and researched in university departments of language, literature and linguistics the world over. The high academic profile it enjoys is mirrored in the number of its dedicated book-length publications, research journals, international conferences and scholarly associations. Far from moribund, modern stylistics is positively flourishing and the lists of almost every major academic publisher are now populated by textbooks, monographs, collections, handbooks, companions and dictionaries of stylistics. Moreover, this exponential growth in academic research is evidenced by a proliferation of subdisciplines, where stylistic methods are enriched and enabled by theories of discourse, culture and society. For example, feminist stylistics, cognitive stylistics and discourse stylistics are established branches of contemporary stylistics that have been sustained by insights from, respectively, feminist theory, cognitive psychology and discourse analysis. And where new techniques and applications have been incorporated into research in linguistics, stylistics has embraced these models in, for example, its subdisciplines of multi-modal stylistics and corpus stylistics.

Stylistics has also become a much-valued method in language teaching and language learning, and stylistics in this 'pedagogical' role, with its close attention to the broad resources of the system of language, enjoys particular pride of place in the linguistic armoury of learners of second languages. Indeed, stylistics in this context is often the 'go to' model for beginning students of English literature – so much so that there are many university departments of English around the world that are now *de facto* departments of stylistics. Finally, stylistics often forms a core component of many contemporary creative writing courses, an application not surprising given the discipline's emphasis on techniques of creativity and invention in language.

So much then for the current 'health' of stylistics and the prominence it enjoys in modern scholarship. It is now time to say a little more about what exactly stylistics is and what it is for. Stylistics is a method of textual interpretation in which primacy of place is assigned to *language*. The reason why language is so important to stylisticians is because the various forms, patterns and levels that constitute linguistic structure are an important index of the function of the text. The text's functional significance as discourse acts in turn as a gateway to its interpretation. While linguistic features do not of themselves constitute a text's 'meaning', an account of linguistic features nonetheless serves to ground a stylistic interpretation and to help explain why, for the analyst, certain types of meaning are possible. The preferred object of study in stylistics is literature, whether that be institutionally sanctioned 'Literature' as high art or more popular 'noncanonical' forms of writing. The traditional connection between stylistics and literature brings with it two important caveats, though. The first is that creativity and innovation in language use should not be seen as the exclusive preserve of literary writing. Many forms of discourse (advertising, journalism, popular music – even casual conversation) often display a high degree of stylistic dexterity, such that it would be wrong to view dexterity in language use as exclusive to canonical literature. The second caveat is that the techniques of stylistic analysis are as much about deriving insights about linguistic structure and function as they are about understanding literary texts. Thus, the question 'What can stylistics tell us about literature?' is always paralleled by an equally important question 'What can stylistics tell us about language?'.

In spite of its clearly defined remit, methods and object of study, there remain a number of myths about contemporary stylistics. Most of the time, confusion about the compass of stylistics is a result of confusion about the compass of language. For instance, there appears to be a belief in many literary critical circles that a stylistician is simply a dull old grammarian who spends rather too much time on such trivial pursuits as counting the nouns and verbs in literary texts. Once counted, those nouns and verbs form the basis of the stylistician's 'insight', although this stylistic insight ultimately proves no more far-reaching than an insight reached by simply intuiting from the text. This is an erroneous perception of the stylistic method and it is one which stems from a limited understanding of how language analysis works. True, nouns and verbs should not be overlooked, nor indeed should 'counting' when it takes the form of directed and focussed quantification (see further strand 12). But the purview of modern language and linguistics is much broader than that and, in response, the methods of stylistics follow suit. It is the full gamut of the system of language that makes all aspects of a writer's craft relevant in stylistic analysis. Moreover, stylistics is interested in language as a function of texts in context, and it acknowledges that utterances (literary or otherwise) are produced in a time, a place, and in a cultural and cognitive context. These 'extra-linguistic' parameters are inextricably tied up with the way a text 'means'. The more complete and context-sensitive the description of language, then the fuller the stylistic analysis that accrues.

The purpose of stylistics

Why should we do stylistics? To do stylistics is to explore language, and, more specifically, to explore creativity in language use. Doing stylistics thereby enriches our ways of thinking about language and, as observed, exploring language offers a substantial purchase on our understanding of (literary) texts. With the full array of language models at our disposal, an inherently illuminating method of analytic inquiry presents itself. This method of inquiry has an important reflexive capacity insofar as it can shed light on the very language system it derives from; it tells us about the 'rules' of language because it often explores texts where those rules are bent, distended or stretched to breaking point. Interest in language is always at the fore in contemporary stylistic analysis which is why you should never undertake to do stylistics unless you are interested in language.

Synthesising more formally some of the observations made above, it might be worth thinking of the practice of stylistics as conforming to the following three basic principles, cast mnemonically as three 'Rs'. The three Rs stipulate that:

- ❏   stylistic analysis should be rigorous
- ❏   stylistic analysis should be retrievable
- ❏   stylistic analysis should be replicable.

To argue that the stylistic method be *rigorous* means that it should be based on an explicit framework of analysis. Stylistic analysis is not the end-product of a disorganised sequence of *ad hoc* and impressionistic comments, but is instead underpinned by structured models of language and discourse that explain how we process and understand various patterns in language. To argue that stylistic method be *retrievable* means that the analysis is organised through explicit terms and criteria, the meanings of which are agreed upon by other students of stylistics. Although precise definitions for some aspects of language have proved difficult to pin down exactly, there is a consensus of agreement about what most terms in stylistics mean (see A2 below). That consensus enables other stylisticians to follow the pathway adopted in an analysis, to test the categories used and to see how the analysis reached its conclusion; to retrieve, in other words, the stylistic method.

To say that a stylistic analysis seeks to be *replicable* does not mean that we should all try to copy each others' work. It simply means that the methods should be sufficiently transparent as to allow other stylisticians to verify them, either by testing them on the same text or by applying them beyond that text. The conclusions reached are principled if the pathway followed by the analysis is accessible and replicable. To this extent, it has become an important axiom of stylistics that it seeks to distance itself from work that proceeds *solely* from untested or untestable intuition.

A seemingly innocuous piece of anecdotal evidence might help underscore this point. I once attended an academic conference where a well-known literary critic referred to the style of Irish writer George Moore as 'invertebrate'. Judging by the delegates' nods of approval around the conference hall, the critic's 'insight' had met with general endorsement. However, novel though this metaphorical interpretation of Moore's style may be, it offers the student of style no retrievable or shared point of reference in language, no *metalanguage*, with which to evaluate what the critic is trying to say. One can only speculate as to what aspect of Moore's style is at issue, because the stimulus for the observation is neither retrievable nor replicable. It is as if the act of criticism itself has become an exercise in style, vying with the stylistic creativity of the primary text discussed. Whatever its principal motivation, that critic's 'stylistic insight' is quite meaningless as a description of style.

Unit A2, below, begins both to sketch some of the broad levels of linguistic organisation that inform stylistics and to arrange and sort the interlocking domains of language study that play a part in stylistic analysis. Along the thread, unit B1 explores further the history and development of stylistics, and examines some of the issues arising. What this opening unit has sought to demonstrate is that in the decades after Lecercle's broadside, stylistics as an academic discipline continues to flourish. In that broadside, Lecercle also contends that the term *stylistics* has 'modestly retreated from the titles of books' (1993: 14). Lest they should feel afflicted by some temporary loss of their faculties, readers might just like to check the accuracy of this claim against the title on the cover of the present textbook!

STYLISTICS AND LEVELS OF LANGUAGE

In view of the comments made in A1 on the methodological significance of the three Rs, it is worth establishing here some of the more basic categories, levels and units of analysis in language that can help organise and shape a stylistic analysis. Language in its broadest conceptualisation is not a disorganised mass of sounds and symbols, but is instead an intricate web of levels, layers and links. Thus, any utterance or piece of text is organised through several distinct *levels of language*.

Levels of language

To start us off, here is a list of the major levels of language and their related technical terms in language study, along with a brief description of what each level covers:

Level of language	Branch of language study
The *sound* of spoken language; the way words are pronounced.	phonology; phonetics
The patterns of *written* language; the shape of language on the page.	graphology
The way words are constructed; words and their constituent structures.	morphology
The way words combine with other words to form phrases and sentences.	syntax; grammar
The words we use; the vocabulary of a language.	lexical analysis; lexicology
The *meaning* of words and sentences.	semantics
The way words and sentences are used in everyday situations; the meaning of language in context.	pragmatics; discourse analysis

These basic levels of language can be identified and teased out in the stylistic analysis of text, which in turn makes the analysis itself more organised and principled, more in keeping so to speak with the principle of the three Rs. However, what is absolutely central to our understanding of language (and style) is that these levels are interconnected: they interpenetrate and depend upon one another, and they represent multiple and simultaneous linguistic operations in the planning and production of an utterance. Consider in this respect an unassuming (hypothetical) sentence like the following:

(1)   **That puppy's knocking over those potplants!**

In spite of its seeming simplicity of structure, this thoroughly innocuous sentence requires for its production and delivery the assembly of a complex array of linguistic components. First, there is the palpable physical substance of the utterance which, when written, comprises *graphetic substance* or, when spoken, *phonetic substance*. This 'raw' matter then becomes organised into linguistic structure proper, opening up the level of *graphology*, which accommodates the systematic meanings encoded in the written medium of language, and *phonology*, which encompasses the meaning potential of the sounds of spoken language. In terms of graphology, this particular sentence is written in the Roman alphabet, and in a 10 point emboldened 'palatino' font. However, as if to echo its counterpart in speech, the sentence-final exclamation mark suggests an emphatic style of vocal delivery. In that spoken counterpart, systematic differences in sound sort out the meanings of the words used: thus, the word-initial /n/ sound at the start of 'knocking' will serve to distinguish it from, say, words like 'rocking' or 'mocking'. To that extent, the *phoneme* /n/ expresses a meaningful difference in sound. The word 'knocking' also raises an issue in *lexicology*: notice for instance how contemporary English pronunciation no longer accommodates the two word-initial *graphemes* <k> and <n> that appear in the spelling of this word. The <kn> sequence – originally spelt <cn> – has become a single /n/ pronunciation, along with equivalent occurrences in other Anglo-Saxon derived lexis in modern English like 'know' and 'knee'. The double consonant pronunciation is however still retained in the vocabulary of cognate languages like modern Dutch; as in 'knie' (meaning 'knee') or 'knoop' (meaning 'knot').

Apart from these fixed features of pronunciation, there is potential for significant variation in much of the *phonetic* detail of the spoken version of example (1). For instance, many speakers of English will not sound in connected speech the 't's of both 'That' and 'potplants', but will instead use 'glottal stops' in these positions. This is largely a consequence of the phonetic environment in which the 't' occurs: in both cases it is followed by a /p/ consonant and this has the effect of inducing a change, known as a 'secondary articulation', in the way the 't' is sounded (Ball and Rahilly 1999: 130). Whereas this secondary articulation is not necessarily so conditioned, the social or regional origins of a speaker may affect other aspects of the spoken utterance. A major regional difference in accent will be heard in the realisation of the historic <r> – a feature so named because it was once, as its retention in the modern spelling of a word like 'over' suggests, common to all accents of English. Whereas this /r/ is still present in Irish and in most American pronunciations, it has largely disappeared in Australian and in most English accents. Finally, the articulation of the 'ing' sequence at the end of the word 'knocking' may also vary, with an 'in' sound indicating a perhaps lower status accent or an informal style of delivery.

The sentence also contains words that are made up from smaller grammatical constituents known as *morphemes*. Certain of these morphemes, the 'root' morphemes, can stand as individual words in their own right, whereas others, such as prefixes and suffixes, depend for their meaning on being conjoined or bound to other items. Thus, 'potplants' has three constituents: two root morphemes ('pot' and 'plant') and a suffix (the plural morpheme 's'), making the word a three morpheme cluster. Moving up from morphology takes us into the domain of language organisation known as the *grammar*, or more appropriately perhaps, given that both lexis and word-structure are normally included in such a description, the *lexico-grammar*. Grammar is organised hierarchically according to the size of the units it contains, and most accounts of grammar would recognise the sentence as the largest unit, with the clause, phrase, word and morpheme following as progressively smaller units (see further A3). Much could be said of the grammar of this sentence: it is a single 'clause' in the indicative declarative mood. It has a Subject ('That puppy'), a Predicator (''s knocking over') and a Complement ('those potplants'). Each of these clause constituents is realised by a phrase which itself has structure. For instance, the verb phrase which expresses the Predicator has a three part structure, containing a contracted auxiliary '[i]s', a main verb 'knocking' and a preposition 'over' which operates as a special kind of extension to the main verb. This extension makes the verb a *phrasal verb*, one test for which is being able to move the extension particle along the sentence to a position beyond the Complement ('That puppy's knocking those potplants over!').

A semantic analysis is concerned with meaning and will be interested, amongst other things, in those elements of language which give the sentence a 'truth value'. A truth value specifies the conditions under which a particular sentence may be regarded as true or false. For instance, in this (admittedly hypothetical) sentence, the lexical item 'puppy' commits the speaker to the fact that a certain type of entity (namely, a young canine animal) is responsible for the action carried out. Other terms, such as the superordinate items 'dog' or even 'animal', would still be compatible in part with the truth conditions of the sentence. That is not to say that the use of a more generalised word like, say, 'animal' will have exactly the same repercussions for the utterance as *discourse* (see further below). In spite of its semantic compatibility, this less specific term would implicate in many contexts a rather negative evaluation by the speaker of the entity referred to. This type of implication is *pragmatic* rather than semantic because it is more about the meaning of language in context than about the meaning of language *per se*. Returning to the semantic component of example (1), the demonstrative words 'That' and 'those' express physical orientation in language by pointing to where the speaker is situated relative to other entities specified in the sentence. This orientational function of language is known as *deixis* (see further A7). In this instance, the demonstratives suggest that the speaker is positioned some distance away from the referents 'puppy' and 'potplants'. The deictic relationship is therefore 'distal', whereas the parallel demonstratives 'This' and 'these' would imply a 'proximal' relationship to the referents.

Above the core levels of language is situated *discourse*. This is a much more open-ended term used to encompass aspects of communication that lie beyond the organisation of sentences. Discourse is context-sensitive and its domain of reference includes pragmatic, ideological, social and cognitive elements in text processing. That means that an analysis of discourse explores meanings which are not retrievable solely through the linguistic analysis of the levels surveyed thus far. In fact, what a sentence 'means' in strictly semantic terms is not necessarily a guarantor of the kind of job it will do as an utterance in discourse. The raw semantic information transmitted by sentence (1), for instance, may only partially explain its discourse function in a specific context of use. To this effect, imagine that (1) is uttered by a speaker in the course of a two-party interaction in the living room of a dog-owning, potplant-owning addressee. Without seeking to detail the rather complex inferencing strategies involved, the utterance in this context is unlikely to be interpreted as a disconnected remark about the unruly puppy's behaviour or as a remark which requires simply a verbal acknowledgment. Rather, it will be understood as a call to action on the part of the addressee. Indeed, it is perhaps the very obviousness in the context of what the puppy is doing *vis-à-vis* the content of the utterance that would prompt the addressee to look beyond what the speaker 'literally' says. The speaker, who, remember, is positioned deictically further away from the referents, may also feel that this discourse strategy is appropriate for a better-placed interlocutor to make the required timely intervention. Yet the same discourse context can produce any of a number of other strategies. A less forthright speaker might employ a more tentative gambit, through something like 'Sorry, but I think you might want to keep an eye on that puppy . . .'. Here, indirection serves a politeness function, although indirection of itself is not always the best policy in urgent situations where politeness considerations can be over-ridden (and see further thread 9). And no doubt even further configurations of participant roles might be drawn up to explore what other discourse strategies can be pressed into service in this interactive context.

Summary

The previous sub-unit is no more than a thumbnail sketch, based on a single illustrative example, of the core levels of language organisation. The account of levels certainly offers a useful springboard for stylistic work, but observing these levels at work in textual examples is more the starting point than the end point of analysis. Later threads, such as 6 and 7, consider how patterns of vocabulary and grammar are sorted according to the various *functions* they serve, functions which sit at the interface between lexico-grammar and discourse. Other threads, such as 10 and 11, seek to take some account of the cognitive strategies that we draw upon to process texts; strategies that reveal that the composition of a text's 'meaning' ultimately arises from the interplay between what's in the text, what's in the context and what's in the mind as well. Finally, it is fair to say that contemporary stylistics ultimately looks towards *language as discourse*: that is, towards a text's status as discourse, a writer's deployment of discourse strategies and towards the way a text 'means' as a function of language in context. This is not for a moment to deny the importance of the core levels of language – the way a text is constructed in language will, after all, have a crucial bearing on the way it functions as discourse.

The interconnectedness of the levels and layers detailed above also means there is no necessarily 'natural' starting point in a stylistic analysis, so we need to be circumspect about those aspects of language upon which we choose to concentrate. Interaction between levels is important: one level may complement, parallel or even collide with another level. To bring this unit to a close, let us consider a brief illustration of how striking stylistic effects can be engendered by offsetting one level of language against another. The following fragment is the first three lines of an untitled poem by Margaret Atwood:

You are the sun
in reverse, all energy
flows into you . . .
             (Atwood 1996: 47)

At first glance, this sequence bears the stylistic imprint of the *lyric poem*. This literary genre is characterised by short introspective texts where a single speaking voice expresses emotions or thoughts, and in its 'love poem' manifestation, the thoughts are often relayed through direct address in the second person to an assumed lover. Frequently, the lyric works through an essentially metaphorical construction whereby the assumed addressee is blended conceptually with an element of nature. Indeed, the lover, as suggested here, is often mapped onto the sun, which makes the sun the 'source domain' for the metaphor (see further thread 11). Shakespeare's sonnet 18, which opens with the sequence 'Shall I compare thee to a summer's day?', is a well-known example of this type of lyrical form.

Atwood however works through this generic convention to create a startling re-orientation in interpretation. In doing so, she uses a very simple stylistic technique, a technique which essentially involves playing off the level of grammar against the level of graphology. Ending the first line where she does, she develops a linguistic *trompe l'oeil* whereby the seemingly complete grammatical structure 'You are the sun' dis-integrates in the second line when we realise that the grammatical Complement (see A3) of the verb 'are' is not the phrase 'the sun' but the fuller, and rather more stark, phrase 'the sun in reverse'. As the remainder of this poem bears out, this is a bitter sentiment, a kind of 'anti-lyric', where the subject of the direct address does not embody the all-fulfilling radiance of the sun but is rather more like an energy-sapping sponge which drains, rather than enhances, the life-forces of nature. And while the initial, positive sense engendered in the first line is displaced by the grammatical 'revision' in the second, the ghost of it somehow remains. Indeed, this particular stylistic pattern works literally to establish, and then reverse, the harmonic coalescence of subject with nature.

All of the levels of language detailed in this unit will feature in various places around this book. The remainder of this thread, across to a reading in D2 by Katie Wales, is concerned with the broad resources that different levels of language offer for the creation of stylistic texture. Unit B2 explores juxtapositions between levels similar in principle to that observed in Atwood and includes commentary on semantics, graphology and morphology. In terms of its vertical progression, this section feeds into further and more detailed introductions to certain core levels of language, beginning below with an introduction to the level of grammar.

A3 GRAMMAR AND STYLE

When we talk of the *grammar* of a language we are talking of a hugely complex set of interlocking categories, units and structures: in effect, the *rules* of that language. In the academic study of language, the expression 'rules of grammar' does not refer to prescriptive niceties, to the sorts of proscriptions that forbid the use of, say, a double negative or a split infinitive. These so-called 'rules' are nothing more than a random collection of *ad hoc* and prejudiced strictures about language use. On the contrary, the genuine grammatical rules of a language are *the* language insofar as they stipulate the very bedrock of its syntactic construction in the same way that the rules of tennis or the rules of chess constitute the core organising principles of those games. This makes grammar somewhat of an intimidating area of analysis for the beginning stylistician because it is not always easy to sort out which aspects of a text's many interlocking patterns of grammar are stylistically salient. We will therefore use this unit to try to develop some useful building blocks for a study of grammar and style. The remainder of this thread examines patterns of grammar in a variety of literary texts, culminating, across in D3, with a reading by Ronald Carter which explores patterns of grammar in a 'concrete' poem by Edwin Morgan. But first, to the basics.

A basic model of grammar

Most theories of grammar accept that grammatical units are ordered hierarchically according to their size. This hierarchy is known as a *rank scale*. As the arrangement below suggests, the rank scale sorts units in a 'consists of' relationship, progressing from the largest down to the smallest:

> sentence (or clause complex)
> clause
> phrase (or group)
> word
> morpheme

As the rank scale indicates, the *morpheme* (see A2 above) is the smallest unit in grammar simply because it has no structure of its own; if it did, it would not be the bottom-most unit on the scale. Arguably the most important unit on the scale is the *clause*. The clause is especially important because it is the site of several important functions in language: it provides *tense*; it distinguishes between positive or negative *polarity*; it provides the core or 'nub' of a proposition in language; and it is where information about grammatical 'mood' (about whether a clause is declarative, interrogative or imperative) is situated. The clause will therefore be the principal focus of interest in the following discussion.

For our purposes, we can distinguish four basic elements of clause structure. These are the *Subject* (S), the *Predicator* (P), the *Complement* (C) and the *Adjunct* (A). Here are some examples of clauses which display an 'SPCA' pattern:

	Subject	Predicator	Complement	Adjunct
(1)	The woman	feeds	those pigeons	regularly.
(2)	Our bull terrier	was chasing	the postman	yesterday.
(3)	The Professor of Necromancy	would wear	lipstick	every Friday.
(4)	The Aussie actress	looked	great	in her latest film.
(5)	The man who came to dinner	was	pretty miserable	throughout the evening.

These examples highlight grammar's capacity to embed units of different sizes within one another. Notice for example how the elements of clause structure are 'filled up' by other units, like words and phrases, which occur lower down on the rank scale. Indeed, it is a defining characteristic of clause structure that its four basic elements are typically realised by certain types of phrases. For instance, the Predicator is always filled by a *verb phrase*. The Subject is typically filled by a *noun phrase* which is a cluster of words in which a noun forms the central component. The key nouns in the phrases which express the Subjects above are, respectively, 'woman', 'terrier', 'Professor', 'actress' and 'man' . The Complement position is typically filled either by a noun phrase or, as in examples (4) and (5), by an *adjective phrase* where an adjective, such as 'great' and 'miserable', features as the prominent constituent in the cluster. Finally, the Adjunct is typically filled either by an *adverb phrase* or by a *prepositional phrase*. The Adjunct elements in examples (1), (2) and (3) are all of the adverbial type. Prepositional phrases, which form the Adjunct element in (4) and (5), are clusters which are fronted by a preposition and which are normally rounded off by a noun or phrase, as in 'in (preposition) her latest film (noun phrase)'. The rule which stipulates that a verb phrase must fill up the Predicator slot is a hard and fast one, whereas the rules about what sorts of phrases go into the other three slots are less absolute and are more about typical tendencies. Later in this unit, a little more will be said about phrases (also known as 'groups') and their significance in stylistic analysis, but for the moment we need to develop further our account of clauses.

Tests for clause constituents

We can test for the Subject, Complement and Adjunct elements of clause structure by asking various questions around the verb – assuming of course that we can find the verb! Here is a list of useful tests for sorting out clause structure:

Finding the Subject: it should answer the question 'who' or 'what' placed *in front of* the verb.

Finding the Complement: it should answer the question 'who' or 'what' placed *after* the verb.

Finding the Adjunct: it should answer questions such as 'how', 'when',
                                'where' or 'why' placed after the verb.

Thus, the test for Subject in example (1) – '*who or what?* feeds those pigeons regularly' – will confirm 'The woman' as the Subject element. Alternatively, the test for Complement in example (2) – 'The man who came to dinner was *what?* throughout the evening' – will confirm the adjective phrase 'pretty miserable' as the Complement.

There is another useful test for elements of clause structure which can also be used to adduce further information about grammatical structure. Although this test will feature in a more directed way in unit B3, it is worth flagging it up here. The test involves adding a 'tag question' to the declarative form of a clause. The examples provided thus far are declarative because all of their Predicator elements come after the Subject, in the form that is standardly (though not always) used for making statements. Adding a tag, which may be of positive or negative polarity, allows the speaker or writer to alter the function of the declarative. Thus:

> (1a)   The woman feeds those pigeons regularly, doesn't she?

> (2a)   Our bull terrier was chasing the postman yesterday, was it?

There are several reasons why the tag is a useful tool for exploring grammatical structure. For one thing, it will always repeat the Subject element as a pronoun ('she', 'it') and it will do this irrespective of how complicated or lengthy the Subject is. It also draws out an important aspect of the Predicator in the form of an auxiliary verb ('does', 'was') which supplies amongst other things important information about tense and 'finiteness' (see further B3 and C3). The slightly awkward thing about the 'tag test' is that the questioning tag inverts the word order and often the polarity of the original clause constituents. However, if you have the good fortune to be Irish, then the Hiberno-English dialect offers an even more straightforward mechanism for testing elements of the clause. Adding an Hiberno-English emphatic tag (eg. 'so she does'; 'so it was') to the end of a declarative will repeat the Subject as a pronoun without affecting word-order or changing the polarity of the original. Thus:

> (3a)   The Professor of Necromancy would wear lipstick every Friday, so she would.

The tag test, whether in the questioning or the emphatic form, still works even when the Subject element is relatively 'heavy'. In a sequence like

> (6)   Mary's curious contention that mackerel live in trees proved utterly
>   unjustified.

the appending of 'did *it*?', 'didn't *it*?' or 'so *it* did' renders down to a simple pronoun the entire sequence 'Mary's curious contention that mackerel live in trees'. This structure, which incidentally contains an embedded clause of its own, is what forms the Subject element in (6).

The tag test can usefully differentiate between other types of grammatical structures. For example, in each of the following two examples, the Subject element is expressed by *two* noun phrases. If this is your book, write in an appropriate tag after each of the examples in the space provided:

(7)   My aunt and my uncle visit the farm regularly, _____

(8)   The winner, a local businesswoman, had donated the prize to charity, _____

Clearly, the application of our 'who or what?' test before the verb will reveal the Subject elements in (7) and (8) straightforwardly enough, but what the tag test further reveals is that the Subjects are of a very different order. In (7), the two noun phrases ('My aunt' and 'my uncle') refer to *different* entities which are brought together by the conjunction 'and'. Notice how the tag will yield a plural pronoun: 'don't *they*?' or 'so *they* do'. The grammatical technique of drawing together different entities in this manner is known as *coordination* (and see further B3). In the second example, the tag test brings out a singular pronoun only ('had *she*?', 'so *she* had') which shows that in fact the two phrases 'The winner' and 'a local businesswoman' refer in different ways to the *same* entity. The term for a grammatical structure which makes variable reference to the same entity is known as *apposition*.

Variations in basic clause structure

Whereas most of the examples provided so far exhibit a basic SPCA pattern of clause structure, it is important to note that this configuration represents only one of a number of possible combinations. Other types of grammatical *mood*, for example, involve different types of clausal patterning. A case in point is the *imperative*, which is the form typically used for requests and commands. Imperative clauses like 'Mind your head' or 'Turn on the telly, please' have no Subject element, a knock-on effect of which is that their verb always retains its base form and cannot be marked for tense. *Interrogatives*, the form typically used for asking questions, do contain Subject elements. However, many types of interrogative position part of the Predicator in front of the Subject thus:

(3b)   Would the Professor of Necromancy wear lipstick every Friday?

When there isn't enough Predicator available to release a particle for the pre-Subject position, a form of the pro-verb 'do' is brought into play:

(1b)   Does the woman feed those pigeons regularly?

By way of footnote, the use of the verb 'do' for this purpose is a relatively recent development in the history of English language. In early Modern English, the SP sequence was often simply inverted to make an interrogative, as in the following absurdly anachronistic transposition of (4):

(4a)   Looked the Aussie actress great in her latest film?

Declarative clauses may themselves display significant variation around the basic SPCA pattern. Pared down to its grammatical bare bones, as it were, a clause may realise S and P elements only, as in 'The train arrived' or 'The lesson began'. Occasionally a clause may contain two Complements. This occurs when one of the C elements is a 'direct object' and the other an 'indirect object', as in 'Mary gave her friend a book' or 'Bill told the children a story'. Notice however that both examples will still satisfy our test for Complement in that the test question is answered *twice* in each case: 'Mary gave *who? what?*', 'Bill told *who? what?*'.

✪ Activity

Adjunct elements are many and varied in terms of the forms they take and of the type of information they bring to a clause. They basically describe the *circumstances* (see A6) that attach to the process related by the clause and for that reason they can often be removed without affecting the grammaticality of the clause as a whole. Here is an example of a clause with an SPAAAA pattern. Try to sort out the four Adjuncts it contains by asking the test questions: 'how?' 'where?' 'when?' and 'why?':

(10) Mary awoke suddenly in her hotel room one morning because of a knock on the door.

What the forgoing discussion illustrates is that, strictly speaking, neither the Subject, Complement nor Adjunct elements are essential components of clause structure. The situation regarding the Predicator element is not quite so clear-cut, however, and there has been much debate among grammarians about the status of 'P-less' structures. Impacting on this is the fact that much of our everyday language use involves a type of grammatical abbreviation known as *ellipsis*. For instance, if A asks 'Where are the keys?' and B answers 'In your pocket!', then B's response, while lacking a Predicator, still implicitly retains part of the structure of the earlier question. In other words, even though B's elliptical reply amounts to no more than a simple prepositional phrase, it still presupposes the elements of a full-blown clause. The term *minor clause* is conventionally used to describe structures, like this one, which lack a Predicator element. It is important to acknowledge minor clauses not only because these elliptical structures play an important role in much spoken interaction but also because, as the other units in this thread will argue, they form an important locus for stylistic experimentation. Finally, as a general rule of thumb, when analysing elements which *are* present in a text, there can only be one Subject element and one Predicator element of structure in any given clause. There may however be up to two Complement elements and any number of Adjunct elements.

Quite how clause structure and other types of grammatical patterning function as markers of style will be the focus of attention across the remainder of this strand, and indeed for part of unit C4 also. Next up in this introductory section of the book is the topic of sound and rhythm as it intersects with style in language. The following unit introduces therefore some key concepts used by stylisticians in their investigations of phonology and metrical patterning.

RHYTHM AND METRE   A4

Literature is, by definition, written language. This truism might suggest then that literature is not a medium especially well suited to exploration either at the linguistic level of phonology or in terms of its phonetic substance. However, sound patterning plays a pivotal role in literary discourse in general, and in poetry in particular. Attention has been given elsewhere (unit C2) to the techniques writers use for representing *accent*, one aspect of spoken discourse, in prose fiction. This unit deals more directly with the issue of sound patterning in literature and it introduces core features, like *rhythm* and *metre*, which have an important bearing on the structure and indeed interpretation of poetry.

Metre
When we hear someone reading a poem aloud, we tend to recognise very quickly that it is poem that is being read and not another type of text. Indeed, even if the listener cannot make out or, as is often the case for young readers, the listener doesn't understand all the words of the text, they still know that they are listening to poetry. One reason why this rather unusual communicative situation should arise is because poetry has *metre*. A pivotal criterion for the definition of verse, metre is, most simply put, an organised pattern of strong and weak syllables. Key to the definition is the proviso that metrical patterning should be *organised*, and in such a way that the alternation between accentuated syllables and weak syllables is repeated. That repetition, into a regular phrasing across a line of verse, is what makes *rhythm*. Rhythm is therefore a patterned movement of pulses in time which is defined both by periodicity (it occurs at regular time intervals) and repetition (the same pulses occur again and again).

Let us now try to work through these rather abstract definitions of metre and rhythm using some textual examples. In metrics, the *foot* is the basic unit of analysis and it refers to the span of stressed and unstressed syllables that forms a rhythmical pattern. Different sorts of metrical feet can be determined according to the number of, and ordering of, their constituent stressed and unstressed syllables. An *iambic* foot, for example, has two syllables, of which the first is less heavily stressed than the second (a 'de-dum' pattern, for want of a more formal typology). The *trochaic* foot, by contrast, reverses the pattern, offering a 'dum-de' style of metre. Here is a well-known example of the first type, a line from Thomas Gray's 'Elegy Written in a Country Churchyard' (1751):

(1)   The ploughman homeward plods his weary way

In the following annotated version of (1), the metrical feet are segmented off from one another by vertical lines. Positioned below the text are two methods for capturing the alternation between strong (s) and weak (w) syllables:

(1a) The plough I man home I ward plods I his wea I ry way
        w   s   w   s   w   s   w   s   w   s
        de dum   de   dum   de   dum   de dum de dum

As there are five iambs in the line, this metrical scheme is *iambic pentameter*. Had there been six feet, it would have been iambic *hexameter*, four feet, iambic *tetrameter*, three feet . . . well, you can work out the rest by yourself. What is especially important about metre, as this breakdown shows, is that it transcends the lexico-grammar (see A2). Metrical boundaries are no respecters of word boundaries, a consequence of which is that rhythm provides an additional layer of meaning potential that can be developed along Jakobson's 'axis of combination' (see B1). That extra layer can either enhance a lexico-grammatical structure, or rupture and fragment it. In respect of this point, it is worth noting the other sound imagery at work in the line from Gray. *Alliteration* is a type of rhyme scheme which is based on similarities between consonants. Although rhyme is normally thought of as a feature of line endings, the internal alliterative rhyme in (1) picks out and enhances the balancing halves of the line through the repetition of, first, the /pl/ in 'ploughman' and 'plods' and, later, the /w/ in 'weary' and 'way'. In terms of its impact on grammatical structure, the first repetition links both Subject and Predicator (see A3), while the /w/ consolidates the Complement element of the clause; taken together, both patterns give the line an *acoustic punctuation*, to use Carter and Nash's term (Carter and Nash 1990: 120). A rearrangement of the line into a structure like the following

(1b) The ploughman plods his weary way homeward

will make the acoustic punctuation redundant because the Adjunct 'homeward', which had originally separated the Subject and Complement, is simply no longer there. And of course, this rearrangement collapses entirely the original metrical scheme.

Here are some more examples of metrical patterning in verse. The following fragment from Tennyson's *Lady of Shallott* (1832) is a good illustration of a trochaic pattern:

(2) By the margin, willow veiled
     Slide the heavy barges trailed

Using our model of analysis, the first line of the couplet can be set out thus

(2a) By   the I margin I willow I veiled
        s   w   s   w   s   w   s   w
       dum de   dum de dum de dum de

and this will reveal, amongst other things, that (2) is an example of trochaic *tetrameter*.

The following line from W. H. Auden's poem 'The Quarry' represents another, slightly more complicated, type of versification:

(3) O what is that sound that so thrills the ear

This sequence, on my reading of it, begins with an *offbeat*. An offbeat is an unstressed syllable which, depending on the metrical structure of the line as a whole, is normally placed at the start or the end of a line of verse. In the initial position, an offbeat can act like a little phonetic springboard that helps us launch into the metrical scheme proper. Here is a suggested breakdown of the Auden line:

(3a)   O | what is that | sound that so | thrills the ear
       w   s   w   w   s   w   w   s   w   w
       de dum de de   dum de de dum de de

Here the three metrical feet contain three beats apiece, and in a strong-weak-weak configuration which is known as a *dactyl*. That makes the line as whole an example of *dactylic trimeter*.

Issues

The example from Auden raises an interesting issue to do with metrical analysis. I am sure that for many readers their scansion of (3) brings out a different metrical pattern, with stress on words other than or in addition to those highlighted in (3a). A strong pulse might for example be preferred on 'ear', giving the line an 'end-weight' focus, or maybe even on 'so' which would allow extra intensity to be assigned to the process of thrilling. In spite of what many metricists suggest, metrical analysis is not an exact science, and these alternative readings are in my view perfectly legitimate. Basically, while conventional phrasing dictates certain types of metrical scheme, readers of poetry have a fair amount of choice about exactly how and where to inflect a line of verse.

A contributing factor in reader choice is that the distinction between strong and weak syllables is relative, and not absolute. Consider again the line from Shakespeare's sonnet 18 which was mentioned briefly in unit A2:

(4)   Shall I | compare | thee to | a sum | mer's day?

The line's five metrical feet, with stress falling on the second element, clearly make it iambic pentameter. However, this classification tends to assume that all accentuation is equal, an interpretation which is not necessarily borne out when reading the line aloud. Whereas in the fourth foot ('a sum') the contrast in stress is clear, in the first foot ('Shall I'), the second beat is only marginally more accentuated, if at all, than the first beat. The second foot ('compare') exhibits a degree of contrast somewhere between the fourth and the second, while the third foot seems to have little accentuation on either syllable. In other words, there are about four *degrees* of accentuation in this line, which we might order numerically thus:

(4)   Shall I | compare | thee to | a sum | mer's day?
         3   4   1   4   1   2   1   4   1   4

Although the degree of contrast within metrical feet may be variable, what is important in metrical analysis is that the contrast itself be there in the first place, whatever the relative strength or weakness of its individual beats. (See further Fraser 1970: 3–7)

embellishment, and so risks attracting a rebuke like 'so what?' from an interlocutor. Reading between the lines of Labov's study, the narrator of (2) seems to have felt some discomfort about the episode narrated and was therefore rather reluctantly lured into telling the story. It may have been this factor which constrained the development of a fully articulated narrative.

There is clearly, then, more to a narrative than just a sequence of basic clauses of the sort evidenced in examples (1) and (2). However, the task of providing a full and rigorous model of narrative discourse has proved somewhat of a challenge for stylisticians. There is much disagreement about how to isolate the various units which combine to form, say, a novel or short story, just as there is about how to explain the interconnections between these narrative units. Moreover, in the broad communicative event that is narrative, narrative *structure* is only one side of a coin of which narrative *comprehension* is the other (see further thread 10). Allowing then that a fully comprehensive description is not achievable, the remainder of this introductory unit will establish the core tenets only of a suggested model of narrative structure. It will point out which type of individual stylistic framework is best suited to which particular unit in the narrative model and will also signal whereabouts in this book each of the individual units will be explored and illustrated.

It is common for much work in stylistics and narratology to make a primary distinction between two basic components of narrative: narrative *plot* and narrative *discourse*. The term *plot* is generally understood to refer to the abstract storyline of a narrative; that is, to the sequence of elemental, chronologically ordered events which create the 'inner core' of a narrative. Narrative *discourse*, by contrast, encompasses the manner or means by which that plot is narrated. Narrative discourse, for example, is often characterised by the use of stylistic devices such as flashback, prevision and repetition – all of which serve to disrupt the basic chronology of the narrative's plot. Thus, narrative discourse represents the realised text, the palpable piece of language which is produced by a story-teller in a given interactive context.

The next step involves sorting out the various stylistic elements which make up narrative discourse. To help organise narrative analysis into clearly demarcated areas of study, let us adopt the model shown in Figure A5.1.

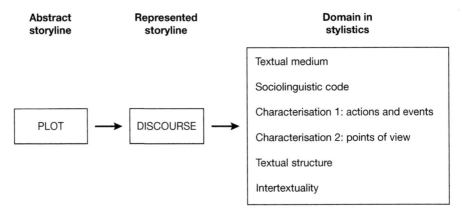

Figure A5.1 A model of narrative structure

Beyond the plot–discourse distinction, the categories towards the right of the diagram constitute six basic units of analysis in narrative description. Although there are substantial areas of overlap between these units, they nonetheless offer a useful set of reference points for pinpointing the specific aspects of narrative which can inform a stylistic analysis. Some further explanation of the units themselves is in order.

The first of the six is *textual medium*. This refers simply to the physical channel of communication through which a story is narrated. Two common narrative media are film and the novel, although various other forms are available such as the ballet, the musical or the strip cartoon. The examples cited thus far in this unit represent another common medium for the transmission of narrative experience: spoken verbal interaction. The concept of textual medium, in tandem with the distinction between plot and discourse, is further explored in B5.

Sociolinguistic code expresses through language the historical, cultural and linguistic setting which frames a narrative. It locates the narrative in time and place by drawing upon the forms of language which reflect this sociocultural context. Sociolinguistic code encompasses, amongst other things, the varieties of accent and dialect used in a narrative, whether they be ascribed to the narrator or to characters within the narrative, although the concept also extends to the social and institutional registers of discourse deployed in a story. This particular narrative resource is further explored in C2.

The first of the two characterisation elements, *actions and events*, describes how the development of character precipitates and intersects with the actions and events of a story. It accounts for the ways in which the narrative intermeshes with particular kinds of semantic process, notably those of 'doing', 'thinking' and 'saying', and for the ways in which these processes are attributed to characters and narrators. This category, which approaches narrative within the umbrella concept of 'style as choice', is the main focus of attention across the units in strand 6.

The second category of narrative characterisation, *point of view*, explores the relationship between mode of narration and a character's or narrator's 'point of view'. Mode of narration specifies whether the narrative is relayed in the first person, the third person or even the second person, while point of view stipulates whether the events of story are viewed from the perspective of a particular character or from that of an omniscient narrator, or indeed from some mixture of the two. The way speech and thought processes are represented in narrative is also an important index of point of view, although this stylistic technique has a double function because it relates to actions and events also. Point of view in narrative is examined across strand 7, while speech and thought presentation is explored in strand 8.

Textual structure accounts for the way individual narrative units are arranged and organised in a story. A stylistic study of textual structure may focus on large-scale elements of plot or, alternatively, on more localised features of story's organisation; similarly, the particular analytic models used may address broad-based aspects of narrative coherence or they may examine narrower aspects of narrative cohesion in organisation. Textual structure (as it organises narrative) is the centre of interest in units B5 and C5, while the reading that rounds off this strand, by Donald Hardy, probes a key stylistic feature of narrative structure, the *narrative gap*.

The term *intertextuality*, the sixth narrative component, is reserved for the technique of 'allusion'. Narrative fiction, like all writing, does not exist in a social and historical vacuum, and it often echoes other texts and images either as 'implicit' intertextuality or as 'manifest' intertextuality. In a certain respect, the concept of intertextuality overlaps with the notion of sociolinguistic code in its application to narrative, although the former involves the importing of other, external texts while the latter refers more generally to the variety or varieties of language in and through which a narrative is developed. Both of these constituents feature in units C1 and C2.

A6   STYLE AS CHOICE

Much of our everyday experience is shaped and defined by actions and events, thoughts and perceptions, and it is an important function of the system of language that it is able to account for these various 'goings on' in the world. This means encoding into the grammar of the clause a mechanism for capturing what we say, think and do. It also means accommodating in grammar a host of more abstract relations, such as those that pertain between objects, circumstances and logical concepts. When language is used to represent the goings on of the physical or abstract world in this way, to represent patterns of experience in spoken and written texts, it fulfils the *experiential* function. The experiential function is an important marker of style, especially so of the style of narrative discourse, because it emphasises the concept of *style as choice*. There are many ways of accounting in language for the various events that constitute our 'mental picture of reality' (Halliday 1994: 106); indeed, there are often several ways of using the resources of the language system to capture the *same* event in a textual representation. What is of interest to stylisticians is why one type of structure should be preferred to another, or why, from possibly several ways of representing the same 'happening', one particular type of depiction should be privileged over another. Choices in style are motivated, even if unconsciously, and these choices have a profound impact on the way texts are structured and interpreted.

✪ Activity   A short illustrative exercise might help underscore this idea of 'choice' in textual representation. First of all, look closely at the three line drawings, A, B and C, which are arranged on the next page in chronological sequence. Then write down a short narrative, of no more than five sentences, describing what you see in the pictures. We shall have cause to return to this exercise in other places in the book (C7, C12), so a stylistic analysis will not be offered here. However, you might at this stage want to reflect on some aspects of your composition. For example, did you give a name to the particular activity portrayed? Did you use any technical vocabulary to refer to the paraphernalia of the activity portrayed? Did you attempt to locate the three pictures in a particular place or time? And did you decide to make up names for the two protagonists depicted?

The particular grammatical facility used for capturing experience in language is the system of *transitivity*. In the present account, the concept of 'transitivity' is used in an

A

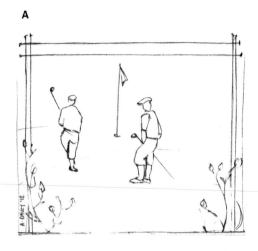

B

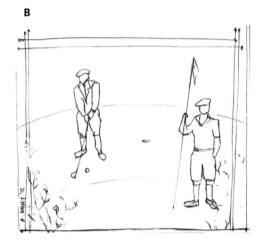

C

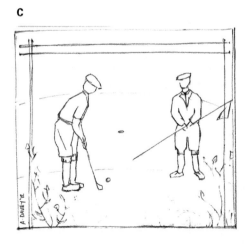

expanded semantic sense, much more so than in traditional grammars where it simply serves to identify verbs which take direct objects. Transitivity here refers to the way meanings are encoded in the clause and to the way different types of *process* are represented in language. Transitivity normally picks out three key components of processes. The first is the process itself, which is typically realised in grammar by the *verb phrase* (see A3). The second is the *participant(s)* associated with the process, typically realised by *noun phrases*. Perhaps less importantly for stylistic analysis, transitivity also picks out the *circumstances* associated with the process. This third element is typically expressed by *prepositional* and *adverb* phrases which, as we saw in A3, fill up the Adjunct element in clause structure.

Linguists working with this functional model of transitivity are divided about how exactly to 'carve up' the experiential function. How many sorts of experience, for example, should the system distinguish? How easy is it to place discrete boundaries around certain types of human experiences when those experiences tend to overlap or shade into one another? In the brief account of transitivity that follows, six types of process are identified, although the divisions between these processes will always be more provisional than absolute.

Material processes, the first of the six, are simply processes of *doing*. Associated with material processes are two inherent participant roles which are the *Actor*, an obligatory role in the process, and a *Goal*, a role which may or may not be involved in the process. The following two examples of material processes follow the standard notation conventions which place the textual example above its individual transitivity roles:

(1)   I   nipped   Daniel.
      Actor   Process   Goal

(2)   The washing machine   broke down.
      Actor   Process

Mental processes constitute the second key process of the transitivity system and are essentially processes of *sensing*. Unlike material processes which have their provenance in the physical world, mental processes inhabit and reflect the world of consciousness, and involve cognition (encoded in verbs such as 'thinking' or 'wondering'), reaction (as in 'liking' or 'hating') and perception (as in 'seeing' or 'hearing'). The two participant roles associated with mental processes are the Sensor (the conscious being that is doing the sensing) and the Phenomenon (the entity which is sensed, felt, thought or seen). Here are illustrations of the three main types of mental process:

(3)   Mary   understood   the story.   (cognition)
      Sensor   Process   Phenomenon

(4)   Anil   noticed   the damp patch.   (perception)
      Sensor   Process   Phenomenon

(5)   Siobhan   detests   paté.   (reaction)
      Sensor   Process   Phenomenon

The roles of Sensor and Phenomenon relate exclusively to mental processes. This distinction is necessary because the entity 'sensed' in a mental process is not directly affected by the process, and this makes it of a somewhat different order to the role of Goal in a material process. It is also an important feature of the semantic basis of the transitivity system that the participant roles remain constant under certain types of grammatical operation. Example (5), for instance, might be rephrased as 'Paté disgusts Siobhan', yet 'Siobhan' still remains the Sensor and 'Paté' the Phenomenon.

A useful check which often helps distinguish material and mental processes is to test which sort of present tense best suits the particular example under analysis. The 'natural' present tense for mental processes is the simple present, so the transformation of the past tense of example (3) would result in 'Mary understands the story'. By contrast, material processes normally gravitate towards the present continuous tense, as in the transposition of (2) to 'The washing machine is breaking down'. When transposed to the present continuous, however, mental processes often sound odd: 'Siobhan is detesting paté', 'Anil is noticing the damp patch' and so on.

There is a type of process which to some extent sits at the interface between material and mental processes, a process which represents both the activities of 'sensing' and 'doing'. *Behavioural* processes embody physiological actions like 'breathe' or 'cough', although they sometimes portray these processes as states of consciousness as in 'sigh', 'cry' or 'laugh'. They also represent processes of consciousness as forms of behaviour, as in 'stare', 'dream' or 'worry'. The key (and normally sole) participant in behavioural processes is the Behaver, the conscious entity who is 'behaving':

(6)	That student	fell asleep	in my lecture again.
	Behaver	Process	Circumstance

(7)	She	frowned	at the mess.
	Behaver	Process	Circumstances

The role of Behaver is very much like that of a Sensor, although the behavioural process itself is grammatically more akin to a material process. Thus, while both examples above display many of the characteristics of mental processes, our 'tense' test satisfies the criteria for material processes: 'That student is falling asleep . . .'; 'She is frowning . . .'. Admittedly, the distinction in meaning between mental and behavioural processes is often very slight, but a recent advertisement for the BBC's classical music station, Radio 3, is a beautifully nuanced illustration, respectively, of the two types of process: 'It's amazing what you *hear* when you *listen*'.

Close in sense to mental processes, insofar as they articulate conscious thought, are processes of *verbalisation*. These are processes of 'saying' and the participant roles associated with verbalisation are the Sayer (the producer of the speech), the Receiver (the entity to which the speech is addressed) and the Verbiage (that which gets said). Thus:

(8)	Mary	claimed	that the story had been changed.
	Sayer	Process	Verbiage

(9) The minister announced the decision to parliament.
     Sayer   Process   Verbiage   Receiver

Notice how the Verbiage participant, which, incidentally, is not a term used in any derogatory sense, can cover either the 'content' of what was said (as in 8) or the 'name', in speech act terms, of what was said (as in 9). It is also important to note that the process of saying needs to be interpreted rather broadly, so that even an inanimate Sayer can be accommodated: 'The notice said be quiet'.

Now to an important and deceptively complex category: *relational processes*. These are processes of 'being' in the specific sense of establishing relationships between two entities. Relational processes can be expressed in a number of ways, and not all of the numerous classifications which present themselves can be accommodated here. There is however general agreement about three main types of relational process. An *intensive* relational process posits a relationship of equivalence, an 'x *is* y' connection, between two entities, as in: 'Paula's presentation was lively' or 'Joyce is the best Irish writer'. A possessive relational process plots an 'x *has* y' type of connection between two entities, as in 'Peter has a piano' or 'The Alfa Romeo is Clara's'. Thirdly, *circumstantial* relational processes are where the circumstantial element becomes upgraded, as it were, so that it fulfils the role of a full participant in the process. The relationship engendered is a broad 'x *is at/is in/is on/is with/* y' configuration, realised in constructions like 'The fête is on all day', 'The maid was in the parlour' or 'The forces of darkness are against you'.

This seemingly straightforward three-way classification is rather complicated by the fact that it intersects with another distinction between *attributive* and *identifying* relational processes. This means that each of the three types come in two modes, yielding six categories in total. The grid shown in Table A6.1 will help summarise this classification. In the attributive mode, the entity, person or concept being described is referred to as the Carrier, while the role of Attribute refers to the quality ascribed to that Carrier. The Attribute therefore says what the Carrier is, what the Carrier is like, where the Carrier is, what it owns and so on. In the identifying mode, one role is identified through reference to another such that the two halves of the clause often refer to the same thing.

Table A6.1 Relational processes grid

Type	Mode attributive	identifying
intensive	Paula's presentation was lively	The best Irish writer is Joyce Joyce is the best Irish writer
possessive	Peter has a piano	The Alfa Romeo is Clara's Clara's is the Alfa Romeo
circumstantial	The fête is on all day	The maid is in the parlour In the parlour is the maid

This means that unlike attributive processes, all identifying processes are reversible, as the grid above shows. In terms of their participant roles, one entity (the Identifier) picks out and defines the other (the Identified). Thus, in the pattern:

(10)	Joyce	is	the best Irish writer
	Identified	Process	Identifier

the sequence 'the best Irish writer' functions to identify 'Joyce' as the key representative of a particular class of individuals. The alternative pattern, 'The best Irish writer is Joyce', simply reverses the sequence of these two participant roles.

Existential processes constitute the sixth and last category of the transitivity model. Close in sense to relational processes, these processes basically assert that something exists or happens. Existential processes typically include the word 'there' as a dummy subject, as in 'There was an assault' or 'Has there been a phone call?', and they normally only contain one participant role, the 'Existent', realised respectively in these examples by 'an assault' and 'a phone call'.

In another sense, the existential process leads us right back to the material process, the category with which we began this review of the system of transitivity. Significantly, both types of process can often accommodate a question like 'what happened?', the response to which results in two possible configurations. Thus, both 'X assaulted Y' and 'There was an assault' would offer a choice of responses to this hypothetical question. However, what happens in the existential version is that no role other than Existent is specified, and that role, moreover, is filled by a *nominalised* element which is created by converting a verbal process into a noun (see C3).

It is worth reemphasising this idea of 'style as choice' in transitivity, and in this respect consider an anecdotal example. When questioned about some rowdiness that resulted in a slight injury to his younger brother, my (then five year old) son replied: 'There was a nip'. This is an interesting experiential strategy because it satisfies the question 'what happened' while simultaneously avoiding any material process that would support an explicit Actor role. It manages in other words to sidestep precisely the configuration displayed in example (1) above, 'I nipped Daniel', where the role of Actor is conflated with the speaker. Another strategy might have been to create a passive, as opposed to active, construction, wherein the Goal element is brought into Subject position and the Actor element removed from the clause entirely ('Daniel was nipped'). However, because the passive still supports the question 'by whom?', this configuration retains a degree of *implicit* agency. The general point is that transitivity offers systematic choice, and any particular textual configuration is only one, perhaps strategically motivated, option from a pool of possible textual configurations.

The core processes of transitivity, arranged so as to capture their interrelationship to one another, are summarised in Figure A6.1. The transitivity model has proved an important methodological tool in stylistics and in more general investigations of text. The remainder of this strand surveys some developments in this area and goes on to examine patterns of transitivity in a variety of texts. The thread concludes with a reading by Deirdre Burton (D6) which applies the model to a passage from Sylvia Plath's novel *The Bell Jar*.

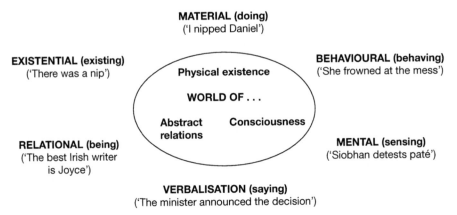

Figure A6.1   A model of transitivity

A7   **STYLE AND POINT OF VIEW**

The *perspective* through which a story is told constitutes an important stylistic dimension not only in prose fiction but in many types of narrative text. Much of the feel, colour or texture of a story is a direct consequence of the sort of narrative framework it employs. A story may for instance be told in the first person and from the viewing position of a participating character-narrator whose account of actions and events is the one we must as readers share. Alternatively, the story might be narrated in the third person by a detached, invisible narrator whose 'omniscience' facilitates privileged access to the thoughts and feelings of individual characters. Yet further permutations are possible. We may encounter a kind of 'restricted omniscience' where a third-person narrator, although external to the action of the story, comes across as unable or reluctant to delve at will into the thoughts and feelings of characters. These issues of narrative organisation are very much at the heart of story-telling and, as noted in A5, function as an important index of characterisation in fiction. The umbrella term reserved for this aspect of narrative organisation is *point of view*.

Point of view in fiction

Much has been written on point of view by stylisticians and narratologists, such that there is now a proliferation of often conflicting theories, terms and models. In these circumstances, the best way to develop an introduction to point of view will be by going straight to a textual example from which can be garnered some basic categories and principles. Below is a passage from Iain Banks's novel *The Crow Road* which raises a number of interesting general issues concerning point of view in fiction. Kenneth McHoan, one of the novel's central characters, has just returned from

university to his home town of Gallanach, and this episode details his arrival in the
rural village station.

> He rested his arms on the top of the wall and looked down the fifty feet or so to the
> tumbling white waters. Just upstream, the river Loran piled down from the forest in a
> compactly furious cataract. The spray was a taste. Beneath, the river surged round the
> piers of the viaduct that carried the railway on towards Lochgilpead and Gallanach.
>   A grey shape flitted silently across the view, from falls to bridge, then zoomed, turned
> in the air and swept into the cutting on the far bank of the river, as though it was a soft
> fragment of the train's steam that had momentarily lost its way and was not hurrying to
> catch up. He waited a moment, and the owl hooted once, from inside the dark constituency
> of the forest. He smiled, took a deep breath that tasted of steam and the sweet sharpness
> of pine resin, and then turned away, and went back to pick up his bags.
>
>   (Banks 1993: 33)

A good general technique for the exploration of point of view in a piece of narrative
is to imagine it as if you were preparing to film it. That is, try to conceive a particular
episode, as a director might, in terms of its visual perspective, its various vantage points
and viewing positions. There are often clear textual clues about where to point your
camera, so to speak, and about how a visual sequence should unfold. This passage works
extremely well in this respect insofar as it abounds in point of view markers that work
to structure the panoramic sweep of the narrative camera. There will be more on these
markers shortly, but a feature of more general interest is the way this passage offers an
almost model explication of a core distinction in point of view theory. This is the
distinction in a story between *who tells* and *who sees*. It is clear from this passage that
whereas a detached, omniscient narrator *tells* the story, it is a particular character who
sees the unfolding scene described. Although this is not the pattern for the whole of
Banks's novel – most of it is written in the first person, in fact – there is a marked
limiting of narrative perspective, in this instance at least, to that of an individual
character within the story. We see what McHoan sees, and we see it in the gradual and
accumulative unfolding of the focal points that are reflected in his visual purview.
Following the relevant terminology, that makes the character of McHoan, even if
momentarily, the *reflector of fiction*.

Even working from so short an extract, there is much more that can be said on the
general dynamic of point of view in narrative fiction. We have established that the third
person narrator is external, detached, situated outside the story as such. In the sense
that its narrator is 'different' from the exegesis that comprises the story, this makes
the narrative *heterodiegetic*. However, had the events described been narrated directly
in the first person by McHoan himself, the narrative would be *homodiegetic*.
A homodiegetic narrator is one who is internal to the narrative, who is on the 'same'
plane of exegesis as the story.

The distinction between heterodiegesis and homodiegesis can be explored by
transposing the text between first-person and third-person modes of narration. This
is a very useful exercise in terms of what it can reveal about point of view, and it is
often surprisingly easy to carry out a transposition in those instances where a third

person narrative employs a reflector of fiction. Converting the character of McHoan into an internal, homodiegetic narrator requires very little alteration to the text. Indeed, most of the passage can stay exactly as it is, as this checklist of third-to-first-person transpositions shows:

> I rested **my** arms on the top of the wall [. . .] I waited a moment [. . .] I smiled, took a deep breath [. . .] and went back to pick up **my** bags.

The smoothness and facility of transposition shows just how strongly in the reflector mode the original passage is; in effect, nothing is narrated that has not been felt, thought or seen by McHoan. (Indeed, the passage reverberates with references to its reflector's senses of taste, sight and hearing.) However, a first person version makes for a very different narrative in other respects. For a start, it brings us psychologically much closer to the central character. In consequence, it loses much of the space, the often ironic space, that can be placed by a writer between the narrator of a story and a character within that story. There will be more on this issue later in this strand, but for now it is worth developing yet further features of general interest in the passage.

Throughout the Banks extract, as noted above, there are stylistic cues about the viewing position it privileges. These cues are a result of the combination of two levels of language: the semantic principle of *deixis* (see unit A2; and further B7) and the use of certain types of grammatical *Adjunct* (see units A3 and B3). The first of these, deixis, works primarily by situating the speaking voice in physical space. In the passage, the reflector of fiction forms a deictic centre, an 'origo', around which objects are positioned relative to their proximity or distance to the reflector. Notice, for instance, how certain verbs of directionality express movement *towards* the speaking source: eg. '[A grey shape] zoomed . . .'. Alternatively, movement *away* is signalled when, near the end of the passage, the reflector 'turned away' from the scene and when he 'went back' (not 'came back') to pick up his bags. This deictic anchoring is supplemented by groups of Adjuncts which express location and spatial relationship. These units of clause structure are normally expounded by prepositional and adverb phrases indicating place and directionality, of which a selection from the passage includes but is not restricted to:

[looked] down
Just upstream
[piled] down
Beneath
across the view
from falls to bridge
into the cutting
on the far bank of the river
from inside the dark constituency of the forest.

The umbrella term *locative expression* (Fowler 1996: 157) is used to cover grammatical units, such as those listed, which provide an index of location, direction and physical setting in narrative description.

Lastly, there is in the passage an occurrence of a particular, specialised point of view device which merits some comment. The term *attenuated focalisation* refers to a situation where point of view is limited, even if temporarily, to an impeded or distanced visual perspective. Lexical items which signal that such a restricted viewing has occurred are nouns with generalised or unspecific reference like 'thing', 'shape' or 'stuff'. Consider this sequence from the passage:

A grey shape flitted silently across the view . . .

McHoan sees something which (at that point) he can't make out, and that blurring of vision is relayed as attenuated focalisation. However, the restriction in point of view is only temporary and, as is often the case when this technique is deployed, is soon resolved. Interestingly, whereas most attenuation is resolved when an indistinct object comes into shaper focus visually, the status of the shape is resolved here by recourse to another mental faculty, through auditory and not visual identification:

. . . the owl hooted . . .

Attenuated focalisation often works subtly in relaying the impression that we are momentarily restricted to the visual range of a particular character. As always in point of view analysis, transposition exercises will accentuate the technique and its stylistic effect. Consider, for example, how the impact would be nullified had the sequence been reversed in the first instance; that is, had the item 'owl' replaced 'shape' thus: 'A grey owl flitted silently across the view'.

In sum, this unit has laid some foundations for a description of point of view in narrative. Working from a single passage, some general categories for a model of point of view have been proposed. Across the thread, the model will be progressively refined and reviewed as further categories are added and further passages analysed. The reading which informs this unit is Mick Short's study of narrative viewpoint in Irvine Welsh's controversial novel *Marabou Stork Nightmares*.

REPRESENTING SPEECH AND THOUGHT   A8

An important preoccupation of modern stylistics has been its interest in the way in which speech and thought is represented in stories. In other words, stylisticians are keen to examine the methods which writers use for transcribing the speech and thoughts of other people, whether these people be imagined characters in a novel or, in the case of everyday 'social' stories, real individuals. While it is true that a great deal of what makes up a story is action and events (see A6), it is also the case that stories contain a great deal of reported speech and thought. And this is as true of news reporting as it is of prose fiction – much of what makes up the 'news', for instance, is a record of what politicians and other public figures (allegedly) say and think.

The presentation of speech and thought is not straightforward. There is an array of techniques for reporting speech and thought, so it makes sense as stylisticians to be aware of and to have at our disposal a suitable model that in the first instance enables us to identify the modes used, and in the second, enables us to assess the effects in the ways these modes are used. The first step towards the development of this model is taken in the next sub-unit which provides a brief outline of the principal categories of speech and thought presentation.

The speech and thought model

The most influential framework for the analysis of speech and thought representation in narrative fiction is undoubtedly that developed by Mick Short and his co-researchers. Leech and Short's textbook (Leech and Short 1981) contains the first systematic account of this important narrative technique and their account is rich in illustrative examples. More recently, much work has been carried out by stylisticians on the way speech and thought is presented in discourse genres beyond those conventionally classed as literary. As our chief concern here is to develop a set of tools that can be used relatively comfortably by the student of language and stylistics, the brief summary of the model provided in this unit will of necessity be kept as simple as possible. To this effect, reference will be made principally to the introductory treatments of the subject in Leech and Short (1981) and Short (1996).

Beginning with the categories of *speech* presentation, the 'baseline' form against which other forms are often measured is *Direct Speech* (DS). In this mode, the report*ed* clause, which tells us what was said, is enclosed within quotation marks, while the report*ing* clause (which tells us who did the reporting) is situated around it. The following two examples of Direct Speech (DS) illustrate how the reporting clause in this mode may be either put in front of, or, as is more common, placed after the quoted material:

(1)   She said, 'I'll come here tomorrow.'

(2)   'I'll come here tomorrow,' she said.

Direct Speech stands in contrast to (though is systematically related to) an altogether more remote form of reporting known as *Indirect Speech* (IS). Here is the equivalent Indirect form of the examples above:

(3)   She said that she would go there the following day.

The method for converting Direct forms into Indirect ones requires you to carry out a series of simultaneous grammatical operations. These are summarised as follows:

Stage 1:   Make the reported material distant from the actual speech used.
Stage 2:   Alter pronouns by shifting 1st and 2nd person pronouns ('I', 'you', 'we') into 3rd person forms ('he', 'she', 'it' or 'they').

Stage 3:   Switch deictic words (see A7) from their proximal forms into their distal forms.

Stage 4:   Change the direction of movement verbs.

Stage 5:   Place tenses in their 'backshifted' forms. For example, if the primary tense is the simple present (eg. 'know') the backshifted tense will be the simple past ('knew'). Through this process, a modal verb like 'will' becomes 'would', 'does' becomes 'did', 'must' becomes 'had to', 'is' becomes 'was' and so on. If the primary tense is already the past ('knew') the backshifted tense will be past perfect ('had known').

When these steps are carried out, the following changes are brought about to the report in our Direct Speech example:

Direct form	Indirect form
'I'	'she'
' 'll' (will)	'would'
'come'	'go'
'here'	'there'
'tomorrow'	'the following day'

A further operation may be carried out on both the Direct and the Indirect forms above to render them into their corresponding 'Free' variants. This involves removing the reporting clause and removing, if present, any inverted commas. If this operation is only partially followed through, then various intermediate forms present themselves. Here are the 'Free' versions, along with possible subvarieties, of both the DS and IS forms introduced above:

Free Direct Speech (FDS):

(4)   I'll come here tomorrow, she said.

(5)   'I'll come here tomorrow.'

(6)   I'll come here tomorrow. (freest form)

Free Indirect Speech (FIS):

(7)   She would be there the following day.

(8)   She would be there tomorrow. (freest form)

The categories available for presenting *thought* in narrative fiction are formally similar to those for speech. Here are examples of the four main types:

Does she still love me? (Free Direct Thought: FDT)

He wondered, 'Does she still love me?' (Direct Thought: DT)

Did she still love him? (Free Indirect Thought: FIT)

He wondered if she still loved him. (Indirect Thought: IT)

It is important to note that in spite of their formal similarities, there are significant conceptual differences between the speech and thought modes. Whereas speech could be overheard and reported by any bystander to an interaction, the presentation of thought is somewhat 'counterfeit' insofar as it presumes entry into the private consciousness of a character. To this extent, the presentation of thought in stories is ultimately an artifice (see Short 1996: 290).

There is one more important category of speech and thought presentation which we can add to our model. This is manifested in its speech and thought variants as, respectively, Narrative Report of Speech (NRS) and Narrative Report of Thought (NRT). This technique involves a narrator reporting that speech or thought has taken place but without offering any indication or flavour of the *actual* words used. Here are two Narrative Report transpositions, one for speech and one for thought, of the basic examples given above:

(9)   She spoke of their plans for the day ahead. (Narrative Report of Speech)

(10) He wondered about her love for him. (Narrative Report of Thought)

Unlike the more explicit modes discussed above, where it is possible to work out the 'words' in which something was said or thought, this mode can be used to summarise whole stretches of reported speech or thought. That is not to say that the NRS and NRT modes are always more 'economical' than their more explicit counterparts – in fact, it is sometimes easier to report verbatim what someone has uttered than to try to look for alternative ways of capturing what they have said.

Practice

The practical work suggested in unit C8 of this thread is very detailed, requiring some fine distinctions to be drawn between various modes of speech and thought presentation, so this is a good place to begin firming up your knowledge of how the basic speech and thought categories work. Admittedly a departure from the overall format of this introductory section, the remainder of this unit therefore develops a short transposition exercise which is designed to test the categories introduced thus far.

Examples a–e listed below are all written in the Direct mode of speech or thought presentation. Working from these base forms, try to convert the five examples into their equivalent Free Direct, Indirect and Free Indirect modes. Some suggestions on how to proceed are offered below the examples:

a   'I know this trick of yours!' she said. [said to a male addressee]
b   'Can you get here next week?' he asked. [said to a female addressee]
c   'Why isn't John here?' she asked herself.
d   She said, 'We must leave tonight.'
e   'Help yourselves,' he urged them.

It is probably most straightforward if you convert them into their Free Direct counterparts first of all. Then, going back to the Direct forms, convert these into their Indirect variants using the five sets of criteria provided in the sub-unit above. It should also be possible to get from the Free Direct variants to their equivalent Free Indirect forms by following these same criteria. That said, there are certain types of grammatical patterns which block some transpositions and you may come up against some of them here. If so, try to account for any problems you encounter. Can you construct some NRS and NRT forms for a–e also? For solutions and commentary, go to the web resources that accompany this book.

Across the remainder of this strand, we will see how speech and thought presentation can be aligned with broader issues to do with narrative communication. In B8, additional refinements are made to the speech and thought model. Further along the strand, unit C8 offers a workshop programme which is designed to develop awareness of the way speech and thought presentation can be used in literary narrative. Unit D8 comprises a reading by Joe Bray which examines the interconnection between thought presentation and empathy.

DIALOGUE AND DISCOURSE   A9

The late 1970s and early 1980s witnessed a new interest among stylisticians in the role of *dialogue* in literature. This interest was paralleled by a concern with literature's status as *discourse*; that is, as a form of naturally occurring language use in a real social context. Thus, the emerging field of *discourse stylistics* was defined largely by its use of models that were interactive in their general bearing and which situated the units of analysis for literary discourse in a framework of utterances as opposed to sentences (see A2). The concept of the 'literary speech situation' (Pratt 1977: 100–19) required for its exploration the methods of pragmatics, politeness theory, conversation analysis and speech act theory. Given this new orientation in research method, it was no coincidence that there developed in parallel a particular interest in the interactive dynamic of drama dialogue, and for this reason much early work in discourse stylistics has come to be associated with the study of dialogue in plays (See Burton 1980; Short 1989; Simpson 1989). To reflect these trends in stylistics, this thread focuses generally on *dialogue*, and more particularly, on dialogue in plays.

Dialogue in drama
It is important to think carefully about what we mean when we talk of literature as *interaction*. We need for instance to separate out the types of interaction that go on between characters within a text from the sort of higher-order interaction that takes place between an author and a reader. In the context of drama dialogue, Short argues that interaction works mainly on two levels, with one level of discourse embedded inside another. He suggests the schema shown in Figure A9.1 as a way of configuring the structure of dialogue in plays. Short's schema is useful in a number of ways. It shows how the utterances that pass from one character to another become part of what the playwright 'tells' the audience. It also differentiates two sets of interactive contexts: the fictional context surrounding the characters within the world of the play, and the 'real'

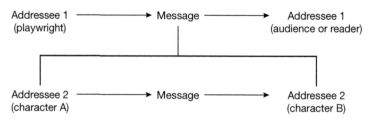

Figure A9.1 Dialogue in plays: from Short (1989: 149)

context framing the interaction between author and reader. From this, it holds that the features that mark social relations between people at the character level become messages *about* those characters at the level of discourse between author and reader/ audience.

This is not to say the levels of discourse portrayed by the schema are absolutely rigid. For example, reported speech (see A8), where one character reports the words of another on stage, opens up a further, third layer of embedding. By contrast, the use of soliloquy tends to break down the layering pattern because the words of a character, while remaining 'unheard' by other interlocutors on the stage, are relayed directly to the reader/audience. Whatever the precise characteristics of its embedding, verbal interaction in plays nonetheless requires for its understanding and interpretation the same rules of discourse that govern everyday social interaction. In other words, the assumptions we make about dialogue in the world of the play are predicated upon our assumptions about how dialogue works in the real world (see further B9).

Understanding dialogue in drama:
context, structure, strategy

It was observed in unit A2 that *discourse* is a relatively fluid and open-ended level of language organisation that encompasses aspects of communication that go beyond the structure of words and sentences. In this respect, it is not that easy to find a compact, workable model of discourse that can be readily pressed into service for the exploration of dramatic dialogue. However, one principle that is common to many models of discourse analysis is the understanding that all naturally occurring language takes place in a *context* of use. We can divide up the notion of context into three basic categories:

Physical context: This is the actual setting in which interaction takes place. Physical context may be constituted by the workplace, the home environment or by a public area. In face-to-face conversation, speaker and hearer share the same physical context, although in some forms of spoken interaction, such as broadcast or telephone talk, speaker and hearer are physically separated.

Personal context: This refers to the social and personal relationships of the interactants to one another. Personal context also encompasses social networks and group membership, the social and institutional roles of speakers and hearers, and the relative status and social distance that pertains between participants.

Cognitive context: This refers to the shared and background knowledge held by participants in interaction. Cognitive context, which is susceptible to change as interaction progresses, also extends to a speaker's world-view, cultural knowledge and past experiences (see further A10).

Against this sketch of interactive context, we can begin to plot some principles of dialogue. One approach that I have found to be reasonably effective, though in no way a canonical or definitive method of analysis, is to conceptualise dialogue in terms of two axes. These intersecting axes – let us call them *structure* and *strategy* – are organised along the lines of the Jakobsonian 'axis of combination' and 'axis of selection' introduced in unit B1. From this perspective, an utterance can be analysed either in terms of its linear placement along an axis of combination or in terms of its status as a strategic choice from the axis of selection. Put another way, the axis of combination forms a structural frame along which units of dialogue are strung in an 'a *and* b' relationship, while the axis of selection connects elements of discourse in an 'a *or* b' relationship.

To illustrate more clearly how this conceptual model works, consider the following hypothetical exchange in which a speaker, who for the sake of argument needs to get a taxi home, decides to borrow some money from a close acquaintance:

(1)   A: Could you lend me five pounds, please?
      B: Umm, OK. [hands money to A]

The two utterances in (1) combine to form a jointly produced unit of discourse called an *exchange*. Here the speaker's request prompts a reaction from the hearer, expressed through both a verbal act ('Umm, OK') and the non-verbal act of handing over the money. This 'request and reaction' pattern is a common exchange type, as are other familiar two-part pairings like 'question and answer' and 'statement and acknowledgement'.

Of course, this simple exchange pattern may have been realised through other structural permutations, through other variations along the axis of combination as it were. For instance:

(2)   A: Could you lend me five pounds, please?
      B: What d'ye wannit for?
      A: I need to get a taxi home.
      B: Umm, OK. [hands money to A]

Here, the progress of the exchange is delayed by speaker B's request for clarification. This utterance prompts a little mini-exchange, known as an *insertion sequence*, which, until it is completed, holds up the progression of the main exchange.

The axis of selection, with its focus on strategy, emphasises the 'tactical' nature of discourse. In this respect, the form of A's utterance represents just one choice from a pool of options that are available to speakers. More direct choices present themselves, as do more indirect ones:

discourse and social interaction have found their way into stylistics, both as a tool for exploring the interactive dimension of literary discourse in the broader sense and as a method for examining patterns of dialogue between fictional characters in the narrower. In this unit, attention focusses on a yet further development in stylistics which has had a profound impact on the direction the discipline has taken in the twenty-first century. This development has come to be known as the 'cognitive turn' in stylistics, and its broad rationale is the basis of this unit.

Cognitive models in and for stylistic analysis

As highlighted by Henry Widdowson's reading in D1, stylistics has since its earliest days set great store by the use of detailed linguistic analysis as a basis for the interpretation of literary texts. This focus on the methods of compositional technique has tended to make stylistics *writerly* in its general theoretical orientation. However, what has largely been missing from this approach has been any account of the mental processes that inform, and are affected by, the way we read and interpret literary texts. Stylistics has in other words lacked a *readerly* dimension. In the last decade of the previous century, stylisticians began to redress the 'writerly bias' in stylistics by exploring more systematically the cognitive structures that readers employ when reading texts. In doing so, they borrowed heavily from developments in cognitive linguistics and Artificial Intelligence, and this new emphasis in research method saw the emergence of *cognitive stylistics* or *cognitive poetics*. While cognitive stylistics is intended to supplement, rather than supplant, existing methods of analysis, it does aim to shift the focus away from models of text and composition towards models that make explicit the links between the human mind and the process of reading.

A further stimulus to the cognitive turn was provided by the object of analysis itself, literature. As noted from strand 1 onwards, a core assumption in much stylistic work has been that there is simply no such thing as a 'literary language'. This ground rule has been important polemically because it positions stylistics in direct counterpoint to the sort of literary criticism that places 'the language of literature' beyond the reach of ordinary users of ordinary language. It does, however, come at a price in that it tends to make harder the task of finding out what it is that makes literature *different* from other forms of social discourse. With its focus on the process of reading rather than writing, cognitive stylisticians have addressed precisely this problem in their work, arguing that literature is perhaps better conceptualised as a way of reading than as a way of writing. Furthermore, exploring fully this way of reading requires a thorough overhaul of existing models of stylistic analysis.

This search for new models was to go beyond even those models of pragmatics and discourse analysis that had become a familiar part of the stylistics arsenal since the 1980s. Moving away from theories of discourse, the new orientation was to models which accounted for the stores of knowledge which readers bring into play when they read, and on how these knowledge stores are modified or enriched as reading progresses. To bring this discourse-cognitive interface into sharper focus, let us consider the following seemingly rather banal utterance whose full significance will emerge shortly:

(1)   Could I have a pint of lager, please?

Across the previous thread, we looked at how spoken utterances might be interpreted in terms of either discourse strategy or discourse structure. An example like this was developed in A9, where observations were made on its various tactical functions in verbal interaction. We might indeed make a number of similar inferences about the pragmatic function of the utterance above. For instance, the utterance, with its conventionally indirect form-to-function pattern, is of the 'choice 1' variety on the strategic continuum (see A9). Furthermore, its illocutionary force as a request is confirmed by the particle 'please', which, along with the reference to a quantity of alcoholic drink within the utterance, would lead to the fairly unexceptional deduction that it is uttered by a single speaker in some kind of public house.

However, what an analysis of discourse would *not* account for is the way we are able to store a mental picture of a 'pub' which can be activated for the understanding of this utterance in context. This mental picture develops out of past experience of such places, experience gathered either through direct contact or through indirect sources. In other words, even if the pub as a social phenomenon does not feature in your own culture, your experience of, say, Western film, television and literature may have provided sufficient input to form an image schema which, if only weakly held, is still susceptible to ongoing modification as more new information comes in.

Whatever the precise type of primary input, it is clear that we can form a mental representation which will specify what a certain entity is, what it is for, what it looks like and so on. This image has been rendered down from multiple experiences into a kind of idealised prototypical image, an image which we might term an *idealised cognitive model*. An idealised cognitive model (ICM) contains information about what is typical (for us) and it is a domain of knowledge that is brought into play for the processing and understanding of textual representations. These domains of knowledge are also accompanied by conceptual slots for the things that routinely accompany the mental representation; the mental representation for the pub would, for instance, include an entry for 'roles' like barman, customer, waiter, bouncer and so on, as well as one for 'props' like tables, optics, chairs, a bar and so on (Schank and Abelson 1977: 43; and see B10). Of course, ICMs differ between subjects, so the props for one individual prototypical representation of a pub might include, say, traditional carved panelling and old oak tables while, for another, the inventory could contain a pool table, a wide-screen television or a games machine. Importantly, ICMs are subject to modification in the course of an individual subject's experience and development. For example, I once had cause to visit a pub in the west of Ireland which doubled up both as a grocery shop, and, more improbably, as a funeral parlour. Amongst other things, this experience caused me to revise my mental model of the pub: the less typical representation interacted with the prototype leading to a modified ICM. Yet I was still able to 'make sense' of the newly experienced pub-cum-funeral-parlour because I was able to structure the new knowledge in terms of the older, familiar ICM. In a dynamic process of conversion, transference between concepts leads us constantly to modify our ICMs as new stimuli are encountered.

When it comes to reading and interpreting texts, it is important to bear in mind that ICMs may be activated often by only the most minimal syntactic or lexical marker in a text. This is not surprising. After all, it would be odd indeed if, for every time we heard the word 'pub', we required for its understanding the provision of a contextualising text like the following:

> (2) The term 'pub' is a contraction of 'public house'. Pubs are premises licensed for the consumption of alcohol and soft drinks. In Western cultures which have no prohibition on alcohol, pubs are establishments which are open to the public, although localised restrictions apply to the admission of minors. Licensed premises may be housed in a variety of building designs which vary in character and theme, although most contain a bar across which drinks, and possibly light snacks or meals are served . . .

There is simply no end to the amount of context that could be provided here, but the point is that such context is unnecessary because the domains of knowledge that comprise ICMs allow us to take cognitive short-cuts when we interpret language. We do not, in other words, need to have a fully elaborated *textual representation* of a concept in order to set in motion a *cognitive representation* of that concept.

Summary

This unit has addressed the broad tenets of a cognitive approach to style. Coverage has however been rather sketchy because little explicit information has been provided either on key models of cognitive stylistic analysis or on the main practitioners in the field. To address this, the cognitive theme will be elaborated further in two different directions. Horizontally, unit B10 surveys some of the key developments in this branch of stylistics and introduces a variety of models of analysis. Further across the strand, C10 develops some practical activities for cognitive stylistic analysis which take account of the ideas introduced both here and in B10. The strand concludes with a reading by Barbara Dancygier that draws on 'conceptual blending theory' in a directed cognitive stylistic analysis of travel writing literature. Vertically, the cognitive theme is developed in A11 where attention focusses on one of the most important devices we use to transfer, modify or blend mental constructs. This device is metaphor which, along with the related concept metonymy, plays a pivotal role in contemporary cognitive stylistic analysis.

A11 METAPHOR AND METONYMY

An important feature of cognitive stylistics has been its interest in the way we transfer mental constructs, and especially in the way we map one mental representation onto another when we read texts. Stylisticians and cognitive poeticians have consistently drawn attention to this system of conceptual transfer in both literary and in everyday discourse, and have identified two important tropes, or figures of speech, through which this conceptual transfer is carried out. These tropes are *metaphor* and *metonymy* and this unit will introduce these core concepts in cognitive stylistics.

Metaphor

A metaphor is a process of mapping between two different conceptual domains. The different domains are known as the *target* domain and the *source* domain. The target domain is the topic or concept that you want to describe through the metaphor while the source domain refers to the concept that you draw upon in order to create the metaphorical construction. Thus, in an expression like:

(1)   She really blew her lid.

the target domain is our understanding of the concept of anger because it is the concept we wish to describe through the metaphor. The source domain for the metaphor can be conceptualised as 'heated fluid in a container' because that is the concept which provides the vehicle for the metaphorical transfer. The metaphor as a whole can be represented, using the standard notation of small capital letters, by the formula: ANGER IS A HEATED FLUID IN A CONTAINER. This type of formulation is useful because it abstracts out of the particular linguistic structure of the metaphor its underlying organisation.

Importantly, the relationship between metaphor and linguistic form is an indirect one, which means that we can express the same conceptual metaphor through a variety of constructions. Consider, for instance, an alternative version of example (1):

(2)   Talk about letting off steam . . . She really blew her lid, I mean really blew her top. She just exploded!

Although this example comprises four grammatical clauses, this is not to say that it contains four metaphors. All of the clauses in fact express the same source and target domain, which means that the single underlying conceptual metaphor ANGER IS A HEATED FLUID IN A CONTAINER is being played out through a variety of linguistic constructions.

In his influential study of the poetic structure of the human mind, Gibbs (1994) highlights the important part metaphor plays in our everyday conceptual thought. Metaphors are not some kind of distorted literal thought, but rather are basic schemes by which people conceptualise their experience and their external world. Figurative language generally, which also includes irony (see the special web strand on style and humour), is found throughout speech and writing; moreover, it does not require for its use any special intellectual talent or any special rhetorical situation (Gibbs 1994: 21). Indeed, the fact that many metaphors pass us by in everyday social interaction is well illustrated by this unwitting slip by a venerable British sports commentator:

(3)   We didn't have metaphors in my day. We didn't beat about the bush.

Metaphor is simply a natural part of conceptual thought and although undoubtedly an important feature of creativity, it should not be seen as a special or exclusive feature of literary discourse. For instance, examples (4) to (6) below, which embody the same conceptual metaphor, are from a variety of print and broadcast media covering the conflict in Iraq in 2003:

(4)   The third mechanised infantry are currently clearing up parts of the Al Mansur Saddam village area.

(5)   The regime is finished, but there remains some tidying up to do.

(6)   Official sources described it as a 'mopping up' operation.

Examples (4) to (6) rehearse the same basic metaphor through three different linguistic realisations. The experience of war, which is the topic that forms the target domain of the metaphor, is relayed through the idea of cleaning, which is the concept that provides the source domain. The metaphor might thus be represented as: WAR IS CLEANING. Given its context, the ideological significance of this metaphor is worth commenting on. It suggests that the conflict is nothing more than a simple exercise in sanitation, a perspective which, it has to be said, is unlikely to be shared by military personnel on the opposing side. In an effort presumably to allay domestic worries about the progression of the conflict, the British and American press are playing down both the extent and intensity of the conflict through this strategically motivated metaphor.

If we accept that metaphors are part and parcel, so to speak, of everyday discourse, an important question presents itself. Are there any qualitative differences in the sorts of metaphors that are found in different discourse contexts? An important criterion in this respect is the degree of *novelty* exhibited by a metaphor. As with any figure of speech, repeated use leads to familiarity, and so commonplace metaphors can some-times develop into idioms or fixed expressions in the language. The commentator's reference to 'beat about the bush' in (3) is a good example of this process. However, what arguably sets the use of metaphor in literature apart from more 'idiomatised' uses of the trope is that in literature metaphors are on the one hand typically *more novel* and on the other typically *less clear* (Kövecses 2002: 43). Writers consciously strive for novelty in literary expression and this requires developing not only new conceptual mappings but also new stylistic frameworks through which these mappings can be presented. This theme of novelty in metaphor is taken up in B11.

Metonymy

In contrast with metaphor, *metonymy* is based on a transfer within a single conceptual domain. Staying within the boundaries of the same domain, metonymy involves transpositions between associated concepts and this commonly results in transfer between the part and the whole, a producer and the produced, an institution and its location and so on. Metonymy in which the part stands for the whole – a trope known as *synecdoche* – is found in expressions like 'hired hand' or 'a fresh pair of legs'. Alternatively, constructions where a location substitutes for the particular institution which it houses can be found in expressions like 'Buckingham Palace is thought to be furious' or 'The Pentagon refused to comment on the story'. Metonymies where the producer of something is associated with what is produced occur in expressions like 'Have you read the new Kate Atkinson?' or 'There's a good Spielberg on tomorrow night'. Importantly, the notation convention used for capturing metonymy, in contrast to that for metaphor, draws on the connecting particle FOR. This is intended to express intra-domain substitution as opposed to the cross-domain transfer in metaphorical mapping. Using small capitals, metonymic formulae for the examples introduced thus far can be expressed, for example, as PRODUCER FOR PRODUCED (as in the Spielberg example), LOCATION FOR INSTITUTION (the Pentagon example), and so on.

Other metonymies are more contextually dependent for their interpretation, as in, say, 'The lead guitar has gone AWOL' where a more contingent 'stands-for' relationship pertains between the musician and the particular instrument played. In general, whereas a metaphor assumes a certain distance between the concepts it embodies, between its target and source, a metonymy upgrades certain salient characteristics from a single domain to represent that domain as a whole.

It is not always easy to spot the difference between metaphor and metonymy but a useful test to distinguish one trope from the other is to try to convert the expression into a *simile*. A simile makes an explicit connection between two concepts through the use of the IS LIKE formula. Applying the test serves therefore to draw attention to the conceptual space between a target and a source domain in metaphor, but the same test will collapse when applied to metonymy. For example, (1) and (4) to (6) convert easily into similes, as in, respectively:

(1′)   ANGER IS LIKE A HEATED FLUID IN A CONTAINER

(4′) to (6′)   WAR IS LIKE CLEANING

By contrast, the metonymy 'hired hand' cannot support the parallel simile 'A worker is like a hand', nor does 'a fresh pair of legs' convert to 'A substitute is like a pair of legs'. The same restriction blocks the conversion of the other metonymies noted above, as in: 'A musician is like a lead guitar', 'A monarchy is like Buckingham Palace', 'Spielberg is like a film' and so on.

Like metaphors, metonymies find their expression in everyday discourse practices. A metonymy that became briefly popular in Britain some years ago began life when a notoriously combative midfielder, employed by a wealthy English football club, criticised certain of that club's fans for their less than committed support of the team. He described them as the sort of people who would eat prawn sandwiches during the half time interval, behaviour which he at least considered unworthy of real soccer fans. The British sports pundits quickly seized on this figure of speech, and within a few months, a novel metonymy had found its way into media and popular discourse. The term 'prawn sandwich' had come to stand for any effete or whimpish football fan, while expressions like 'They're just a bunch of prawn sandwiches' could be said of any set of supporters, and not just those who comprised the original referents of the phrase.

Metonymy has an important stylistic function. In unit B6 it can be seen how *meronymic agency* is a type of transitivity process which involves the part 'standing for' the whole in such a way as to place a human body part, rather than a whole person, in the role of an Actor, Sensor, Sayer and so on. Metonymy also plays an important role in the technique of *caricature*. Caricature is a form of metonymic distortion, much favoured by satirical humorists, which involves the distortion of some aspect of human appearance, normally physiognomy, such that this exaggerated body part assumes a prominence sufficient to symbolise the whole being. For example, most caricatures of former British Prime Minister Margaret Thatcher played, according to Garland (1988:

77), on her bouffant hair and pointed nose. This gradually shaded into ever more grotesque representations until the nose and hair themselves became the visual embodiment of the politician (see further chapter five of Simpson (2003)).

Summary

This introductory unit is developed further in B11, where amongst other things the important issue of novelty as a feature of literary metaphor is explored. Unit C11 offers a range of practical suggestions covering both metaphor and metonymy, while the thread concludes, in D11, with a reading by Peter Stockwell on the theory of metaphor.

NEW DIRECTIONS IN STYLISTICS: CORPUS APPROACHES

Given the numerous and diverse developments throughout the discipline, one might reasonably ask, where next for the practice of stylistics? This is an important question because it connects with, on the one hand, the internal dynamic of stylistic method-ology, and on the other, the external influence on stylistics of new research paradigms. With regard to the former, the stylistic method is very much accumulative rather than substitutive in the sense that its analytic techniques accrue and mount up in tandem with the forward momentum of the discipline. For instance, in a survey article charting recent innovations in the field (Simpson 2012), I sorted, according to theme, all of the publications in a key stylistics journal over a two-year period. Tellingly, coverage was broad and many papers aligned (mercifully) with the areas of interest represented across this book. This included articles whose primary stimulus was a more 'traditional' topic of inquiry as well as articles whose principal impetus stemmed from a more recently conceived framework of analysis. Thus, a paper on metrical structure (see A4) in the journal was flanked by an essay on narrative stylistics (A5) and a study of fictional dialogue (A9), while a study of grammatical patterns in poetry (B2) kept company, in the same issue, with papers on conceptual blending theory (D10), multimodal stylistics (D9) and the use of computerized corpora in stylistic analysis (see below). This shows that no one model or approach will single-handedly answer all the questions we have about the idea of 'style'. It also shows that the central precepts of stylistics do not become outmoded as the field develops. Stylistics is therefore accumulative in that its models of analysis, far from having some kind of fixed 'sell-by date', are honed, tested and re-evaluated as part of a natural intellectual progression.

With respect to the external developments that have significantly enriched the methods of stylistic analysis, there is one particular advance that merits special attention and as such will be a fitting way to complete this textbook. Innovations in com-putational technology have facilitated the electronic generation and development of *corpora*. The availability of corpora, which are large collections of computer-readable texts that can include entire literary works, has enabled stylisticians to use corpus software to produce some very broad, yet rigorous, analyses of sometimes eye-watering swathes of textual material. This groundbreaking method has become known as *corpus stylistics* and it is the focus of the remainder of this strand.

Corpus stylistics

Let us begin this sub-unit with some informal exercises and commentary before progressing to the more robust procedures involved in using corpora in stylistics. First of all, think about what the English word *treacherous* means. If asked by someone who didn't know its meaning, could you provide a short definition of the word? And what sort of definition would a dictionary offer? Informal observation suggests that people will quite confidently describe this adjective as meaning 'disloyal', 'dangerous' or 'untrustworthy' when said of a person or indicating a character trait. An uncontroversial result perhaps, but let me present the following scenario. In the month of December 2011, I heard (or read) the word *treacherous* twenty-three times in print and broadcast news outlets from British media. You might want politely to deduce from this that I should get out more, but ironically, this was relevant to the matter at hand because Britain in this period was afflicted by a sustained and unprecedented period of very cold weather. News items and weather reports carried warnings about the weather, very commonly couched in expressions like the following:

Activity ✪

UK prepares for *treacherous* weather conditions.

On Monday, many roads across north Wales remained *treacherous*.

Treacherous black ice causes travel chaos.

This raises some interesting issues about what words mean, what they mean in particular contexts and, no less importantly, what we *think* words mean. The word *treacherous* has clearly shifted in sense towards a broader metaphorical usage that captures the menace and danger of weather rather than of people. This metaphorical sense may even have become the dominant usage, although we would need more evidence to support this hypothesis. And garnering evidence to test hypotheses like this – which probe the meanings of words in their everyday contexts of use – is precisely the task of corpus approaches to language study.

Consider another example, in this instance based on Louw (2011). The following two sequences of text are structurally isomorphic passive clauses, differing only in terms of the gender of their subject pronouns:

He was approached . . .

She was approached . . .

However, when these structures are retrieved from language corpora, there seems to be rather more going on. For instance, the structure with the male pronoun commonly develops a process that is beneficial in some way to the referent embodied by the pronoun. Examples of this include attested sequences like:

He was approached by the film director Danny Boyle . . .

He was approached by global accountancy firm PwC

He was approached to take over at Stamford Bridge next season . . .

In all instances, the process leads to some kind of advantage or benefit for the male individual involved. However, occurrences of the structure with the female pronoun are different, often alarmingly so. Examples in Louw's corpus include the following:

She was approached by a man who grabbed her bag.

. . . in Cork city centre when she was approached by the pervert.

. . . she was approached by three men who attacked her.

Clearly, in all the cases here the consequences of the 'approach' are far from beneficial to the female represented by the pronoun. Yet this is not an absolute distinction because there were some instances in Louw's corpus where the process *did* have positive consequences for the woman: '[she] was just 15 when she was approached to be a model'. Importantly though, this counter-example does not mean that the entire argument collapses; it is rather the type of exception that proves the rule. The corpus analysis is designed to show trends, broad tendencies and repeated patterns across banks of language data, so the evidence it adduces is not limited to a possibly 'one off' occurrence of a particular feature of language.

Corpus-based stylistic research may be modern in terms of its technology, but in spirit it follows in a long-established tradition of linguistic inquiry. The grammarian J. R. Firth's famous axiom was that 'you shall know a word by the company it keeps', and the importance of *collocation* (the company a word keeps) has remained at the fore of the neo-Firthian tradition of linguistics since the late 1950s (see unit D1). This has far-reaching implications for stylistic analysis because to talk of the 'meaning' of a piece of language is contingent on how real people actually use it in connected patterns of discourse and in real contexts of use. The historical development of the language form across different language communities is patently relevant also to our understanding of its meaning. King James II's (apocryphal) reaction to seeing, for the first time, Sir Christopher Wren's new cathedral included the approbatory adjectives 'amusing, awful and artificial' – words whose meaning in the late seventeenth century were, respectively 'capturing attention', 'inspiring awe' and 'displaying art'.

One of the main stylistic applications of corpus techniques is to set patterns in a literary text against those found in general corpora of the language. This cross-referencing offers clear points of contrast between so-called everyday language and the, perhaps more nuanced, variants that mark a particular writer's craft. In the context of the remarks made across units B1 and C1, any discussion of foregrounding or deviation in literature is after all contingent upon, and relative to, some form of quantitative observation about what is 'normal' in language. Another stylistic application is when the corpus itself comprises literary works, perhaps the entire output of a single writer that might run into the millions of words (see further B12). This facilitates an evidence-based description of the writer's style which is grounded in retrievable procedures and which at times flies in the face of received critical wisdom about this or that writer's technique. Just how a corpus stylistic analysis can be designed and implemented is the substance of the remainder of this unit.

Methods in corpus stylistics

There are a number of conveniently available corpora that provide an opportunity to test and practice some of the methods set out here. In the main, these corpora are derived from written texts, such as newspapers, textbooks or legal documentation, and from transcriptions of spoken discourse, ranging from broadcast talk to everyday social interaction. And as noted, there are corpora devoted exclusively to the published output of individual literary authors. Access to corpora is variable and may require support through subscription from an academic institution. However, the *British National Corpus* (BNC) is a one-hundred-million-word bank of data whose website offers some access for those who are not formally registered, while the *Corpus of Contemporary American* (COCA) is a freely searchable corpus of 450 million words. *Early English Books Online* (EEBO) is a very large bank of early literary texts where the texts themselves are presented in facsimile versions, if available, of their original manuscript forms. The *International Corpus of English* (ICE) includes different varieties from around the world, such as Indian English, Canadian English and New Zealand English. *WebCorp* is an extremely useful and user-friendly facility for deriving linguistic data from the internet. It offers many advantages over more standard search engines, such as Google or Bing, which are not really designed as corpus linguistic tools.

After finding a suitable corpus, the next stage is to probe the occurrences of words and their collocates. This is of course integrally dependent on the purpose of the stylistic analysis (see B12) and it will be guided by whatever argument the corpus evidence is designed to support. It is important also to consider different grammatical forms of the same lexeme, known as *lemmas*. A lemma is the particular form chosen by convention to represent a lexeme and is the one listed as the default entry in a dictionary. However, if we wanted to explore the occurrence in a corpus of, for example, the verb *choose*, then we need to take into consideration its other grammatical variants, *chose, choosing* and *chosen*.

Exploring collocation involves appending to our key search term a specified amount of text on either side of it. This will reveal a window of 'co-text' around the key word, and the pattern that emerges is vertically arranged in alphabetical order and horizontally laid out normally as a nine to fifteen-word sequence of text (see further below). This pattern is described as the *Key Word in Context* (KWIC) and the repeated combinations and collocations that are revealed in this way offer some compelling insights into the 'real' company that the word keeps. To the far left of this results window is information on the origin of each example; that is, on whether the data was spoken or written and on the particular register or genre of discourse in which it is framed. The KWIC layout means that the analyst has a bird's eye view of the word in context and does not have to read the many and varied texts from which the data is taken.

It is important to think carefully and selectively about stipulating a specified amount of text around a search term. A search for a very common word in English, such as the lemma *warm*, will yield an overpowering set of results: in COCA, the number of occurrences is 33,495. However, with the simple addition of the preposition 'to', deriving the collocation 'warm to', the occurrences become very much reduced. Here is the results window for the first eleven of the 323 patterns found in COCA:

The real key is get the water	warm to	105, 110 degrees, mix it in your mixer
temperatures in upper Cook Inlet usually	warm to	14–17 Celsius (Bakus *et al.*, 1979)
ranging from one to five. (e.g. , 1 =	warm to	5 = cold , 1 = sharp to 5 = dull
than any hit since Titanic, but it's hard to	warm to	a business franchise
Cardinal McCarrick did	warm to	a question about his colleagues
After all she says, who wouldn't	warm to	a story that celebrates the magic of love
to clutch someone	warm to	allay the emptiness and isolation
call them lesbians if they didn't	warm to	amorous advances
Not a tear; it was too	warm to	be a tear
turned back to her, and she grew	warm to	be under his scrutiny
from being an object to keep you	warm to	being recognized as art

As this data set is intended as an illustration of the basic procedure, it is not a particularly interesting corpus analysis in and of itself. Nonetheless, it is worth noting how the alphabetical organisation on the vertical plane begins (on the fourth entry down) only after all three numerical collocates are completed. Notice also how the KWIC layout is no respecter of grammatical boundaries: the 'to' particle in some instances (e.g. the 7th and 11th sequences) marks the onset of a new clause and so is not really part of the search phrase proper. In some cases, the lemma *warm* is a verbal form, in others, an adjectival form (and you can work out which is which by yourself!). Finally, some of the verbal forms are literal in meaning when they refer to the heating of liquids (e.g. 'get the water warm . . .') but others are non-literal, idiomatic uses as in 'they didn't warm to amorous advances'. This second type draws its experiential basis from the functioning of the human body and so is, of course, metaphorical; in this instance, expressing the conventional metaphor INTIMACY IS HEAT (and see further B12).

Although necessarily rudimentary in its coverage, this unit has introduced some of the basic tenets of the corpus stylistic method. Unit B12 assesses what stylisticians have done with these techniques and with computer-readable texts, while unit C12 suggests a number of related activities, applications and exercises. The strand concludes with a corpus-driven study of Dickens's fiction by Michaela Mahlberg and Catherine Smith.

Section B

DEVELOPMENT

DOING STYLISTICS

DEVELOPMENTS IN STYLISTICS

This unit looks at some of the important influences on stylistics that have helped to shape its development over the years. From the Classical period onwards there has been continued healthy interest among scholars in the relationship between patterns of language in a text and the way a text communicates. The Greek rhetoricians, for example, were particularly interested in the tropes and devices that were used by orators for effective argument and persuasion, and there is indeed a case for saying that some stylistic work is very much a latter-day embodiment of traditional rhetoric. However, there is one particular field of academic inquiry, from the early twentieth century, that has had a more direct and lasting impact on the methods of contemporary stylistics. This field straddles two interrelated movements in linguistics, known as Russian Formalism and Prague School Structuralism. Of the former movement, key figures include Viktor Shklovsky and Boris Tomashevsky; of the the the latter, Jan Mukarovsky and Wilhem Mathesius. One scholar, whose work literally links both movements, is Roman Jakobson, who moved from the Moscow circle to the Prague group in 1920. Many of the central ideas of these two schools find their reflexes in contemporary stylistics and two of the more durable theoretical contributions are the focus of this unit. These are the concept of *foregrounding* and the notion of the *poetic function* in language.

Foregrounding

Foregrounding refers to a form of textual patterning which is motivated specifically for literary-aesthetic purposes. Capable of working at any level of language, foregrounding typically involves a stylistic distortion of some sort, either through an aspect of the text which deviates from a linguistic norm or, alternatively, where an aspect of the text is brought to the fore through repetition or parallelism. That means that foregrounding comes in two main guises: foregrounding as 'deviation from a norm' and foregrounding as 'more of the same'. Foregrounding is essentially a technique for 'making strange' in language, or to extrapolate from Shklovsky's Russian term *ostranenie*, a method of 'defamiliarisation' in textual composition.

Whether the foregrounded pattern deviates from a norm, or whether it replicates a pattern through parallelism, the point of foregrounding as a stylistic strategy is that it should acquire salience in the act of drawing attention to itself. Furthermore, this salience is motivated purely by literary considerations and as such constitutes an important textual strategy for the development of images, themes and characters, and for stimulating both effect and affect in a text's interpretation. Foregrounding is not, therefore, the simple by-product of this or that writer's idiosyncratic predilections in style. For example, Jonathan Swift, a writer with much to say about language and style, was reputedly never very fond of words which were made up of only one syllable. Whereas the relative scarcity of monosyllabic words in Swift's work might therefore be noticeable or salient, it is rather more a consequence of the personal stylistic foibles of the writer than of a carefully modulated design in literary foregrounding. In sum, if a particular textual pattern is not motivated for artistic purposes, then it is not foregrounding.

The theory of foregrounding raises many issues to do with the stylistic analysis of text, the most important of which is probably its reliance on the concept of a 'norm' in language. Given the functional diversity of language, it is very difficult – if not impossible – to say what exactly a 'normal' sentence in English actually is. This constitutes a substantial challenge to foregrounding theory because the theory presupposes that there exists a notional linguistic yardstick against which a particular feature of style can be measured. A related issue concerns what happens when a once deviant pattern becomes established in a text. Does it stay foregrounded for the entire duration of the text? Or does it gradually and unobtrusively slip into the background?

One way of addressing these important questions is through a short illustration. Unit C8 of this book develops a workshop in practical stylistics which is based on a passage from Ernest Hemingway's novella *The Old Man and the Sea* (1952). That passage arguably typifies Hemingway's written style, a style which literary critics have described with epithets like 'flat', 'dry', 'restrained', 'journalistic' or even 'tough guy' (see C8). These observations are largely based on a perceived scarcity of adjectives in the writer's work, which is correlated with the 'machismo' feel of much of his narrative style. It is indeed true that in the first few lines of the passage analysed in C8, almost all of the nouns receive *no* adjectival modification at all: 'the tuna', 'the stern', 'the gaff', 'the line' and 'the fish'. Let us accept for the moment, then, that this marked non-adjectival pattern is foregrounded because it deviates from our expectations about the 'normal' style of twentieth-century prose fiction.

Such an interpretation immediately raises two interconnected problems. The first, as noted above, concerns the degree to which the 'no-adjective' pattern is able to stay foregrounded before it gradually slips into the background. The second is about what would happen should a phrase that *did* contain adjectives suddenly appear in the text; that is, should a structure occur whose very use of adjectives goes against the foregrounded pattern. As it happens, there is elsewhere in the novella a rather startling example of such a deviation. When a poisonous jellyfish approaches the old man's boat, the narrative refers to it as 'the purple, formalised iridescent gelatinous bladder of a Portuguese man-of-war' (Hemingway 1960 [1952]: 28). This is stylistically somewhat of a quantum leap insofar as the simple article-plus-noun configuration gives way here to a sequence of not one but *four* adjectives which are built up before the main noun ('bladder'). The old fisherman's superstitious mistrust of this dangerous animal, this 'whore of the sea' as he puts it, is captured in a stylistic flourish and with a type of hyperbole that would not be out of place in a D. H. Lawrence novel. The upshot of this is that foregrounding can be seen to work on two levels, both across and within texts. Whereas Hemingway's so-called 'flat' noun phrases may be foregrounded against the notional external stylistic backdrop of the twentieth-century novella, their repetition in the text develops a norm which is itself susceptible to violation. This type of secondary foregrounding, known as *internal foregrounding*, works inside the text as a kind of deviation within a deviation. Moreover, it is clear that foregrounding does not stand still for long and that a writer's craft involves the constant monitoring and (re)appraisal of the stylistic effects created by patterns in both the foreground and in the background. The concept of foregrounding will be further explored and illustrated in B2.

Jakobson's 'poetic function'

In a famous paper, that still reverberates in much of today's stylistic scholarship, the structuralist poetician Roman Jakobson proposes a model of language which comprises six key functions (Jakobson 1960). These are the *conative, phatic, referential, emotive, poetic* and *metalingual* functions of language. Alongside the referential function (the content carrying component of a message) and the emotive function (the expression of attitude through a message), there is one function that stands out in respect of its particular appeal to stylisticians. This is the poetic function, which Jakobson defines thus: 'the poetic function projects the principle of equivalence from the axis of selection into the axis of combination' (Jakobson 1960: 358). This rather terse formula is not the most transparent definition you are likely to come across in this book, so some unpacking is in order. As a short demonstration of the formula at work, consider first of all the following example which is the opening line of W. H. Auden's elegiac poem 'In Memory of W. B. Yeats' (1939). A key verb in the line has been removed and you might wish to consider what (sort of) word would make an appropriate entry:

> He _____ in the dead of winter

There are clearly many items that might go into the slot vacated in the line. That said, some words, if semantically compatible, can be ruled out on the grounds of inappropriateness to the context: the euphemistic cliché 'passed away' or the crudely informal idiom 'kicked the bucket' are unlikely to be strong contenders in the context of an poetic elegy. You may instead prefer to settle on a verb like 'died', a contextually neutral form which is more in keeping with the poem's obvious funereal theme. However, the missing verb is actually 'disappeared', reinstated here for clarity:

> He disappeared in the dead of winter

The technique of blanking out a word in a line, a *cloze test* in stylistics parlance, is to force us to think about the pool of possible lexical entries from which a choice is ultimately made. This pool of available words is what Jakobson means by his term 'axis of selection'. What is significant about Auden's selection, one word taken from many possibilities, is that it engenders a series of resonances across the line as a whole. Notice for example, how the three syllable word 'disappeared' creates associative phonetic links with other words in the line. Most obviously, its initial and final consonant /d/ alliterates with those in the same position in the word 'dead' later in the line. Possibly more subtly, its third, stressed syllable (disappeared) contains a diphthong, the first element of which is the vowel /iː/, the same as the vowel in 'He'. This type of vowel harmony, known as *assonance*, further consolidates points of equivalence across the poetic line.

However, there are also semantic as well as phonetic transferences in the line. Notice how it is the season, winter, which takes over the semantic quality of death and, when positioned together in the same grammatical environment, the words 'dead' and 'disappeared' enable new types of signification to emerge. More specifically, the parallel drawn between the words opens up a *conceptual metaphor* (A11), where the concept of death is represented in terms of a journey. In fact, we commonly invoke this DEATH IS A JOURNEY metaphor in everyday interaction when we talk of the 'dearly departed', or of someone 'passing away' or 'going to a final resting place'. The point about Auden's technique, though, is that this is a novel metaphor (B11), suggesting the sense of being lost or of straying from a journey, and this is brought about subtly by the implied connection between the process of disappearing, and the references to death and the seasons elsewhere in the same line. In sum, the way Auden uses language is a good illustration of Jakobson's poetic function at work: the particular language patterns he develops work to establish connections (*a principle of equivalence*) between the words he chooses from the pool of possible words (*the axis of selection*) and the words that are combined across the poetic line (*the axis of combination*).

Summary

It is important to footnote the foregoing discussion with a rider. Whereas many of the precepts of both the Formalist and Prague School movements have had a significant bearing on the way stylistics has developed, this is not for a moment to say that stylisticians have embraced these ideas unequivocally, unanimously or without debate. We have already touched upon some of the theoretical problems associated with the theory of foregrounding, and in this context, stylisticians like van Peer (1986) and Cook (1994) have made advances in solidifying the foundations of this generally useful concept. Amongst other things, their work has incorporated cognitive and psychological models of analysis to explain how text-processors perceive foregrounding in texts (see further B10). Moreover, corpus techniques (A12) offer a valuable tool for assessing recurring patterns of style across large swathes of text, and this gives stylisticians a more solid empirical basis upon which to make generalisations about what particular writers actually do with language.

Application of the concept of the poetic function in language also brings with it an important caveat. Although not articulated especially clearly by Jakobson, it is essential to view the poetic function not as an exclusive property of literature but rather as a more generally creative use of language that can pop up, as it were, in a range of discourse contexts. One consequence of seeing the poetic function as an exclusively literary device is that it tends to separate off literature from other uses of language, and this is not a desired outcome in stylistic analysis. This latter issue will come more to the fore in the next unit along this strand, C3, while the unit below provides an opportunity, through the analysis of a short poem, to investigate and illustrate further the concept of foregrounding.

B2   LEVELS OF LANGUAGE AT WORK: AN EXAMPLE FROM POETRY

This unit, which investigates patterns of language in a single short text, forms a useful intersection between the two areas of interest raised in units B1 and A2. On the one hand it offers a chance to illustrate some basic principles of foregrounding in the context of literary discourse; on the other it develops further the main remit of this thread by exploring how different levels of language can be pressed into service in stylistically significant ways. These themes will be worked through jointly as the unit progresses.

On e e cummings's 'love is more thicker than forget'
The following untitled poem was published in 1939 by the American poet e e cummings:

> love is more thicker than forget
> more thinner than recall
> more seldom than a wave is wet
> more frequent than to fail
>
> it is most mad and moonly
> and less it shall unbe
> than all the sea which only
> is deeper than the sea
>
> love is less always than to win
> less never than alive
> less bigger than the least begin
> less littler than forgive
>
> it is most sane and sunly
> and more it cannot die
> than all the sky which only
> is higher than the sky
>   (cummings 1954 [1939]: 381)

This text – a love poem, of sorts – shall in the absence of a formal title be referred to from now on as 'love is more thicker'. It certainly bears many of the familiar stylistic imprints of its author, notable among which is the conspicuous spelling and orthography resulting from the removal of standard punctuation devices such as commas, full stops and capital letters. It also contains a number of invented words, *neologisms*, such as the adjectives 'sunly' and 'moonly', as well as the verb 'unbe' which suggests a kind of reversal in sense from 'being' to 'not being'. Perhaps even more markedly, the poem treats existing words in the English lexicon, especially adjectives and adverbs, in a striking and colourful way. In counterpoint to this more 'deviant' strand of textual structure, there is nonetheless a high degree of regularity in the way other aspects of the poem are crafted. Observe, for example, the almost mathematical symmetry of the stanzaic organisation, where key words and phrasal patterns are repeated across the four verses. Indeed, all of the poem's constituent clauses are connected grammatically to the very first word of the poem, 'love'.

Choosing models for analysis

In order for a solid basis for interpretation to be built, we need to be both clear and precise about what resources of language cummings uses, so the preceding rather informal description needs to give way to a more rigorous account of linguistic technique. To do this requires that we step back from the text for a moment in order to pinpoint more narrowly which aspects of language, in particular, the poet is manipulating. *Adjectives*, for a start, have already been highlighted as one of the main sites for stylistic experimentation in the poem. Constituting a major word class in the vocabulary of English, adjectives ascribe qualities to entities, objects and concepts, familiar examples of which are words like *large, bright, good, bad, difficult* and *regular*. A notable grammatical feature of adjectives, and one which cummings exploits with particular stylistic force, is their potential for *gradability*. Many English adjectives can be graded by extending or modifying the degree or intensity of the basic quality which they express. A useful test for checking whether or not an adjective is gradable is to see if the intensifying word 'very' can go in front of it. Indeed, all of the adjectives cited thus far satisfy this test: 'a *very bright* light', 'the *very good* decision', 'this *very regular* routine' and so on. The test does not work for another group of adjectives, known as *classifying adjectives*, which specify more fixed qualities relative to the noun they describe. In the following examples, insertion of 'very' in front of the classifying adjectives 'former' and 'strategic' feels odd: 'the *very former* manager', 'those *very strategic* weapons'.

A special feature of gradable adjectives, whose significance to 'love is more thicker' is shortly to become clear, is their capacity to compare objects and concepts through expressions of *comparative, superlative, equal* and *inferior* relationships. Thus, a comparative form of the regular adjective *large* can be formed by adding the inflectional morpheme *er* to form 'larger', while a superlative form adds *est* to form 'largest'. Comparative and superlative gradation of irregular adjectives involves a change in the whole stem of the word: thus, 'good' becomes respectively 'better' and 'best'. If on the other hand the adjective contains more than one syllable, then the comparative and superlative forms normally require the introduction of a separate word, as in '*more* regular' or '*most* difficult'. Finally, adjectives may be graded to signal equal relationships ('as bright as . . .', 'as difficult as . . .') as well as inferior or negative, as opposed to positive, relations ('less/least large', 'less/least regular').

Another notable feature of adjectives, again pertinent in the present context, is the way the grammar of English allows for material to be placed *after* the adjective in order to determine more narrowly its scope of reference. Compare for instance the following sentences:

(1)   The pilot was *conscious*.

(2)   The pilot was *conscious of his responsibilities*.

Clearly, very different meanings can be assigned to the adjective *conscious* in the two examples. Whereas the adjective on its own in (1) suggests (mercifully) a general state of being awake, in the second example the appended phrase targets more specifically a special kind of awareness on the part of the pilot. Thus, in a sentence like 'Mary is now *much better at maths*' the main adjective signalling Mary's general improvement ('better') is bounded on *both* sides by other elements. These elements comprise the intensifier 'much' and the scope defining element 'at maths':

intensifier	adjective	scope
much	better	at maths

Notice here how the loss of this final scope element would invite a very different interpretation, or at least a much less specific interpretation, for the clause as whole.

Exploring levels of language in 'love is more thicker'

Let us return now to the cummings text, and in particular, to his manipulation of the features of grammar and vocabulary pinpointed above. To some extent, 'love is more thicker' is an object lesson in how *not* to form adjective phrases in English. Much of what the poet does is arguably either grammatically redundant or semantically anomalous. Not intended as a sleight on this style of writing, this comment requires some explanation. For a start, cummings constantly 'reduplicates' the grammatical rules for comparative and superlative gradation. In spite of their one-syllable status, adjectives like 'thick' and 'thin' receive *both* the inflectional morpheme *and* the separate intensifier ('*more* thicker'). However, no sooner is this pattern introduced in the poem, than it is thrown off course by a number of secondary operations which constitute good examples of *internal foregrounding* (see B1). For a start, superlative forms of other one-syllable adjectives like 'mad' and 'sane' do *not* receive the inflectional morpheme (as in 'maddest' or 'sanest') but are instead fronted, more unusually, by separate words: 'most mad' and 'most sane'. Thereafter, a further variation on the pattern emerges where markers of both positive and inferior relations are mixed together in the *same* adjective phrase. Notice how, for example, 'big' is converted to 'less bigger' and, even more oddly, 'little' to 'less littler'. It is as if many of the grammatical structures in the poem are designed to push in two different directions simultaneously, creating a textural frame which, the more it advances, the more it tends to self-nullify.

These are by no means all of the lexical and grammatical operations cummings employs, nor indeed are they even all of the tweaks performed on the structure of adjective phrases. The scope element, introduced above as the device that 'rounds off' the meaning of the adjective phrase, also comes in for particular enhancement in the poem. Take first of all the conventional usage of the structure, as embodied in the proverb 'Blood is thicker than water'. Here the comparative adjective 'thicker' connects up the entity 'blood' with the key item in the scope element, 'water'. Moreover, so that the adjective can, as it were, do its job, the entities thus compared need to be compatible at least in some measure – both blood and water are liquids, for example, and it is their relative viscosity that forms the nub of the comparison. A comparison of 'love' might therefore reasonably anticipate another noun element which derives from the broad compass of human emotion, yet nothing of the sort is offered by cummings. Instead, it is verbs, of all things, which often fill the position reserved for the compared entity. Consider the opening sequence of the poem in the context of the structural formula set up in B2:

intensifier	adjective	scope
more	thicker	than forget

Here the adjective phrase works ostensibly to develop a comparison of the noun 'love'. That noun represents the abstract domain of human experience, yet the grammatical relationship into which it is projected involves a comparative adjective standardly used to describe solids and liquids. Odder again is that the scope of reference of that adjective is specified not by another noun from the same broad set as 'love' but by a verb referring to a mental process.

Other eye-catching patterns litter the poem, one of which emerges in the second and third lines of the first stanza and is sustained for the remainder of the poem. Eschewing adjectives completely in this case, cummings inserts *adverbs of time-relationship*, like 'seldom', 'always' or 'never', into the main slot in the adjective phrase frame. Adverbs have a markedly different grammatical function from adjectives. Whereas adjectives describe qualities, adverbs normally describe circumstances. The adverbs employed here are of a specific type in that they provide circumstantial information about the duration and time-frame in which a verbal process did or did not take place. Furthermore, many of these adverbs function to communicate *negative* time relationships, and when piled up on one another, words like this can make a text very hard to unravel conceptually. For example, if someone were to remark of the book you are currently reading that 'This is a book you must not fail to miss', you might initially interpret this as a solid endorsement of the work in question. However, closer scrutiny will reveal that the remark means precisely the opposite; that is, that you should endeavour at all costs to avoid this book. In terms of discourse processing, then, the cumulative build up of words like 'fail', 'seldom', 'forget' and 'less' – words denoting a kind of negative semantic space – creates a complex interpretative framework which makes the text in certain respects almost impenetrable as a unit of meaning.

This framework is further problematised by other semantic devices in the poem. One such technique is *tautology* which in common parlance means saying the same thing twice and which is embodied in everyday phrases like 'War is war' or 'If she goes, she goes'. Many of cummings's comparative and superlative structures are full-blown logical tautologies simply because they replicate the basic premises of the proposition. Notice how the *same* entities are positioned either side of the adjectival structure in 'the sea is . . . deeper than the sea' or 'the sky is . . . higher than the sky'. In the strictest sense, these comparisons aren't comparisons at all because their underlying logical structures fail to establish new propositions. Other features embedded in the semantic fabric of the text include *lexical antonyms*, words of opposite meaning like the adjectives 'thicker' and 'thinner', the adverbs 'never' and 'always' and even the adjectival neologisms 'sunly' and 'moonly'. Antonyms are one way of establishing cohesion in a text, and perhaps rather ironically here, these opposites help shore up the poem's cohesive organisation when, so to speak, chaos is breaking out elsewhere in the grammatical system. Through its interplay between the levels of semantics, lexis and grammar, then, 'love is more thicker' is a poem which is strongly cohesive on the one hand but which still seems to resist interpretation on the other.

Stylistic analysis and interpretation

It is admittedly not easy, when faced with complex language like this, to discuss either *what* a text means or indeed *how* a text means. However, it is important to stress that, in spite of the veritable semantic labyrinth that is 'love is more thicker', the poem still does *communicate*. Indeed, a case could be made for arguing that it is the very opacity, the very indeterminacy of its linguistic structure which acts out and parallels the conceptualisation of love that cummings seeks to capture and portray. The individual stylistic tactics used in the poem, replicated so vigorously and with such consistency, all drive towards the conclusion that love is, well, incomparable. Every search for a point of comparison encounters a tautology, a semantic anomaly or some kind of grammatical *cul de sac*. Love is at once more of something and less of it; not quite as absolute or certain as 'always' but still more than just 'frequent'. It is deep, deeper even than the sea, and then a little bit deeper again.

Perhaps more contentiously, a case might be made for suggesting that many localised stylistic features hint at the struggle of an innocent trying to find some resource in the language system that adequately captures this aspect of felt emotion. Notice for example how the grammatical reduplication echoes the expressions of a child trying to come to grips with the irregularities of English; 'worsest', 'more badder' and 'baddest' are, after all, common developmental errors and these have close stylistic analogues in the poem. In many respects, this is a 'meta-poem', a poem about trying to write a poem. It seeks on the one hand to capture the world of human understanding and relation-ships, although the difficulty of the linguistic exercise draws attention in turn to the difficulty in mediating that world through language. This lack of reconciliation between form and content is mirrored in the way the resources of the language system are deployed. Buried in the semantics of the poem is its central enigma, acted out in the very contradictions ascribed to the poem's central theme, the experience of love.

Much of the internal dynamic of cummings's poem is sustained by the subversion of simple and everyday patterns of language, and it is the distortion of these commonplace routines of speech and writing that deliver the main stylistic impact. In a sense, there is nothing to be scared of in a text like 'love is more thicker' simply because, as analysis reveals, the grammatical patterns of English upon which it is based are in themselves straightforward. That is why it is important to be precise in stylistic analysis, and indeed, as noted in A1, it is an important part of the stylistic endeavour that its methods probe the conventional structures of language as much as the deviant or the distorted. In any case, to say that the language of this particular poem is 'deviant' is both a sweeping and contingent categorisation. Foregrounding never stays still for long, and once a striking pattern starts to become established in a text, so, by imputation, it begins to drift towards the background as new patterns take its place. There is also, as noted, a high level of symmetry in the poem, which means that the technique of foregounding-through-deviation is supplemented by foregounding-through-more-of-the-same (B1). Finally, I hope this exercise has demonstrated the importance of making the analysis retrievable to other students of style, by showing how not just one level, but multiple levels of language organisation simultaneously participate, some in harmony and some in conflict, in creating the stylistic fabric of a poem.

SENTENCE STYLES: DEVELOPMENT AND ILLUSTRATION   B3

This unit sets out to achieve two main goals. Focussing exclusively on grammar, it narrows down the broader perspective adopted in B2, which was principally interested in how various levels of language function in textual patterning. This unit also dovetails with other units in this strand both by offering a number of extensions to the model of grammar developed in A3 and by paving the way for the practical stylistic exercise that will be undertaken in C3.

Sentence types

The principal focus of attention thus far in our study of grammar and style has been on the clause and on the units which are situated beneath it on the rank scale (see A3, and also B2). So far, little attention has been paid to the highest unit of organisation in grammar, the sentence. Also known as the 'clause complex', the sentence is a far from straightforward category. Grammarians are divided about its importance with some arguing that it is really only an extension of the clause and others that it comprises a genuine unit with its own elements of structure. Whatever its precise theoretical status, the sentence is nonetheless a significant feature in the organisation of style and is worth elaborating upon in a little more detail here.

The most 'simple' type of sentence structure is where the sentence comprises just *one* independent clause. Here are two sentences, each containing a single clause apiece:

(1)   He ate his supper. He went to bed.

Not surprisingly, the term for sentences which are so constructed is *simple sentence*. A good technique for conceptualising sentence structure (and this will come more to the fore as we look at other types) is to imagine a sentence as a box whose housing forms a grammatical boundary and whose contents are variable. The conceptual structure of (1) would therefore be as two boxes placed side-by-side but without any formal linkage between them:

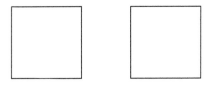

Although circumspection is always advised in generalisations about the effects of grammatical patterns, one of the stylistic functions of the simple sentence is often to engender a frenetic or fast-paced feel to a passage of description. Consider to this effect the following extract from Jerome K. Jerome's novel *Three Men in a Boat*. The novel's first person narrator has just been perusing a medical encyclopaedia only to convince himself that he suffers from all but two of the numerous ailments listed therein:

> I tried to examine myself. I felt my pulse. I could not at first feel any pulse at all. Then, all of a sudden, it seemed to start off. I pulled out my watch and timed it. I made it a hundred and forty-seven to the minute. I tried to feel my heart. I could not feel my heart. It had stopped beating.
>
> (Jerome 1986 [1889]: 5)

Most of the sentences in this short passage are made up of a single independent clause. In this narrative context, their sense of speed and urgency helps deliver a melodramatic mock tension as the hypochondriac narrator's self-examination unfolds.

The term *compound sentence* is used to describe structures which have more than one clause in them, and where these clauses are of equal grammatical status. Compound sentences are built up through the technique of coordination (see A3) and they rely on a fixed set of coordinating conjunctions like *and*, *or*, *but*, *so*, *for*, and *yet*. Each of examples 2–4 are *single* compound sentences which contain within them *two* coordinated clauses:

(2)   He ate his supper and he went to bed.

(3)   He ate his supper so he went to bed.

(4)   He ate his supper but he went to bed shortly after.

The best way of conceptualising the structure of compound sentences, using the 'boxes' analogy, is to imagine them as linked together like square beads on string, thus:

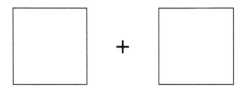

Compound sentences can perform a variety of functions, and the symmetrical nature of the connection between their units makes them a favoured style in material designed for junior readers. This fragment from a popular nursery rhyme is a compound sentence containing three coordinated clauses:

(5)   He huffed and he puffed and he blew the house down.

A similar technique of coordination is at work in this sequence from Hemingway's *The Old Man and the Sea*:

> They sat on the terrace and many of the fishermen made fun of the old man and he was not angry.
>
> (Hemingway 1960: 3)

Notice how this is coordination of the most basic sort. The direct coordinator *and* takes precedence over an 'adversative' conjunction like *but*, even when one might expect the latter. The adversative would after all impart some sense of contrast between the last two conjuncts – 'many of the fishermen made fun of the old man *but* he was not angry' – yet the narratorial perspective is kept almost wilfully non-interpretative here (see further C8).

Complex sentences involve two possible structural configurations, but their main informing principle is that the clauses they contain are in an asymmetrical relationship to one another. The first configuration involves *subordination*, where the subordinate clause is appended to a main clause. To form this pattern, subordinating conjunctions are used and these include *when, although, if, because* and *since*. As further variations on the sample sentences used so far, consider the following examples which are all two-clause complex sentences:

(6)   When he had eaten his supper, he went to bed.

(7)   Having eaten his supper, he went to bed.

(8)   Although he had just eaten his supper, he went to bed.

(9)   If he has eaten his supper, he must have gone to bed.

The conceptual structure for the subordinate relationship is to imagine that one box leans on another thus:

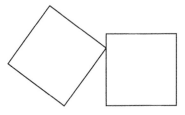

The main clause is the supporting box which, if taken away, will cause the (subordinate) box leaning on it to topple.

The second type of complex sentence involves the *embedding* of one structure inside another. To put it another way, this pattern involves taking a unit at the rank of clause and squeezing it inside another clause. This means that the embedded clause has had to be pulled down a rank ('downranked') in order to fit inside a structure of equal size. Here are some examples of complex sentences containing downranked clauses:

(10) Mary realised he had eaten his supper.

(11) She announced that he had gone to bed.

(12) That he had eaten his supper was obvious to everyone.

Highlighting the capacity of grammar to embed units within other units of varying sizes, the 'boxes' analogy conceives this structure conceptually as:

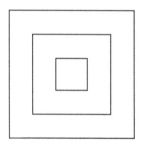

The outside box is the main clause and nested inside it is any number of downranked clauses. You can test for the main elements in each of examples (10) to (12), sorting out which is the matrix clause and which is the embedded, by using the various grammatical tests provided in A3.

Trailing constituents and anticipatory constituents

Although coordination between clauses is a founding principle of compound sentences, the same operation can be performed on other grammatical ranks. For example, words and phrases, as opposed to clauses, may be coordinated, as indicated by the following well-known couplet from Shakespeare's *Macbeth:*

> Tomorrow, and tomorrow, and tomorrow,
> Creeps in this petty pace from day to day.
>   (*Macbeth*, V.v.19–20)

Here, three occurrences of the temporal adverb 'tomorrow' are tied together with the coordinating conjunction 'and' to form an Adjunct. As the play draws to its conclusion, the grim inevitability of its denouement is signalled in this sequence of repetition, delivered here with an almost laboured monotony. The inexorability of the passage of time is picked up again at the end of the sequence with the repetition of another temporal adverb in the Adjunct 'day to day'. Thus, grammatical structure works to create temporal 'book-ends' around the main Predicator ('Creeps in') and Subject ('this petty pace') elements. The stylistic effectiveness of this configuration can be tested simply by pulling it apart; the following 'unravelled' version has little impact and nor does it seem to make much sense:

> This petty pace creeps in from day to day
> Tomorrow, and tomorrow, and tomorrow.

This point leads to another issue about grammatical patterning which concerns the positioning of various elements of clause structure in a particular text. Imagine the Subject, Predicator and Complement elements of a main clause as the hub around which satellite structures, principally Adjuncts and subordinate clauses, can be placed. In the Shakespeare example, Adjuncts are placed on either side of that hub. In such situations, where the weighting of elements on either side of a Subject and Predicator is balanced, we use the term *equivalent constituents* to explain this stylistic technique. However, the following sequence, which is the opening two lines of Michael Longley's poem 'The Ghost Orchid' displays a rather different pattern:

> You walked with me among water mint
> And bog myrtle when I was tongue-tied . . .
>   (Longley 1995)

The two Adjunct elements, filled by the prepositional phrases 'with me' and 'among water mint and bog myrtle', along with the subordinate clause ('when I was tongue tied'), come after the hub of the clause. *Trailing constituents* is the term used in stylistics for units which follow the Subject and Predicator in this way.

Finally, to the reverse technique, where Adjuncts and subordinate clauses are placed before the main Subject-Predicator matrix. When this occurs, the initial elements are known as *anticipatory constituents*. Here is good illustration of the principle at work in a piece of narrative description from Joseph Conrad's novella *The Secret Sharer*. The anticipatory constituents have been highlighted:

> *On my right hand* there were lines of fishing-stakes resembling a mysterious system of half submerged fences . . . *To the left* a group of barren islets had its foundations set in a blue sea . . . *And when I turned my head to take a parting glance*, I saw the straight line of the flat shore . . . *Corresponding in their insignificance to the islets of the sea*, two small clumps of trees . . .
>   (Conrad 1995 [1912]: 1)

These initial elements serve to orientate each sequence of unfolding description within the spatial perspective of the first person narrator. In their analysis of the grammar of this same passage, Leech and Short (1981: 83–9) note how the description is etched with meticulous detail in such a way that we are able to construct in our mind's eye the whole topography as perceived by the passage's lone human observer.

Illustrating grammar in action: Dickens's famous fog

Thus far in our developing model of grammar, short illustrations from literary texts have been used to illustrate each of the various categories introduced. In order to show how a range of devices of grammar can work simultaneously in a text, it will be useful to close this unit by focussing on a slightly longer passage. Much beloved of stylisticians because of its foregrounded patterns of language, this text is the second paragraph of Charles Dickens's novel *Bleak House*, reproduced here with sentences numbered for convenience:

(1) Fog everywhere. (2) Fog up the river, where it flows among green aits and meadows; fog down the river, where it rolls defiled among the tiers of shipping, and the waterside pollutions of a great (and dirty) city. (3) Fog on the Essex Marshes, fog on the Kentish heights. (4) Fog creeping into the cabooses of collier-brigs; fog lying out on the yards, and hovering in the rigging of great ships; fog drooping on the gunwales of barges and small boats. (5) Fog in the eyes and throats of ancient Greenwich pensioners, wheezing by the firesides of their wards; fog in the stem and bowl of the afternoon pipe of the wrathful skipper, down in his close cabin; fog cruelly pinching the toes and fingers of his shivering little 'prentice boy on deck. (6) Chance people on the bridges peeping over the parapets into a nether sky of fog, with fog all round them, as if they were up in a balloon, and hanging in the misty clouds.

(Dickens 1986 [1853]: 49)

Rather than attempt to tease out every significant stylistic feature of this famous paragraph – such an undertaking would on its own take up a whole unit and more – we shall restrict ourselves to analysis of just five noteworthy grammatical patterns in this text. Commentary on these patterns will be kept brief.

Feature 1
A key stylistic feature is the way the central noun 'fog' is elaborated (or perhaps more accurately, 'un-elaborated') throughout the passage. It is a resource of grammar that nouns commonly enter into combinations with other words so that any particular or special quality they possess can be identified and picked out. Thus, in a phrase like 'the thick grey fog nearby', the grammatical slots around the word 'fog' are filled up by a determiner ('the'), two adjectives ('thick grey') and an adverb ('nearby'). However, none of the available slots are thus filled in the passage and this marked absence of grammatical modification makes the central noun, 'fog', emerge as stark, undifferentiated and (literally) undetermined. Its characterless quality is reinforced by comparison, in that many other nouns in the passage receive precisely this sort of grammatical modification: eg. 'green aits', 'waterside pollutions' and 'a great (and dirty) city'.

Feature 2
A popular interpretation of this passage is to see it as a text with 'no verbs'. This is not strictly accurate, however, because only in the first three sentences and in part of sentence (5) have verbs been excised completely. In any case, there are plenty of verbs in the numerous subordinate clauses in the passage. A more rigorous stylistic description would therefore stipulate that the passage displays a restricted verbal development in its main clauses. In the opening sentences, the Predicator element has been ellipsed completely, and this takes with it all sense of verbal process. Later in the passage, from sentence (4), part of the Predicator element is offered, but significantly, one key element is omitted. This element, known as the *finite*, is often expressed by auxiliary verbs and it serves to provide, among other things, tense, polarity and grammatical agreement with the Subject. By offering only the main verbal component in 'lying', 'creeping' and 'pinching', Dickens effectively splits the Predicator in two so that we get a sense of ongoing process, but no indication of tense. Trying out the tag

tests developed in unit A3 is revealing in this respect. Applied to the sequence 'Fog creeping into the cabooses of collier-brigs', the tag test would pick out 'Fog' as Subject without any trouble, but the absence of a finite verbal particle creates problems in choosing a tense for the tag:

Fog creeping into the cabooses of collier-brigs [wasn't it?/isn't it?]

Fog creeping into the cabooses of collier-brigs, [so it is/so it was]

So while these clause patterns indicate both a basic verbal process and the location of that process, they offer no indication of tense, a consequence of which is that it is difficult to establish a time frame for the events narrated. Whereas the fog's omnipresence in the spatial context is well grounded, there is little sense of concrete anchoring in the corresponding temporal context.

Feature 3

The passage abounds in 'trailing constituents' in which grammatical build-up takes place towards the right of the main Predicator position. These clauses contain numerous subordinate clauses and Adjuncts of location, so again, and sustaining feature 2, the narrative is rich in detail about place but low in detail about time. The amount of information contained in these trailing constituents also brings into sharper relief the very sparseness of the material that is positioned to the left of the Predicator slot. Furthermore, the grammatical 'sprawl' that is brought about by these trailing constituents also facilitates an interesting textual ambiguity. In the sequences '. . . it flows . . .' and '. . . it rolls defiled . . .' (2), the pronoun 'it' serves a possible dual reference with respect to its two potential antecedents in the main clause. Is it the fog that flows and rolls, or is it the river? My own interpretation is that the ambiguity is motivated, and that it works to underscore the very blurring and indeterminacy that is ascribed to the core visual elements in the scene.

Feature 4

There is a gradual narrowing of spatial focus as the passage progresses. Whereas the first Adjunct declares that the fog is, well, everywhere, subsequent Adjunct elements move progressively right down into the localised, even microscopic, environment of the stem and bowl of the skipper's pipe. In tandem with this progressive narrowing through Adjuncts, the processes embodied by the related verbs in the main clauses also undergo an interesting change. In experiential terms (see unit A6), the processes associated with 'fog' are initially intransitive in that they do not impact upon a Goal. Here are four such examples, piled up in parallel in the fourth sentence: '. . . *creeping* into the cabooses . . . *lying* out on the yards . . . *hovering* in the rigging . . . *drooping* on the gunwales . . .'. However, just as the overall spatial focus narrows, so the transitivity pattern shifts to a Goal-directed one, as in 'fog cruelly *pinching* the toes and fingers . . .' (5). It is notable that the adverb 'cruelly' is the only instance where a grammatical element (here an Adjunct) is wedged between the 'Fog' and its following Predicator. It seems that the longer the passage goes on, the more menacing and spiteful the fog becomes.

Feature 5

The final sentence of the passage offers a good illustration of *internal foregrounding* (see B1). The pattern established from sentence 1 through to 5 gradually forms its own text-internal norm, so to keep us on our interpretative toes, as it were, Dickens subverts the pattern in the sixth sentence. This he does by creating a different Subject element and by shifting the lexical item 'fog' to the right of the Predicator. That said, 'fog' still receives no grammatical modification and therefore still maintains its undefined, indefinite feel. By showing how a pattern initially built through parallelism and repetition can ultimately be turned on its head, this fifth stylistic feature illustrates well the fluid and dynamic properties of foregrounding.

Summary

As one works through a text like the *Bleak House* passage, it is always important to remember that style comes from the totality of interrelated elements of language rather than from individual features in isolation. While it is not feasible to cover every aspect of language in an analysis, a useful way of dealing with this problem is to make up some sentences that you feel would be at odds with the stylistic techniques used in the passage under examination. This exercise, used extensively in a number of other units, helps tease out through contrast the features that *are* in the text. Here for example is a sample of utterly 'non-fog' language which unravels several of the five features identified above. You can work out which ones by yourself:

> Across the Essex Marshes, a thick choking fog of indistinct proportion was sweeping in.

In the context, a thoroughly un-Dickensian sentence to be sure.

A number of the features addressed here and in unit A3 are explored further in the practical activity developed in C3 while aspects of Dickens's prose feature in the survey of corpus stylistics across strand 12. In the following unit, attention focuses on another of the core levels of language as it applies to stylistic analysis. This is the level of sound.

B4 INTERPRETING PATTERNS OF SOUND

Unit A4 established a set of basic principles for the analysis of metre and rhythm in poetry. Continuing this theme, the present unit will raise and explore some issues concerning the significance of patterns of sound for stylistic analysis. In particular, this unit should encourage us to think about how, as stylisticians, we make connections between, on the one hand, the physical properties of the sounds represented *within* a text and, on the other, the non-linguistic phenomena situated *outside* a text to which these sounds relate.

Onomatopoeia

Onomatopoeia is a feature of sound patterning which is often thought to form a bridge between 'style' and 'content'. It can occur either in a *lexical* or a *nonlexical* form, although both forms share the common property of being able to match up a sound with a nonlinguistic correlate in the 'real' world. Lexical onomatopoeia draws upon recognised words in the language system, words like *thud*, *crack*, *slurp* and *buzz*, whose pronunciation enacts symbolically their referents outside language. Nonlexical onomatopoeia, by contrast, refers to clusters of sounds which echo the world in a more unmediated way, without the intercession of linguistic structure. For example, the mimicking of the sound of a car revving up might involve a series of nonlexical approximations, such as *vroom vroom*, or *brrrrm brrrrm*, and so on. As nonlexical onomatopoeia is explored in depth in reading D4, the remainder of this unit will concentrate mainly on the stylistic importance of lexical onomatopoeia.

The role that lexical onomatopoeia plays in the stylistic texture of poetry makes for an important area of study. The lexicon can be exploited for its imitative potential, with individual words being pressed into a kind of onomatopoeic service on the basis of their particular phonetic profiles. Random or happenstance sequences of sound can thus acquire a mimetic function in particular discourse contexts. Let us develop these observations by considering two short fragments of poetry, both of which display marked sound symbolism. The first is from Stephen Spender's poem 'Pylons' and the second from Gerard Manley Hopkins's 'The Windhover'. In both examples, the relevant sequences are highlighted:

(1)   [The valley . . . and the green chestnut . . .]
      Are mocked dry like the parched bed of a brook.

(2)   Brute beauty and valour and act, *oh, air, pride, plume, here*
      Buckle! [. . .]

In the sense that patterns of sound palpably evoke the visual elements of their respective descriptions, both examples are, to my ear, good illustrations of poetic onomatopoeia at work. The example from 'Pylons' is *alliterative* (see A4) because it foregrounds a certain type of consonant in order to ascribe a quality of aridity to the entity it describes. Note the dominance of the voiceless stops /k/ and /t/ in this line, supplemented by voiced stops /b/ and /d/ and the voiceless affricate consonant /tʃ/ in 'par*ch*ed'. Note also that because of their immediately preceding phonetic environment, the spelled 'd's at the end of both 'mocked' and parched' are, when read aloud, assimilated to the voiceless variant /t/. (This is a good illustration, worth noting in passing, of the sometime disparity between written language and spoken language.) Notably absent from the line are the conventionally 'softer' sounds like the fricatives /s/ and /z/, or 'slushier' sounds like the fricative /ʃ/ which is (significantly) found in a word like 'lu*sh*'. My point is that Spender foregrounds a particular set of consonant sounds in order to embody the dryness, the very desiccated quality of the empty brook that his poetic line describes.

The example from Hopkins represents a different kind of onomatopoeia, built not through consonant harmony but by a kind of vowel 'disharmony'. The highlighted words in (2) are describing the path of the windhover (a species of falcon) as it flies at speed through the air. If you try to sound out these words you may notice that the vowel progression between them is almost discordant, with the articulation of each new vowel representing a different place and manner of articulation in the oral cavity. Although accents of English vary, an informal approximation of the six relevant vowels would be: oh – eh – aye – oo – eea – uh. This sequence is a nexus of phonetic contrasts, between front and back vowels (eh/oo), between open and close vowels (uh/*eea*), between lip-rounded and unrounded vowels (oo/eh) and between shorter monophthongs (oh and uh) and longer diphthongs (aye and eea). My interpretation is that the constant shift in type of articulation, from high to low, back and forth and so on, follows the movement of the bird itself, such that the crisscrossing in phonetic space becomes a mirror of the angles, the spiralling and the swooping, that the windhover makes as it flies through the air. In sum, vowel mimesis works onomato-poetically by mediating with the nonlinguistic world. And because examples (1) and (2) both use sound symbolism to invite from the reader an affective response to a text, they can be said to express poetic *phonaesthesia*.

The 'phonaesthetic fallacy'

Did you find my interpretation of sound symbolism in (1) and (2) convincing? Can phonetic detail be matched up with a text in such a way? Or perhaps the interpretation reads too much into a few simple vowels and consonants? So were my views mere hunch?

    The simple truth of the matter is that in phonetics there is simply no such thing as a 'dry' consonant or a 'flying' vowel, and such impressionistic labels have no place whatsoever in the systematic study of speech sounds. If such direct connections could be made, it would mean that every time we encountered a consonant configuration like that in (1) we would instantly think 'dry', or every time we came across a sequence of vowels like that in (2) we would think of a bird's flight through the air. We need look no further than the preceding paragraph of this sub-unit for proof of this point. In the second sentence, beginning 'Can phonetic detail . . .', there were actually more of the so-called dry /k/, /t/ and /tʃ/ consonants than there were in the Spender line. You can go back and count them yourself, but the point is that you are unlikely, even when reading this sentence again, to conclude that it is a particularly 'dry' piece of prose. More tellingly, the final sentence of the previous paragraph has exactly the same progression of vowels as the Hopkins line:

oh	eh	aye	oo	eea	uh
so	were	my	views	mere	hunch?

You may have experienced a number of reactions to my sentence – what poor prose style, what a lame rhetorical question and so on – but I would be very surprised indeed if you felt that its sound structure mirrored the shimmering flight path of the European falcon as it flies, spectacularly and fleet of wing, across the horizon.

    Clearly, there is a certain risk in trying to connect up directly a particular feature of sound in a text with nonlinguistic phenomena outside the text, and the sort of interpretative practice which does make such direct connections might be termed the *phonaesthetic fallacy*. This is not to say that my feelings or intuitions about examples (1) and (2) were in any sense wrong; it is rather that my analysis drew an uncomfortably direct parallel between these intuitions and the raw linguistic material of the text. In other words, the fallacy lies in the assumption that language functions unproblematically as a direct embodiment of the real world.

The phonaesthetic fallacy, if not articulated in precisely the same terminology as here, is a serious issue for stylistic analysis. Nash talks of it as something that teachers of language and literature have come to dread when dealing with the interpretation of phonetic features in literary texts (Nash 1986: 130). Attridge notes as a failing in much traditional literary criticism that it uses aspects of sound to evoke directly the meaning of the text: a practice evident in common critical comments like 'rhythmic enactment' or 'appropriate sound-patterns' (Attridge 2004). So let me try then to set out some basic principles about the interpretation of sound symbolism that will help avoid the interpretive pitfall that is the phonaesthetic fallacy.

We need first of all to make the assumption that a particular piece of language is *intended* to be performed mimetically. If this function is not understood, then we simply do not seek out sound symbolism. The conventions of reading textbooks differ from those governing the reading of poetry, which is why (I assume) you were not primed to search out mimetic sound patterns in the earlier paragraph. Second, we should never lose sight of the text immediately surrounding the particular feature of style under consideration, the *co-text* in other words. In the Hopkins example, for instance, the salient items are preceded by a very different stylistic pattern, where coordination ('Brute beauty *and* valour *and* act') suggests a perhaps more languid precursor to the contrasting brisker and more strident delivery invited of the highlighted sequence. Related to this point, and echoing units A2 and B2, we need also to think about how a relevant feature is paralleled by other levels of language. In Hopkins, again, note how the disharmony at the phonetic level is underscored by the mixture of grammatical forms that carry these sounds, a mixture which comprises an uncoordinated sequence of nouns, verbs and adverbs and which is even fronted by a nonlexical expressive particle, 'oh'.

There are also conventions for reading sound imagery, such that certain types of sounds are conventionally interpreted in certain ways. Moreover, onomatopoeia works on the reader's familiarity with the entity described which means that we need to know that we are being told about, say, a dry brook or the flight path of a falcon, before we can search out a correspondence in sound. Attridge adopts the useful phrase *heightened meaning* to explain how onomatopoeic conventions work (Attridge 2004: 150). Phonetic and semantic properties interact with one another, and in a way that mutually reinforces and intensifies both aspects of language. Thus, the so-called 'dry' consonants in Spender are conventionally understood as heightening the semantic quality of aridity. This explains why a word like 'waterless', which contains 'softer' consonants like /w/, /l/ and /s/, would not have had the same impact even though it is semantically compatible in the context. It would simply not *heighten* meaning in the way that the word 'parched' does.

We cannot cut sound symbolism adrift from its overall discourse context because – and this is a point that extends to all stylistic practice – the linguistic system does not embody the real world directly. Meanings are signalled only indirectly, so it is a guiding principle of stylistic analysis to be cautious about treating any aspect of language as if it bears an inherent relationship with a given or felt experience. Taking these cautionary observations on board, unit C4 offers a programme for the analysis of a short poem by Michael Longley, in which sound symbolism is one of various levels of language explored. In the reading by Derek Attridge which supplements this unit, the emphasis on patterns of sound is maintained, with the focus on nonlexical as opposed to lexical onomatopoeia.

DEVELOPMENTS IN STRUCTURAL NARRATOLOGY

In unit A5, a distinction was drawn between the concepts of narrative *plot* and narrative *discourse*. It should be noted that this distinction, like many terms developed in this book, mirrors and to some extent simplifies a number of various parallel categories available in the stylistics literature. With particular respect to narrative analysis, my ordering of the elements *plot* and *discourse* is designed to correspond to other comparable pairings like *fabula* and *sjuzhet*, *histoire* and *discours*, and *story* and *discourse*. Whatever the precise terminology, the main point is that the first term in each pair captures the abstract chronological configuration of the core elements of plot and the second the discourse in and through which that plot is realised. The many and varied linguistic-stylistic permutations that are afforded by narrative discourse are covered in strands 6, 7 and 8, but in this unit the emphasis will be strictly on narrative *plot*. The unit begins by reviewing an important *structuralist* model of narrative and then continues with an application of it to two narrative texts.

An important feature of the narrative schema set out in A5 was its acknowledgment that narrative may be encoded in a variety of textual media, which include but are not restricted to film, cartoon, ballad, comic strip, prose fiction and oral vernacular. The two narrative texts that are to come under scrutiny here are 'celluloid' narratives, one film and the other animation, although both narratives have direct counterparts in prose fiction. There will be more to say on these texts shortly, but first to the model of analysis.

Propp's morphology of the folktale
In what became an influential study in structuralist narratology, the Russian scholar Vladimir Propp published in 1928 a 'morphology' of the fairy tale (or the 'folktale', in his terms). Propp's interest is principally in extrapolating out of a corpus of 115 actual stories a kind of blueprint for the folktale as a whole. Although this blueprint does not constitute an analysis of any individual story, its categories are designed so as to capture all of the possible elements available to *any* fairy story. The result of the study

is a finite list of *thirty-one* narrative functions, no less, and these functions are undertaken by *seven* basic types of character roles.

The way Propp sets about developing his list of narrative functions is to isolate from his corpus the recurring components of each fairy tale. Acknowledging that the names of the particular 'dramatis personae' may change from story to story, Propp argues that it is the question of *what* a tale's characters do that is important, not so much *who* does it or *how* it is done (Propp 1966 [1928]). This orientation therefore requires the rendering down of narratives into their raw, basic constituents, producing a kind of grammar of narrative which is indeed indicated by the reference to 'morphology' in the title of Propp's study.

According to Propp, a tale usually begins with some sort of initial situation after which some or all of the thirty-one narrative functions follow. The first function, for example, is where one of the members of a family, normally the character role of 'Hero', absents himself from home. This 'absentation' (*sic*) may be precipitated by the death of parents or by some similar calamity, whereupon the Hero may go to war, to the forest or even, curiously, to work. The second narrative function involves an interdiction being addressed to the Hero, normally taking the form of a warning that danger is present and including some instruction about what *not* to do. Following from the interdiction is the narrative function: 'violation of the interdiction'. For example, in the Walt Disney cartoon *Beauty and the Beast*, the Beast warns Beauty not on any account to go into the west wing of the castle (the interdiction), whereupon Beauty, er, goes into the west wing of the castle. The fourth of Propp's functions sees the arrival of the character role of 'Villain'. The Villain attempts to make 'reconnaissance' on the Hero, finding out about his whereabouts or about some vulnerability or weakness. And thus the pattern of the model develops, up to a total of thirty-one possible narrative plot functions.

Now, the point of Propp's model is not to imply that *all* narratives realise *all* functions. Nor is it to suggest that all narratives, in their manifestation as discourse, follow a straightforwardly linear chronology. Suffice it to say, there are numerous stylistic devices which give a stamp of originality to narrative as far as the actual telling of the story is concerned (see strands 6, 7 and 8). However, what Propp's model does is to try to define a genre of narrative discourse, the fairy tale, through a circumscribed set of core organisational parameters. How those parameters might be applied to more contemporary narratives is the focus of the next sub-unit.

The morphology of contemporary narrative

Thus far, the Proppian morphology may look at first glance like a rather antiquated analytic model, a model whose scope of reference embraces nothing more than the quaint oral narratives of a then fledgling Soviet Union. True, contemporary narratives do seem a long way off from the Russian folk story of the 1920s. However, as with any sound theoretical model, it is a central precept of the Proppian framework that it should have universal relevance. That means that it is designed to have the explanatory power to account for folk narratives beyond the specific corpus used in the design of the model, and even for narratives that had not even come into being at the time the model was developed.

Let us consider, in turn, two cases where the application of the Proppian model offers some interesting insights about narrative structure. Both film narratives, the first is Disney's cartoon *The Jungle Book* which is based, rather loosely it has to be said, on Rudyard Kipling's 'Mowgli stories'. The second is Chris Columbus's feature film *Harry Potter and the Philosopher's Stone* which is based, more closely this time, on the first instalment of J. K. Rowling's hugely successful series of 'Harry Potter' novels. What follows is a short exploration of the types and degree of coalescence that there is between the core categories of Propp's model and the key plot advancing functions of both films.

First of all, to Disney's animated film *The Jungle Book* which was released in 1967. Realising the first of Propp's functions, absentation, Mowgli the 'mancub' is displaced from his parents and home and is found wandering in the jungle. Mowgli, clearly fulfilling the character role of 'Hero', then acquires a Helper, a character role dually occupied by Bagheera the panther and later by Baloo the bear. Both friends warn Mowgli of the dangers of being in the jungle on his own (the 'interdiction' function), advice which of course Mowgli ignores (violation of the interdiction). Numerous other Proppian functions are realised thereafter. In a famous and hugely comic scene from the film, the Villain, Shere Khan the tiger, carries out reconnaissance on the Hero by interrogating the snake, Kaa. The Villain then attempts to take possession of the Hero (the sixth of Propp's functions) but in the course of the struggle injures Baloo, Mowgli's protector. This second event realises the eighth function of the model where the Villain hurts a member of the Hero's circle of family and friends. Hero and Villain eventually join in combat (function sixteen), and in the course of the struggle Mowgli uses fire (function twelve, the intercession of a magical agent) in order to scare off Shere Khan (function eighteen, the Villain is vanquished). Mowgli, having been enticed by the 'water girl' and her song, eventually goes back to the 'man village', and so the film concludes with the realisation of function twenty, the Hero returning home, and with perhaps the suggestion that the Hero will eventually be married or crowned (function thirty-one).

Clearly, not all of the thirty-one plot advancing functions are present in Disney's cartoon, but those that are realised square very closely indeed with the key Proppian categories. This is not to suggest that the makers of Disney's film worked to any kind of explicit blueprint of narrative structure – a copy of Propp is unlikely to have been to hand in the production process! The main issue is really about what makes a good story. Disney's cartoon draws out, from a finite list of universalised functions, a specific selection of plot advancing devices. What is interesting is that even though their particular settings, 'dramatic personae' and historical periods may change, a great many Disney films work to the same basic plot typology.

Columbus's film *Harry Potter and the Philosopher's Stone* (2000) is some fifty minutes longer than *The Jungle Book* and is pitched at older viewers, so its even fuller display of Proppian functions is perhaps no surprise. A running commentary on all realisations in the film would be rather dull, so Table B5.1 shows the main connections between Propp's model and the narrative functions realised in *Harry Potter*. The left of the table displays a category of the model, numbered in accordance with Propp's own sequence of functions, and on the right of the table is a short summary of the relevant plot development and character role as realised in the film. It is noticeable

Table B5.1 Propp's model and *Harry Potter and the Philosopher's Stone*

Propp's function	Narrative event in *Harry Potter and the Philosopher's Stone*
1. Hero absents himself	Harry Potter [Hero] has been orphaned and is forced to live in the home of his cruel aunt and uncle, the Dursleys.
2. Hero receives interdiction	Harry is told by the Dursleys *not* to go to Hogwart's school of wizardry
3. Interdiction is violated	Harry goes to Hogwart's school of wizardry
6. Villain attempts to deceive or to take possession	Unknown to all, Voldemort [Villain] has taken over the body of Professor Quirrel.
8. Villain harms member of Hero's family	Harry learns that Voldemort has killed his parents.
9. This harm made known: Hero goes/ is sent on a mission	Harry embarks on a mission to recover the philosopher's stone.
12. Hero gets helper and/ or magical agent	Harry receives (unexpectedly) a top-of-the-range broomstick, a Nimbus 2000.
25. Difficult task is set for Hero	Harry is charged with retrieving the 'golden snitch' in a game of Quidditch.
14. Hero uses magical agent.	Harry uses the Nimbus 2000 in the Quidditch game.
26. Task is accomplished.	Harry successfully retrieves the golden snitch.
16. Hero and Villain join in combat	Harry and Voldemort join combat.
17. Hero is branded	Harry has acquired a lightning-shaped scar through an earlier encounter with Voldemort.
28. False Hero is exposed	Quirrel exposed as the host of Voldemort.
29. False Hero is transformed	Quirrel transformed into dust during the combat.
18. Villain is defeated	Voldemort is defeated.
30. Villain is punished	Voldemort forced to leave the body of his dead host.
19. Initial misfortune is set right.	In the Hogwart's school competition, Harry's house Gryffindor is reinstated above their cheating rivals Slytherin.
20. Hero returns home	Harry leaves Hogwart's for the summer recess.

that certain of the narrative functions in the film are slightly out of kilter with the sequence developed in Propp. For example, Harry's parents have been killed by Voldemort prior to the first action of the film, yet Harry only later discovers this and to some extent relives the episode through flashback. Nonetheless, the sometime reordering and indeed repetition of the core narrative functions is precisely what the Proppian model seeks to accommodate, and in actual narrative discourse the use of flashback, prevision and other devices are markers of individuality in the story (see B7). It is interesting also that in neither of the two films are *all* of Propp's thirty-one functions drawn upon, but as we have seen, not all functions are needed to create a coherent narrative. What the identification of features shows, especially in the context of the *Harry Potter* checklist, is that many of the archetypical patterns that inform fairy stories are alive and well in certain genres of contemporary narrative. Admittedly, both film texts examined here are magical, mythical adventures much in the vein of the folktale, so the success with which the Proppian model can accommodate *all* narrative genres remains to be proven. Nonetheless, a narrative genre like the Western, whether embodied in film or prose media, seems an obvious candidate for scrutiny, as might the romance, the detective story or the science fiction story. Moreover, in film criticism, cross-comparisons between different genres of film often focus on their shared narrative elements. The plot of Disney's feature-length animation *The Lion King*, for instance, is often likened to that of Shakespeare's *Hamlet*. This says as much about the narrative structure of *Hamlet* as it does about Disney's cartoon, and a Proppian breakdown of the core organising units of Shakespeare's play would make for an intriguing stylistic analysis. In all, the import of Propp's model is not to suggest that all narratives are the same, but rather to explain in part why all narratives are different.

The focus in the next unit along this thread explores narrative through another type of textual medium, the narrative of everyday spoken interaction. The unit below concentrates on narrative as discourse and assesses some of the developments that have taken place in the use of transitivity for narrative analysis.

STYLE AND TRANSITIVITY

Writing about narrative, the American novelist Henry James once posed a pair of rhetorical questions: 'What is character but the determination of incident? What is incident but the illustration of character?'. The integration of 'character' and 'incident' may at first glance seem a curious alignment, but closer scrutiny suggests that James's formula serves very much as a template for the analysis of *transitivity* in narrative. In the model proposed in unit A5, it was suggested that a principal mode of narrative characterisation is the transmission of 'actions and events'. This mode refers to the way character is developed through and by the semantic processes and participant roles embodied in narrative discourse. Character may for instance be determined by degree of influence on narrative incidents, by degree of active involvement in the forward momentum of the plot. Alternatively, character may be determined by detachment from narrative incident, by the positioning, say, of an individual as a passive observer of the events that unfold around them. As noted here and elsewhere, the linguistic framework which encompasses this aspect of narrative organisation is transitivity and this unit will review two of the various applications this model has received in narrative stylistics.

Developments in the analysis of style and transitivity

Over the years, stylisticians have returned regularly to the transitivity model in their analyses of text, and especially in their analyses of narrative text. One particular study, recognised as one of the key early essays in modern stylistics, was conducted by the eminent functional linguist M. A. K. Halliday (1971), architect of the very model of transitivity which informs this strand. In that now classic paper, Halliday applies the framework to William Golding's novel *The Inheritors* and explores, amongst other things, the linguistic patterns which encode the 'mind-styles' of the various Neanderthal peoples who inhabit the story. Whereas the bulk of the novel is narrated from the perspective of Lok, one of a primitive group of Neanderthals, the later stages of the book see Lok and his people supplanted by a more advanced tribe. Halliday argues that choices in transitivity reflect this transition. The behaviour of Lok's tribe is depicted as discontinuous and rather aimless, where physical action rarely affects objects in the immediate environment. In more explicitly experiential terms (see A6), 'Lok language' is marked consistently by material processes which realise an Actor element but no Goal element, in clauses like: 'A stick rose upright' or 'The bushes twitched'. Significantly, these Goal-less processes make the action specified seem self-engendered, even when it is clear from the narrative context that they are brought about by the external agency of Lok's enemies. Lok's failure to see a 'joined up' world of actions and events is therefore conveyed through systematic choices in transitivity, although no such failure in understanding is embodied by the transitivity patterns of the more advanced tribe whose way of configuring the world is, according to Halliday, more like our own.

Halliday's study is important in a number of respects. By using narrative discourse as a test site for a particular model of language, it illustrates well the usefulness of stylistic analysis as a way of exploring both literature *and* language. It also shows how intuitions and hunches about a text (and yes, stylisticians rely on intuitions and hunches) can be explored systematically and with rigour using a retrievable procedure of analysis. That is not to say, however, that Halliday's pioneering analysis was entirely flawless in its design or uncontroversial with respect to the scholarly reception it received. By suggesting that the text's linguistic structure embodies its meaning as discourse, Halliday does make a very strongly 'mimetic' (see B4) claim about the explanatory power of the transitivity model. He argues for instance in respect of 'Lok language' that it is no doubt 'a fair summary of the life of the Neanderthal man' (1971: 350). The methods employed in his study, and this sentiment in particular, are what stimulated Stanley Fish's well-known critique of stylistics, facetiously entitled 'What is stylistics and why are they saying such terrible things about it?', which followed in the wake of Halliday's analysis (Fish 1981: 59–64). Although this is not the place to review that debate in detail, Fish's attack continues to attract rebuttals from stylisticians to the present day, and the polemic has proved important in helping shape the way stylisticians think about the connections between analysis and interpretation (see the further reading suggestion for this unit given at the end of the book).

Several years after Halliday's study, Kennedy used the transitivity model to explore a key passage from Joseph Conrad's novel *The Secret Agent* (Kennedy 1982). In this climactic scene of the story, Mrs Verloc, who has just discovered that her husband has been involved in the death of her brother Stevie, kills a seated Mr Verloc with a carving knife. What is of particular interest to Kennedy is the manner by which Mr Verloc's death is described. For example, in over four hundred words of narrative description, it is striking that no mental processes at all are attributed to Mrs Verloc, giving little if any indication of what this character feels, thinks or perceives. Moreover, although one would anticipate that Mrs Verloc would feature in some material processes – she is after all the 'doer' of the killing – very few of the processes that are realised are Goal-directed. Instead, Goal-less patterns like the following are common: 'She started forward . . .', 'she had passed on towards the sofa . . .'. Mrs Verloc is thus represented as a character whose actions are done seemingly without reflection and without directly affecting the entities (including her husband) that surround her.

The pattern of transitivity which defines Mr Verloc is rather different. He participates in a few non-Goal directed material processes, such as 'He waited . . .' or 'He was lying on his back . . .'. In fact, some of these sequences, like 'He stared at the ceiling', would be coded in the later version of the transitivity model (see A6) as *behavioural* processes insofar as they tend to straddle the interface between material and mental processes. However, the overwhelming majority of the processes ascribed to Verloc are full-blown mental processes which feature him in the role of Sensor and which normally include a Phenomenon element. Patterns like the following are the norm: 'Mr Verloc heard the creaky plank in the floor'; 'He saw partly on the ceiling and partly on the wall the moving shadow of an arm'; 'Mr Verloc [recognised] the limb and the weapon.'. Thus, Verloc is portrayed as someone who is thoroughly aware of everything that is going on around him, yet in spite of his mental acuity, paradoxically, is unable to instigate the action necessary to prevent his own death. By contrast, his wife is portrayed as an insensate being, and as a being whose physical actions rarely influence any external objects in her environment.

The question which these two different characterisations-in-transitivity raise, then, is how is it that Mr Verloc comes, as it were, to be dead? One technique Conrad uses is simply to push the narrative forwards by using material processes with non-human Actors. In this respect, the sequence 'the carving knife had vanished' is especially revealing. A similar technique is the use of the passive (see A6) which allows the deletion of any human Actor that might be responsible for a process: 'The knife was already planted in his breast' is, again, a telling sequence. So, while Mrs Verloc may in the strictest sense be the killer of Mr Verloc, that is not what the transitivity profile of Conrad's text asks us to see.

Conrad employs a further stylistic technique known as *meronymic agency*, the use of which to some extent unites the interests of both Kennedy and Halliday. A slightly misleading term in that 'metonymy' (A11) is the concept which informs it, meronymic agency involves the part 'standing for' the whole in such a way as to place a human body part, rather than a whole person, in the role of an Actor, Sensor, Sayer and so on. This technique stands in contrast to the default position, known as *holonymic agency*, where the participant role is occupied by a complete being. Although not articulated explicitly in either paper, much of what Mrs Verloc does and most of what Lok does is, in experiential terms, carried out through the intercession of their body parts. For instance, it is Mrs Verloc's hand, never 'Mrs Verloc', which acts in key Goal-directed processes in the passage like 'Her right hand skimmed lightly the end of the table' and 'a clenched hand [was] holding a carving knife'. By contrast, Lok's nose and ears seem to do most of the work for him: 'His nose smelled this stuff', 'His ears twitched' and so on. Although these meronyms do different stylistic jobs in their respective narrative contexts, this type of agency is a recurring feature in the transitivity profile of many types of prose fiction. The (literal) disembodiment of a character often makes what they do, say or think appear involuntary, cut adrift from conscious intervention. It can also serve to differentiate the character experientially from other characters who are portrayed, say, in holonymic terms. Importantly, the technique sometimes connects a style of writing with a particular literary genre. This particular theme is resumed across the way in unit C6 where some observations are made on how the transitivity model can be extended to account for these broader dimensions of style. In the unit below, attention turns to the concept of point of view, which is a facet of narrative characterisation which complements well patterns of transitivity.

APPROACHES TO POINT OF VIEW   B7

The first unit along this thread introduced some basic terms and categories for the study of point of view in narrative. It was noted in that unit that a great deal has been written on, and various models have been proposed for, the stylistic analysis of point of view in prose fiction. This unit provides an opportunity to review some important developments in point of view studies as well as to 'tidy up' theoretically some of the competing models of analysis.

Planes of point of view in narrative fiction

In an influential publication on prose composition, the narratologist Boris Uspensky proposed a four-way model for the study of point of view in fiction (Uspensky 1973). This model was later revised and refined by Roger Fowler (Fowler 1996 [1986]: 127–47) so it is probably best to refer to this composite framework of analysis as the 'Fowler-Uspensky model'. The four components identified by the Fowler-Uspensky model of point of view are as follows:

(i)   point of view on the *ideological* plane
(ii) point of view on the *temporal* plane
(iii) point of view on the *spatial* plane
(iv) point of view on the *psychological* plane

The broad compass of the model has proved significant in shaping much stylistic work on point of view because it helps sort out different components in narrative organisation. However, certain aspects of it are rather confusing and the review which follows will suggest some simplification and realignment of its four categories. But first, to definitions of the four categories themselves.

Point of view on the ideological plane

The term *ideology* has a wide scope of reference. It refers to the matrix of beliefs we use to comprehend the world and to the value systems through and by which we interact in society. It follows then that the concept of point of view on the ideological plane refers to the way in which a text mediates a set of particular ideological beliefs through either character, narrator or author. Of authorial ideology, Fowler notes how Tolstoy's Christianity, Lawrence's celebration of sexuality and Orwell's hatred of totalitarianism shape respectively the ideologies articulated in their work. Narratives also manifest ideology at the level of character, where the ideas expressed by fictional characters serve as vehicles for ideologies which may or may not accord with those of the real author. For example, the character of 'the Citizen' in the 'Cyclops' episode of Joyce's *Ulysses* is portrayed as a republican ideologue whose short-sighted and philistine outlook cuts across the other ideological positions set up in and by the text. Indeed, it is a tenet of the Fowler-Uspensky model that the more the different value systems articulated in a work compete with one another then the richer and more interesting becomes the work itself.

In the course of his adaptation of Uspensky's ideas on ideological point of view, Fowler makes the telling comment that a novel 'gives an interpretation of the world it represents' (1996: 130). This immediately begs the question: what sort of narrative, whether prose fiction or an oral story of everyday experience, does *not* give an interpretation of the world it represents? Furthermore, what type of text – drama, poetry or prose – is *not* ultimately enshrined in some framework of ideology? These are important questions and they highlight the problems that are attendant on trying to align a particularised narrative technique like point of view with an all-embracing concept like 'ideology'. Indeed, the domain of ideology is so broad that just about any aspect of narrative can be brought within its compass, whether it be a facet of narrative 'voice' like author, narrator, character or persona, or an element of narrative 'preoccupation' like emblem, theme, motif, and most important of all, characterisation. What has tended to happen in much narrative stylistics is that ideological point of view has become an all too accommodating 'bucket category' into which more narrowly defined elements of narrative organisation are placed. A result of this practice is that some of the more subtle nuances of textual meaning are glided over. In sum, the concept of ideological point of view, if tempting as an analytic tool, needs to be treated with some caution because it is simply too wide to have much explanatory power. A good case for a fully workable category of ideological point of view remains to be made.

Point of view on the temporal plane

If the first category of the point of view model tends to be rather too broad to be usefully serviceable, the second tends arguably to be somewhat misplaced in the overall context of narrative. Point of view on the temporal plane, in the terms of the Fowler-Uspensky model, is about the way relationships of time are signalled in narrative. Temporal point of view envelops a whole series of stylistic techniques such as *repetition*, *analepsis* (flashback) and *prolepsis* (prevision or flashforward). In the reading which comprises unit D7, Mick Short examines a number of these aspects of temporal point of view in Irvine Welsh's novel *Marabou Stork Nightmares*. Welsh's narrative exploits narrative time relationships in challenging ways; beginning in the narrating present, it relives the bulk of the story, including a parallel fantasy narrative, as flashback. Another temporal technique, known as *duration* (Genette 1980: 86), relates to the temporal span of a story and accounts for our impression of the way certain events may be accelerated or decelerated. Whereas the entire sweep of, say, Joyce's *Ulysses* is confined to a single day, one paragraph of Virginia Woolf's *To the Lighthouse* marks a twenty-year interval – two extremes of the concept of duration. Temporal point of view basically covers any kind of manipulation of time sequence in narrative, explaining how certain events might be relayed as remote or distant, others as immediate or imminent.

Temporal point of view is certainly an important narrative category, but the question is still begged as to where precisely it should be situated in a multi-dimensional narrative model of the sort proposed in A5. In fact, if we think through the organisation of that model, temporal point of view seems to be less about focalisation and viewpoint and rather more about narrative structure; it does after all encompass the structural segments and sequential progression of the time-line of a narrative. Much of what is analysed under the umbrella term 'temporal point of view' is to do with temporal organisation as it relates to narrative structure. My suggestion is, again, to approach this admittedly useful concept with some caution.

Point of view on the spatial and psychological planes

If the first two categories of the Fowler-Uspensky model are not exactly watertight theoretically, the good news, so to speak, is that the remaining two, spatial and psychological point of view, really do embody the core characteristics of the concept. Exploration of these two categories will take us through to the end of this unit. Spatial point of view, as demonstrated in unit A7, is about the narrative 'camera angle' and is a device which has palpable grammatical exponents in deixis and in locative expressions. The passage from Iain Banks's *The Crow Road*, where the character of McHoan acted as reflector, illustrated well how these linguistic markers work to establish spatial point of view in a text. However, there were in addition to those indices of physical viewpoint a number of other stylistic markers, such as references to the reflector's senses, thoughts and feelings, which suggested that a more internalised, psychological perspective had been adopted. Uspensky classifies such cases where 'the authorial point of view relies on an individual consciousness (or perception)' as point of view on the *psychological* plane (Uspensky 1973: 81). This formula also hints (in its reference to 'perception') that spatial viewpoint is really one dimension of the broader technique of psychological point of view.

To develop further this idea of the interplay between spatial and psychological point of view, consider by way of illustration the following passage from Ian McEwan's novel *Amsterdam*. In this episode Rose Garmony, an eminent surgeon whose politician husband has just become embroiled in a political scandal, awakes to find nine members of the press outside her London apartment:

> ... she stared down at the group – there were nine of them now – with controlled fascination. The man had collapsed his extendable pole and had rested it against the railings. One of the others was bringing a tray of coffees from the takeaway shop on Horseferry Road. What could they ever hope to get that they didn't already have? And so early in the morning. What sort of satisfaction could they have from this kind of work? And why was it they looked so alike, these doorsteppers, as though drawn from one tiny gene puddle of humanity?
>
> (McEwan 1998: 94–5)

What happens in this passage is that spatial perspective dovetails with and indeed shades into psychological perspective. Rose Garmony is clearly the reflector of fiction throughout the passage, and her viewing position is established early on with locative expressions like 'down at the group' and deictic markers referring, for instance, to one member of the group 'bringing' (as opposed to 'taking') a tray of coffees. Like an establishing shot in visual film narrative, Rose's demeanour is caught as she stares down at the group; thereafter, a point of view shot shows us what she sees. However, the overall dynamic of point of view development does not stop there. The sequence beginning 'What could they ever hope . . .' marks a further shift into the conscious thought processes of Rose Garmony as she watches the paparazzi outside her home, a pattern which is sustained for the remainder of the passage. Her thoughts are tracked by means of a special mode of thought presentation known as Free Indirect Thought, on which there will be more in the unit below.

It is important to stress that the type of point of view development identified in the McEwan passage, where a spatial perspective shifts almost seamlessly into the cognitive field of a character, is an extremely common progression in prose fiction. Whereas the passage is focalised entirely from Rose's point of view, the slip from her role as anchor for spatial viewpoint into her role as conscious thinker is almost imperceptible, and is in part achieved through the particular device employed for representing her thoughts. This suggests that there are good grounds for subsuming the category of spatial point of view into the broader category of psychological point of view. In fictional narrative, psychological point of view is an extremely rich site for stylistic creativity and this issue will be explored more fully along this strand in C7. The unit below considers some of the key techniques of speech and thought presentation, one of which has already been hinted at in this unit.

TECHNIQUES OF SPEECH AND THOUGHT PRESENTATION   B8

Unit A8 introduced a basic model for assessing how speech and thought is represented in narrative while in B7 some observations were made on different planes of point of view in prose fiction. This unit offers, amongst other things, an opportunity to 'marry' both topics by examining the way both narratorial viewpoint and character perspective can be mediated through techniques of speech and thought presentation. The following sub-unit will look at the more indirect techniques, dealing particularly with the special category of Free Indirect Discourse. Then, attention focuses on some of the more direct forms of speech and thought presentation, with particular emphasis on the Free Direct mode, in both its speech and thought guises. The final sub-unit offers a short commentary on the connections between point of view and speech and thought presentation.

Indirect discourse presentation

Whatever the particular category used, all of the techniques of speech and thought presentation represent a shift away from basic narrative structure towards the discourse of a particular character. The external narrative structure onto which the modes of speech and thought are grafted is referred to as Narrator's Representation of Action (NRA). It describes the actions, perceptions and states that occur in the world of the fiction; it basically encompasses all non-speech and non-thought phenomena (see Short 1996: 292). As noted in the first unit of this strand, the most 'minimal' transition into a character's speech or thought is where a narrator reports that speech or thought has taken place but offers no indication or flavour of the *actual* words used. Narrative Report (of speech/thought) thus marks the first step away, as it were, from NRA and although it is often used to summarise whole stretches of reported speech or thought, that is not the only narrative function it serves. Consider the following episode from Henry Fielding's novel *Tom Jones*. Here the eponymous hero, although required to leave the room midway through the encounter, finds himself momentarily in the company of some 'great personages':

> . . . the conversation began to be, as the phrase is, extremely brilliant. However, as nothing past in it which can be thought material to this history, or indeed, very material in itself, I shall omit the relation; the rather as I have known some very fine polite conversation grow extremely dull, when transcribed into books [. . .]
>
> He [Tom Jones] was no sooner gone, than the great personages who had taken no notice of him present, began to take much notice of him in his absence; but if the reader hath already excused us from relating the more brilliant part of this conversation, he will be very ready to excuse the repetition of what may be called vulgar abuse . . .
>
> (Fielding 1970 [1749]: 277–8)

Fielding rather subtly uses the Narrative Report of Speech (NRS) mode both as a mechanism for compressing a sequence of extended dialogue and as an ironising device to critique the 'great personages'. With characteristically false modesty, Fielding's narrator politely demurs from transcribing such reputedly 'fine' talk thereby portraying as arid and effete the conversation of the assembled socialites.

Of all the categories of the speech and thought framework, there is one mode that has come under particular scrutiny from a stylistic perspective. This mode is Free Indirect Discourse (FID), a term which usefully subsumes both its speech (FIS) and thought (FIT) variants. The importance of this narrative technique is evidenced in the existence of numerous other terms for it, such as *erleßte rede*, 'indirect interior monologue' and *style indirect libre*. What is of especial interest to stylisticians is the impression this mode gives of both a character and narrator speaking simultaneously, through a kind of 'dual voice' (yet another term for FID!). Recalling the definition offered in A8, this mode displays all the features of indirectness but, crucially, it lacks a reporting clause and inverted commas. Consider the following brief example of the technique 'at work'. In this passage from Malcolm Lowry's novel *Under the Volcano*, M. Laruelle is contemplating his future in Mexico just before, in the second paragraph, his thoughts turn abruptly and rather more trivially towards the weather:

> Yet in the Earthly Paradise, what had he done? He had made few friends. He had acquired a Mexican mistress with whom he quarrelled, and numerous beautiful Mayan idols he would be unable to take out of the country, and he had –
> M. Laruelle wondered if it was going to rain . . .
>
> (Lowry 1984 [1947]: 16)

To give some idea of how effective this first paragraph of FIT is and of how smoothly it blends, or gives the impression of blending, both narrator and character voices, it is worth rewriting it in another mode. A useful technique in stylistic analysis, the transposition of a passage into other structural possibilities often sheds light on the subtleties of its textual composition. If for example the passage were written as Direct Thought (see the criteria in A8), the result would be rather more stilted and contrived in feel:

> 'Yet in the Earthly Paradise, what have I done?' he wondered. 'I have made few friends', he thought to himself. He pondered, 'I have acquired a Mexican mistress with whom I quarrel . . .'

Alternatively, a Free Direct version (see A8), which would dispense with both reporting clauses and inverted commas, would certainly add some immediacy to the narrative representation:

> Yet in the Earthly Paradise, what have I done? I have made few friends. I have acquired a Mexican mistress with whom I quarrel . . .

With respect to Lowry's original, however, the stylistic force of the Free Indirect mode inheres in its seeming coalescence of the thoughts of the character with the structural framework, including deixis and tense, of a third-person heterodiegetic narrative. This coalescence results in an apparent blurring of focus where it is often difficult to distinguish whether the thoughts relayed are to be attributed to a participating character or to the external third-person narrator. This explains to some extent the jolt delivered by the second paragraph as it shifts into the Indirect Speech mode: the dual voice of FIT evaporates as the narrative thread is brought more tightly under the control of the narrator. In fact, such is the schism between the IS and FIT modes here that it even suggests that M. Laruelle is someone other than the reflector of fiction in the paragraph preceding.

These general principles of FID apply to third-person narratives, narratives which offer the opportunity to fashion a seeming split between the voices of character and narrator. What, then, of first-person narratives where narrator and character may be one and the same entity? In other words, how does FID work in *homodiegetic* as opposed to heterodiegetic fiction? To answer these questions, consider first of all the following extract from a homodiegetic narrative written in the first person:

> Wednesday. In the afternoon, Haze (Common-sensical shoes, tailor-made dress) said she was driving downtown to buy a present for a friend of a friend of hers, and would I please come too because I have such a wonderful taste in textures and perfumes. 'Choose your favourite seduction,' she purred.
>
> (*Lolita*; Nabokov 1986 [1955]: 50)

Here, in what is a very common type of staged progression in narrative, a sequence begins in Indirect Speech ('Haze said she was driving downtown'), then 'slips' into more free and more direct forms, before culminating in Direct Speech ('Choose your favourite seduction', she purred.). This sequence contains a transitional sequence of FIS: 'Would I please come too because I have such a wonderful taste in textures and perfumes.' Now, the criteria for identifying FID in a first-person, as opposed to third-person, narrative are slightly different because of a variation in the overall pronoun system of the homodiegetic narrative. In reported speech, any second person pronouns used to address the character-narrator are switched, not to the third person, but to the *first* person. Whereas the FIS sequence highlighted does *not* capture the exact words that would have been said to the narrator, a Direct Speech rendition of it would ('Will *you* please come too . . .'), thereby bringing it into line with the actual DS sequence following ('Choose *your* favourite seduction'). So although much of its stylistic import remains the same, Free Indirect Discourse in first-person narratives behaves structurally rather differently from that used in third-person narratives (and see further the activities appended to the readings in unit D8).

Direct discourse presentation

The Free Direct modes of speech and thought presentation have a very different kind of stylistic currency compared to their counterparts in the Free Indirect modes. For example, Free Direct Thought (FDT) is the mainstay of the so-called 'stream of consciousness' technique of prose writing. This technique involves supplementing FDT with a type of grammatical abbreviation known as *ellipsis*, to produce a fast-paced flow of sometimes fragmentary or partial thoughts as they enter the consciousness of

DIALOGUE IN DRAMA

Across in A9, a model for the analysis of dialogue was suggested which comprised two principal methodological orientations. The first of these involves a focus on the way spoken discourse is *structured*; on how it is organised in a linear fashion and how its various components are bolted together. A structural analysis of discourse thus seeks to explore the connection (or sometimes, lack of connection) in dialogue between questions and answers, statements and acknowledgements, requests and reactions, and so on. The second orientation involves the study of discourse in terms of *strategy*. Here attention is focussed on the way speakers use different interactive tactics at specific points during a sequence of talk. As observed in A9, the axis of selection forms a strategic continuum ranging from 'direct' to 'indirect', along which different types of utterances can be plotted in terms of their varying degrees of politeness.

If not always signalled in precisely these terms, most stylistic research on drama dialogue over the years has focussed on one or the other planes of organisation. The main thrust of this work, again not always flagged up explicitly, has been both to explain how characterisation is created through patterns of language and to highlight the points of departure and/or intersection between the discourse world of the play and the discourse situation of the world outside the play. This short unit surveys some of the issues and developments arising from this research in discourse stylistics.

The strategies of dialogue

Analysing play dialogue in terms of discourse *strategy* often involves cross-reference between the character level and the higher-order interactive level of playwright and audience/reader (see A9). Not surprisingly, many interesting insights have come from studies of the 'Theatre of the Absurd' where particularly rich comparisons can be drawn between the discourse worlds inside and outside the play. The tradition of absurd writing is characterised by a preoccupation with the apparent futility of human existence, and this often manifests in play talk that, when compared to the socio-linguistic routines of everyday verbal interaction, stands out as deviant, anti-realist or just plain daft.

Here is a brief and relatively straightforward example of how our expectations about discourse routines can act as a context-framing device for interpreting play dialogue. In the following scene from N. F. Simpson's absurdist play *One Way Pendulum*, a courtroom has been hastily assembled inside a domestic living room to facilitate Mr. Groomkirby's 'swearing in' ceremony:

> *The Usher enters followed by Mr. Groomkirby, whom he directs into the witness box.*
> *Mr. Groomkirby takes the oath.*
> Mr. Groomkirby: (*holding up a copy of 'Uncle Tom's Cabin'*)
>   I swear, by Harriet Beecher Stowe, that the evidence I shall give shall
>   be the truth, the whole truth, and nothing but the truth.

| Judge: | You understand, do you, that you are now on oath? |
| Mr. Groomkirby: | I do, m'lord. |

(N. F. Simpson 1960: 60)

A courtroom is institutionally sanctioned to deal exclusively with legal proceedings, and is manifestly not the sort of thing that can be set up by anybody in, for example, a domestic living room. Furthermore, there are established procedures for ritualised activities such as the swearing-in of witnesses, and shared assumptions between participants about the way these routines are conducted thus form part of the cognitive context of the courtroom. Although Mr. Groomkirby's 'swearing-in' contains many instantly recognisable formulaic structures such as ' . . . the truth, the whole truth and nothing but the truth . . .', the use of *Uncle Tom's Cabin* clearly violates the pragmatic conditions which govern this ritual. These conditions, known as *felicity conditions* (Austin 1962: 39), proscribe the swearing in of a witness by anything other than a designated religious text – irrespective of its literary merit. What operates in the discourse world inside the play, then, is thoroughly at odds with the sanctioned routines of the world *outside* the play.

As a footnote to this commentary, it is worth noting how the judge expresses no surprise at the general procedures of Groomkirby's swearing-in ceremony. Were the judge to have outlawed *Uncle Tom's Cabin* and declared the swearing-in inadmissible, as presumably any judge in the 'real' world would do, then this appeal to everyday modes of conduct would have lessened greatly the absurdity of the sequence. The responses of interlocutors at the character level to something that is unanticipated at the higher-order interactive level, such as the Judge's reaction to Mr. Groomkirby's use of *Uncle Tom's Cabin*, is often an important index of dramatic genre. Absurdist, as opposed to realist, drama tends to make use of a special kind of incongruity that comes from a mismatch between communicative strategy and discourse context, often deriving from fictional speakers *not* observing the familiar or expected routines that are cued by everyday discourse contexts. And these incongruities often have humorous outcomes (see further the special web strand on style and humour).

The structure of dialogue

One of the most significant studies of the structures of play talk is Deirdre Burton's book on dialogue and discourse (Burton 1980). Burton investigates a number of play texts using a variety of different models in conversation analysis and speech act theory (see for example C5). Her book culminates with a lengthy breakdown of Harold Pinter's play *The Dumb Waiter* (1960) using a single model of discourse structure, although it has to be said that the more eclectic chapters leading up to this analysis offer rather more stylistic insight than this longer analysis. That aside, the thrust of her structural analysis is very much in keeping with the rationale of stylistics in that it seeks to base interpretation on rigorous and retrievable methods of analysis.

As an illustration of the sorts of issues Burton's study raises, consider the following short extract from *The Dumb Waiter*:

| GUS: | I want to ask you something. |
| BEN: | [no response] |

The restaurant script is a knowledge structure which is activated by an essential precondition – that is, wanting to eat. The script is sustained further as a 'giant causal chain' by accompanying conceptual slots such as *roles*, which include sub-entries like WAITER and CUSTOMER, or *props*, with entries like TABLE and MENU (Schank and Abelson 1977: 43; and see A10). Importantly, scripts allow for new conceptualisations of objects within them just as if these objects had been previously mentioned, such that 'objects within a script may take 'the' without explicit introduction because the script itself has already implicitly introduced them' (Schank and Abelson 1977: 41). The precise nature of conceptualisations varies from one individual to another, and there is no obvious upper limit to the number of conceptualisations that can be invoked for every script. This potentially endless list of specifiable features has resulted in some criticism of the Schank and Abelson model, the theoretical implications of which must be left aside for now (see Stockwell 2002: 75–89 for a useful survey of the model).

Although superseded to some extent by more recent developments in cognitive linguistics (see D10), application of the schema model represented an important move in stylistics, away from a linguistic and text-based approach and towards a cognitive and expectation-based approach to literary discourse. One of the most significant of these applications is Cook's (1994) assimilation of schema theory with Formalist and Structuralist concepts like *deviation* and *foregrounding* (see B1). An important assumption of the AI approach is that we draw on schemata to help establish coherence in textual interpretation. However, according to Cook, the primary function of certain kinds of discourse is to effect a change in the schemata of their readers, and preeminent among these is literary discourse which often works to *disrupt* and then *refresh* schemata (1994: 191). Cook accepts that other forms of discourse, such as jokes and advertisements, can also refresh schemata. He even gives an example from Stephen Hawking's *A Brief History of Time* as an illustration of 'extreme schema disruption' in which the remarkable suggestion that time can go backwards is expressed in lucid and unremarkable prose. Discourse like this, which disrupts and refreshes schemata, stands in direct contrast to discourse in which schemata are *preserved*. For example, in the outline in A10 of the *pub schema* (for that is what it was), reference was made to the way this ICM might be modified and revised in the wake of new incoming information. But the addition of, for example, a new prop to the schema (such as an entry for WIDE-SCREEN TELEVISION) is more an extension to the schema rather than a disruption. Cook's general point is that because literary texts affect our schemata in special ways and on a number of levels, traditional stylistic concepts like *foregrounding* and *defamiliarisation* are better located in a framework of cognition than in a framework of language.

Text worlds and narrative comprehension

Let us begin with a seemingly tangential observation. British television runs a popular hospital drama called *Casualty* in which stories about the professional and personal entanglements of the medical staff are intermingled with stories of various emergencies that befall ordinary members of the public. Many episodes begin with a series of unrelated mini-narratives involving assorted luckless characters whose actions will lead inexorably towards the accident that takes them to the casualty department. What is intriguing is how, as viewers of the programme, we are able to track the progress of these various mini-narratives, which are patched together through a technique called 'parallel editing', when only one of the stories is in frame at any one time. It is also intriguing that we expect *not* to be returned to any of these stories at the same point at which we left – it would be thoroughly disorientating if we were. Clearly, we have some cognitive faculty that not only allows us to track the progression of character and narrative, but also to make inferences about the forward development of a plot even when it is, so to speak, un-narrated. This sub-unit will focus on two developments in cognitive stylistics that are linked by an interest in narrative, character and plot, and which, if only implicitly, address the sorts of issues just raised about narrative understanding.

The first model derives from the pioneering work on *text worlds* by Paul Werth (Werth 1999; and see Gavins (2005) for a compact introduction). Werth seeks to account for the conceptual space that links narrative levels, and to this effect he proposes three 'worlds' of discourse. The first is the *discourse world* which is the immediate, higher-order actual space that is inhabited by an author and a reader. Understanding of this world by the reader is founded on 'real' external circumstances and requires direct perception backed up by knowledge of the elements perceived (Werth 1999: 17). The discourse world is an important determinant of how we read a text because it contains all of the objects and elements immediately manifest to the participants in the language event. The significance of this was brought home (somewhat inadvertently) in a study by Canning and Simpson (2012) of informants' reactions to lines of poetry. Respondents were asked to complete a cloze test (see unit B1) of the opening line of Theodore Roethke's poem 'Dolour', which goes, 'I have known the inexorable sadness of _____ '. The responses garnered from under-graduate students and from young adult Facebook members rarely deviated from the set: 'loss', 'love' and 'death'. However, when the same experiment was replicated with a group of female prisoners, in the presence of a warder and in a room with iron bars on the windows, some new predictions tellingly appeared: 'prison' and 'jail'.

Through the discourse world is constructed a *text world*. A text world is a 'total construct' which requires for its understanding memory and imagination, rather than direct perception. Text worlds as conceptual spaces are defined *deictically* and *referentially*, and are anchored by references to the world depicted by the discourse (Werth 1999: 52). For example, in this segment from near the opening of James Kelman's *How Late it Was, How Late*, the central character Sammy awakes in a lane after a two-day drinking binge:

> He was here, he was leaning against auld rusty palings, with pointed spikes, some missing or broke off. And he looked again and saw it was a wee bed of grassy weeds, that was what he was sitting on. His feet were back in view.
>
> (Kelman 1998: 1)

Notice how deictic references like 'here' and 'in view' pick out spatial location, while the adverb of time relationship 'again' and the past progressive verbs 'was leaning' and 'was sitting' signal temporal connections between events in the text world. Referential information, in the pronouns and noun phrases 'He', 'auld rusty palings', 'a wee bed of grassy weeds' and 'his feet', serves to identify the entities present in the text world and their relationship to one another.

The third type of conceptual space in Werth's typology is a *sub-world*. Sub-worlds are established when a character projects thoughts and reflections, perhaps through a flashback or prolepsis (B7), to create another conceptual space inside the text world. This projection forms a distinct situation of its own, because it sets up a reality outside the parameters of the existing text world. For instance, in Ian McEwan's *Atonement*, the character-narrator Robbie Turner, finding himself in a desperate flight from an attack by the Luftwaffe, imagines the safety afforded by nearby trees:

> But the woods were near, there would be streams and waterfalls and lakes in there. He imagined a paradise.
>
> (McEwan 2001: 238)

Notice here the hypothetical modal 'would' and the counterfactive predicator 'imagined' which, through the thoughts of Robbie, engender a world shift away from the primary text world and into an 'enactor-accessible' epistemic sub-world (see Gavins 2007: 114). The deictic signature 'in there' consolidates this projection. Some further suggestions about how to identify text world and sub-world defining elements are set out in unit C10.

The second key model of conceptual tracking is the framework of narrative comprehension developed by Emmott (1997). Emmott, as with Werth, is interested in the way the reader can hold more than one context at once while concentrating on one context in particular. Emmott develops the term *binding* to describe how episodic links between people and places are established in a text, and how these links create a context which is monitored by the mind. Characters are bound into a mental frame at the point at which they enter a fictional place. This process is distinguished in Emmott's model from the process of *priming* which describes the process by which one particular contextual frame becomes the main focus of attention for the reader (Emmott 1997: 123). As any sentence of narrative normally follows only one event in one context, that frame is the reader's main context and is therefore primed.

The question arises, then, as to what we do with the other narrative strands that have been bound into the story but which have been temporarily left alone by the narrator. Emmott points out that characters remain in a fictional place until there is an indication that they need to be 'bound out'. So for example in the hospital drama referred to above, a number of characters are bound into a variety of fictional places as each episode begins. We develop a mental frame to track these fictional characters and locations even when they are not primed, and indeed, we assume that the characters remain in place until we receive an explicit signal that they should be bound out. Unit C10 provides an opportunity to develop through textual analysis the concepts of binding and priming in more detail.

Summary

Like all models in stylistics, cognitive models are designed to facilitate the process of interpretation by helping us understand how we read texts. What distinguishes cognitive from other sorts of stylistic models is that the main emphasis is on mental representation rather than on textual representation. Finding the right balance on the cognitive–textual continuum is important, because a stylistic analysis can go too far in either direction. To be overly text-based risks losing sight of what readers do when they read, and this makes our stylistic analysis look as if it holds good for all readers in all reading contexts. To be overly cognitive risks losing sight of the way a text is made, and this tends to mask stylistic subtlety and creativity in textual composition.

The cognitive stylistic theme is sustained in C10 where a selection of practical activities are provided which probe the concepts developed here and in A10. The unit below takes the cognitive model in a different direction by focussing on the interconnections between style and conceptual metaphor.

STYLES OF METAPHOR

This unit looks at some of the ways in which the study of metaphor has developed within cognitive stylistics. In unit A11, brief reference was made to the idea of *novelty* as a feature of metaphor in literature, and the following sub-unit will explore this issue in greater depth. Later in the unit, attention turns to a short poem by Roger McGough which, amongst other things, serves as a good illustration of some of the connections that can be drawn between metaphor and style.

Metaphors in everyday discourse and in literary discourse

The idea that a particular metaphor is 'novel' can be understood in a number of ways. It can be understood as referring for example to the newness or uniqueness of a conceptual mapping between a source and target domain, or alternatively, to a striking method of expression which a writer uses to relay a metaphor. However, taking the idea further requires that we work from the background assumption that most metaphorical mappings are transmitted through familiar, commonly occurring linguistic expressions. For instance, the metaphor IDEAS ARE FOOD is relayed through a variety of everyday constructions like 'I can't stomach that idea', 'Your theory's half-baked' or 'His story is pretty hard to swallow' and so on. It is interesting that the pattern in such metaphors involves the mapping between an abstract target domain (IDEAS) and a more physical source domain (FOOD). This pattern of 'concretisation', where we try to capture the essence of an abstraction by recasting it in the terms of something more palpable, is replicated in a great many metaphorical constructions and it offers an important insight into the way the human mind works.

The process of concretisation underscores the fact that metaphorical mapping is a conventional way of thinking and is not something remote to human thought.

Not surprisingly then, many metaphors have become embedded over time into fixed expressions like *idioms*. Idioms are conventionally defined as clusters of words whose meaning cannot be read off their constituent parts, although it is important not to lose sight of the often metaphorical origin of a particular idiom. A good illustration of this principle of 'metaphoricity' is provided in the following slip of the tongue, said by a journalist of an overworked sports personality:

> (1)   He's burning the midnight oil at both ends.
>   (from Simpson 1992b)

In this example, two expressions embodying one conceptual metaphor have been unwittingly merged. The metaphor which is evoked is ENERGY IS A BURNING FUEL and it is commonly transmitted through idioms like 'burn the midnight oil' and 'burning the candle at both ends'. The popular term for this sort of slip, a 'mixed metaphor', is something of a misnomer because, as observed, this is really a blend of two idioms which draw on the same metaphor. But most importantly, the example explains well the cognitive basis of idioms by showing how the same conceptual storage system can contain related sets of fixed expressions.

To return to the issue of novelty, it is against this background of everyday metaphorical mapping that writers of literature seek not only to establish new connections, and new types of connection, between target and source domains, but also to extend and elaborate upon existing metaphors in various ways. Consider for instance the following fragment from Craig Raine's poem 'An Enquiry into Two Inches of Ivory':

> (2)   . . . the vacuum cleaner grazes
>   over the carpet, lowing, . . .
>   (Raine 2000 [1979]: 26)

Here the target domain is an everyday domestic appliance and the source domain a familiar bovine animal. The source domain, as with many metaphorical expressions, is evoked by verbs which specify some action of the target ('grazes' and 'lowing'), so the overall metaphorical formula can be captured as: A HOUSEHOLD APPLIANCE IS A FARMED ANIMAL. As far as the novelty of the metaphor is concerned, it is the mental coalescence, or 'conceptual blending', of the familiar entities that offers a fresh perspective on an otherwise prosaic object like the humble vacuum cleaner. It is noticeable also that the two concepts in (1) are physical (one animate, the other not) so the transition between target and source is not like the process of concretisation seen above in the examples of everyday metaphorical mapping.

As a footnote to this discussion, it is worth reemphasising that novelty in stylistic expression cannot remain novel indefinitely, and what is foregrounded in an original context of use will become part of the background as time goes by (see B1). Indeed, many of our common sayings and figures of speech originated from creative metaphors in literature. The expressions 'cold comfort', 'a tower of strength' and 'to the manner born' may have little impact nowadays, but all of them saw their first use in the plays of William Shakespeare (and see further the 'Issues to consider' at the end of reading D12).

Metaphor and style

The following poem is by the Liverpudlian poet Roger McGough:

40   –   LOVE

middle	aged
couple	playing
ten	nis
when	the
game	ends
and	they
go	home
the	net
will	still
be	be
tween	them

(McGough 1971)

In this poem, McGough employs a range of linguistic-stylistic devices to relay a single underlying conceptual metaphor. Whereas the target domain is our understanding of a human relationship, the source domain for the metaphor comes from games and sport, yielding the formula: A HUMAN RELATIONSHIP IS A GAME OF SPORT. Regarding the source domain, we often apply concepts drawn from games and sports to a whole host of target domains – the game of chess alone services a great many metaphors in many different cultures. However, what is particularly marked about the McGough poem is the way this conceptual metaphor is sustained by patterns of graphology and other levels of language (see A2). Using this variety of devices, McGough develops the basic metaphor through two processes known as *extending* and *elaboration* (Kövecses 2002: 48; Semino 2008: 25, 45). Extending a metaphor means expressing it through linguistic resources that introduce new conceptual elements from the source domain. The extension often results in several words from the source domain being used across different clauses in the text. In the poem, McGough extends the source domain from the more general concept of sport to one specific type of sport, and this enables yet further stylistic-expressive possibilities in the way the target domain is subsequently developed. The particular spatial organisation of tennis, with its back and forth movement between ball and players, is captured stylistically by the break up of the text into two columns, and this forces the reading of the text into a similar to and fro movement. Put another way, both sides of the game of love, as it were, are embodied in a textual layout which serves as an *orientational metaphor*. Conventional orientational metaphors use the idea of space as a vehicle for tracking human emotion, where GOOD IS UP ('I feel on top of the world') and BAD IS DOWN ('He's pretty low these days'). Unlike these vertical metaphors, McGough's orientation is horizontal, and this directionality embodies not only the emotional to and fro but the sense of implicit conflict that exists between the couple.

A range of levels of language are also exploited in order to *elaborate* the underlying conceptual metaphor in the poem. Elaboration involves capturing an existing component of the source domain in an unusual or unconventional way. For example, at one point in David Lodge's novel *Thinks,* a character-narrator describes her feelings of depression through the clause: 'I languished at the bottom of deep hole, like the shaft of a waterless well . . .'. According to Semino, this is a creative elaboration of the conventional metaphor UNHAPPY IS DOWN, of the sort captured in more everyday generic expressions like 'I'm feeling low' (Semino 2008: 46). And with the inclusion of the simile in the same clause, further scope is offered for potential cognitive associations and stylistic effects.

In the McGough poem, once the source domain has been extended to tennis, special features of this domain, such as its *props* (see A10 and B10), can acquire extra signification in the metaphorical mapping. The net which serves as the physical barrier in a tennis court symbolises a spiritual and emotional barrier between the estranged couple. Similarly, the numerical scoring system used in tennis allows for further elaboration, where the reference to '40' in the title parallels the age of the couple and, even more fortuitously, the reference to 'love' allows a metaphorical projection from the sport domain to the more abstract target domain of human relationships. Derived from the French *l'oeuf* on account of the resemblance of an egg to the zero symbol, the tennis-domain 'love' facilities a pun because it allows more than one sense to be projected. The score in the game of love for the middle aged couple is, it seems, at zero.

Throughout the poem, a variety of devices enable a conceptual projection to be made from the physical body of the poem into the more abstract world of human relationships. In sum, McGough's text illustrates well the idea of novelty in metaphor because it offers both a new type of conceptual mapping between a source and target domain as well as a striking method of expression to relay the metaphor.

The broad themes raised in this unit are translated into a set of practical activities across in C11, where some of the ideas developed in A11, including those on metonymy, are also reintroduced. The reading that concludes this strand, by Peter Stockwell, examines an important issue in the theory of metaphor which relates to how the two concepts involved in a metaphorical mapping are affected by the mapping process. Metaphor will also feature in the next unit in this strand, where a survey is offered of some key research developments in corpus stylistics.

B12   DEVELOPMENTS IN CORPUS STYLISTICS

The main challenge for corpus stylistic research is to make the computer work for the analyst and not the other way around. Some years ago I attended a lecture on corpus linguistics where the speaker had amassed a huge bank of English prose writing straddling the eighteenth and nineteenth centuries. The corpus results revealed broad, yet significant, syntactic changes in the texts and showed a marked transformation in clausal patterning across a time span of one hundred years. Excitedly, I asked the speaker a number of questions. What did the results reveal about the shared literary motifs, themes and preoccupations in the two periods? Did the grammatical evidence suggest a shift in writers' perceptions of their own craft, perhaps from objective to subjective concerns? Or was the nuanced movement in style itself a subtle portent of the coming of the Romantic Movement in literature? My admittedly rambling questions were greeted by both the speaker and the chair of the session with a mixture of boredom and incredulity. The results, they argued, were straightforward: the computer had spoken. My questions were irrelevant because a large bank of electronic texts had produced a body of data, and this data was of itself the end point of the study. But to my mind, my stylistically focussed questions were, and still are, the only sort of questions worth asking.

Corpus stylistics in action

Mercifully, corpus stylistic research is fully cognizant of the need to balance quantitative analysis with a broader conceptualisation of the relationship between language, style and creativity. This means framing a hypothesis or research question about a literary text or an individual writer's style *in advance of* bringing corpus tools to bear in stylistic analysis. For example, in an expansive corpus-assisted analysis of the work of Charles Dickens, Mahlberg never loses sight of the 'why' of Dickens's particular and arresting literary technique (Mahlberg 2013). Mahlberg draws on an enormous quantitative base, comprising twenty-three works by Dickens himself and twenty-nine texts by other nineteenth-century writers, yet the core framing questions of stylistics, such as the relationship between language, characterization and the creation of fictional worlds, remain the bedrock of the investigation. Take for instance Mahlberg's exploration in the corpus of the collocates of the phrase *as if.* Earlier stylistic research has suggested that Dickens uses a style of 'sinister grotesquerie' to portray characters externally, without psychological interpretation but with heightened attention to their physical peculiarities (Fowler 1996: 179; see also unit C7). A corpus-assisted approach facilitates exploration of generalisations like this because it drills down into the texts *en bloc* to test for the stylistic indicators and markers of this perceived stylistic tendency. Mahlberg's exploration of *as if* reveals, amongst other things, that this pattern is associated with the voice of the narrator and is frequently used to make reference to body language and the outward features of fictional characters. The five-word span to the left of the phrase reveals a predominance of certain types of action verbs alongside body part noun collocates, as in:

Mr Barkis turned his eyes upon me *as if* for my assent . . .

He made up his mouth *as if* to whistle . . .

Mr Slackbridge shook his head, *as if* he would shake it off.

A related pattern is the presence of the lemma *look* as a left-collocate of *as if,* which in Dickens's prose foregrounds the sense of external description taking precedence over psychological interpretation. The occurrence of *look* often describes the appearance registered by a character's face, rather than a consciously directed movement of the eye:

> Ralph <u>looked</u> *as if* he did not quite understand the observation.

> 'No,' said he, <u>looking</u> *as if* he hardly understood me.

The evidence such data offers clearly grounds and consolidates the perhaps more hazy impressions about style that we might intuit from a literary text. But the crucial impact of such an approach is that it provides, in an instant, an aerial perspective on the entire body of a writer's work. It is worth recording, for example, that the short illustrations from Dickens above are taken from *five* different and, in the main, very long novels. It is a curious feature of the corpus method that it simultaneously offers both the micro-detail of a text's composition and a bird's eye view of the broader patterns in language that often elude direct observation.

Developments in corpus stylistics

It may not seem so at first, but the corpus-assisted method lends itself well to the investigation of metaphor in literature. Tracking metaphorical patterns in a corpus may appear difficult because the identification of source and target domains arguably rests on judicious and intuitive decisions by the stylistician. However, Semino's ground-breaking work on metaphor includes much that is corpus-based (Semino 2008). For example, Semino uses *WordSmith Tools* (Scott 1999) to probe the collocates of the word *rich* in a sub-corpus of the BNC. Her reasons for doing so are to explore the metaphor A PURPOSEFUL LIFE IS A BUSINESS (as evidenced in everyday expressions like 'She has a rich life', 'It is time to take stock of my life', 'It was an enriching experience' and so on). Semino takes issue with the linguistic evidence offered by Lakoff to explain the basis of this metaphor (Lakoff 1993), notably with Lakoff's assertion that the main activity through which one acquires what one wants is business. Using corpus tools, Semino considers both the noun and verb forms of *rich*, ruling out seven of the 139 instances found because they were first or second names. Of the remaining 132 tokens, sixty-one were non-metaphorical in that they were genuine indicators of fiscal wealth (e.g. 'The Tories are for the rich and Labour are for the poor'). The remaining instances were metaphorical, as in the following patterns:

> Gemsbok national park is *rich* in wildlife

> . . . the *rich* culture of its architectural heritage

> . . . we have a *rich* reserve of good will

> a voice high in pitch but *rich* in timbre

> (after Semino 2008: 193–4)

Contrary to the position adopted by Lakoff on this word, *rich* not only signals positive evaluation in all four examples but connotes a sense of plenty or abundance across a variety of target domains. In relation to the specific target domains here, *rich* captures, respectively, an abundance of a particular form of life, a noted skill in craft and design, a positive personal attribute and a cherished resonance in the human voice. Semino's evidence therefore challenges the claim that the pattern 'rich life' is best captured through Lakoff's formula A PURPOSEFUL LIFE IS A BUSINESS. The corpus analysis reveals that the phrase 'rich life' is not even in the top fifty collocates in the BNC. Instead, the word 'rich' is conventionally used metaphorically to describe the qualities of abundance, intensity and variety across a much broader set of target domains. On the basis of her corpus results, Semino is able to conclude that if there is such a conceptual metaphor as A PURPOSEFUL LIFE IS A BUSINESS, then the evidence for it needs to be found elsewhere (2008: 196).

The concept of *semantic prosody* (Sinclair 1996; Louw 1993, 2000) marks another important development in corpus stylistics. A semantic prosody is a form of meaning that is established through the proximity of a consistent series of collocates. Not intended in the sense of intonation or patterned versification, a semantic prosody expresses the attitude of the speaker or writer, either positive or negative, to the situation expressed by the recurrent language pattern. Such meanings are therefore collocational (in that they derive from the company the words keep) but also *hidden* and *subtextual* in that they derive not from the words' traditionally understood meanings but from the frequent collocates in their proximity. (In fact, some steps were taken towards a characterisation of semantic prosody in A12, in the discussion of the collocates of 'was approached').

Louw (2007) offers a semantic-prosodic analysis of the seemingly uncontroversial phrase 'natural justice'. On first inspection, 'natural justice' is a positive thing, the dispenser of which is a good citizen and the recipient a clear beneficiary. However, corpus analysis reveals that its context of use is less straightforward. Louw observes (2007: 360) that in spite of it being an outcome that one would aspire to, *natural justice*, in almost all judgments reported in the press, is something that is *not* the outcome – that is, something that has been refused or withheld. Whereas in legal textbooks the concept is represented unproblematically as a natural aspiration of the judicial process, the most common collocates in the press reports are *denied* and *breached*. Louw suggests (personal communication) that the expression may now be 'D-noticed', in the sense that various governments have advised editors against publishing the phrase in their newspapers.

Stylistic applications of semantic prosody theory are useful because, on the one hand, they support idea of literature as *difference* and, on the other, help probe the idea of *subtext* in literary composition. To take one example only, Louw and Milojkovic (2013) probe collocational patterns in W. B. Yeats's poem, 'The Circus Animals' Desertion' (1939). They look at many patterns in the poem, including the opening clause 'I sought a theme', which, they argue, is a marked deviation from the ordinary use of the phrase 'sought a'. But how is this rather bold claim justified? Louw and Milojkovic offer evidence from the 44.5-million-word Times corpus, which reveals seventy-nine occurrences of the phrase. In all instances of 'sought a', the entity actually being sought is very specific, in spite of the indefinite article which precedes it. This is clear in examples like 'Buckingham Palace *sought a* correction', 'The young couple *sought a* mortgage', '[he] *sought a* court order', '[she] *sought a* divorce' and so on. Unlike Yeats's formulation, the sought object in the corpus is always singular, tangible and specific. The sought object in Yeats's poem is, by contrast, elusive, and as the poem progresses, the search for 'a theme' ultimately proves to be in vain, with the poet's determined search for the unknown and the unknowable leading to a creative impasse.

Corpus analysis: checks and balances

It is worth closing this unit by reverting to the caveat expressed at its start: the computer should work for the analyst and not the other way around. The evidence a bank of data can offer an analysis of style is only as good as the corpus on which it is built, so caution always needs to be exercised when looking at the results from even very large corpora. In particular, care needs to be taken in assessing both the *topicality* and the *generic source* of the occurrences in the corpus. For instance, Mahlberg (2011), in her exploration of British broadsheet newspapers, notices a marked increase in certain collocates of the word 'hand'. Examples such as 'hand *gels*' and 'hand *sanitisers*' reflected the topicality of the news because these patterns were added to the corpus in the wake of the swine flu epidemic of 2009. (And see also A12 for the discussion of the topicality of *treacherous*).

Consider now some issues relating to the *generic source* of corpus data. In a study of the ways in which ordinary users of language describe different types of *irony*, I used the BNC to test the occurrence of this lemma alongside its leftwards-situated adjectival modifiers, as in 'tragic irony', 'bitter irony' and so on (Simpson 2011). In raw terms, with fourteen occurrences in total, the most common phrasal pattern proved to be '*heavy* irony' and the first ten of these are produced in Table B2.1.

The information preceding the KWIC window is rather telling. The third column from the left reveals that all instances come from written fictional prose. The abbreviated coding in the second column allows us to track the original texts, which, as it happens, are all popular romance novels. The coding also shows that four of the occurrences are actually from the same text (JY8). This creates a problem for interpretation because the result is clearly skewed markedly upwards by its frequent occurrence in a certain type of prose fiction. It is therefore not the case *per se* that 'heavy' is the most common modifier of 'irony' in the language as a whole; rather, there is some evidence that the expression 'heavy irony' is a common, and perhaps hackneyed collocation which is shared and borrowed by authors of a particular *genre* of writing.

This generic source aside, corpus evidence nonetheless raises interesting questions and frequently opens up other areas for investigation. For example, do the results in the table suggest a gendered distinction where it is the male 'lead' in these popular romances who is normally the gatekeeper of *irony*? And does the romantic heroine tend to be the recipient of irony or on the receiving end of related strategies like *sarcasm* and *teasing*? These are genuine research questions and, with a KWIC analysis of these italicised lemmas, are amenable to corpus-assisted stylistic analysis. More practical suggestions along these lines are suggested in unit C12.

Table B12.1 Occurrence of *irony* in the BNC

1	ADA	W_fict_prose	much of the 'coincidence' (as they will put it, with **heavy irony**, drawing out each syllable like bubble-gum) that Miller also appears to share the
2	CEY	W_fict_prose	'By appointment only? Like the Queen?' Nicky asked, with **heavy irony**. 'Yes, if you like,' Constance replied sharply. 'I
3	G1A	W_fict_prose	South America. The intention is to curb the spread of package-tour baroque and **heavy irony**. Ah, the propinquity of cheap life and expensive
4	GUD	W_fict_prose	been nothing dramatic, no great debate, just a lot of jokes and **heavy irony** to start with, then a gradual, gentle separation. Plus, of course,
5	HA7	W_fict_prose	too much if I finish my coffee, though?' he said with **heavy irony**. 'Oh, please don't hurry on my account.' 'I
6	JXX	W_fict_prose	incisive mind I've been hearing so much about lately?' Ignoring the **heavy irony** of his voice, and deciding that she was just too weary to rise to
7	JY8	W_fict_prose	just when do you expect the cavalry to arrive?' he countered with **heavy irony**. She flushed angrily, refusing to back down on a point of principle.
8	JY8	W_fict_prose	&equo; 'Don't go overboard with the gratitude,' he rejoined with **heavy irony**. 'I said thanks. What would you have me do?' she
9	JY8	W_fict_prose	. ' 'I'm looking forward to it!' Paige returned with **heavy irony**, and dropped the receiver back on its rest in an aura of disbelief.
10	JY8	W_fict_prose	hand finally. 'That much was always obvious,' he said with **heavy irony**. 'And begs the question, why not?' She rubbed at her

Section C

EXPLORATION

INVESTIGATING STYLE

IS THERE A 'LITERARY LANGUAGE'?

As far as most stylisticians are concerned, the short answer to the question which heads this unit is 'no'. That is to say, there exists no feature or pattern of language which is inherently or exclusively 'literary' in all contexts. This may seem a curious stance to adopt given stylistics' close association with literary discourse. After all, literature offers the chance to explore language that is out of the ordinary, language which is often the preeminent embodiment of the creative spirit. It is also the case that there have been, over the centuries, certain conventions in writing styles that mark certain literary epochs, such as the alliterative style of the Anglo-Saxon poem, the sonnet form of later periods in literary history, or, later again, forms like the novel and the novella. However, these forms of writing are more representative of specific codes or conventions of use which may change over time, rather than confirmation of the existence of a special language which in its very essence is immutably, and for all time, 'literary'.

The question now begged is why, if there is such widespread rejection of the concept within stylistics, does the issue of 'literary language' need to be discussed or even mentioned? The answer to this question is the main focus of this unit. In the following sub-unit, some of the broader theoretical consequences of the 'literary language' debate are framed, while the sub-unit after that makes use of a short poem to extend and explore this problematic concept in a more practical and directed way.

The 'literary language' issue

Contemporary stylistics' resistance to a distinct form of 'literary language' might on the face of it seem like a rather cynical snipe at the many literary critics who believe the opposite; at those who believe not only that there exists a literary language, but that literature can be defined by its use of this special language. Let me address this issue by making three basic points.

One of the most important concerns in the practice of stylistics is that the language used in literary texts should not be cut adrift from its reflexes in the common resources of everyday discourse. Stylistics is interested in what writers do *with* and *through* language, and in the raw materials out of which literary discourse is crafted. As noted across the strand in A1, the tools of modern linguistics are drawn from the full system of language and discourse, so it makes sense that those same tools be used to see what writers do against this broader context. The aim is not to sequester off into a special category significant aspects of literary style, but rather to look for the origins of this style in the overall totality of discourse.

Following directly from this is a second point. If we describe this or that piece of discourse as 'literary language', we immediately place a linguistic boundary around it. In fact, to set down stylistic parameters around a form of discourse is in some respect to codify it as a *register*, thereby making it a language variety that regularly co-occurs with a particular situation (see C2). But it is the very freedom of linguistic possibility which is an index of creativity in language, not the presence of a fixed set of linguistic guidelines within which a writer must work. To argue for the existence of a distinct literary register is effectively to argue for a kind of cliché, because it would involve reining stylistic expression into a restricted set of formulaic prescriptions.

A third issue raised by the literary language debate is somewhat more ideological than methodological in its general bearing. To claim that literary language is special, that it can somehow be bracketed off from the mundane or commonplace in discourse, is ultimately to wrest it away from the practice of stylistics. Followed through, such a move assumes that whereas language scholars might be better equipped to investigate forms of discourse like journalism or everyday conversation, it should fall to the literary critic alone to deal with the special language of literature. As the critic F. W. Bateson once noted (1966: 464), the rather mechanical procedure of the stylistician is no match for the sensitivity of the critic.

I am reminded here of a curious episode which is germane to the present discussion. Some years ago, I approached a publisher who held copyright on the work of a well-known British poet. My request indicated the few lines of text required and included a sample of the proposed stylistic exercise, part of which involved a cloze test of the sort developed in B1. Not only was my request for permission refused point blank, it was accompanied by the following rather sniffy rejoinder: 'we cannot possibly countenance such a travesty of lines as magical and special as these'. At the risk of seeming to work out a personal angst in print, the relevance of the story is that it shows precisely what can happen when the language which writers use is hived off into a separate and indeed hallowed category. The 'travesty' (the stylistic analysis, in other words!) was considered irreverent because it tried to lay bare the very subtleties in expression the poet was conveying in language, yet to this self-appointed guardian of literary probity, my methods had clearly violated something that was deeply sacrosanct. It is worth noting that the injunction did not come from the poet himself – ironically, it is my experience that poets are often intrigued by what stylisticians have to say about their style.

Probing 'literary language'

This short sub-unit explores further the problematic issue of 'literary language'. To start us off, you will find below two-thirds of a poem. The name of its author, and the reason why you have been given only two of its three stanzas will emerge later, but as you read it through try to identify any features of textual construction, words or phrases, that you feel are 'literary' or that you would normally associate with literature. Below the poem are some more detailed tasks which you can work through.

Activity

One Perfect Rose

A single flow'r he sent me, since we met.
　　All tenderly his messenger he chose;
Deep-hearted, pure, with scented dew still wet –
　　One perfect rose.

I knew the language of the floweret;
　　'My fragile leaves,' it said, 'his heart enclose.'
Love long has taken for his amulet
　　One perfect rose.

✪ Activity With respect to the poem, consider the following questions:

- ❑ How many speakers are there in the poem and how can we work this out from the text?
- ❑ When is the poem set, and how do we know?
- ❑ What sort of vocabulary is used by the poet? That is, is it modern or archaic, formal or conversational?
- ❑ Can you identify a rhyme scheme in the poem? If so, what sort of scheme is it?
- ❑ Can you spot any marked or unusual features of grammar (see A3) in the poem?

My own response to these questions are that the text as it stands satisfies many of the generic conventions of a lyric love poem (see A2). A single speaker expresses an emotional state, and mediates this through the popular symbol of the rose. Other devices work to sustain this reading and to suggest that this is the written style of a bygone era. Some of the vocabulary is clearly archaic, as in the obsolete diminutive form 'floweret' or the contracted form 'flow'r'. The rhyme scheme is tightly configured into an *abab* pattern, and is maintained even on the trisyllables 'floweret' and 'amulet'. In terms of its grammatical organisation, many of the poem's clauses are structured in such a way as to bring to the front elements other than the grammatical Subject. In fact, the clause 'All tenderly his messenger he chose' is particularly marked in this respect because it is fronted by two elements, an Adjunct and then a Complement, with the Subject occurring in a later position (cf. 'He chose his messenger all tenderly'). No doubt many more features could be identified which, in the conventional sense of the term, make this text feel like 'literary' writing.

With its third stanza now reinstated, read the poem again. Think particularly about how the addition of the final verse impacts on your initial reaction to and interpretation of the first two verses. Once you have read it, go back and reconsider your answers to the set of questions listed above.

One Perfect Rose

A single flow'r he sent me, since we met.
　All tenderly his messenger he chose;
Deep-hearted, pure, with scented dew still wet –
　One perfect rose.

I knew the language of the floweret;
　'My fragile leaves,' it said, 'his heart enclose.'
Love long has taken for his amulet
　One perfect rose.

Why is it no one ever sent me yet
　One perfect limousine, do you suppose?
Ah no, it's always just my luck to get
　One perfect rose.

The general tenor of the third stanza is a long way indeed from the discourse of the seventeenth- or eighteenth-century love poem, although it does create a humorous play on that discourse frame. In fact, the poem was written in 1926 by the American wit and socialite Dorothy Parker. What Parker does is to use a kind of style-shift for comic effect where the echoes of the lyric genre in stanzas one and two give way in the third stanza to an altogether more prosaic style of language. Constructions like 'Ah no', 'just my luck' and 'do you suppose' signal an informal register of discourse while in grammar the Subject is brought back to its more common first position in the clause ('. . . no one ever sent me yet . . .').

But the heart of the issue, as far as present discussion is concerned, is that it is simply not feasible to say that, in comparison with the third, the first two stanzas are 'literary language'. It is more the case that a convention of writing is echoed, and then is ultimately brought into collision with, the more contemporary idiom projected in the third verse. If asked outside this context which of the words 'floweret' or 'limousine' you considered to be 'literary', you would have probably opted for the first one, but as we have just seen both words are perfectly capable of being pressed into service in a poem. It is a question therefore of how these words function in context, not of how this or that word sounds in isolation, which is important. By exploiting a formal convention of writing of the sort mentioned earlier, Parker sets up a twist in expectation that works for comic effect. Echoing other discourses in new contexts is an important way of generating irony (see the special web strand on style and humour), but here the echo only becomes clear when the shift in style is delivered in the third stanza. Parker's poem is a good illustration, then, of how discourse is open to constant reinvigoration and transformation over time. Highlighting this principle, the theoretician Michel Foucault develops the term *transdiscursivity* to describe how the rules of discourse formation in one era become detached from its 'ulterior transformations' in later developments (Foucault 1986: 145–6).

Summary

A position which regards literary discourse as impervious to or resistant to linguistic analysis is utterly at odds with the rationale of modern stylistics. Stylistics is about interrogating texts, about seeing a text in the context of its other stylistic possibilities. One of the most effective ways of understanding how a text works, as Pope notes (1995: 1–2), is to challenge it, to play around with it or to intervene in its stylistic make-up in some way. Upholding the view that 'literary language' is somehow outside the boundaries of the overall language system does little to enable or facilitate this sort of textual intervention.

It makes sense therefore to treat the concept of 'literary language' with a healthy degree of scepticism. Indeed, a somewhat more useful way of approaching the issue of stylistic creativity, whether it be found in literature or in other types of discourse, is through the concept of *literariness*, a term first coined by Roman Jakobson. Literariness is a property of texts and contexts and it inheres in patterns of language in use as opposed to patterns of language in isolation. Crucially, in keeping with Jakobson's other important term, the poetic function (B1), literariness is not exclusive to literature. It is instead a principle of expressiveness that transcends literature into many types of discourse contexts of which journalism and advertising discourse are just two preeminent examples. Literariness also accommodates a text's capacity to absorb other voices and styles, the sorts of textual techniques witnessed in the example from Dorothy Parker. This particular theme, the 'multivoicedness' of literary discourse, is the main focus in the following unit.

C2

STYLE, REGISTER AND DIALECT

This unit explores a passage from Irvine Welsh's controversial novel *Trainspotting* and develops a sociolinguistically orientated activity based around variations in dialect, register and style. In order to help focus that analysis, the following sub-unit introduces some general categories of language variation.

Varieties of language

One of the six components of the model of narrative introduced in A5, *sociolinguistic code* is a term referring to the pool of linguistic varieties that both derive from and shape the social and cultural backdrop to a text. Sociolinguistic code is a key organising resource not just for narrative but for all types of literary discourse. In the case of monolingual writing in English, that code will remain largely within the parameters of a single language and its subvarieties, although in bilingual writing it is common for any number of indigenous language varieties to intermix, and often alongside a 'superstrate' language like English. Chicano literature, from the border regions of Mexico and the USA, draws on a sociolinguistic code which combines Spanish, English and localised American-Indian forms, while in the Nigerian literary context (embodied in the work of Wole Soyinka, for example), Standard English is mixed with West African Pidgin English and the indigenous African language, Yoruba. The term *code-switching* is normally used to explain transitions between distinct languages in a text, and literary code-switching is a sophisticated technique which signals movement between different spheres of reference and has important consequences for a range of thematic intentions (see further Hess 1996: 6 and Pratt 1993: 177).

Literary works which remain within the compass of a single language may still exhibit marked variation in terms of their use of sociolinguistic code. What follows is a summary of a number of key dimensions of such intra-lingual variation.

Idiolect

It a truism of modern linguistics that no two speakers use language in exactly the same way. We all have our own linguistic mannerisms and stylistic idiosyncrasies, and the term reserved for an individual's special unique style is *idiolect*.

Accents and dialects

Influenced and shaped by the regional origins and socioeconomic background of their speakers, dialects are distinguished by patterns in grammar and vocabulary while accents are distinguished through patterns of pronunciation. The Standard English dialect and the Received Pronunciation accent (see Table C2.1) represent jointly the high-prestige varieties of British English, although these are far outnumbered (in terms of numbers of speakers) by many non-standard regional varieties. Two further points of special relevance to stylistic analysis are worth making here:

(i) It is popularly yet wrongly assumed that Standard English is not really a dialect at all, but that this variety along with its high-prestige counterpart accent, RP, simply constitute 'real' English. A consequence of this is that when critics discuss the representation of 'dialect' in literature – as in, say, the novels of Thomas Hardy – they tend to be talking rather more narrowly about the regional, non-standard dialects, often of a rural and particularly conservative type, which are used by particular fictional characters. But *all* speech and writing is framed in a dialect of some sort, whether it be standard or non-standard, high-prestige or low-status.

(ii) Given that accent is a variety of language defined through *pronunciation*, it might seem that the study of accent has no place in the stylistic analysis of written literary discourse. However, writers make use of any number of often ingenious techniques for representing features of spoken discourse in print. For example, in the Irvine Welsh novel from which the passage used below is taken, the nuances of spoken Edinburgh vernacular are captured through a variety of orthographic techniques:

   a   Vowel lengthening, which is a characteristic of all varieties of Scots English, is relayed by doubling the vowels in spelling, so that *got* becomes 'goat', *off* becomes 'oaff' and so on.

   b   A feature widespread in Scots English is an older style vowel pronunciation which dates back to the time of Chaucer. Whereas most contemporary British accents now have diphthongs in words like *about* and *down*, their realisation in Scots is as long monophthongs, represented in spellings like 'doon' and 'aboot'.

   c   A particular feature of the low-status variety of Scots English targeted by Welsh (a feature it shares, curiously, with London's Cockney English) is 'L-vocalisation'. This involves the realisation of the /l/ sound as a vowel rather than a liquid consonant, such that *ball* becomes 'baw', *always* 'eywis', *football* 'fitba' and so on.

Table C2.1   Standard and non-standard accents and dialects

	Accent (varieties of pronunciation)	Dialect (varieties of grammar and vocabulary)
Standard:	Received pronunciation (RP)	Standard English
Non-standard:	Regional Accents ('Scouse', 'Cockney'; 'Belfast'; 'Glaswegian' and so on)	Regional Dialects ('Scouse'; 'Cockney'; 'Belfast'; 'Glaswegian' and so on)

Register

Whereas a dialect is a linguistic variety that is defined according to the user of language – it tells you things about their social and regional background – a *register*, on the other hand, is defined according to the *use* to which language is being put. In other words, a register shows, through a regular, fixed pattern of vocabulary and grammar, what a speaker or writer is doing with language at a given moment. Registers are often discussed in terms of three features of context known as *field*, *tenor* and *mode*. Field of discourse refers to the setting and purpose of the interaction, tenor to the relationship between the participants in interaction and mode to the medium of communication (that is, whether it is spoken or written). For example, if we take a particular field of discourse like *chemistry*, and specify that the language event take the form of written interaction between a student and lecturer, then these parameters will strongly constrain the sort of text-type that is anticipated. Only the first of the following two sequences is appropriate to the demands of this discourse context:

(1)   A quantity of copper sulphate crystals was dissolved in a beaker containing 200ml of H_2O. The aqueous solution was then heated.

(2)   I was just sayin', Jimmy, that me and my mate Will were putting some copper sulphate stuff into a jug of water the other day. It was bloody great fun.

The vocabulary and grammar of (1) confirm its field of discourse as science and its mode as written discourse. Moreover, the use of the *passive voice* (see A6) without any explicit interpersonal markers and terms of address, suggests a relatively formal tenor of discourse. By contrast, it is the very presence of first person pronouns, along with evaluative adjective phrases ('bloody great'), that makes the second example inappropriate to the context of formal scientific prose but appropriate to the context of a spoken narrative of personal experience. Notice also how tenor of discourse is made more informal in (2) through both the *vocative* (the term of direct address, 'Jimmy') and the swear word ('bloody'). In that they can occur in all social and regional dialects, swear words and taboo language generally are important features of register, and not, as is commonly assumed, of dialect.

Antilanguage

Antilanguages are the semi-secretive languages born out of subcultures and alternative societies. These societies, 'antisocieties', are consciously established as alternatives to mainstream society such that their relationship to the dominant social order is one of resistance, even active hostility. Antilanguages are therefore typically characterised by references to proscribed drugs, to alternative sexual behaviours or more generally to the various activities of a criminal underworld (Halliday 1978). Antilanguages play an important part in, and often dominate completely, the style of literary works which are thematically concerned with such subcultures and antisocieties. Notable examples of such fiction are William Burroughs's *The Naked Lunch* (1959), Hubert

Selby Jnr's *Last Exit to Brooklyn* (1966), and Anthony Burgess's antilanguage novel *sine qua non, A Clockwork Orange* (1962). The most important process in the formation of an antilanguage is *relexicalisation* which involves recycling established words in the language into new structures and meanings. For example, in Welsh's novel, there are numerous coded antilanguage references to proscribed drugs, to types of criminal activity and to the police and other figures of authority. Relexicalisation in the 'drugs' field of discourse alone is heavily foregrounded, with a single page of text likely to produce items such as the following and more: *skag, works, smack, gear, speedball, shootin gallery, cookin up* and *shootin home.*

Levels of style in Irvine Welsh's *Trainspotting*

If we accept the argument made both along this thread and in unit C1, that literary discourse has the capacity to stack up or absorb other varieties of language, the difficulty that then presents itself is how to separate out in a rigorous way these various elements in stylistic analysis. In the stylistic analysis of sociolinguistic code, for example, we need to identify and explore the connections between features like accent, register or antilanguage in a text. The following exercise is designed as one method for helping to tease out these stylistically significant varieties of language.

Below you will find a passage from Irvine Welsh's novel *Trainspotting*. This episodically written novel is set in Edinburgh, and follows the interconnected lives of a group of drug addicts and that of their violent and psychotic friend, Frank Begbie. The novel's 'hero' is its first person narrator, Mark Renton. More intelligent and articulate than his peers, Renton manages ultimately to break free from the strictures of this drug-ridden, repressed existence. In this particular episode, Renton and Spud Murphy, having stolen books to sustain their heroin habit, find themselves in a Magistrate's court defending a charge of shoplifting. They are watched from the public gallery by their friends Sick Boy and Begbie. Although Spud is sent to Saughton prison, Renton is released subject to his participation in a drugs rehabilitation programme. Read the passage through a couple of times. You could even try to read it aloud!

Activity

Courting Disaster

The magistrate's expression seems tae oscillate between pity n loathing, as he looks doon at me n Spud in the dock.

– You stole the books from Waterstone's bookshop, with the intention of selling them, he states. Sell fuckin books. Ma fuckin erse.

– No, ah sais.

– Aye, Spud sais, at the same time. We turn aroond n look at each other. Aw the time we spent gittin oor story straight n it takes the doss cunt two minutes tae blow it.

The magistrate lets oot a sharp exhalation. It isnae a brilliant job the cunt's goat, whin ye think aboot it. It must git pretty tiresome dealin wi radges aw day. Still, ah bet the poppy's fuckin good, n naebody's asking the cunt tae dae it. He should try tae be a wee bit mair professional, a bit mair pragmatic, rather than showin his annoyance so much.

– Mr Renton, you did not intend to sell the books?

Summary

The purpose of this exercise has been to try to develop some systematic methods for exploring how multiple and higher-order levels of style can work in a text. The grid devised to help itemise the main categories of the analysis can of course be modified to accommodate different types of sociolinguistic code in other contexts of writing. Whereas Welsh's novel is principally 'monolingual' in the sense that it exploits sociolinguistic variation in and around a single language, the grid can be extended to account for literary code-switching which straddles different languages. And it can also work for both poetry and drama, as well as for works of prose fiction.

There are a number of advantages to being rigorous in the identification of the various styles employed in a literary text. The procedure serves well to illustrate in practice the concept of *polyphony*. Coined by the Russian theoretician Mikhail Bakhtin, polyphony refers to a quality of 'multi-voiced-ness' which is displayed by certain genres of discourse. These genres, known as 'complex speech genres', arise in the artistic discourses of 'more complex and comparatively highly developed and organised cultural communication' (Bakhtin 1986: 62). Bakhtin adds that during the process of their formation, complex speech genres 'absorb and digest various primary (simple) genres that have taken form in unmediated speech communion' (62). Literary discourse is a preeminent example of a complex speech genre and the principle of polyphony is situated at its core. Irrespective of how the academic literary institution views Irvine Welsh's work, the stylistic activity suggested here does indeed highlight this writer's capacity to build a text through multiple and varied aspects of language and style.

C3 GRAMMAR AND GENRE: A SHORT STUDY IN IMAGISM

This unit experiments with grammatical patterns in poetry in order to help us think about the processes involved in translating experiences and thoughts into the type of text that is a poem. The activity proposed here draws principally on the concepts introduced and developed across units A3 and B3, and it will also feed into unit D3, an article by Ronald Carter which offers a detailed stylistic analysis of grammatical patterns in modern poetry.

From experience to language

Below you will find part of a letter that was penned in 1911 by a well-known American writer to his friend. It tells of an experience that befell the writer while he was resident in Europe. Read the letter through carefully:

> For well over a year I have been trying to make a poem of a very beautiful thing that befell me in the Paris Underground. I got out of a train at, I think, La Concorde, and in the jostle I saw a beautiful face, and then, turning suddenly, another and another, and then a beautiful child's face, and then another beautiful face. All that day I tried to find words for what this made me feel. That night, as I went home along the Rue Raynouard I was still trying. I could get nothing but spots of colour. I remember thinking that if I had been a painter I might have started a wholly new school of painting.

This is the inspiration, the 'felt experience', that prompted the writer eventually to construct a poem. Before we move on to look at this poem, think of the sort of poem that *you* might produce if you had had such an experience in the Underground. If you were asked specifically to produce a short poem of only a few lines, what sort of imaginative impulse would you draw upon? Here are some further questions that might shape and influence your creative thinking:

Activity

(i)   Would you, as the writer does in his letter, position yourself as a 'voice' in the poem? (Notice the 'I' pronouns in the letter which locate the writer as the authorial source for the text.)
(ii) Would you situate your poem in a specific time and place (as, again, the writer does)?
(iii) What type of evaluative vocabulary would you use to capture the impact of this experience on you?
(iv) Would you address your poem to an imagined reader, through markers of direct address such as 'you'? Or would you instead prefer to depersonalise it, making it stand as a more generalised statement for all readers?
(v)   What sort of sound and rhythm structure (if any) would you use? Would you try to adopt a formal metrical scheme or instead prefer to render it in 'free verse'? (See unit A4.)

Jot your poem into the box below (if this is your book, of course). Don't feel you have to shape a complete and rounded piece of poetry – you may simply have some ideas for fragments or particular constructions of language that might begin to capture the experience. We shall return to this exercise shortly.

Probing grammatical patterns, back to front

Your next task is to look at the following text, which is a complete but very short poem (including its title). The poem has been grammatically 'scrambled' in that the *noun phrases* and *prepositional phrases* (see A3) which comprise it have been jumbled up. Orthography (the capitals, punctuation and so on which normally signal line endings and sentence boundaries) has been stripped away, so that all that you are left with is a collection of unordered phrases.

Activity

Referring where possible to the grammatical information provided in units A3 and B3, now try to reassemble the poem into some form of coherent unit. What kind of grammatical steps are necessary for such a reconstruction? What aspects of language are responsible for the difficulties (if any) that you encounter? Before proceeding to the next sub-unit, write your reconstruction in the box below the text.

in the crowd
the apparition
in a station
petals
of these faces
of the metro
on a wet black bough

Grammar and literary genre

On the basis of some give-away lexical items like 'station' and 'metro' in the scrambled poem, you may indeed have begun to suspect some connection between this text and the letter writer from earlier. But before we explore that connection, let us reflect for a moment on your reconstruction work. There are indeed many ways of bolting together the phrases that comprise this poem, resulting in a number of possible permutations. This comes about largely because of the absence in the original of one crucial grammatical feature, which we shall consider shortly. Here first of all is the unadulterated text. And in the commentary that follows, consider how it compares to both your own poem and your rearrangement.

In a Station of the Metro

The apparition of these faces in the crowd;
Petals on a wet, black bough.
                    (Pound 1969 [1912])

One important aspect of the grammar of this short couplet, which is based loosely on the seventeen syllable Japanese *haiku* poem, is that it contains no verbs. With that go many contingent structures such as finiteness, tense (and time reference) and propositional value (which means that you cannot 'argue' with the ideas expressed here) (see units A3 and B3). From this, other aspects of clause structure collapse: a grammatical Subject cannot be formed, nor can Complement elements be positioned relative to a verb. What remains is pared down to its stylistic 'bare bones', so to speak, encoding a sequence of phrases to do with things and their locations. Gone, for instance, are the self-referential pronouns ('I') which so characterised the letter; gone also are the explicit references to time which were signalled through finite verb forms (eg. 'I *have been trying*'; 'I *think*'; 'I *got out*') and temporal Adjuncts ('over a year'; 'that night'; 'all that day'). Notice also how the repetitions ('a beautiful face') and parallel formations ('another and another') of the letter give way to the most minimal and sparsest of lexis in the poem. Yet this is not to say, in terms of the ideas discussed in unit A6, that the absence of verbs means that there are no *processes* in the poem. There is one clear example of *nominalisation*, where a noun embodies a process of action. As in unit A6, you can test a text for nominalisation by asking the question 'what happened?' and seeing if, in the reply, any nouns slot into the frame 'there was a(n) _____'. Here, that question would be answered by the word 'apparition', so it is not the case that nothing happens, it is just that the happening has been made a 'thing' and has been cut adrift from any agency and from any locus in time. It is interesting also that even the deictic word 'these' (unit A2) suggests proximity to a speaking source even though explicit reference to that speaker has been erased.

What remains, in the light of these grammatical operations, is the sparest juxtaposition of a statement of experience and a statement of interpretation. The relationship between the two is a metaphorical one (see unit A11) in that it involves a conceptual mapping between two domains: the perceived experience encoded in the first line, and its mapping in the second onto a metaphorical plane. The result is a frozen crystallised moment, cut adrift from time but very much an instantiation of things and place. An 'image', rather than a proposition.

In stylistic terms, this short poem does indeed appear to embrace the credentials of the Imagist movement in poetry, which flourished for a few years from 1910 and of which Ezra Pound was a preeminent figure. Pound described an image as 'an intellectual and emotional complex in an instant of time' and characterised Imagist poetry by its exactitude of vocabulary, its hard and clear images presented 'instantaneously', and its direct treatment of the 'thing'. To what extent did your own poem, based on the experience in the Metro, embody (if at all) any of these features? Did you put a personal subject into your poem, and was that subject a speaking or narrating voice? Was your own poem more contemplative and meditative, more 'lyrical' in the sense of a single speaker reflecting on thoughts and emotions? And finally, if your own poem had none of the stylistic markers of of Imagism, what literary genre *did* it embody?

In this unit, our principal aim has been to examine the connection between stylistic technique, as it translates to grammatical experimentation, and literary genre. That is one of the themes that will be resumed across the book in the reading in D3. In the next unit, C4, the focus will shift to exploring patterns of sound and metre in poetry.

C4   **STYLES IN A SINGLE POEM: AN EXPLORATION**

This unit offers a set of framing questions designed to help organise the exploration of a single literary text from multiple stylistic perspectives. The text selected for analysis is Michael Longley's short poem 'The Comber', which appears in his collection *The Weather in Japan* (2000). The questions asked of the text cover a range of stylistic models, which include, but are not restricted to, the material on sound and rhythm which was developed along this strand. They also bring in grammar (thread 3) and other levels of language (thread 2), although later threads in the book will no doubt offer yet further models of analysis. The set of questions posed in the following sub-unit are picked up in the web material which accompanies this book, where some advice and commentary is offered on the various activities suggested.

Going to work on a poem

(✪ Activity)   First of all, read the poem closely:

> *The Comber*
>
> A moment before the comber turns into
> A breaker – sea-spray, raggedy rainbows –
> Water and sunlight contain all the colours
> And suspend between Inishbofin and me,
> The otter, and thus we meet, without my scent
> In her nostrils, the uproar of my presence,
> My unforgivable shadow on the sand –
> Even if this is the only sound I make.
>
> (Longley 2000)

Now work through the questions, and if you have to, double-check their terms of reference by looking again at the other units to which they relate. For the most part, you can deal with the questions in any order, although it is important to recognise that a particular feature of language targeted in one activity will always intersect with features of language covered in the other activities.

Question 1: what can we say about general patterns of grammar in the poem?
(Refer to units A3, B3 and C3 when undertaking these activities)

Identify the main clauses in the poem, and any subordinate clauses that are placed around them. (Remember, there can only be one S element and one P element in any main clause). What pattern emerges as the overall grammatical system of the poem? For example, where are units like Adjuncts and subordinate clauses positioned? Do they function as anticipatory, trailing or equivalent constituents?

Question 2: what can we say about foregrounded patterns of grammar in the poem?
(Refer to units B1 and A3 when undertaking these activities.)

Identify any sequences which break from the basic grammatical pattern you have identified for the poem as a whole. For example, are there any places in the poem where clause structure gives way to sequences of phrases which are *not* connected to a Subject and Predicator element?

Question 3: what can we say about sound and rhythm in the poem?
(Refer to units A4 and B4 when undertaking these activities)

Identify any significant aspects of sound patterning in the poem. Does the poem display a dominant metrical pattern? Or is its versification based more on the rhythm of natural speech than on a formal metrical scheme? In other words, is the poem written in *free verse*?

Does the poem contain any significant features of sound symbolism like onomatopoeia? If so what, what is the function of these devices in the poem?

The term *grammetrics* describes the convergence between grammatical structure and rhythmical structure. Can you identity any significant coalescence(s) of grammar and metre in the poem?

Question 4: what can we say about the graphology of the poem?
(Refer to units A2 and B2 when undertaking these activities)

How is the poem as language 'on the page' formally organised? What impact does its visual arrangement have on other levels of language? In particular, how does the graphology of the poem complement (or interfere with) its grammatical organisation?

Question 5: what can we say about vocabulary and word-structure in the poem?
(Refer to this thread and to units A2 and B2 when undertaking these activities)

Are there any individual words or word-structures that are foregrounded? Does anything deviate from the ordinary, and if so, how does it intersect with other levels of language like sound and rhythm?

Question 6: in what other ways might the poem have been written?

(Refer to unit B3 and to any other units of the book which contain rewrites and transposition exercises)

How might the poem read if its basic stylistic organisation (at any level of language) were altered? In particular, what would happen if its grammatical structure were rearranged into a more linear representation?

Summary

This unit has interrogated a single text using a set of questions which draw on material from a number of units in the book. Other questions could of course be asked of the same text. The poem's organisation as *narrative* represents one such line of inquiry. It is noticeable, for instance, that the conjunction 'before' near the start of the poem signals a so-called 'previous to given time' relationship. This means that the later event (the comber turning into a breaker) is relayed first and, in an inversion of natural narrative ordering, the earlier event ('water and sunlight contain . . .') is relayed second. However, developing further this sort of angle requires a fuller account of the organisation of narrative. Providing such an account is the remit of the next unit.

A SOCIOLINGUISTIC MODEL OF NARRATIVE

This unit makes some practical suggestions for exploring further the structure of narrative. It draws upon one particular model of narrative: the framework of *natural narrative* developed by the sociolinguist William Labov. Labov's concept of narrative structure, which has already featured in this strand (A5), has proved a productive model of analysis in stylistics. After a brief sketch of the model, some narrative texts will be introduced and some practical activities developed around them.

Labov's narrative model

The enduring appeal of Labov's model of natural narrative is largely because its origins are situated in the everyday discourse practices of real speakers in real social contexts. Working from a corpus of hundreds of stories told in the course of casual conversation by informants from many different backgrounds, Labov isolates the core, recurrent features that underpin a fully formed natural narrative. Six key categories are rendered down from this body of data (Labov 1972: 359–60). Each of these categories serves to address a hypothetical question about narrative structure ('What is this story about?', 'Where did it take place?' and so on) so each category fulfils a different function in a story. Table C5.1 lists the six categories, the hypothetical questions they address and their respective narrative functions. The table also provides information on the sort of linguistic forms that each component typically takes. With the exception of Evaluation, the categories listed on the Table are arranged in the sequence in which they would

Table C5.1 Labov's model of natural narrative

Narrative category	Narrative question	Narrative function	Linguistic form
ABSTRACT	What was this about?	Signals that the story is about to begin and draws attention from the listener.	A short summarising statement, provided before the narrative commences.
ORIENTATION	Who or what are involved in the story, and when and where did it take place?	Helps the listener to identify the time, place, persons, activity and situation of the story.	Characterised by past continuous verbs; and Adjuncts (see A3) of time, manner and place.
COMPLICATING ACTION	Then what happened?	The core narrative category providing the 'what happened' element of the story.	Temporally ordered narrative clauses with a verb in the simple past or present
RESOLUTION	What finally happened?	Recapitulates the final key event of a story.	Expressed as the last of the narrative clauses that began the Complicating Action.
EVALUATION	So what?	Functions to make the point of the story clear.	Includes: intensifiers; modal verbs; negatives; repetition; evaluative commentary; embedded speech; comparisons with unrealised events.
CODA	How does it all end?	Signals that a story has ended and brings listener back to the point at which s/he entered the narrative.	Often a generalised statement which is 'timeless' in feel.

occur in a typical oral narrative. Evaluation tends to sit outside the central pattern because it can be inserted at virtually any stage during a narrative. Evaluation is also the most fluid of the narrative categories stylistically: it may take a variety of linguistic forms depending on what particular evaluative job it is doing. However, the insertion of evaluative devices is generally very important as it helps explain the relevance of the central, reportable events of a story. A fully formed narrative will realise all six categories, although many narratives may lack one or more components.

Putting the model to work: a natural narrative

Below you will find a transcription of a story recorded during linguistic fieldwork in Northern Ireland. Although narrative analysis was not the primary aim of the fieldwork, the resulting interviews often involved informants telling of amusing episodes that had happened to them. This story, which took well under a minute to tell, is a fairly compact example of a natural narrative – even if the storyteller has a somewhat sniffy attitude to the events described. In the transcription, pauses are indicated by three dots while other relevant glosses are placed in square brackets. Beside each chunk of the story are five boxes, corresponding to five of Labov's categories. Evaluation has not been included because, as noted above, this component tends to permeate the other categories and can occur throughout a narrative. Read the story through now and identify which category is which by writing (if this is your book) the name of the component in the box to the right of the relevant piece of text:

. . . well erm a weird one [i.e. episode] happened to me a couple of years back . . .	
y'know when I was working in Belfast at the time . . . I was out for erm out for a drive in the car the weekend y'know of the May Bank holiday I think it was . . .	
erm . . . I picked up a hitchhiker thumbing a lift to Derry, rounabout Toome [a village] . . . I wouldn't often do that, mind you , but well I didn't mind the company that day. Rounabout Magherafelt [another village], yer man puts a cigarette in his mouth and looks at me, like sort of inquring y'know . . . so I pushed in the dashboard lighter in the . . . [inaudible] When it popped out, I handed it to him but, b'Jesus, after him lighting the fag he sorta glanced around like puzzled and ye wouldn't believe it, he opened the window on his side and . . .	
chucked the bloody lighter out into the field!	
There's not much you can say about a thing like that, is there?	

Now go through the story again, this time underlining the Evaluation devices the narrator uses. How much variety is there in the linguistic forms that are used for narrative Evaluation? And what would be lost from this story if Evaluation was not there?

Stylistics and natural narrative

Stylisticians have made much of the Labovian model, not least because it enables rigorous comparisons to be drawn between literary narrative on the one hand and the social stories told in everyday interaction on the other. However, the model's simple six-part structure tends to make it best suited to literary narratives that are (literally) short, which is why stylistic applications have tended to concentrate either on narrative texts of only a hundred words or so (eg. Simpson 1992a) or on 'narratives within narratives' such as the sorts of stories told by individual characters within a longer novel or play (eg. Toolan 2001: 150–9). Although the general application of the Labovian model to a full-length novel is theoretically viable (see Pratt 1977: 38–78), the replication of its six basic components, sometimes over many hundreds of pages of text, means that the results of a direct analysis can be less than exhilarating. However, the seeking out of shorter literary texts for natural narrative analysis is, it has to be said, rather like the drunk man who loses his keys on the way home one evening and who, on retracing his steps, looks for them only under lamplight. So with a theoretical disclaimer duly delivered, what follows is a practical narrative exercise based around a short 'narrative within a narrative'.

The passage below is from Eugene Ionesco's absurdist play *The Bald Prima Donna*, a play which satirises, after a fashion, its author's perception of the social and intellectual sterility of the English middle classes (see Burton 1980: 24). In this episode, two couples, Mr and Mrs Smith and Mr and Mrs Martin, engage in a bizarre story telling round in which Mrs Martin is encouraged to recount a narrative of personal experience about something 'interesting' that befell her. Read the passage through, concentrating particularly on the story told, across several speaker turns, by Mrs Martin:

| Activity |

MR MARTIN: [*to his wife*] Tell them, darling, what you saw today.

MRS MARTIN: Oh no, I couldn't. They'd never believe me.

MR SMITH: You don't think we'd doubt your word! [. . .]

MRS MARTIN: [*graciously*] Well, then! Today I witnessed the most extraordinary incident. It was absolutely incredible [. . .] As I was going to the market to buy some vegetables, which are still going up and up in price . . .

MRS SMITH: Yes, where on earth's it going to end!

MR SMITH: You mustn't interrupt, my dear. Naughty girl!

MRS MARTIN: In the street, outside a restaurant, was a gentleman, respectably dressed and about fifty years old, perhaps less, who was . . . Well, I know you'll say that I'm making it up: he was kneeling on the ground and leaning forward.

MR MARTIN: ⎫
MRS SMITH: ⎬ Oh!
MR SMITH: ⎭

MRS MARTIN: Yes! Leaning forward!

MR MARTIN:
MRS SMITH: } It can't be true!
MR SMITH:

MRS MARTIN: Yes! Leaning forward he was! I went right up to him to see what he was doing . . .

MR MARTIN:
MRS SMITH: } What ? What?
MR SMITH:

MRS MARTIN: His shoelaces had come undone and he was tying them up!

MR MARTIN:
MRS SMITH: } Fantastic!
MR SMITH:

MR SMITH: If I'd heard that from anyone else, I'd never have believed it.

(Ionesco 1963 [1958]: 98–9)

 Activity Now work through the following tasks which relate to the delivery, content and reception of Mrs Martin's 'shoelaces' story.

❏ What elements of the six-part Labovian model can you identify in Mrs Martin's story?
❏ Labov notes that it is understood among interactants that a narrative of personal experience must have a central reportable event. What is the central reportable event of Mrs Martin's story?
❏ To what extent does the category of Evaluation feature in Mrs Martin's story? In other words, what tactics does she use to ward off the 'so what' question? How many (and what sort of) Evaluation devices can you identify?
❏ With reference to the reaction her story draws from her interlocutors, is Mrs Martin's story successful *within* the interactive world of the play? That is, does it work at the *diegetic* (see A7) level?
❏ Going on your own reactions to it, to what extent is Mrs Martin's story successful *outside* the world of the play? In other words, does it work at the *extradiegetic* level?
❏ Following from the previous point, would you expect an audience (or readers of the play) to react in the same way as Mrs Martin's co-conversationalists to the story? How have the requirements for successful story-telling in the real world been transformed in the world of the absurd? Accepting that you may not have found it especially funny, can this piece of dialogue's potential for humour be explained by reference to this transformation?
❏ Ionesco's professed aim in this play is to break down the cliché-ridden and formulaic 'social language' that typifies polite bourgeois society (Ionesco 1964). How successful is this sort of dialogue in accomplishing this aim?

Drama dialogue is explored in depth across thread 9, where a range of stylistic issues and interests are covered. In the next three units the attention shifts away from the more structural aspects of narrative to consider models for the analysis of narrative as discourse. *Transitivity* is the first of those models.

TRANSITIVITY, CHARACTERISATION AND LITERARY GENRE

This unit offers some practical activities based around the model of transitivity developed in A6 and B6. It details first of all a stylistic experiment where transitivity can be used to highlight techniques of characterisation in narrative. It then widens the scope of the analysis to illustrate the ways in which transitivity can work as an important marker of literary genre.

Transitivity profiles

Some years ago, I co-authored an article with Martin Montgomery which examined a range of narrative devices, including patterns of transitivity, in Bernard MacLaverty's novel *Cal* (Simpson and Montgomery 1995). The implications of the article for the present unit will be clear soon. As far as our analysis of transitivity was concerned, we noted how certain types of process functioned to cast the novel's central character, Cal, as a rather ineffectual and passive observer on the events around him. Specifically, Cal is often represented as the Sensor in mental processes of perception or as the Actor in material processes which are not Goal-directed. Here is a flavour of the transitivity framework through which Cal the character is portrayed. Using the material provided in units A6 and B6, you should be able to identify the process types by yourself:

> A. Several times Cal saw the yellow Anglia pass in the opposite direction and followed it with his eyes. During the day he occasionally saw Marcella's child playing in the back garden or heard her prattling from another room when he was standing having a cup of tea in the kitchen. He also heard again the stomach-churning bubble of coughing from somewhere in the house.
>
> (MacLaverty 1984: 69)

In essence, Cal's actions are portrayed through a regular pattern of transitivity choices, a *transitivity profile* in other words. The transitivity profile embodied by a text is a generally useful indicator of character in prose fiction.

Part of the impetus for the Simpson and Montgomery paper referred to above came, like many publications in stylistics, from experience of teaching a text to students. In this particular case, our work on the MacLaverty novel took the form of a workshop on stylistics with thirty or so fluent speakers of English as an additional language. With respect to the idea of the transitivity profile, we were struck by how quickly the participants, while reading a novel, came to intuit a kind of stylistic template for the delineation of character. Evidence for this template came in the shape of an experiment involving pairs of related sentences, with one member of the pair a real sentence in the novel and the other a fake. On the basis of the short passage above, you may already be able to make reasonably strong predictions about which of these sentences 'fit' the novel and which do not:

(1a) The big one grabbed Cal.
(1b) Cal grabbed the big one.

(2a) She noticed that Cal was crying.
(2b) Cal noticed that she was crying.

(3a) Crilly handed two photographs to Cal.
(3b) Cal handed two photographs to Crilly.

(4a) He [Cal] moved his mouth to smile and the muscles of his face responded properly.
(4b) He [Cal] moved his mouth to smile but the muscles of his face would not respond properly.

The actual *Cal* sentences are 1a, 2b, 3a and 4b. Remarkably, the workshop participants, who had read the novel only once and without any accompanying stylistic explication, were *all* able to identify the correct sentences. (How did *you* fare?). It is not that the remaining sentences are 'impossible' or 'wrong' as such; it is more that they come across as stylistically anomalous, as incongruent with the overall tenor of characterisation in the novel. As suggested in A5, the relationship between transitivity and characterisation is a close one, and the usefulness of a simple exercise like this, where a set of actual patterns are paralleled by a set of variant patterns, is that it can bring this relationship to the forefront of the analysis. The exercise can also be replicated on any narrative text, and even on some non-narrative texts. What happens is that over the course of a narrative, which may span many hundred of pages of prose, certain elements are experientially foregrounded while others are suppressed. While we cannot expect to remember every sentence in a story, we do seem to develop a sense of a transitivity profile, a profile based on broad process and participant types as they relate to individual characters.

Genre

We can develop further the idea of the transitivity profile by moving up from the narrower features of characterisation to the broader area of literary *genre*. This move works on the premise that the styles of individual genres of literature, such as the popular romance, the Gothic horror tale, the fairy tale, the 'hard boiled' detective novel and so on, are in part defined by special and recurrent configurations of transitivity. Focussing on the first two of the literary genres just cited, you will find below two passages for analysis. The first is from a 'Mills and Boon' popular romance and the second from Bram Stoker's classic horror story *Dracula*:

B. Suzie closed her eyes, knowing that she should make the effort to go upstairs and go to bed, but reluctant to move. When she heard Carlos' deep voice, it was obvious he was standing very near to her. Her eyes flickered open to see him leaning over her, his face close to hers [. . .]

   And then his mouth was on hers, taking her by surprise and stopping her breath. His arms locked around her, pulling her close. Like a knife, a sudden panic cut through Suzie's body as her brain screamed out the message that this was wrong –

wrong! She struggled futilely against him, trying desperately to push him away, knowing full well that if she succumbed she would be lost and knowing also that she was fighting against herself. Even as her common sense told her this was pointless and wrong, her lips parted under his as if by a will of their own . . .

(*Escape to Love* by Claudia Jameson;
cited in Nash 1990: 141)

C. There lay the Count, but looking as if his youth had been half-renewed, for the whole hair and moustache were changed to dark iron-grey; the cheeks were fuller, and the white skin seemed ruby-red underneath; the mouth was redder than ever, for on the lips were gouts of fresh blood, which trickled from the corners of the mouth and ran over the chin and neck. Even the deep, burning eyes seemed set amongst swollen flesh, for the lids and pouches underneath were bloated. It seemed as if the whole, awful creature were simply gorged with blood; he lay like a filthy leech, exhausted with his repletion.

(Stoker 1998 [1897]: 51)

First of all, work through the two passages following this set of general exercises:

 Activity ✪

(a) Analyse the transitivity patterns in the two extracts, looking closely at:
   (i) The types of *processes* that are present.
      (Specify whether they are material, mental, behavioural and so on (see A6))
   (ii) The types of *participants* associated with each of the processes.
      (Identify participant roles like Actor, Goal, Sensor and so on (A6))
   (iii) Any special *types* of participant role.
      (See for example if you can distinguish *meronymic* agency from *holonymic* agency (see B6))
(b) What does your analysis of transitivity reveal about the key stylistic characteristics of each of the two genres of writing?

Having undertaken an analysis of the broader patterns, consider now the following issues and sub-activities which are directed more specifically to each of the passages:

Passage B:
(a) A generally useful framing question for the analysis of transitivity is to ask: *who or what does what to whom or what?* (and see further the reading by Deirdre Burton in D6). The question provides useful orientation for the Mills and Boon passage, where it can help distinguish the two characters through the sorts of actions they perform. In a sense, the question helps differentiate who *does* from who *thinks*.

(b) A related issue in transitivity analysis concerns the success or failure of a semantic process. It is common for narrative description to indicate that a character *attempts* to carry out a process, but that the process either fails, or ends up being self-directed. In a self-directed material process, for example, the Actor and Goal become the same entity. Notice how in example (4b) from *Cal*, the process attributed to Cal as Actor is not only self-directed ('He moved his mouth to smile') but it fails as well ('the muscles of his face would not respond . . .').

(c)   Look again at the Mills and Boon passage exploring the issues raised in (a) and (b). Is it true to say that its romantic heroine is portrayed as 'helpless'? And if so, is the portrayal of a female central character in this way sexist?

Passage C:

(a)   The framing question set out for passage B obviously works better for material processes which express action than it does for relational processes which represent states of being. Not much seems to happen by way of physical action in the passage from *Dracula* and you may have found this passage more difficult to analyse for this reason. However, transitivity still has an important part to play even in heavily descriptive passages like text C. Furthermore, relational processes, of which there are many in C, are very much tied up with the sense of stasis in the scene and with the image of inertia and repletion which is attributed to the vampire.

(b)   In the light of the observations in (a), look again at the relational processes in C. Remember, this process type is not just coded through the verb 'to be' but through a variety of intensive verbs like 'seem', 'appear', 'become' and so on. The participant roles for these processes include the elements Carrier and Attribute. What sort of entities make up the Carrier element and what sort of descriptions (Attributes) are attributed to them? Does the pattern you uncover give the impression of the Count as a whole being, or is his portrayal delivered in a more corporeally fragmented way?

(c)   While transitivity is undoubtedly an important feature of style, it forms only part of the overall organisation of narrative discourse. Passage C offers a good illustration of how the experiential function is supplemented by other aspects of language, most notably markers of the *interpersonal* function (and see further C7). Notice for example how the narrator modulates his description of the vampire's post-prandial torpor. This is a narrator who seemingly struggles to make sense of the awful events in front of him, and this stamp of uncertainty and bewilderment is, in true Gothic horror style, manifested in heavily foregrounded references to visual appearance and to the interpretation of visual appearance. Look again at the passage and see how many of these archetypal markers of horror writing you can identify.

This unit has illustrated some of the ways in which the model of transitivity can usefully be employed in the study both of characterisation and of literary genre. Of course, the practical activities offered here are no more than a snapshot of a type of analysis that can be extended to many other styles of writing; nor are they intended to suggest that the experiential function is the only component of narrative that can offer insights into characterisation and genre. The interpersonal function of language, as signalled in the activities based around text C, plays an important role in the organ-isation of narrative discourse. This theme is developed further in the next unit.

EXPLORING POINT OF VIEW IN NARRATIVE FICTION

This unit is designed to explore further the concept of point of view by building on the observation, made towards the end of C6, that the *interpersonal* function of language works in parallel with the experiential function in the overall stylistic make-up of a narrative text. The synthesis of the two functions is an important marker of style in its own terms, and the regular co-occurence of certain functional patterns often serves to distinguish different genres of writing. Unit B7 introduced and reviewed four principal types of point of view. The conclusion to that review was that, of the four types surveyed, *psychological* point of view is the pivotal term of reference for this dimension of narrative organisation. This unit offers the opportunity to develop some practical work around the key interpersonal features which serve to mark out psychological point of view in narrative. The unit also pays particular attention to the way point of view intersects with the stylistic concept of *mind style*.

Modality and style

The *interpersonal* function, as the term itself suggests, is about how we orientate, shape and measure our utterances as discourse. This function is expressed principally by the grammatical system of *modality* which is that part of language which allows us to attach expressions of belief, attitude and obligation to what we say and write. Modality is therefore the grammar of explicit comment, and it includes signals of the varying degrees of certainty we have about the propositions we express, and of the sorts of commitment or obligation that we attach to our utterances.

A useful way of fleshing out this rather abstract definition of modality, and in a way that helps align it with the concept of psychological point of view, is to consider some alternative types of modal patterning in a short sample narrative. The three invented 'mini-stories' that follow were scrawled on the back of a napkin in a British airport late one November evening some years ago. No more than the slightly deranged ramblings of a stylistician at a loss for something to do, these narratives make no claim whatsoever to any kind of literary accomplishment, although they do serve a useful purpose in sketching some basic concepts in modality and style. With all disclaimers delivered, consider the first version:

(1)   *In the Heathrow cafeteria*
      What a nuisance! The bally London to Tunis flight had been delayed, *quelle surprise*. The tannoy sheepishly attributed this to the late arrival of an incoming flight. Fog is normally the problem at this time of year.

I needed a robust coffee, so I felt I had to confront the busy cafeteria. A lone waitress patrolled the tables.

'What'll it be?' she asked, harassed.

'Strong coffee please,' I replied.

Her face tightened in a way that registered the request as unreasonable. She eventually brought to me, in a flowery mug, a pale grey liquid which I understood was to pass for filter coffee.

This is a homodiegetic narrative where actions and events are relayed through a first person 'participating' narrator. So much is obvious, but it is the manner by which these actions and events are relayed that is rather more significant here. The narrator of (1) tells you not only what happens but also what he thinks. Throughout, interpretations and interpolations are offered as to why events unfold in the way they do, with the narrator cooperatively orientating what they say towards an implied reader. Text (1) thus embodies a particular type of modal framework which in narrative discourse is marked by certain key expressions. The narrator, for example, expresses clearly their own desires, duties, obligations and opinions in relation to events and other characters: 'I *needed* a coffee'; 'I *felt I had to* confront the busy cafeteria' and so on. Modality which expresses desire and obligation is known as *deontic* modality. Notice also that the narrator of (1) – and this self-analysis is not to suggest any craft in its creation – employs a generic sentence in the sequence 'Fog is normally the problem at this time of year'. This key marker of narratorial modality, which is always expressed through the time-less simple present tense, allows the narrator confidently to represent what they say as a universal truth. The text is also rich in what Uspensky (1973) calls *verba sentiendi*. These are words denoting thoughts, feelings and perceptions, as embodied in mental processes like 'I felt . . .' or 'I understood . . .'. Overall, the text is dominated by clearly articulated personal interpretations of felt experience where the narrator makes sense of the experience before relaying it. Following the taxonomy presented in Simpson (1993) for the reminder of this sub-unit, let us adopt the term *positive shading* for this type of modal pattern.

Consider now another version, another embodiment in discourse as it were, of the same basic narrative *plot*. Here the first person narrator appears to have a little more trouble in making sense of and relaying experience:

(2)   *In the Heathrow cafeteria*
The London to Tunis flight must have been delayed because the tannoy said something about the late arrival of another flight. Perhaps it was fog?

I must have been hungry, or maybe thirsty, because I found myself in a large busy room whose appearance suggested it was a cafeteria. A woman, in the attire of a waitress, patrolled the tables.

'What'll it be?' she asked, as if harassed by my presence.

'Strong coffee please,' I seem to recall saying.

Her face tightened as though she found my request unreasonable. She eventually brought to me, in a flowery mug, a pale grey liquid which must have been filter coffee.

The overall interpersonal dynamic of this (admittedly bizarre) piece of narrative is very different from (1). This is a narrator who *tries* to make sense of the world around him, but does so with only limited success. His account is marked by *epistemic* modality which refers to the system of modal markers used for signalling judgments of belief, certainty or truth. Epistemic modality works principally in (2) to foreground the narrator's efforts to interpret and make sense of what he sees and hears: '[the] flight *must have been* delayed . . .'; '*Perhaps* it was fog . . .' and so on. The passage is also rich in 'words of estrangement' (Fowler 1996) which reinforce the narrator's seeming uncertainty about what is going on around him. A consequence of this is that description tends to rely on the narrator's interpretation of external appearance; notice how it is the appearance of the room which suggests it was a cafeteria, and the woman's attire that suggests she was a waitress. To accommodate this sort of modal framework, where the epistemic system is heightened as the narrator struggles to make sense of the world, let us reserve the term *negative shading*.

Finally, consider a third variant:

(3)   *In the Heathrow cafeteria*
       The London to Tunis flight had been delayed. The tannoy referred to the late arrival of an incoming flight. I went into a cafeteria. A woman patrolled the tables.
           'What'll it be?' she said.
           'Strong coffee please,' I said.
           Her face tightened. She eventually brought me a mug of coffee.

This version is characterised by, if anything, a marked absence of narratorial modality. It is constructed entirely from *categorical assertions*; that is to say, from raw propositions which have no trace of explicit modal comment. Because they are stripped of modality, categorical assertions are in a certain respect non-negotiable, and the removal of interpersonal markers in (3) explains in part why it is much shorter than the first two versions. In this type of modal framework (or, better, 'demodalised' framework), the narrator withholds subjective evaluation in favour of an ostensibly more 'neutral' description of events. Straightforward physical description dominates, while there is little or no attempt at any psychological development or interpretation. Even the reporting clauses which are used to relay sequences of Direct Speech (see thread 8) have been stripped of their adverbial embellishments, so that nothing other than the most basic of reporting verbs remain. Let us refer to this type of modal framework as *neutral shading*.

Before we move to consider the significance of this exercise and of the three narrative modalities identified, it is worth noting that transpositions to third person variants are possible with all three texts. In other words, the same basic modal framework can be transferred across into corresponding heterodiegetic modes. For example, version 2 might be rewritten thus:

(2a)   *In the Heathrow cafeteria*
       The London to Tunis flight must have been delayed because the tannoy said something about the late arrival of another flight. Perhaps it was fog?

Simpson must have been hungry, or maybe thirsty, because he found himself in a large busy room whose appearance suggested it was a cafeteria. A woman, in the attire of a waitress, patrolled the tables.

'What'll it be?' she asked, as if harassed by his presence.

'Strong coffee please,' he replied.

Her face tightened as if she found his request unreasonable. She eventually brought to him, in a flowery mug, a pale grey liquid which must have been filter coffee.

In this version, the original narrator of (2) becomes a character within the story, a character who in fact occupies the role of reflector of fiction (see A7), while the new narrator is 'heterodiegetic' in the sense of being different from and external to the story. Although the negatively shaded modality follows the transposition, the source of the epistemic warrant for what is narrated is now less clear. Is it the reflector of fiction who is the 'bewildered' focaliser here? Or is it the external, non-participating narrator? Or is it even some combination of both? Both of the other original versions can be similarly transposed, so that the same modality (of lack of it) carries over into the third person framework. Again, the same questions are raised about where the source for the modal comment should be situated. Basically, the third person framework offers two options: either align the modality with the external narrator or locate it in the viewpoint of the character-reflector. This means that the point of view model becomes a little more complex when applied specifically to the third person mode because it offers two variants for each of the three modal possibilities. It also means that there is considerable scope for ambiguity, and sometimes for irony, in this mode, because we are often less certain about whose point of view exactly is being relayed in third person narratives.

Modality and psychological point of view

This sub-unit outlines some practical activities that follow from the point of view rewrite exercise undertaken above. Before going on to consider some of the implications of the exercise for passages of 'real' fiction, it will be worth recapping upon and tightening up the three basic types of modal patterning identified thus far in our survey:

Positive shading: this is a narrative modality where the narrator's desires, duties, obligations and opinions of events are foregrounded. The *deontic* modal system is prominent and the narrative is rich in generic sentences and in *verba sentiendi* (words denoting thoughts, feelings and perceptions). Positive shading is perhaps the most common point of view modality, underpinning a great many first and third person fictional works.

Negative shading: this is a narrative modality where an often 'bewildered' narrator (or character) relies on external signals and appearances to sustain a description. The *epistemic* modal system is foregrounded and the narrative is rich in 'words of estrangement'. The narrator's uncertainty about events and about other characters' motivations is often expressed through structures based on human perception (*as if; it seemed; it appeared to be*, etc.). Negative shading often characterises 'existentialist' or 'Gothic' styles of narrative fiction.

Neutral shading: this style is characterised by a complete absence of narratorial modality and is typified by *categorical assertions* where the narrator withholds subjective evaluation and interpretation. This type of shading often comprises 'neutral' physical description at the expense of psychological development. Neutral shading embodies the principle of 'objective realism' in fiction and it corresponds to what the narratologists Genette (1980) and Rimmon-Kenan (1983) have called 'external' focalisation. Given the often sparse feel this mode engenders, narratives written entirely in a neutrally shaded modality are rare.

It is, of course, possible for a literary text to shift from one pattern to another, even while a particular pattern dominates overall.

You will find below seven passages of prose fiction. The passages are not ordered in any particular or significant sequence, and the only thing to bear in mind is that there are present at least two representatives of each of the three categories of modal shading. As you work through each passage, follow the guidelines below:

(i)   Identify (as far as you can tell) the narrative *mode* in which the passage is written. That is, say whether it is first person or third person.
(ii) Identify the *dominant* type of modal shading in each passage. Do not try to analyse the passage on a sentence by sentence basis, but rather pick out the modal framework which best describes the passage as a whole. Highlight any of the tell-tale devices that help confirm your interpretation.
(iii) If you identify a passage as third person, try to work out whether its modality (ie. the attitudes, opinions and beliefs it expresses) comes from (a) an external heterodiegetic narrator who is situated *outside* the story or (b) from an individual character, a reflector of fiction (A7), who is situated *inside* the story.
(iv) Wherever feasible, think of the stylistic impact of both the narrative mode and the point of view framework that each writer has chosen. What would happen if either the narrative mode or the particular modal shading were altered?

Seven passages

   a) Shaking off from my spirit what *must* have been a dream, I scanned more narrowly the real aspect of the building. Its principal features seemed to be that of an excessive antiquity. The discolouration of ages had been great. No portion of the masonry had fallen; and there appeared to be a wild inconsistency between its still perfect adaptation of parts, and the crumbling of the individual stones. Beyond this indication of extensive decay, however, the fabric gave little token of instability. Perhaps the eye of a scrutinising observer might have discovered a barely perceptible fissure [. . .]

> (*The Fall of the House of Usher,*
> Edgar Allan Poe 1986 [1839])

b) In my younger and more vulnerable years my father gave me some advice that I've been turning over in my mind ever since.

'Whenever you feel like criticising any one,' he told me, 'just remember that all the people in this world haven't had the advantages that you've had.'

He didn't say any more, but we've always been unusually communicative in a reserved way, and I understood that he meant a great deal more than that. In consequence, I'm inclined to reserve all judgments, a habit that has opened up many curious natures to me and also made me the victim of not a few veteran bores. The abnormal mind is quick to detect and attach itself to this quality when it appears in a normal person [. . .]

(*The Great Gatsby*, F. Scott Fitzgerald 1994 [1925])

c) The fat white circles of dough lined the pan in rows. Once more Sethe touched a wet forefinger to the stove. She opened the oven door and slid a pan of biscuits in. As she raised up from the heat she felt Paul D behind her and his hands under her breasts. She straightened up [. . .]

(*Beloved*, Toni Morrison 1987)

d) Someone must have been telling lies about Joseph K., for without having done anything wrong he was arrested one fine morning. His landlady's cook, who always brought him his breakfast at eight o'clock, failed to appear on this occasion. That had never happened before. K. waited for a little while longer, watching from his pillow the old lady opposite, who seemed to be peering at him with a curiosity unusual even for her, but then, feeling both put out and hungry, he rang the bell. At once there was a knock at the door and a man entered whom he had never seen before in the house. He was slim and yet well knit, he wore a closely fitting black suit, which was furnished with all sorts of pleats, pockets, buckles, and buttons, as well as a belt, like a tourist's outfit, and in consequence looked eminently practical, though one could not quite tell what actual purpose it served.

'Who are you?' asked K., half raising himself in bed. But the man ignored the question, as though his appearance needed no explanation.

(*The Trial*, Franz Kafka 1985 [1925])

e) He [Strether] was to to delay no longer to reestablish communication with Chad, and [. . .] he had spoken to Miss Gostrey of this intention on hearing from her of the young man's absence. It was not, moreover, only the assurance so given that prompted him; it was the need of causing his conduct to square with another profession still – the motive he had described to her as his sharpest for now getting away [. . .] He must do both things; he must see Chad, but he must go. The more he thought of the former of these duties the more he felt himself make a subject of insistence of the latter.

(*The Ambassadors*, Henry James 2001 [1903])

f) We were in a garden in Mons. Young Buckley came in with his patrol from across the river. The first German I saw climbed over up the garden wall. We waited till he got one leg over and then potted him [. . .] Then three more came over further down the wall. We shot them. They all came just like that.

(from a story in *In Our Time*, Ernest Hemingway 1925)

g) Different though the sexes are, they intermix. In every human being a vacillation from one sex to the other takes place, and it is only the clothes that keep the male or female likeness, while underneath the sex is the very opposite of what it is above.

(*Orlando*, Virginia Woolf 1998 [1928])

Commentary

I hope your analysis of the sample passages above will have underscored the stylistic significance of modal shading as a marker not only of point of view but of narrative style more generally. As with all the units in this Exploration section, I do not propose to provide a circumscribed set of 'answers', and in any case my own interpretation counts as just one of many possible interpretations that can be systematically reached on the basis of a stylistic analysis. I will however footnote briefly one of the passages, the Toni Morrison excerpt c), because of the particularly interesting issues it raises.

On the grounds that it is devoid of any modality at all, my analysis suggests that this passage embodies neutral shading. Whereas its narrative mode is third person, its point of view is aligned, significantly, with the reflector of fiction. That is to say, in spite of the third-person framework, the narrative camera angle assumes the vantage point of a particular character, here Sethe, and it is her experience of events which is recorded and relayed. (Notice how this is established by the word 'felt', the one verb of perception in the passage.) Interestingly, this generally 'flat' modal framework tends in this discourse context to make the central character seem numb, and very much acquiescent to the advances of Paul D. We are given no information as to whether she welcomes or is offended by his advances, the sort of information that would be communicated precisely by a positively shaded modality. Prior to this point in the novel, we have learned of Sethe's experience of having to have sex with a stonemason simply to get an engraving on a dead child's headstone, and this and other traumatic events may have rendered her emotionally dead, and unable or unwilling to react to the events around her. This is not to argue, though, that the modality of the novel as a whole is neutrally shaded nor indeed that this character's perceptions of the world are always relayed in this way. It is very much in the idiom of the 'postmodern' novel, of which *Beloved* is a preeminent example, that it tangles up different domains of discourse and allows its characters to migrate between different text worlds (McHale 1987). To my mind, variable narrative focalisation is just one of the reflexes of the post-modernist 'style', such as it is, where the oscillations in point of view give rise to many alternating viewing positions and modalities.

Mind-style and point of view

The concept of *mind-style* forms a natural intersection with point of view in fiction, so this is a good place to develop some practical exercises that meld the two concepts. Roger Fowler coined the term – now often expressed as two separate words – in his study of style in prose fiction, where he defines mind-style as 'any distinctive linguistic presentation of an individual mental self' (1977: 103; and see also the important accounts in Semino 2002; 2007). In its broader sense, the term encompasses the general markers of style which bias a narrative towards a particular character's point of view, but the concept most productively captures the special and often rather *restricted* cognitive perspective of a particular narrator-character. This sense of a 'consistently restricted' mind-style (Fowler 1977: 105) is important because choices in vocabulary, grammar and other stylistic markers effectively limit the narrative to the perspective of that reflector. This 'focalised ignorance' (Hardy 2005: 374) is delivered in such a way as to invite, or indeed to demand, a 'seeing beyond' by the reader of the limited understanding and world-view of the character-narrator.

★ Activity

Over in unit A6, a short exercise was developed around three pictures. Without any further commentary at this stage, consider the following passage, which is the first paragraph of William Faulkner's novel, *The Sound and the Fury* (1980 [1931]):

> Through the fence between the curling flower spaces, I could see them hitting. They were coming toward where the flag was and I went along the fence. Luster was hunting in the grass by the flower tree. They took the flag out, and they were hitting. Then they put the flag back and they went to the table, and he hit and the other hit. Then they went on, and I went along the fence and they stopped and we stopped and I looked through the fence while Luster was hunting in the grass.

Bearing in mind that this is the beginning of the novel, now follow through these preliminary exercises:

(a) What activity is the first person narrator describing?
(b) Who or what is Luster?
(c) Highlight any aspects of language that seem to arrest the reading process or that seem to restrict your understanding of this narrative.
(d) As a narrative opening, how effective is this paragraph? That is, how adequate is the information given on the characters involved in the scene, their identities and activities, and their immediate physical environment?

After working through tasks 1–4, go back to the short narrative that you composed in response to the three pictures in unit A6. Astonishingly, your own text and the lines from Faulkner to all intents and purposes describe the same thing, a game of golf. However, Faulkner's narrative (or at least this part of the novel) is delivered from the perspective of Benjy Compson – an adult who, in today's parlance, suffers from acute learning difficulties. Crucially, with Benjy as the reflector of fiction, the restricted mind-style that emerges requires considerable cognitive input from the reader in order to 'see beyond' Benjy's limited, and limiting, description of the golfers. In short, this is a pre-eminent example of the cognitive-stylistic impact of the intersection between point of view and mind-style.

I do not propose to be programmatic about how the stylistic comparisons between your own text and the lines from Faulkner might be drawn. The supplementary questions posited after the pictures in unit A6, alongside the tasks set out above, will guide these comparisons. However, it is worth looking briefly at the onward progression of Faulkner's opening paragraph because it raises even more tasks for stylistic exploration. Here now are the first four paragraphs of Faulkner's *The Sound and the Fury*; after reading them through closely, work through the additional tasks posted below the text:

> Through the fence between the curling flower spaces, I could see them hitting. They were coming toward where the flag was and I went along the fence. Luster was hunting in the grass by the flower tree. They took the flag out, and they were hitting. Then they put the flag back and they went to the table, and he hit and the other hit. Then they went on, and I went along the fence and they stopped and we stopped and I looked through the fence while Luster was hunting in the grass.
>
> 'Here, caddie.' He hit. They went away across the pasture. I held to the fence and watched them going away.
>
> 'Listen at you now.' Luster said. 'Ain't you something, thirty-three years old, going on that way. After I done went all the way to town to buy you that cake. Hush up that moaning. Ain't you going to help me find that quarter so I can go to the show tonight.'
>
> They were hitting little, across the pasture. I went back along the fence to where the flag was. It flapped on the bright grass and the trees.

Additional tasks

A   The grammar of the passage

   (i)   Identify any transitive verbs that are presented without Goal elements (see A6).
   (ii) Identify any (multi-component) *noun phrases* (see strand 3) that function as circumlocutions. Compare this with the way you 'named' the things and activities in the pictures.
   (iii) Identify any repeated patterns, especially coordinated ('beads on a string') sentence structures (see again strand 3).
   (iv) Identify any unresolved pronominal reference – that is, pronouns whose referent or antecedent is not clear or obvious.

B   Coherence and co-text

   (i)   In spite of its rendering in the voice of what one critic has called a 'congenital imbecile', what cues about the story's setting and context can we pick up in the sequences of reported speech (see A8) in the passage?
   (ii) Related to (i), do any features of dialect locate the passage in a particular time and place?
   (iii) Overall, is the passage *in its entirety* really just the uninformative rambling of an imbecile?

Summary

There are many novels which embrace striking mind-styles and the methods developed in this unit can be usefully put in place as basic research tools for further study. More generally, looking at how particular patterns of point of view mark out specific genres of narrative fiction also offers scope for further research. Another fruitful line of investigation would be to see if additional modal frameworks could be developed, beyond the three proposed earlier in this unit, which could more subtly delineate types of writing style. Some more general issues to do with narrative viewpoint are raised in Mick Short's reading, D7, which completes this thread.

C8   **A WORKSHOP ON SPEECH AND THOUGHT PRESENTATION**

This workshop programme is designed to encourage you to use your stylistic analyses in tandem with your affective responses to literary texts and to enable you to challenge and (re)evaluate some of the literary critical commentaries that have been written on the texts you are studying. Before moving onto the more practical aspects of the programme, it is worth introducing here the short passage that will form the nucleus of the workshop activity. It is taken from American writer Ernest Hemingway's short novel (or novella) *The Old Man and the Sea* (see also unit B1). The intention will ultimately be to place this passage against a series of literary-critical comments about the novella and then to use an analysis of speech and thought presentation as a way of reappraising these critical comments and of reaching more systematic interpretations about Hemingway's narrative technique.

The passage itself is taken from the lengthy central section of the story which covers the time the old man spends at sea during his struggle with the huge marlin that he has hooked. This particular episode occurs early in the morning of the second day of his battle with the fish (thus explaining the references in the text to 'the line' slanting into the water). He is confronted with two practical problems: eating the small tuna that he caught the day before and solving the problem of his cramped left hand. The passage is quite neatly rounded in that it stretches from the preparatory stages to the completion of the old man's meal. To facilitate subsequent referencing to the passage, lines have been numbered. Read the passage now. Don't worry about locating any stylistic features in the passage at this stage and don't feel you that are being asked to make any kind of interpretative judgment about the text.

The Text

He knelt down and found the tuna under the stern with the gaff and
drew it toward him keeping it clear of the coiled lines. Holding the line with
his left shoulder again, and bracing on his left hand and arm, he took the
tuna off the gaff hook and put the gaff back in place. He put one knee
on the fish and cut strips of dark red meat longitudinally from the back of   5
the head to the tail. They were wedge-shaped strips and he cut them from
next to the back bone down to the edge of the belly. When he had cut six
strips he spread them out on the wood of the bow, wiped his knife on his
trousers, and lifted the carcass of the bonito by the tail and
dropped it overboard.   10

'I don't think I can eat an entire one,' he said and drew his knife
across one of the strips. He could feel the steady hard pull of the line and
his left hand was cramped. It drew up tight on the heavy cord and he
looked at it in disgust.

'What kind of a hand is that,' he said. 'Cramp then if you want.   15
Make yourself into a claw. It will do you no good.'

Come on, he thought and looked down into the dark water at the
slant of the line. Eat it now and it will strengthen the hand. It is not the
hand's fault and you have been many hours with the fish. But you can
stay with him for ever. Eat the bonito now.   20

He picked up a piece and put it in his mouth and chewed it slowly. It
was not unpleasant.

Chew it well, he thought, and get all the juices. It would not be bad
to eat with a little lime or with lemon or with salt.

'How do you feel, hand?' he asked the cramped hand that was   25
almost as still as rigor mortis. 'I'll eat some more for you.'

He ate the other part of the piece that he had cut in two. He chewed
it carefully and then spat out the skin.

'How does it go, hand? Or is it too early to know?'

He took another full piece and chewed it.   30

'It is a strong full-blooded fish,' he thought. 'I was lucky to get him
instead of dolphin. Dolphin is too sweet. This is hardly sweet at all and all
the strength is still in it.'

There is no sense in being anything but practical though, he
thought. I wish I had some salt. And I do not know whether the sun will rot   35
or dry what is left, so I had better eat it all although I am not hungry. The
fish is calm and steady. I will eat it all and then I will be ready.

'Be patient, hand,' he said. 'I do this for you.'

I wish I could feed the fish, he thought. He is my brother. But
I must kill him and keep strong to do it. Slowly and conscientiously he ate   40
all of the wedge-shaped strips of fish.

He straightened up, wiping his hand on his trousers.

Hemingway (1976 [1952]: 47–9)

A workshop on stylistics and literary evaluation

The following five statements, written by different literary critics, are concerned with
aspects of language and style in Hemingway's *The Old Man and the Sea*. Now that you
have read a section of this novella and perhaps formed your own impressions of
Hemingway's style of writing, try to rank the five statements in order of accuracy and
appropriateness. Try to say why you consider a particular remark to be more or less
effective than another:

A   As a matter of fact, Hemingway takes pains to avoid the *mot juste*, probably
     because it sounds too 'literary' to him, preferring the general, unspecific word
     like 'and' . . .

B   . . . there is a really heroic piece of narrative in *The Old Man and the Sea*, told with a simplicity which shows that Mr. Hemingway has forgotten that he is a tough writer . . . the first few pages are almost strangely sentimental with relapses into the 'ands' of children's storybooks.

C   The reader who expects a psychological novel will feel disappointed, despite the superb handling of the material and the style which is classical in its simplicity and force, pure as poetry, sonorous as music, flowing on the rhythms of the sea it describes.

D   The plain, dry, restrained and documentary style succeeds in lending an extraordinary glow and depth to its simple subject matter.

E   [. . .] Hemingway's diction is thin; [. . .] in the technical sense, his syntax is weak; and [. . .] he would rather be caught dead than seeking the *mot juste* or the balanced phrase. Granted [. . .] his adjectives are not colourful and his verbs not particularly energetic.

What my students said

On the basis of their earlier reading of the passage, a group of thirty of my students were asked to rank these statements in the manner detailed above. It has to be said that the students whose comments are reported here found very little of value in any of the critical statements. Statement A was felt to be 'not particularly informative', though it was 'reasonable enough' as far as it went. Statement B was 'too personalised about the writer' but otherwise seemed 'OK'. Statement C fared very badly, and the comment about style 'flowing on the rhythms of the sea' was singled out for particular criticism ('naff'; 'too airy-fairy'; 'completely daft'). Statement D was responded to more positively, although students found it hard to see how a 'documentary style' could make subject matter 'glow'. Opinion was divided on statement E, largely because students felt that it was 'too out of context' to know what the critic was getting at, although 'what he [*sic*] did say might be interesting'. The tutor was rebuked for this oversight and urged to replace statement E with something more accessible in future. Overall, though, there was some measure of agreement across the group of students about the usefulness or otherwise of the five statements. The overall ranking, beginning with the most favoured statement, runs as follows: D, A, E, B, C. How did your own ranking compare with this sequence? We will return to these rankings later.

The analysis of speech and thought presentation

Activity

The next stage of the programme involves an analysis of speech and thought presentation in the passage using the criteria outlined in units A8 and B8. You should refamiliarise yourself with the broad categories introduced in these units before progressing any further. As there are many types of speech and thought modes in evidence, a good idea is to mark up on the text the modes you spot. Try to see how many modes you can identify and how they are used to signal and accommodate different aspects of the story. (A full analysis of the passage in terms of its patterns of speech and thought presentation is provided in the web material which accompanies this book.)

The bigger picture: seeing transitions between speech and thought

Now that you have identified in the passage the many and varied modes of speech and thought presentation, and the patterns of oscillation between these modes, it might be worth trying to see if we can develop a visual representation for the stylistic fabric of the text. Figure C8.1 works as a template for charting the two main directions of narrative organisation in the passage. The horizontal axis on the figure represents the simple forward development of the passage, moving from line 1 through to line 42. The vertical axis marks the transitions between one strand of speech and thought presentation and another, such that every one of the modes realised in the passage can be assigned a position on the vertical axis. Speech modes are plotted above the NRA line on the vertical axis; thought modes below. I have marked up, with dots in the relevant places, the four modes in evidence up to line 16. Using dots to chart subsequent modes, complete the figure. Then, once you are satisfied that all the modes have been plotted on the figure, join up (with a single line moving from left to right) all the modes. Each of the transitions in the passage will now be represented by a through-line connecting each node on the axis. You should end up with a wavy line which intersects with the straight line in the middle.

Activity ✪

Stylistic analysis and critical (re)evaluation

The implications of this figure will be the main issue developed in this part of the workshop programme. First of all, you should reevaluate the five literary-critical comments provided earlier in the light of your analysis of the text and in the light of

Activity ✪

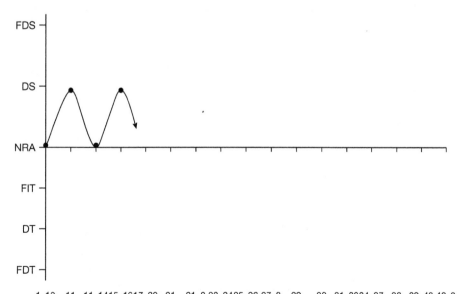

Figure C8.1 Template for charting narrative organisation in the extract from *The Old Man and the Sea*

the visual representation of the narrative texture provided by the figure. Are any of the critical comments, in your opinion, a true reflection of Hemingway's prose style? Do any of the critics come close to giving a genuine insight into the language of this text? Is it true, as most of the critics seem to suggest, that the style of the passage is 'simple'? And, importantly, have you been tempted, since doing your analysis, to modify your initial rankings in any way?

The figure, with its double axis showing narrative development, suggests perhaps a degree of subtlety in narrative organisation that had not hitherto been identified by the critics. The group of students who produced the initial ranking offered some illuminating feedback on the basis of their analysis of speech and thought. For the most part, their analysis only served to consolidate the impression that the critical statements offered little in the way of concrete information about Hemingway's use of language in the passage. Having said that, there was one particular statement that caught the attention of the group when it was set against the figure. This was statement C, which had been resolutely and unequivocally consigned to the bottom of the original ranking list.

The points of intersection between the layout of the figure and critic C's remarks are interesting. The critic suggests that narrative technique is foregrounded at the expense of psychological interpretation, and to the extent that the style of the novella echoes the very physicality of what it sets out to depict. This culminates in the reference to the style 'flowing on the rhythms of the sea it describes'. Although scoffed at initially, this remark, when placed in the context of the completed figure, no longer reads like the critical excess it first seemed. Indeed, it prompts a hypothesis that is both tendentious and fanciful but is nonetheless worth mooting as a point for debate. Consider the following argument. Our figure essentially captures a dual movement in the passage: the linear progression of the text as narrative on one level, and the movement created by oscillations between speech and thought modes on another. There is a curious analogy between this dual movement at the level of narrative structure and the implied movements of the old man and his boat. On the one hand, the boat moves on the sea horizontally – the effect of being dragged by the huge marlin; on the other, it moves up and down vertically as a consequence of the swell of the Gulf Stream. Both types of movement are referred to frequently by the narrator in the novella's central section. Moreover, the particular wave-like pattern of speech and thought presentation identified in our analysis is *only* initiated once the old man sets sail in his boat. Thereafter, it is sustained with almost mathematical consistency during his time at sea. Is it the case, then, that the 'narrative waves' created as stylistic texture are an analogue of the fictional environment portrayed in the story? Has critic C – whose remarks seemed so outlandish at first glance – perhaps stumbled intuitively upon one of the novella's central motifs?

We cannot really answer this question with any degree of certainty. Stylistic categories and affective responses are simply not homologous domains of reference, and the interpretative pathway that connects them is abstract, indirect and multidimensional. That said, my students were noticeably divided in their opinion about the 'narrative wave' argument when it was put to them. Some simply were not convinced by my suggested connection between the stylistic analysis and the physical elements of the fictional world. However, they were hard put to explain *why* they found the theory unconvincing.

Around two-thirds of the group, by contrast, found the theory appealing. There was a general sense that the rhythmical texture displayed by the narrative analysis echoed the very movements of the old man on the sea and, as a consequence, these students wanted to elevate comment C to the top of their ranking. They felt that the critic had had an 'insight' into the style of the story, though they added the proviso that no evidence was offered in support of this insight. As far as the 'narrative waves' idea is concerned, you can decide which side you want to come down on: is the idea a fanciful conceit based on a mere stylistic coincidence, or is it the perception of a deftly crafted *leitmotif* embodying the very essence of the novella? There is no right or wrong answer to this. What is important is that we think of the reasons why we might adopt one position or the other. In other words, we need to ground what we say about the language of a text in a model that does precisely that; we need a language for talking about language, a *metalanguage*, as was argued in unit A1. In this workshop we looked at five rather speculative critical comments which all stressed the supposed 'simplicity' of the story's style. What little stylistic evidence there was on offer tended to be drawn from perceived patterns in vocabulary. Yet parts of speech such as nouns, verbs and adjectives are not necessarily the principal indices of narrative style; nor is the specific connective 'and' about which, frankly, some preposterous comments were made in the critical statements. Indeed, the evidence provided by our analysis and figure suggests a level of complexity and depth in narrative organisation that appears to have eluded the critics completely. That said, the present workshop is not about the validity or otherwise of the 'narrative wave' hypothesis. It is about the way we link analysis and interpretation, the way we present our case to others, and the way we seek to explain how a stylistic analysis can impact on the literary evaluation of a text.

EXPLORING DIALOGUE   C9

An important organising principle across this thread has been the working assumption that dialogue occurs in a discourse context and that the structures and strategies of dialogue need to be investigated with reference to this context. Awareness of context, in its physical, personal and cognitive dimensions, and the forms of communication that are appropriate to it, is what constitutes part of a speaker's communicative competence (see A9). This unit develops a practical activity around this intersection between dialogue, context and communicative competence. In keeping with work in this branch of discourse stylistics (B9), the activity is designed to provide an analytic method for exploring fictional dialogue. By looking at *unusual* dialogue, it also seeks to highlight the underlying patterns of non-fictional interaction through the analysis of fictional communication. It has not escaped discourse stylisticians that the analysis of unusual dialogue is both an important critical tool in its own terms and a useful way of bringing into sharper focus the commonplace routines of discourse that often pass us by in everyday social interaction.

Discourse and context

Not exactly drama dialogue, the passage selected for analysis is part of a well-known comedy sketch from the television series *Monty Python's Flying Circus*. Before the text is introduced, it will be worth undertaking a short contextualising exercise as a preliminary to the analysis. To a certain extent, this is an exercise in communicative competence because it requires the matching up of appropriate forms of discourse to a specific set of contextual variables (see A9). Consider the following set of instructions:

Think about the sort of verbal interaction that would typically take place in the following contextual circumstances:

A. The participants in dialogue are two white middle-class, middle-aged English males. They have never met before. Both are dressed reasonably formally and they both speak with relatively high-prestige southern English accents. These are the only obvious features that they have in common.

B. The physical context of interaction is a plush English public house. The pub is busy, and most seats are taken. Having just brought drinks from the bar, the two strangers end up sitting side-by-side at the same table.

Working from this contextualisation and drawing on the ideas developed in A9 and B9, try to predict:

(i) what sort of dialogue would be likely to ensue between the two men should they decide to talk to one another.

(ii) what sorts of discourse strategies are likely to be used by the respective parties in interaction.

(iii) what sorts of terms of address or politeness tactics would characterise this sort of interaction.

(iv) what sorts of topics of discourse would be considered suitable in this interactive context.

On the basis of your responses to (i–iv) write down a short piece of dialogue that would be typical in this sort of interactive context.

The fragment of dialogue below is the opening of Monty Python's famous 'Nudge Nudge' sketch, first broadcast on BBC2 in 1971. For ease of reference in the transcript, the anonymous characters have been named metonymically through slight differences in their dress, the first man as CRAVAT and the second as TIE. Throughout the interaction, CRAVAT embellishes each of his utterances with highly exaggerated nonverbal gestures that include nudging his interlocutor with his elbow at appropriate cues in his speech. CRAVAT also uses an exclusively sexual nonverbal gesture brought about by crossing his forearms and rapidly raising and lowering one fist. As you read the extract, think about the extent to which your predictions about dialogue and context are fulfilled:

CRAVAT: Is your wife a . . . goer . . . eh? Know what I mean? Know what I mean? Nudge
          nudge. Nudge nudge. Know what I mean? Say no more . . . know what I
          mean?
TIE: I beg your pardon?
CRAVAT: Your wife . . . does she, er, does she 'go' – eh? eh? eh? Know what I mean,
          know what I mean? Nudge nudge. Say no more.
TIE: She sometimes goes, yes.
CRAVAT: I bet she does. I bet she does. I bet she does. Know what I mean. Nudge
          nudge.
TIE: I'm sorry, I don't quite follow you.
CRAVAT: Follow me! *Follow* me! I like that. That's good. A nod's as good as a wink to
          a blind bat, eh?
TIE: Are you trying to sell something?

(Monty Python's Flying Circus 1971)

Commentary: incongruity in discourse

In its day, the Monty Python series marked a radically new comic genre, although their sometimes surreal and dark humour was not to everyone's taste. The 'Nudge Nudge' sketch is archetypally Pythonesque in its design, although, like much of the team's output, its sexism can make it feel uncomfortable by today's standards. That said, it does offer an illuminating example of how to create humour through a simple mismatch between context and utterance. Your own analysis, which was effectively based on the exploration of your communicative competence, may have already gone some way towards explaining the oddity of TIE and CRAVAT's interaction. There are for example very strong interactive constraints on what can be said at the beginning of a conversation between two people who don't know each other, and I imagine that your responses to questions (i) to (iv) above would have predicted a fairly narrowly circumscribed set of utterance types. The sorts of utterances used for conversational openings – what linguists refer to as *phatic communion* – are expected to be neutral and uncontroversial. Thus, interactively 'safe' gambits in the context established in the sketch would include references to the weather ('Nice day') or comments on the shared physical context ('About time someone cleared these glasses'). What is manifestly *not* cued by the context is the interrogation of the interlocutor about his private life. While the marital status of a stranger is obviously a delicate subject, topics concerning sexual behaviour are even more taboo. CRAVAT's thinly veiled insinuations about the sexual behaviour of his interlocutor's wife (about which TIE is perversely slow on the uptake) are thoroughly incongruous in this sort of discourse context.

Of many other discoursal features of stylistic interest, it is worth noting how TIE's apparent bewilderment at CRAVAT's questions impacts on the development of the structure of *exchanges* (see A9 and B9). CRAVAT's initiations tend to be followed by requests for restarts from TIE. TIE's seeming inability to take up CRAVAT's sexual references creates an impasse which leads to repeated loops in discourse structure, and this is further compacted by CRAVAT's single-minded pursuit of the same basic innuendo even beyond those phrases conventionally used as sexual double-entendres ('*Follow* me! I like that'). And it is only after thirty more lines of the same cyclical pattern of discourse that TIE eventually begins to grasp the point when finally, in a comment that summarises the sketch's entire topical drift, he says 'Look, are you insinuating something?'

Summary

Although not drama dialogue *per se*, the Python sketch can be placed, as can many other types of non-dramatic dialogue, in Short's layered interactive schema (see A9). This is particularly useful for interpreting the comic effect of the dialogue. The viewer/reader positioned at the higher interactive level occupies the position of a kind of discoursal 'on-looker'. The communicative competence that organises everyday interaction for the on-looker acts as a frame for interpreting the incongruity of the displayed interaction down at the character level. The greater part of the humour of this Python sketch arguably stems from the mismatch between character speech and the discourse context in which it is embedded within the text. As noted earlier, analysing unusual talk implicitly draws attention to the canonical and the everyday in interaction. Indeed, it may be possible to read this text as, amongst other things, a skit on the repressively mundane trivia that often passes for conversation between non-familiar interactants.

The intersection between style and humour is further addressed in the special web strand accompanying this book, where additional types of comic language are explored. In the following unit, a variety of practical activities are developed, some of which involve the analysis of play dialogue with some attention to humour. However, the methods developed in C10 mark a new perspective, which is altogether more cognitive than discoursal in orientation.

C10 COGNITIVE STYLISTICS AT WORK

This unit offers an opportunity to apply a number of the constructs developed across this strand to different types of literary text. Although no more than a snapshot of the range of methods currently available in cognitive poetics, it should nonetheless signal the type of direction such an analysis might take. A more comprehensive analysis is provided in the reading that accompanies this unit (D10), where Barbara Dancygier draws upon the framework of *conceptual blending theory* in her exploration of Jonathan Raban's travel writing.

Schemas in literary discourse: that restaurant again

Schank and Abelson's 'restaurant script' was touched upon in B10, and given the fame, not to say notoriety, their illustration has acquired over the years, we should probably undertake a stylistic activity that explores this very scenario. As noted, Schank and Abelson build the idea of temporal progression into a script by defining it as a *stereotyped sequence of actions* that define a well-known situation. This ties in well with models of discourse (see C9) which take account of our assumptions about how certain routines of discourse should progress.

Read through the following two extracts from Steven Berkoff's play *Greek* (the extracts are separated by around forty lines of dialogue, which includes interaction between characters other than the two featured here): Activity

(1) *Cafe. Chorus of kitchen cafe menu sounds and phrases.*
    EDDY: One coffee please and croissant and butter.
    WAITRESS: Right. Cream?
    EDDY: Please.
    (. . .)

(2) EDDY: Where's my fucking coffee? I've nearly finished this cheese-cake and then my whole purpose in life at this particular moment will be lost. I'll be drinking hot coffee with nothing to wash it down with.
    WAITRESS: Here you are, sorry I forgot you!
    EDDY: About fucking time!
    WAITRESS: Oh shut your mouth, you complaining heap of rat's shit.

                                                        (Berkoff 1983: 35f)

With respect to the obvious transition in discourse strategies that occur in (2), try to highlight any features of discourse that challenge your understanding of the natural progression of this familiar service encounter. To what extent is Berkoff's dialogue an example of *schema disruption* as described in B10? And to what extent can our predictions about the development of a script (in this case the progression of the restaurant script) be aligned with our predictions about discourse and dialogue (especially politeness strategies)?

Text worlds and sub-worlds: stream of consciousness writing

The second activity suggested in this unit is likely to prove the more difficult. Its purpose is to try to balance the ideas about text worlds and narrative comprehension that were outlined in B10 and to apply them to a short piece of 'stream of consciousness' writing from Joyce's *Ulysses*. Here first of all is the passage in question which, when delivered 'cold' like this, is alarmingly dense:

(3) You might pick up a young widow here. Men like that. Love among the tombstones. Romeo. Spice of pleasure. In the midst of death we are in life. Both ends meet. Tantalizing for the poor dead. Smell of frilled beefsteaks to the starving gnawing their vitals. Desire to grig people. Molly wanted to do it at the window. Eight children he has anyway.

                                                (Joyce 1980 [1922]: 110)

Even though undoubtedly complex as a narrative style, it is still possible to unpack this text stylistically and also to use cognitive models to explain how we might 'make sense' of it. First of all, let me provide the context to (3). Taken from the 'Hades' chapter of the novel, this fragment details Leopold Bloom's visit to Glasnevin Cemetery to attend a funeral. Just prior to this piece of text, Bloom has been in conversation with the cemetery caretaker, John O'Connell. From this verbal encounter, Bloom begins to muse on the implications of O'Connell's job and on how, particularly, such employment might affect one's chances of forming romantic attachments. This is in effect the main *text world* which Joyce has established for Bloom.

Bloom's musings at the level of the text world translate into projections, which as noted in B10, mark out different sub-worlds. Some of these projections are intertextual, which is to say that they evoke other texts and especially other literary works. Others are more of the order of reactions to elements at the text world level, to aspects of Bloom's immediate environment. As a first stage in a cognitive unpacking of the multiple sub-worlds of (3), here is the text again, now in a list format for easier annotation:

(3′) (1)   You might pick up a young widow here.
    (2)   Men like that.
    (3)   Love among the tombstones.
    (4)   Romeo.
    (5)   Spice of pleasure.
    (6)   In the midst of death we are in life.
    (7)   Both ends meet.
    (8)   Tantalizing for the poor dead.
    (9)   Smell of frilled beefsteaks to the starving gnawing their vitals.
    (10) Desire to grig people.
    (11) Molly wanted to do it at the window.
    (12) Eight children he has anyway.

Now go through the text and try to identify the elements which mark out the different sub-worlds which are projected through Bloom's consciousness. Look out for what Werth calls *deictic signatures* (1999: 186) because these alert the reader to the particular narrative world they are currently in. For example, what sort of anchoring function is achieved by the deictic marker 'here' in the first sentence? The next strand to the analysis involves tracking the techniques of *binding* and *priming* as they apply to various characters in the sub-worlds. For example, to whom does the pronoun 'he' refer in the last sentence? Is it to Romeo? If not, what previously 'bound in' character needs to be (re)primed for this reference to make sense?

Bloom's thoughts are not only fixed on ideas about romantic-sexual attachment. He also reflects on death (unsurprisingly given his location) and food (it is after all approaching lunch time – and see reading D4). These preoccupations are ever-present in Bloom's mind but one of the subtleties of Joyce's narrative technique is that these three domains of experience are often carried over in a kind of radial structure from one sub-world to another. You can check the extent of this by going down the text again and marking up any words that refer, either implicitly or explicitly, to either sex, death or food. You may find that the same word cross-refers to more than one experience. If so, to what extent does Joyce establish a *web* of connections in Bloom's consciousness between the three experiential domains on the one hand and the various sub-worlds on the other?

I do not propose to follow through in detail these guidelines for analysis, only to offer some short comments by way of conclusion to this unit. One of the most striking transitions in the passage, to my mind, occurs in the progression from 11 to 12, where one sub-world shifts to another. Throughout the morning, Bloom's thoughts have constantly returned to his wife, Molly, as the reflection on past experience in sentence 11 shows. However, these thoughts are reined in rather abruptly when sentence 12 jolts us into another sub-world space. As well as the change in tense, the pronoun in this final sentence is a good indicator of how the minutiae of textual detail can often have significant implications on the development of text worlds and sub-worlds. The question asked above looked for a referent for the pronoun 'he'. Although the most 'recent' male subject in the text is 'Romeo', we need to look much further back, and this is where the concepts of binding and priming come to the fore. Remember, the concept of binding serves to establish a particular character in a particular place until we receive a signal that that character is to be bound out. Even though many lines of prose have passed since his last mention, we have so far had no indication that John O'Connell is to be bound out of the location of Glasnevin Cemetery. This type of stylistic technique is very much the essence of 'stream of consciousness' as embodied by Joyce's novel. The process of binding involves locating different characters in *different* sub-worlds, such that we need not only to retain and juggle these various planes of textual representation but we need to be able to recall each character's location in each sub-world at a moment's notice.

Finally, in his commentary on this very passage in Joyce's novel, the literary critic Harry Blamires remarks that after the conversation with O'Connell, Bloom's thoughts 'run out *centrifugally* from the figure of O'Connell' (Blamires 1988 [1966]: 37; my emphasis). This is an intriguing comment, but it is also the sort of critical intuition that cries out for support from stylistics, and especially from cognitive stylistics, because it touches on the essence of compositional technique and understanding. I hope that the analytic activities suggested here will have begun to probe the way Bloom's *mind-style* (C7) is developed by Joyce, and I will therefore leave it to you to explain how it might be said that Bloom thinks 'centrifugally'.

EXPLORING METAPHORS IN DIFFERENT KINDS OF TEXTS

Continuing the cognitive-stylistic theme established in C10, this unit offers a selection of practically orientated activities for exploring in texts both metaphor and the related trope, metonymy. The activities suggested make use of a variety of texts because, as observed across the strand, these tropes are endemic to human thought processes.

So while literary texts feature in the unit, the activities themselves tend to emphasise the commonality of metaphor and metonymy as important types of figurative thought.

Metaphor and metonymy

The exercises developed in this sub-unit are more an appetiser than a main course. To start us off, here are five metaphorical mappings, each stripped down into the appropriate small capitals formula: FRUIT IS AN ANCIENT BURIAL GROUND, MEMORY IS GRAMMAR, BOREDOM IS A SOLID MINERAL OBJECT, CONVERSATION IS DAIRY FARMING and POTTERY IS A COLD WOMAN. Whereas many conceptual metaphors, as discussed in B11, are a familiar part of everyday discourse, mappings such as these make a good case for being described as *novel*. The following five fragments are from works by Irish poets. Work through each excerpt, looking out for some structures that may be expressed as similes, and match each one up with one of the five metaphorical formulae above. What are the techniques in language that each poet uses to develop the metaphor? And to what extent can these mappings be considered novel?

 Activity

> Terracotta vases and teapots
> queue beside their warm kiln
> like shivering women
> waiting for the sauna
> > (Katie Donovan [2004] 'The Potter's House')

> Boredom was a rock that rolled between them
> > (Sinead Morrissey [2002] 'Street Theatre')

> Shoppers steer trolleys
> past cairns of avocadoes
> > (Mary O'Donoghue [2004] 'This is Sunday')

> to forget is
> a common verb
> > (Ciaran Carson [2009] 'What Then')

> Our one-way conversation was like milking
> a mastitic cow who regards you
> reproachfully, [. . .]
> > (Catríona O'Reilly [2004] 'To the Muse')

Activity   In the interest of balance, here now are four metonymies, abstracted down into the appropriate formula: MEDIUM FOR COMMUNICATOR, ACCOMPLISHMENT FOR AGENT, ROLE FOR ACTOR and ACTIVITY FOR DURATION. If not exactly 'novel', the type of 'stands-for' relationship embodied by each pattern is certainly less common than those featured in A11. Try to match up the four examples provided below with their corresponding underlying formula:

> Emma Watson just punched Draco Malfoy at the MTV Movie awards. It was awesome.
> > (Online Twitter 'tweet')

It seems like yesterday, even though
That was sixteen hundred and sixty two beers ago.
> (lyrics from the song 'Beers Ago' by Toby Keith)

The radio played a forgotten song.
> (lyrics from the song 'Radar Love' by Golden Earring)

These are impressive line-ups – remember, there are already eleven champions' league medals out there.
> (BBC Radio sports commentator, in advance of a Champions League
> soccer match between Bayern Munich and Barcelona, April 2013)

Metaphor and metonymy in different kinds of texts

Here is a set of ten attested examples of language use which have been taken from a variety of sources. Mixing the 'literary' with the manifestly 'non-literary', the set, which features both metaphor and metonymy, draws in material from journalism, song lyrics, spoken discourse and, of course, literary texts. Instructions about how to organise your analysis follows below the examples.

Examples

1. Downing Street is thought to be furious over the International Development Secretary's radio interview.
> (from British newspaper, *The Guardian*)

2. I have other irons in the fire but I am keeping them close to my chest.
> (British football manager discussing his plans
> for the forthcoming season)

3. My luve is like a red, red rose
That's newly sprung in June:
My luve is like the melodie
That's sweetly played in tune.
> (from a song by Robbie Burns)

4. Top rod for the day was visiting angler Mr. Simpson who had eight trout.
> (*Angling Reports Wales*; Tallylyn)

5. Because I could not stop for Death—
He kindly stopped for me—
The Carriage held but just Ourselves—
And Immortality.
> ('Because I could not stop for Death'
> Emily Dickinson [1890] 1963)

6. Simultaneously the whole party moved toward the water, super-ready from the long, forced inaction, passing from the heat to the cool with the gourmandise of a tingling curry eaten with chilled white wine.
> (*Tender is the Night*, F. Scott Fitzgerald [1934] 1986: 29–30)

7   When the still sea conspires an armor
     And her sullen and aborted
     Currents breed tiny monsters . . .
                (from 'Horse Latitudes' by Jim Morrison of rock band *The Doors*)

8   Of course, with the Soviets' launch of Sputnik, the Americans had been Pearl
     Harbored in space.
                                                    (Arthur C. Clarke, interviewed in 2001)

9   Whether 'tis nobler in the mind to suffer
     The slings and arrows of outrageous fortune,
     Or to take arms against a sea of troubles,
     And by opposing end them?
                                            (from *Hamlet* by William Shakespeare)

10   The exercises developed in this sub-unit are more an appetiser than a main
     course.
                                        (the first sentence of the previous sub-unit)

Instructions

A   For each of 1–10, decide whether the example represents metonymy or metaphor.
     If you are in doubt, you should apply the 'simile test' which was set out in A11.
     If you decide an example is metonymy, follow instruction B below; if metaphor,
     then follow instruction C. Some examples may well exhibit both tropes, in which
     case you will need to follow both A and B in your analysis.
B   Specify which type of associated concept is the vehicle of the metonymy. For
     example, is the metonymy based on a part-for-whole relationship, a location-for-
     institution relationship, or on a more contingent 'one-off' connection between
     the associated concepts?
C   Specify the source domain and the target domain for the metaphor. Follow this
     procedure even if there is more than one metaphor in the example. (Remember,
     the same target domain may be mapped through different source domains.)
     Referring to material in B11 if necessary, try to say if the metaphor has been
     extended or elaborated in any way.

Metaphors in texts and texts as metaphors

This short exercise explores the relationship between metaphor and textual organisation. In narrative fiction, for example, metaphors can be positioned at a number of
levels in the textual hierarchy (see Steen 2005: 305–7). Indeed, the concept of *allegory*
(from the Greek 'allegoria' meaning 'other speaking') represents a very broad metaphorical structure, but one which eliminates overt or direct reference to the target
domain (Crisp 2005: 325). Allegory is therefore a form of metaphor where the frame
contrast is eliminated and where the source domain becomes a fictional world in its
own right (see further below). An *extended metaphor*, by contrast, does make reference
to its target domain. For instance, the eponymous narrator of Lawrence Sterne's novel
Tristram Shandy makes use of extended metaphor through his repeated commentary
on the structure of his own story. This 'meta-discourse' is cast as a JOURNEY metaphor:

Therefore, my dear friend and companion, if you should think me somewhat sparing of my narrative on my first setting out, – bear with me – , and let me go on, and tell my story my own way: – Or, if I should seem now and then to trifle upon the road, – or should sometimes put on a fool's cap with a bell to it, for a moment or two as we pass along, – don't fly off, – but rather courteously give me credit for a little more wisdom than appears on my outside; – and as we jog on, either laugh with me, or at me, or in short, do anything, – only keep your temper.

(Sterne [1749] 2010: 10)

An important framing question for the study of metaphor in prose fiction is to ask where, in relation to the story, is the metaphor positioned. Is it *intradiegetic* in the sense that it is developed by a particular character-narrator within the story, or is it *extradiegetic* because its provenance is in the 'invisible' narrator who is outside the story frame? Or is the metaphor 'external' in the sense that it is 'about' the narrative but it is not part of the story proper? These distinctions may seem a little confusing, so here is a short exercise that may help clarify things. The following four examples all express metaphors and they are all 'to do with' John Steinbeck's novel *Cannery Row* (1945) Keeping a close eye on italicisation, decide on the narrative layer at which each of the metaphors operate: is it external, extradiegetic or intradiegetic? | **Activity** ⭐

(i)   Cannery Row in Monterey in California is a poem, a stink, a grating noise, a quality of light, a tone, a habit, a nostalgia, a dream.

(from page 1 of Steinbeck's novel)

(ii)   *Cannery Row* is full of gems.

(from a print review of Steinbeck's novel)

(iii) The Doc dug himself into Cannery Row. He became the fountain of philosophy and science and art.

[from page 21 of Steinbeck's novel)

(iv)   *Cannery Row* paints a portrait of humanity.

(from an online review of Steinbeck's novel]

An interesting 'sub-exercise' here would be to think about the sheer number of metaphorical mappings embraced by example (i). How many source domains can you spot? From what human senses do (some of) these source domains come? And why would Steinbeck chain all of these mappings together in so seemingly random or haphazard a sequence?

Finally, think about works that you have read that make a good case for being described as allegories. I imagine that George Orwell's novella *Animal Farm* could top the list. But if you were pressed, what would you say Orwell's novel is *about*? Is it about the iniquities of totalitarian Joseph Stalin's Soviet regime in the years preceding the Second World War? Or is it about a bunch of animals on a farm who fall out with each other? There has been some critical commentary around the French title of Orwell's novella: *Union des républiques socialistes animals* (the abbreviation of which is *URSA*). | **Activity** ⭐

Is there a sense in which this title (and its symbolic abbreviation) weakens the allegorical force of Orwell's story?

Metaphor in prose fiction: a single passage

This sub-unit narrows the focus by developing some practical work around a single passage from prose fiction. The passage is from Jeanette Winterson's novel *Written on the Body* (1993). To say that metaphor features in this text is somewhat of an understatement (as you will soon see), but the passage offers an excellent opportunity for a more detailed analysis of metaphorical composition. Analysis of the passage will also help to consolidate many of the concepts introduced across this strand, including those relating to novelty, concretisation, and extending and elaboration in metaphor.

Before you proceed to the Winterson text, read through the following guidelines which will help give shape to your analysis and interpretation of the passage:

(i)   When thinking about metaphor, it is important not to lose sight of the distinction between source and target domains. It is not uncommon to come across a target (that is, the concept you are describing through the metaphor) which has been mapped onto several distinct source domains. The concept of LOVE, for instance, can form the target domain for a range of source domains, and conventional metaphors with this pattern include LOVE IS A BATTLE ('They've been at each other's throats for months'), LOVE IS A JOURNEY ('Our relationship is going nowhere') or LOVE IS A NUTRIENT ('He's sustained by her love') and so on. In the analysis of text, it is important to differentiate sets of metaphors which develop the same target domain from other, unrelated metaphors which develop different target and source domains.

(ii) A key stylistic question that needs to be addressed (and which has featured throughout this unit) concerns the extent to which the mapping between source and target is novel. That is, is the mapping conventional (as in the examples provided for LOVE above) or are the mappings striking or unusual in comparison to what we encounter in day to day language? Another important question concerns the degree of concretisation, or otherwise, embodied by a metaphor. Does the mapping go, for example, from an abstract target to a concrete source domain, or is some other permutation involved?

(iii) Elaboration and extending are two of a number of techniques for embellishing metaphors by making new concepts available for mapping. This is especially common in metaphors containing a broad source domain (involving say, build-ings, food or economic exchange) because part of the mental representation for that domain includes entries for various *props* and *roles* (see A10 and B10). This enables certain individuated concepts within these domains (such as rooms or corridors within a building) to be brought into play to further elaborate the metaphor.

(iv) Metaphors can be *chained*, by which I mean that a source domain from one metaphor may itself be opened up to form the target domain for possibly a whole series of sub-metaphors. For example, a chain for the LOVE IS A NUTRIENT metaphor would mean taking the source domain (the nutrient concept) and making it the target domain for a new metaphorical mapping. (It is worth paying particular attention to the idea of chaining when examining the Winterson passage.)

Working from these four guidelines, now look closely at the passage from *Written on the Body*:

> Misery is a vacuum. A space without air, a suffocated dead place, the abode of the miserable. Misery is a tenement block, rooms like battery cages, sit over your own droppings, lie in your own filth. Misery is a no U-turns, no stopping road. Travel down it pushed by those behind, tripped by those in front. Travel down it at furious speed though the days are mummified in lead. It happens so fast that once you get started, there's no anchor from the real world to slow you down, nothing to hold on to. Misery pulls away the brackets of life leaving you free to fall. Whatever your private hell, you'll find millions like it in Misery. This is the town where everyone's nightmares come true.
>
> (Winterson 1993: 183)

It is worth tying up this unit with a few informal comments on Winterson's technique. Almost theatrical in its style of delivery, the passage develops a single target domain (which you will have identified by now) by mapping it onto an almost bewildering array of source domains, and the sheer exuberance of this style of metaphorisation suggests perhaps some sense of irony (see further the special web strand on style and humour). Not only do the metaphors come thick and fast, but they begin to trip over one another as metaphorical chains develop. Without giving too much away, notice how the reference to the 'tenement block' is developed through the reference to 'rooms', a good example of a source domain being elaborated through one of the concepts it embraces. However, the individuated concept itself plays a role in the development of a new metaphor, where it becomes the target domain of a mapping where 'battery cages' forms the source domain. Thus the passage develops, with a range of stylistic devices being brought into play for the creation of a series of novel metaphors.

The passage raises another, more theoretical issue to do with the stylistic analysis of metaphor. One of the functions of metaphor is to alter or transform our perception of the target domain, while leaving unaltered our perception of the vehicle for the metaphor. With respect to the Winterson text, is it really the case that our perception of the many source domains on display is left unaltered during the mapping? Or is it more the case that our understanding of *both* target and source domains is affected? This very issue is taken up in D11, in a reading by Peter Stockwell, which completes this strand on metaphor and style.

C12   USING CORPORA IN STYLISTIC ANALYSIS

This unit makes some suggestions about how corpus tools might usefully enrich stylistic analysis. The exercises and tasks that follow are not intended to be rigid or programmatic but are designed simply to point to areas where revealing investigations might be carried out. As stressed throughout this strand, corpus tools provide a window (literally) on the frequent collocates of words found in literary texts. The particular word under scrutiny need not of itself be a striking neologism or unique linguistic invention. Indeed, if it were, then it is likely to be a *hapax legomonon*, which is a venerable term still used in corpus analysis for a word or expression that is found only once. For example, an online search for James Joyce's striking lexical compound 'brightwindbridled', describing the crashing of the waves in the Proteus episode of his novel *Ulysses*, will revert only the original word itself, either in an electronic edition of the novel or in a scholarly critique of this section of Joyce's text.

Getting started

While they can at least detect the uniqueness of *hapax legomena* in literature, corpus tools instead come much more to the fore when used to explore patterned combinations of altogether more prosaic words. Now look at some of the poetry covered in Widdowson's reading in unit D1. Robert Frost's 'Dust of Snow' concludes with the sequence, 'And saved some part / Of a day I had rued', in reference to which I offered some follow-up commentary at the end of the reading. It is interesting to probe these patterns through a KWIC analysis, ideally using, in view of the poet's nationality, the bank of American English (COCA). The sequence *and saved some* is a good place to start, and the results will show that this is not a common pattern relative to the size of the corpus. Look at the collocates that appear to the right of *some*. What meaning does *some* typically acquire in the environment of the terms that follow it? Another interesting exercise is to key in the verb *rued* on its own, without any specified additional text. What words (or types of words) typically follow it in the corpus? How many occurrences of *rued* include the word 'day' (as Frost does) within a ten-word span? If your corpus evidence seems to suggest that Frost uses a rather straightforward vocabulary in a fairly straightforward way, think about the grammatical environment of *rued*. Does it ever appear, as it does in Frost, in the final position in a sentence?

Following again from unit D1, the supporting commentary at the end of Widdowson's reading raised some issues to do with collocational 'clashes' in Tennyson's *In Memoriam*. Specifically, discussion focussed on Tennyson's phrases 'bald streets' and 'blank day'. The question posed there was whether or not the common collocates of *bald* embrace the feature /+animate/? What does a corpus word search of 'bald' as an adjectival modifier *actually* reveal? What also does a search of the collocates of 'blank' reveal? Are there any surprising, perhaps figurative, combinations for each term? Does the corpus analysis support Widdowson's description of Tennyson's structures as 'deviant'?

Metaphor and corpora

The discussion in B12 of Semino's work, and in particular her critique of conceptual metaphor theory, illustrates the type of stylistic problem to which corpus tools can be productively applied. The basic technique for corpus-assisted metaphor analysis is to get, so to speak, to the heart of the metaphor by isolating the key words of its source domain. As in Semino's investigation of *rich*, the corpus will reveal the proportion of metaphorical to non-metaphorical usage, and in the case of the former, will reveal the target domains with which the search term is conventionally associated.

Corpus tools also facilitate the exploration of *novelty* in metaphor composition (see B11). The principle of concretisation accepts that the direction of metaphorical mapping conventionally moves from the abstract and experiential to the concrete and the bodily. The perceived wisdom is therefore that developments new to society, such as those in design and technology, will often be mapped through metaphors with source domains in human, perhaps visceral terms. For instance, a military manual of World War Two hardware describes the new Sherman Tank as 'down-to-earth', 'masculine' and the 'backbone of the campaign'. Similarly, in Stephen Spender's poem 'The Pylons', which was touched upon briefly in B4, the eponymous technological constructions are captured by simile thus: 'those pillars / Bare like nude giant girls'.

Against this framework of conventional directionality, it is worth considering the **Activity** ✪

sorts of metaphorical mappings that occur in poems such as 'Thrushes' (1960) by Ted Hughes or 'Trout' (1966) by Seamus Heaney. These poems are easily tracked down so the full texts will not be provided here, but without elaborating too much, the concept of nature in both poems is conceived of in a more novel way than in the conventional mappings above. For instance, with reference to the birds of his title, Hughes asks what 'Gives their days this bullet and automatic / Purpose?'. Heaney's trout is 'a fat gun barrel', with a 'muzzle' capable of firing a 'tracer-bullet'. To get some sense of the creativity in play here, select some of the quoted terms (or other key phrases from either poem) and investigate their occurrences in a broader corpus. To what extent can both poems make a claim for novelty in the metaphorical transferences they embrace? Both texts also re-open the debate in unit C1 about what constitutes 'literary language'. If, in the light of your corpus analysis, the vocabulary used by Heaney and Hughes appears to have more in common with certain manifestly 'non-poetic' genres of discourse, then why are both poets credited with being two of the great creative writers of twentieth-century literature?

Corpus and analysis and literary criticism

It is always interesting to position a stylistic analysis against a literary-critical reading of the same text, either to seek support for the stylistic analysis or to suggest a counter-reading based on the outcome of the stylistic analysis. What unites both approaches is the importance of close reading. I have never encountered a literary critic who did not believe in the importance of close reading, although by the same token, I have never encountered a critic who believed that a close reading could be ably assisted by the use of a computer. With respect to the challenges for corpus stylistics, then, there undoubtedly remains ahead some important dialogue and discussion.

In an important survey of the current theoretical and practical intersections between stylistics and literary criticism, Hall surveys a range of criticism which (ostensibly) sets great store by the close reading of literary texts (Hall 2014). This survey includes literary theorist Eagleton's advice on how to read poetry (2007). Eagleton opens his guide by hectoring undergraduate students on their insensitivity to 'questions of literary form' (2007: 2) before going on to offer his own checklist of key features for reading poems. Eagleton later demonstrates how his checklist works by offering an interpretation of the following poem by Gerard Manley Hopkins:

God's Grandeur

THE WORLD is charged with the grandeur of God.
It will flame out, like shining from shook foil;
It gathers to a greatness, like the ooze of oil
Crushed. Why do men then now not reck his rod?
Generations have trod, have trod, have trod;
And all is seared with trade; bleared, smeared with toil;
And wears man's smudge and shares man's smell: the soil
Is bare now, nor can foot feel, being shod.

And for all this, nature is never spent;
There lives the dearest freshness deep down things;
And though the last lights off the black West went
Oh, morning, at the brown brink eastward, springs—
Because the Holy Ghost over the bent
World broods with warm breast and with ah! bright wings.

(Hopkins 1995 [1877])

In a commentary ungrounded in any linguistic detail and rife with stylistic imprecision, Eagleton ignores his own checklist from the outset by offering an elaborate disquisition on Victorian cultural perceptions of Nature and Roman Catholicism, none of which is observable in the text under scrutiny (2007: 154–5). In his survey article, Hall (2014) offers his own stylistic analysis of the same poem in advance of drawing out acerbically these perceived problems with Eagleton's 'close reading'. Readers are strongly encouraged to read Hall's analysis against the backdrop of Eagleton's, even if only for a clear exposition of the distinctiveness of the stylistic method in the context of literary criticism.

The debate nonetheless raises a number of issues about Hopkins's poem that might suit corpus-assisted exploration. In fact, Hall's own position is that further investigation from this perspective is warranted. In one place, Eagleton, taking his cue from the possible financial intimation in 'charged' in the first line, sees the same fiscal metaphor at work in 'spent' and 'dearest', which both relate back to 'trade' in the first stanza (2007: 155). Without suggesting that this interpretation is necessarily invalid, consider what evidence a corpus analysis would offer here. Look for example at the occurrence of the relevant lemmas in a corpus you have access to, and think of ways of narrowing the search terms by taking your cue from the grammatical environments around these search terms in 'God's Grandeur'. Perhaps more tendentiously, Eagleton suggests that 'bent' may mean 'both literally curved and morally corrupt' (2007: 156). The second meaning is captured in collocations in contemporary vernacular English such as '*bent copper*', but would a corpus analysis bear this sense out? (Hopkins was a Jesuit priest and wrote the poem in 1877). Finally, there is much more in Hopkins's poem that could be explored without necessarily invoking Eagleton's (or Hall's) analysis. For example, are there any 'one-off' hapax legomena in the poem? Or is all of Hopkins's vocabulary attested by corpus analysis? And what other striking linguistic features – such as sound patterns, word formation and grammatical form – embody and determine Hopkins's poetic style?

Corpus techniques: always the right answer?

A position adopted throughout this book, and one revisited at the opening of this strand, is that stylistics develops through an accumulation of different approaches and methods. No single model or framework has all the answers. With regard to the efficacy of the corpus approach, I close this unit on something of a conundrum. This requires the reintroduction from unit C7 of the first three sentences of Faulkner's *The Sound and the Fury*:

 Activity

> Through the fence between the curling flower spaces, I could see them hitting. They were coming toward where the flag was and I went along the fence. Luster was hunting in the grass by the flower tree.

One of the questions posed in C7 of this markedly under-informative opening sequence was about the identity of Luster. Now, in any classroom application of this reading exercise, students (around the world) consistently suppose that Luster is some kind of animal. Subsequent disambiguating text reveals of course that this is not so, but student responses tend to suggest that there must be something about Faulkner's arrangement of words that references familiar patterns and collocations in the language as a whole. Yet support for this interpretation from corpora is not forthcoming. For example, the phrases *was hunting* and *were hunting* predominantly reveal a human agent as their most common leftwards collocate. Think about the implications of this. For example, could the corpus search be narrowed further to incorporate the preposition to the right of the phrase, as in *was hunting in*? If this does not offer an explanation, then what other permutations might productively limit the corpus search? If the corpus-assisted analysis does not satisfactorily explain why readers react in the way they do, then what other aspects of the style of this sequence, including the two sentences that constitute its preceding co-text, might frame such an impression? Or is it simply a conundrum, the resolution of which lies beyond the scope of stylistic analysis? Good luck.

Section D

EXTENSION

READINGS IN STYLISTICS

HOW TO USE THESE READINGS

Throughout this book, and in the Further Reading section in particular, emphasis is put on the importance of supplementing your work in stylistics by reference to original scholarly sources. While this principle applies to all academic study, it sometimes happens that some advanced scholarship is not particularly accessible and its relevance to the task in hand not immediately apparent. Bearing that in mind, what has been assembled here is a broad selection of generally relevant work that has been carried out by well-known stylisticians from around the world. The readings cover an extremely wide array of texts, topics and issues. Some of the readings may be more challenging than others, but not to the extent that they are opaque and inaccessible. Close and extensive reading will always be rewarded because:

❏   it provides you with the necessary background to the history of the discipline;
❏   it familiarises you with the key research areas;
❏   it allows you to see the sorts of methods and approaches that are used by different stylisticians;
❏   it gives you a model for how to express yourself in appropriate academic and scholarly language.

Wherever necessary, contextualisation to individual readings is offered in the form of brief prefatory notes. Additionally, follow-up comments and suggestions for further work are offered under the banner heading 'Issues to consider'.

STYLISTICS AND THE TEACHING OF LITERATURE

The following reading is taken from a classic book in stylistics. Published in 1975, Henry Widdowson's *Stylistics and the Teaching of Literature* set out the case for positioning stylistic analysis centre-stage in the practice of literary criticism. Consolidating a theme developed across this strand, Widdowson locates the study of style in language at a number of intersections between linguistics, creative writing and the teaching of literature. Admittedly, a number of the methods Widdowson employs have been superseded by subsequent innovations in linguistic theory and analysis, and some of the ways in which Widdowson's analyses might be re-appraised in the light of such developments are explored in the commentary following the reading. However, it is important not to lose sight of the ground-breaking nature of Widdowson's argument nor of its place in the history of stylistics. In the period of its publication, the mid-1970s, stylistics was a fledging discipline that had only begun to explore the potential of linguistics in literary study; the study of literature was, by contrast, then well established in the academe.

Throughout this reading, Widdowson conceptualises literature as *discourse*. This means thinking about literary creativity in terms of the job it does with language in context. Supplementing this conceptualisation is the now perennial focus in stylistics where literary discourse is always seen against the more mundane instantiations of everyday language that frame it. If we can understand how we, so to speak, understand the language of literature, then we can make significant advances in both the appreciation and criticism of literature. Widdowson's reading offers many insights into how the 'language code', broadly conceived, provides literary discourse with what he terms its 'basic resources'.

Stylistics and the teaching of literature

Henry Widdowson (reprinted from *Stylistics and the Teaching of Literature*, Harlow: Longman, 1975: 33–40)

Henry Widdowson

[A]n interpretation of a literary work as a piece of discourse involves correlating the meaning of a linguistic item as an element in the language code with the meaning it takes on in the context in which it occurs. This correlating procedure is necessary for the production and reception of any discourse, however, so that the ability to use and comprehend language as communication in general provides the basis for the understanding of literature in particular. I want now to discuss the nature of discourse comprehension in general and then show how the interpretation of literary discourse can be seen as an extension of this ability. [. . .]

It will be useful, to begin with, to make a distinction between two kinds of meaning: that which inheres in linguistic items as elements of the code on the one hand and that which linguistic items assume when they appear in contexts of use on the other. I will use the term *signification* to refer to the first kind of meaning and the term *value* to refer to the second. Let us now consider what is involved in understanding a piece of ordinary – that is to say non-literary – discourse. The following may serve as an example:

> In the north-eastern division of their territory, Bushmen bands are rather larger than elsewhere, numbering on average fifty to sixty persons and each having an hereditary headman. The members of a band are mostly relatives of the headman, together with wives who will have come originally from neighbouring bands. But the size of the group who are actually dwelling together varies from season to season and according to the accessibility of food or some exceptional circumstances. In some tribes a band breaks up in the dry season and the different households scatter in search of game, to come together again only in the rainy season when there is an ample supply of water and edible roots.
> (Barton 1965: 55)

We will begin with a simple observation. The entry for the word *band* in a dictionary will include a wide range of meanings: a flat strip of material, a hoop of metal or rubber, a strip forming part of a hat or dress or shirt, a stripe of different colour or texture, a

Henry Widdowson

company of armed men, robbers or musicians, a group of persons, and so on. These meanings represent the total signification of this word as an item in the code. The context, however, makes it clear which of these meanings is relevant here: in other words, only one of these meanings has the required value and the others are irrelevant. To understand the meaning of *band* in this passage, then, the reader has to select a meaning by matching up code and context. Notice, however, that even if the reader did not know the signification of the word, he would be able to derive its value from the context in which it occurs if he knows the relevant signification of the other items. Thus he knows from the context that a band is a number of persons, that it has a headman, that its members are mostly relatives of the headman, that it is a group of some kind. Most of our vocabulary is acquired in this way by recognising what value words have: we rarely interrupt our reading by referring to a dictionary but rely on the context to provide us with the necessary clues. In fact when asked the meaning of a word by some importunate child or foreigner we tend not to adduce the signification but to give examples of value by providing appropriate contexts.

Sometimes the recognition of value is not simply a matter of selecting the appropriate part of the signification of a lexical item. Consider the item *each* in the above passage, for example. A dictionary will give something like the following signification 'every (person, thing, group) taken separately'. This is of very little help since what the reader wants to know is *which* person, thing or group in the discourse the particular instance of *each* he is concerned with actually refers to. In the present case, for example, it could refer to either *band* or *person* and the reader has to decide whether it has the value 'each band' or 'each person'. Again, establishing value is frequently a matter not of selecting a particular meaning from the semantic complex which constitutes an item's signification but of extending it. Here we get nearer to literary uses of language. Consider the lexical item *break up*, for example. It may happen that the reader has only encountered this expression in reference to concrete and frangible objects (particularly if the reader is a foreign learner) so that for him this reference will constitute its signification, but if he knows the meaning of the expression in this sense he will be able to work out the 'idiomatic' value it has in this particular passage. He will do so by abstracting from the signification some feature which is appropriate to the context: in this case the feature will have to do with the disintegration of something, with the taking apart of some unity. In the code the unity is associated with a concrete mass but this association can be ignored as irrelevant in the context and the notion can be transferred to other things – in this case to a unity represented by a band of persons. The same procedure would enable him to understand the use of *break up* when this item collocates with *meeting* or *negotiation* or *family life*.

The ability of users of a language to give new values to words in actual discourse is, of course, one of the principal factors in linguistic change. Not only poets but all language users create figurative or metaphorical meanings in this way and as these meanings become accepted as part of current usage so they become part of the signification of the lexical item. To take a simple example, the terms *probe* and *freeze* are of very common occurrence in our newspapers, the first meaning *enquiry* and the second *prevention of increase (of wages)*. These meanings can be said to be part of the signification of these items now but when they were first used in these senses their value

Henry Widdowson

represented a figurative extension of the code meaning. As time passes and new uses enter into common custom so particular values become part of signification. This, of course, is why dictionaries have to issue appendices including not only new words but new meanings of old words which are sufficiently established for the lexicographer to accept them as part of the code of the language. It is not always easy, of course, to decide when a certain use warrants a dictionary entry: the borderline between value and signification is often hazy and what sometimes appears to be an original turn of phrase may be of general currency among a certain group of speakers.

The important point to note is the essential naturalness of metaphorical uses of language. The ability to create new values in discourse is part of what we call a person's knowledge of his language and it is not restricted to writers of literature. Grammarians sometimes talk as if it is only poets, children and foreign learners who do not conform to the rules of the language code, but as far as selection restriction rules are concerned at least very few language users are in fact strictly bound by them. It is for this reason that grammars cannot account for all aspects of language use. The widespread 'non-literal' use of language is a fact of considerable importance to the teacher of literature since it points to the possibility of representing literary works not as totally different ways of using language but as extensions of the way language is used in 'everyday' discourse. [. . .]

The question now arises: if poets (and other literary writers) only do what everybody else does, then what is distinctive about literary discourse? Essentially the distinction is that non-literal expressions occur randomly in ordinary discourse whereas in literature they figure as part of a pattern which characterises the literary work as a separate and self-contained whole. What is distinctive about a poem, for example, is that the language is organised into a pattern of recurring sounds, structures and meanings which are not determined by the phonology, syntax or semantics of the language code which provides it with its basic resources.

Consider, for example, the following verse from Tennyson's *In Memoriam*:

He is not here; but far away
The noise of life begins again,
And ghastly thro' the drizzling rain
On the bald streets breaks the blank day.

Here we have a piece of discourse which has the syntactic form of a compound sentence but which is organised phonologically in a way which is not required by the language code. It is divided into metrical lines and arranged into a rhyme scheme. The last line contains only monosyllabic words and these words are arranged so as to create a pattern of alliteration and a metrical line whose rhythm contrasts with those which precede. Over and above the code structure, then, is a linguistic organisation of the poet's own devising and this organisation is an essential part of what he is trying to convey. Except for occasional instances of onomatopoeia the actual sounds of words in a language are not significant of any particular meaning: they are meaningless elements which, when compounded, form words which *are* meaningful. Here, however, they are used to semantic effect: the monosyllabic structure of the words in the last

Henry Widdowson

line and the alliterative pattern they form reinforce the semantic import of the words as lexical items. The desolation that Tennyson feels is conveyed by the sound of the last line as well as by what the words themselves mean. This patterning of sound and sense into a single unit of meaning is the principal reason, of course, why translation of poetry is so extremely difficult. It is also the principal reason why paraphrase (which can be regarded as translation within one language as opposed to across two languages) must always misrepresent poetic meanings.

While it is conceivable, then, that a deviant expression like the *bald streets* or the *blank day* might occur in other forms of discourse as isolated expressions it is the manner in which they combine in this particular line and the manner in which the phonological structure of the line relates to the verse as a whole (and of course how this verse relates to the others in the poem) that characterise the use of these expressions here as literary. And they are understood not simply in terms of what value the individual words have as constituents of these phrases but of what value the phrases themselves take on as elements in a larger pattern.

It is then the correlation of code meanings, or significations, with the contextual meanings that linguistic items acquire as elements of a pattern which yields what value these items have as parts of a discourse. [. . .] [I]n these lines of Tennyson a particular deviation is understood partly by reference to the code and partly by reference to the way it patterns in with the language in the rest of the poem. It should not be supposed, however, that the unique values which linguistic items take on in literary writing are dependent on deviation. Though it is common to find violations of linguistic rules in literature it is neither a necessary nor a sufficient condition for a discourse to be literary that it should be deviant as text. It is not sufficient because, as we have noted, other forms of discourse depart from code rules. It is not necessary because there is a good deal of literature which does not show any marked linguistic oddity, and which cannot be defined satisfactorily in terms of textual deviations. [. . .]

As another example of literary discourse which is not deviant as text we might consider the following simple poem by Robert Frost:

Dust of Snow

The way a crow
Shook down on me
The dust of snow
From a hemlock tree

Has given my heart
A change of mood
And saved some part
Of a day I had rued.

This poem consists of a single sentence which a grammar of English would have little problem in generating. Although there is no deviation, however, the lexical items do take on a unique value in association with each other and with their signification in the code. The word 'crow', for example, signifies a bird of the genus *Corvus*, a black bird of carrion. In this context it is associated with 'dust' and 'hemlock tree' and these words select, as it were, those features of 'crow' which they share. A hemlock tree is the common name given to *Abies Canadensis*, which is a kind of North American pine or spruce. What links the item *crow* with the item *hemlock tree* in the context of the poem, however, is not the information that the former belongs to genus *Corvus* and the latter to the genus *Abies Canadensis*, nor that the former is a bird and the latter a tree but that the crow is black and feeds on corpses and the hemlock tree is, or is thought to be because of its name, poisonous. And these features are all associated with death. The value of the item *dust* now becomes clear as the one which it has in the phrase in the burial service: 'earth to earth, ashes to ashes, dust to dust' and in the passage from *Genesis*: 'For dust thou art, and unto dust shalt thou return'.

The association of these lexical items in this context has the effect of activating those semantic features in their signification which have a common point of reference. Thus the value of each of these lexical items lies in its composite character which represents a reconciling of code and context relations. The crow is at one and the same time a familiar black-feathered bird disturbing the snow on the branches of a tree and, in relation to *dust* and *hemlock* in the poem, a symbol of death. Once this basic value is recognised, one can then go on to impose a more specific interpretation on the poem and suggest that the crow represents a black-frocked priest scattering dust on a coffin. Since poetic meanings are of their very nature unspecific and ambiguous it is always possible for the reader to translate them into precise terms and so adapt them to his own personal vision: there is no such thing as a definitive interpretation. What is important, however (particularly from the teaching point of view) is that the individual interpretation should be based on an understanding of how linguistic items take on particular values in discourse. [. . .]

Literary discourse then is characterised by the creation of language patterns over and above those which are required by the linguistic code and these patterns bestow upon the linguistic items within them certain meanings which, when fused with the signification these items have as code elements, constitute their unique semantic value. I have tried to show how these patterns are formed by phonological means and by the semantic links between individual lexical items. I want now to discuss the patterning of syntactic structures. We can begin with a simple example from Alexander Pope:

> See how the world its veterans rewards!
> A youth of frolics, an old age of cards;
> Fair to no purpose, artful to no end,
> Young without lovers, old without a friend . . .
> (Pope, A. 'Epistle to a Lady', 1743)

Each of the last three lines here consists of two structurally equivalent phrases. Furthermore, the syntactic equivalence is reinforced by semantic links between the lexical items which appear in these structures. Thus *youth* and *old age* are semantically linked as antonyms by virtue of their signification, as of course are *young* and *old*. *Frolics* and *cards* are synonymously related under a general semantic feature such as /+entertainment/ and *lovers* and *friend* are similarly related under some feature such

Henry
Widdowson

as /+ affection/. *Purpose* and *end* are synonyms. It should be noted that in this pattern of syntactic and semantic equivalence, synonymous expressions appear in each case as the second part of each phrase and that these are balanced in the second and fourth lines by antonymous expressions relating to the dichotomy of youth and age. Two items, however, do not fit into this scheme by virtue of their signification: these are the terms *fair* and *artful* occurring in the third line. Now there is no explicit indication whether this line is meant to refer to the 'veterans' in their youth or in their age. But the position in the pattern of these two terms suggests that they are related in the same way as *youth/old age* and *young/old* are related. That is to say, the expressions *fair* and *artful* are conditioned by the context so that they take on particular values: fairness is represented as a quality associated with youth and artfulness as a quality associated with age. We might go on to suggest that the picture that emerges is of women practising the art of coquetry after they have lost the youth and beauty which would enable them to succeed.

What I am suggesting is that a pattern of structural equivalences can condition the lexical items in the structures concerned in such a way that they take on meanings other than those they have in the language code. [. . .]

Issues to consider

As Widdowson's concluding remarks make clear, the gist of this reading tallies implicitly with Jakobson's poetic function of language, discussed earlier in unit B1. Widdowson argues that a great deal of the 'signification' of his literary examples is achieved by structural equivalences that are established by judiciously chosen patterns of language. Importantly, and in the spirit of the commentary in units C1 and C2, this reading also highlights how literary devices operate at different *levels* of language (in this instance, vocabulary, grammar, semantics and sound patterns). It underscores then the importance of identifying and sorting out these levels as a precursor to lucid and coherent stylistic analysis.

Some suggestions follow.

 ❑ Widdowson's analysis of 'Dust of Snow' explores the significance of vocabulary. It is suggested that the words used by Frost acquire 'a unique value in association with each other and with their signification in the code'. In other words, and in line with Jakobson's axiom, the words reach new semantic values through the merger of their general meaning in the language system with the symbolic meaning arising from their alignment with other key words in the poem. A useful exercise, then, is to think about how the text might otherwise have been crafted. Try replacing the core words with synonyms, near-synonyms or items from the same genus or lexical set. You could, for example, replace 'crow' with 'magpie', 'hemlock tree' with 'Canadian spruce' and 'dust' with 'powder'. To all intents and purposes, such changes should not affect the overall narrative dynamic of the poem: it is still the case that the poet/speaker has some snow sprinkled upon him by a bird of carrion which is sitting in the branches of a North American pine tree. But does the poem now 'mean' what it did before? And if not, why not?

❏ Widdowson makes it clear that there is no such thing as a definitive interpretation of a literary text. His own analysis of vocabulary and grammar in 'Dust of Snow' prompts him to identify a funereal theme involving a 'black-frocked priest scattering dust on a coffin'. This however is largely predicated on the patterns of the first stanza, and it does not take into account the structures embodied in the second. A useful avenue for further exploration is to try to use the materials developed across strand 3 of this book to identity the overall grammatical structure of Frost's poem. Widdowson correctly describes the poem as a single sentence – but within this structure there are nested a number of individual clauses, so the breakdown is far from straightforward. Two of these clauses are embedded deep in the structure of noun phrases, but there are two main clauses also. A good starting place is to identify the Subject of the poem as a whole, using the tests offered in unit A3. As it happens, the Subject element is co-extensive with the entire first stanza, and this means that Frost has positioned a major syntactic boundary between his two stanzas. So, to what extent is the funereal theme sustained after this boundary? What do you make of noun phrases like 'my heart' and 'A change of mood'? What does the verb 'saved' mean in the context of the second stanza? Notice also the use of the *past perfect tense* when the speaker talks of 'a day I *had rued*'. This tense form is used in English to describe an activity that has happened in the past but which is now over. So what is it about this day that the speaker *no longer* rues? Is there a case for arguing that the language patterns of the second stanza tend to dissipate some of the symbolic meanings engendered by the first stanza?

❏ Widdowson explores the notions of *semantic anomaly* and the *collocational clash* in his reading. Because they inhere in the juxtaposition in language of un-related concepts, these ideas are in essence a precursor to the analysis of metaphor, a subsequent but major development in stylistics. In a number of places Widdowson explains how all language users (not just poets) create figurative or metaphorical meanings in language and this is an issue which will re-surface across strand 11. The idea of the collocational clash also lends itself well to the sorts of corpus techniques that are developed in strand 12 of the book. For instance, the examples from Tennyson, 'bald streets' and 'blank day', can be probed for common collocates. Widdowson describes these structures as 'deviant' because in the terms of the *selection restriction* model he uses there is an incompatibility between core aspects of the semantic make-up of these words. That is, the word 'bald' carries the feature /+human/, or at least /+animate/, whereas 'streets' yields the feature /+inanimate/. (An overview of the stylistic potential of the selection restriction model can be found in Simpson 1997a: 77–84.) But just how accurate is this characterisation? In your experience, do all of the commonly occurring collocates of 'bald' embrace the feature /+animate/? Some further suggestions about developing a corpus analysis along these lines are offered at the start of unit C12.

Henry Widdowson

STYLE AND VERBAL PLAY

In this light-hearted article from 1992, Katie Wales explores the stylistic strategies pop and rock musicians use when they name their bands. Wales uncovers an array of naming practices, which, even in this relatively narrow sphere of discourse activity, illustrates again how stylistic creativity can work simultaneously on a number of levels of language.

Zodiac mindwarp meets the horseflies

Katie
Wales

Katie Wales (reprinted from *English Today*, 29, January 1992, 50–1)

The world of popular music is all too easily branded as bland by those who dislike it: 'a sameness' that results from its blend of technological reproduction and appeal to mass consumption. However, the *Music Master* database of 1990 lists over 69,000 singles released since the 1950s, and is fascinating reading. What impresses is not only the sheer variety of the recordings, but also the linguistic creativity of the performers: in the names they give themselves. Any readers of *English Today* thinking of launching out on a career in the pop industry will find naming their groups a daunting task, unless they follow certain trends.

The safest line is to choose a popular modifier, like *Big, Beat, Bad, Hot, New, Red, Blue, Little* and *Sweet*. But is this enough to grab the attention of the DJs and your audience? For those who think pop music is a meaningless, repetitive noise, then clearly names like *A-ha, Buppi Buppi K, Blam Blam, Kajagoogoo, Oingo Boingo, Slam Slam, Ya Ya* and *Zaga Zaga* might appeal. Actually, such sound-play forms are quite rare. You might do better by punning: at least you will raise a smile: *Acid Reign, Terry Dactyl, Idol Rich, Split Enz, Well Red, Hear 'N' Aid*, for example. For those who think pop music sounds like the cries and noise of wild animals, it will be no surprise to learn that animal names are much more popular: *Animals, Balham Alligators, Bats, Big Pig, Boomtown Rats, Budgie, Cheetahs, Crickets, Dalmations, Elephant Talk, Frogs, Horseflies, Lions, Monkees, Piranhas, Reptiles, Sharks in Italy, Stingrays, Vipers, Wolfhounds, Zebras*, etc. But perhaps because pop music is to a lot of people's taste, quite a number of names are quite tasty and mouth-watering: *Applejacks, Bananarama, Bread, Blancmange, Bucks Fizz, Candy, Coconuts, Famous Potatoes, Finest Ingredients, Golden Syrup, Hot Chocolate, Scrambled Eggs, Sugar Cubes, Tangerine, Vanilla Ice, Wobbly Jellies, Whiskey & Soda*.

If pop group names are indicative, then the performers have come from a wide range of occupations that they wish to be reminded of: there are *Administrators, Ambitious Beggars, Captains of Industry, Chefs, Dead Milkmen, Diplomats, Engineers, Fire Brigade, Hunters & Collectors, Janitors, a Lecturer, Law Lords, Men at Work, Monks, Police, Scientists, Shop Assistants, TV Personalities, Undertakers, Vets*, and *Waitresses*. The V.I.Ps include *The Royal Family*, and especially the *Queen* and *Prince Charles*. Many would appear to have been artists (*Deep Green, Deep Purple, Frigid Pink, King Crimson, Pink and Black, Simply Red, Vicious Pink, Snowy White, Yello*), scientists (*Air Supply,*

Antenna, Einstein, Flying Saucers, H2O, Silicon Chip), and botanists (*Blue Orchids, Chrysanthemums, Edelweiss, Holly & The Ivys, Little Acorns, Poppies, Persian Flowers, March Violets*). More depressing, however, is to discover just how many are hypochondriacs (*Anorexia, Antidote, Anthrax, Cramps, The Cure, Double Visions, Fatal Microbes, Fear of Flying, Hypertension, Malaria, Mental As Anything, Scars, Sore Throat, Social Illness, Suicidal Tendencies, Talking to Walls, Varukers, Vapors*).

Just from the names alone, there is a truly revealing image presented of late twentieth century society, its social symbols and flotsam and jetsam. Mobility and technology are reflected in transport (*Blue Mercedes, Cars, Fifty-Three Bus, Freight Train, Heathrow Flyers, London Underground, Metro, Taxi*), and all its social ramifications (*Car Crash, Crawling Chaos, Jet Set, Love Train, Taking the Trains Out*). The media of journalism and television are captured in the names that reproduce the catch-words, buzz-words, idioms and collocations that many up-to-date dictionaries try hard to record also: *Alternative TV, Colour Supplement, Local Boy Makes Good, Mystery Guests, Personal Column, Send No Flowers, Small Ads, Tabloids*. Images of other aspects of contemporary society are captured in names like *Neighbourhood Watch, Overdraft, Photofit, Kissing the Pink, State of Play* and the abbreviations *UB 40, UFO and VDUs*.

More general in distribution are the names which repeat the cliches, similes and proverbs of everyday spoken language: *Curiosity Killed the Cat, Hear No Evil, Humble Pie, If All Else Fails, If It Moves, Keep it Dark, Lip Service, Look Before You Leap, Midas Touch, The Name Escapes Me, Scotch Mist, Soft Touch, Tongue in Cheek*. Perhaps some performers are actually ex-linguists, so sharp is their ear for contemporary idiom. Indeed, how else are we to explain names like *ABC, Accent, Bad English, Broken English, Coptic Roots, English Subtitles, Esperanto, Learning Process, Stylistics, Talk Talk, Talking Heads* and *Word of Mouth*. Not to mention: *He She Him; It; Me and You; Thee People; Them; The Who; Who Me;* and *Which is Which*.

Another creative source of naming practice comes from the register we normally associate with linguistic creativity: literary language. *The Bards* and *Poets* join with the *Romantics* and *The Bloomsbury Set*, *Dante* with *Virginia Wolf* (sic), *Keats* and *Milton* with *Shakespear's Sister*, to give us many *Books, Characters* and *Chapter and Verse*, much *Culture* and *Drama*, *Pulp* and *Poesie Noire*, *Science Fiction* and *Symbols*. Here we find (*The*) *Dubliners, Stephen Hero* and *Finnegans Wake, Catch 22, Erewhon, Eyeless in Gaza, Fra Lippo Lippi, Godot, Dorian Gray, Hard Times, Look Back in Anger*, the *Bible* and *Genesis*, the *Odyssey, Romeo and Juliet, Uriah Heep* and *Twelfth Night*. And here we can identify many quotations: *Fiat Lux, Have No Fury, Midnight Oil, Hollow Men, This Mortal Coil*.

From the *Fiction Factory* comes the 'archetypal' story immortalised in pop lyrics themselves: *Boys Meets Girl* on a *Blind Date* after a *Lonely Hearts* advert, *Perfect Strangers* hoping to be *Loveless* and *Lonesome No More*. After a *Long Pursuit* followed by the first *Kiss*, a few *Seconds of Pleasure, Lover Boy* and his *Platinum Blonde* are bitten by the *Love Bug*, full of *Passion* and *Naughty Thoughts*. With *Terms of Endearment* and *Promises, Promises, Super Lover* the *Seducer* with his *Fatal Charm* makes his *Valentine*, his *Venus in Furs*, fall into the *Tender Trap*. And *So to Bed. Tempting Fate*, he agrees to a *White Wedding*, with *Silk* and *Velvets*, and a *Long Honeymoon, Any Day Now*. But *Believe It or Not* soon *Something Happens*: it's a *Love Gone Wrong*, no *Paradise* ahead.

Big Trouble: he doesn't like the *Company She Keeps*; he's been *Caught in the Act* with someone else. They become *Passive Friends*. '*Admit You're Shit*', the *Iron Maiden* says with *Dirty Looks*. The *Lover Speaks*: '*Oh Well*' he concludes.

However, by far the most inventive and colourful naming, and the most productive, evokes the surrealism of science fiction, of fantasy and modernist poetry. The roots of inspiration may well lie in the psychedelic visions of the hippy drug culture of the 1960s, but the witty deviation of the incongruous collocations is eye-catching and mind-bending, like the concepts of Metaphysical poetry. Undoubtedly there is the same kind of 'poor man's poetry' that Eric Partridge and others have associated with slang, in names like the following: *Angels in Aspic, Aztec Camera, Ballistic Kisses, Bone Orchard, Dead Pan Tractor, Digital Dinosaurs, Electric Prunes, Exploding Seagulls, Flaming Mussolinis, Fourteen Iced Bears, Green Telescope, Groovy Chainsaw, Immaculate Fools, Laughing Apples, Lemon Kittens, Lovin Spoonful, Liquid Gold, Magnolia Siege, Leather Nun, Mind Over Muesli, Pink Noise, Glass Ties, Prefab Sprout, Reverend Sunshine, Sad Cafe, Singing Sheep, Soup Dragons, Spandau Ballet, Stone Roses, Suede Crocodiles, Velvet Underground, Voice of the Beehive* and *Wishbone Ash* – a real *Zodiac Mindwarp*!

Issues to consider

As a follow-up to Wales's entertaining paper, readers interested in general issues connected with the language of popular music might wish to consult Trudgill (1983), Simpson (1999), Andres Morrissey (2008), Beal (2009) and Coupland (2011). All of these articles explore, from a language perspective, the singing and performance styles adopted by different pop and rock musicians over the decades. Keeping within the same general field of discourse, Steen (2002a) is an insightful analysis of metaphor in Bob Dylan's song 'Hurricane', while Filardo (forthcoming) uses a number of stylistic frameworks in an analysis of the lyrics of John Lennon's 'Imagine'.

More suggestions follow.

❑ Wales's article concentrates on a field of discourse that is transient by nature, where fashions change almost overnight and an artist's popularity is measured by weeks and not years. What then is the current 'state of play' as far as naming techniques used in rock and pop go? Are the practices identified by Wales still in evidence or are other techniques now used in the names of contemporary pop and rock groups? Do different decades have different characteristic naming practices, for example?

❑ The array of stylistic strategies which Wales uncovers relates exclusively to pop and rock bands, but how widespread are these naming strategies in other musical sub-genres? Are the same tendencies found in the names of, for example, jazz or folk groups? And if not, why not?

❑ What other areas of discourse (outside 'literary' writing) do you know of which make use of similar techniques in linguistic creativity?

❑ Here is a short exercise which builds on the issues raised above. This is a 'word salad' activity which works by bringing together, in a structured way, terms from two fixed, but disparate, lexical sets. As observed in the follow-up to Widdowson's reading in D1, the sorts of semantic anomalies and clashes which emerge are often a cornerstone of the linguistic realisation of metaphor (see strand 11). In this exercise, elements relating to members of the animal kingdom are fronted with adjectival modifiers pertaining to the field of physical geography.

Katie Wales

Imagine you have just formed a rock or pop band. Shuffle each pack of words below, take one member from each set and see what combinations follow. Perhaps in the surreal concoction that emerges from this there might be a good name for your own ensemble, though musical genre may limit the use of some of the wilder combinations (I have yet to hear of a string quartet named 'The Subterranean Wombats'). Try also to explain how the degree of semantic incongruity can vary in different permutations, with some patterns less odd than others. Finally, I should add that one of the possible combinations below has already been taken.

subterranean	wombats
nocturnal	monkeys
arctic	toads
volcanic	skylarks
oceanic	dolphins
stratospheric	worms

TEACHING GRAMMAR AND STYLE

D3

In this reading, comprising an article written by Ronald Carter, two important issues in stylistics are raised. The first is to do with the development of a stylistics of poetry, which Carter addresses by offering a detailed lexico-grammatical analysis of a 'concrete' poem written by Edwin Morgan. The second issue connects explicitly to a theme that resonates through a number of the readings in this section: pedagogical stylistics. Here, Carter elaborates a programme for teaching about grammar in the narrower context and for teaching about language and style in the wider context. Carter's article makes a number of useful proposals for language teaching, emphasising further the importance of pedagogical issues and methods in contemporary stylistics.

A more localised point to note as you read through Carter's article is that he draws on the term *nominal group* in his study. This structure, which is heavily fore-grounded in the poem he analyses, is a cluster of words that has a noun as its main element. To all intents and purposes, then, it means the same thing as *noun phrase*, which is the term that we have been using across the strand to refer to this grammatical feature.

What is stylistics and why can we teach it in different ways?

Ronald Carter

Ronald Carter (reprinted from Mick Short (ed.) *Reading, Analysing and Teaching Literature* Harlow: Longman, 1989: 161–77).

The nature of stylistics

Given that stylistics is essentially a bridge discipline between linguistics and literature it is inevitable that there will be arguments about the design of the bridge, its purpose, the nature of the materials and about the side it should be built from. Some would even claim it is unnecessary to build the bridge at all. In such a situation there is always a danger that stylistics can become blinkered by too close an affiliation to a single mode of operation or to any one ideological position. There is already a considerable division in the subject between literary stylistics (which is in many respects an extension of practical criticism) and linguistic stylistics (which seeks the creation of linguistic models for the analysis of texts – including those conventionally thought 'literary' and 'non-literary'). Such divisions can be valuable in the process of clarifying objectives as well as related analytical and pedagogic strategies, but one result can be the narrowing of classroom options and/or the consequent reduction in the number and kinds of academic levels at which stylistics to literature students can operate. For example, literary stylistics can be more accessible to literature students because it models itself on critical assumptions and procedures already fairly well established in the literature classes of upper forms in schools, whereas the practice of linguistic stylistics tends to require a more thorough acquaintance with linguistic methodology and argumentation. [. . .]

Off Course

[1] the golden flood   the weightless seat
     the cabin song   the pitch black
     the growing beard   the floating crumb
     the shining rendezvous   the orbit wisecrack
[5] the hot spacesuit   the smuggled mouth-organ
     the imaginary somersault   the visionary sunrise
     the turning continents   the space debris
     the golden lifeline   the space walk
     the crawling deltas   the camera moon
[10] the pitch velvet   the rough sleep
     the crackling headphone   the space silence
     the turning earth   the lifeline continents
     the cabin sunrise   the hot flood
     the shining spacesuit   the growing moon
[15]   the crackling somersault   the smuggled orbit
           the rough moon   the visionary rendezvous
           the weightless headphone   the cabin debris

Ronald
Carter

[20]	the floating lifeline	the pitch sleep
	the crawling camera	the turning silence
	the space crumb	the crackling beard
	the orbit mouth-organ	the floating song

Edwin Morgan (1966)

I shall now work through this short text and point to some ways in which it might be explored in the classroom from within an expanded framework for stylistics. [. . .]

Approaches to study and teaching

TEACHING THE GRAMMAR

Most striking here is the consistent pattern of nominal groups across the whole text. In each case the structure is that of **d m h** where d = definite article, m = modifier and h = headword. The predominant modifier of the headwords in the nominal groups of this poem is an epithet. But they are not all of the same type. We distinguish in English (though by no means exhaustively) between three main types of epithet:

e[a]	=	qualitative epithet; e.g. *marvellous, interesting, strong*
e[b]	=	colours; e.g. *red, blue*
e[c]	=	classifying epithet; e.g. *classical, wooden*.

The usual order for these is **a b c**; so that you cannot normally have 'a red, classical, wonderful vase' but you can have 'a wonderful, red, classical vase'. In addition to these epithets English allows numerals, past and present participles (e.g. 'shining' [14] and 'smuggled' [15]) and other nouns (e.g. 'the space walk' [8] – sometimes called nominators) to act as modifiers in the nominal group. What kind of exploitation of these features is made in the text?

Epithet ordering rules do not really surface since only one modifier occurs at any one time. Morgan employs a mixture of modifiers including colours ('the golden lifeline' [8]), nominal modifiers ('the cabin debris' [17]) and participles (e.g. lines 3 & 5). In terms of classes of epithet, classifying epithets (e[c]) seem to predominate: e.g. 'the weightless headphone' (line [17]); 'the floating lifeline' (line [18]); 'the imaginary somersault' (line [66]); even to the extent that the majority of participles are of a classifying kind. In fact, 'the golden lifeline' may be seen to describe a characteristic of the lifeline as much as it does its colour. Thus, one cumulative effect of the use of this structure is that a number of objects are classified and reclassified. Occasionally, a particular qualitative contour is imparted to the things seen but the predominantly defining procedure suggests something more in the nature of an inventory (the run of articles reinforces this) or, more specifically, a ship's log with only occasionally the kind of qualitative reaction allowed in line [6] 'the visionary sunrise'. [. . .]

Other key structural features which must be noted are the absence of a verb and the particular use to which the participles are put. One main result of the omission of a verb is that there are no clear relations between objects. Objects either do not seem to act upon each other or have no particular 'action' of their own. Verbs generally work

Ronald
Carter

to establish a clear differentiation between subject and object and to indicate the processes contracted between them; a resultant effect here is that processes between things become suspended. The poet's suspension of some of the normal rules of grammar can be seen in part, at least, to contribute to this effect. Yet this observation can be countered by a recognition that there are verbs in the poem; for example, the participles already observed (e.g. 'crawling', lines [9] & [19]; 'floating', lines [3] & [21]; 'growing', lines [3] & [14]) are formed from verbs. The difference between the two verbal items in the following sentences:

(i) the world turns   (ii) the turning world

illustrates the point that in the participial form the 'verbs' work both with a more defining or classificatory function and to underline a sense of continuing, if suspended, action. The present participles convey a feeling of things continuing endlessly or, at least, without any clear end.

From a teaching or classroom viewpoint there is much that can be done with the above observations. They can be used in the service of fuller interpretation of the text; they can form the basis of discussion of the function of different parts of speech; and, more specifically, the text can be used to introduce and form the basis of teaching some key structural features of English syntax such as nominal group organisation, participles, verbal relations, etc. There is no reason why a literary text cannot be used to illustrate such features. In fact, one real advantage of such a framework is that grammatical forms are not learned in a rote or abstract way or in relation to made-up examples; instead, grammar is taught in action and in terms of its communicative features (cf. Widdowson 1975). We are made to ask both what is grammatical and, practically, what specific job a grammatical form can do in addition to what the semantic relations are which underlie noun-phrase sequences. This can be of direct value to both native English language students and foreign-language learners of English.

TEACHING THE LEXIS

One procedure here involves discussion and definition of what the individual words mean; it is a conventional and time honoured procedure and is clearly of most practicable use to foreign students. However, the introduction of the notion of lexical collocation can be rather more instructive. Here we are asking more direct questions about 'the company words keep' and exploring the different degrees of acceptability in the semantic fit between lexical items – in this case, between modifier and headword. Such exploration can teach more to foreign students about the meaning of words than dictionary-type definitions; we are forced in relation to this text into explaining, precisely, why 'crackling headphone' (line [11]) contains items which sit more comfortably alongside each other than 'crackling beard' (line [20]) or why 'smuggled' has a greater degree of semantic compatibility with 'mouth-organ' (line [5]) than with 'orbit' (line [15]). Idioms are explained, e.g. 'pitch black' (line [2]), as well as the extent of convertibility of idioms, e.g. 'the pitch sleep' (line [18]) or 'the pitch velvet' (line [10]); the range of meanings or associations carried by particular words can be discussed in relation to collocations such as 'the rough sleep' (line [10]); 'the rough moon' (line

[16]); and the possibilities of metaphoric extension can also be investigated through the uses to which items like 'crawling' or 'crackling' are put e.g. 'the crawling deltas' (line [9]); 'the crackling somersault' (line [15]); 'the crawling camera' (line [19]); 'the crackling beard' (line [20]).

Ronald Carter

One central insight into the structure of the poem which should emerge as a result of such lexico-semantic analysis concerns the concentration of metaphoric extensions, semantic incompatibilities and generally unusual collocational relations in the last six lines of the poem. It is almost as if the typographic inlay at line [15] signals a markedly changed set of relationships between objects and their classifications even though both object and attribute remain fixed and finite. There is thus a basis laid for further interpretative investigation and for conjunction with the syntactic analysis above. [. . .]

THE TEACHING OF TEXT AS DISCOURSE

[. . .] From a classroom viewpoint one of the most instructive and helpful means of distinguishing textual discourse is analysis through a juxtaposition of one discourse with another. In the case of 'Off Course' it may be useful to set it alongside texts containing instructions, or inventories, or lists of participants at a meeting, or even perhaps a recipe. In other words, texts which can be shown to contain linguistic conventions of a similar nature to the poem under consideration. One main aim here should be to focus attention on the nature of the textual organisation of 'Off Course'; as a result, the following features should be discerned:

(i)   readers should be uncertain as to how they are to read it. Across? Or down? The typography is not a reliable guide in this respect.

(ii) the lineation is unusual. There is an unexplained indentation at line [15]. The second column lacks the order and patterning of the first column although there is an equal space between noun phrases in both columns.

(iii) repetition of words is a marked feature although there is never repetition with the same collocational partner. A crisscross patterning occurs across columns, with modifiers sometimes turning up elsewhere as headwords (e.g. 'camera', lines [9] & [19]).

(iv) the relation of the title to the text is not a direct one. Compare this with: 'Chicken and Vegetable Broth'; 'How to Use the Pump'; 'Shopping List' etc.

(v)   the poem has no punctuation.

Once again the discernment of features such as these can be used to augment an interpretation of the text. But it can also be stylistic analysis of the kind that aids recognition of different styles of discourse and their different functions. Such work can be of particular use to the foreign-language learner who in some cases may have to learn totally new sets of conventions for different discourses. How explicitly he or she needs to learn this depends on the teacher's assessment of the needs of the class and the overall aims and objectives of the group's learning, but it can also be valuably underlined how different kinds of literary discourse can create their own rules for their reading, or can set out deliberately to disorientate a reader and how all literary discourse – however

Ronald
Carter

unusual – requires reference to one or other set of norms in order to create effects at all. Learning about the nature of literature involves learning about some of its operations as discourse. Learning about its operation as discourse is one essential prerequisite for reading the sort of concrete poetry of which 'Off Course' is a notable representative text.

[...]

INTERPRETING THE TEXT

For some people this is where we should arrive as well as the whole object of arrival. I've taken a long time to get here in order to try to demonstrate how much linguistic awareness can be derived from an examination of the language of a text as language and to challenge a prevailing view that literary texts cannot 'merely' be used for purposes of developing language competence. For me a stylistic approach to textual or literary interpretation is no more or less than another approach and is valuable only in the sense that it is a valuable activity for some students (but not necessarily for all). It would be wrong for our teaching of stylistics to be dominated by interpretative strategies; otherwise stylistics can become a restricted academic activity – both ideologically and pedagogically.

Put in a crude way, stylistic interpretation involves a process of making equations between, or inferences about, linguistic forms and the meanings contracted by the function or operation of these forms in a literary context. The whole issue of what is precisely involved in this is very complex and stylisticians are as involved as others in debates over what goes on in the process and over how particular interpretative facts can be established in a verifiable way. These issues cannot be addressed directly here although one perspective is offered in the next section; the following comments therefore carry the danger that they are based on assumptions which have not been made particularly explicit.

One of the 'equations' that can be made in relation to 'Off Course' is between the omission of verbs and an impression of weightlessness and suspension in which objects appear to be located in a free-floating relationship with each other and with the space surrounding them. The absence of verbal groups in the poem equates with and produces a sensation of a weightless, suspended condition of outer space where objects float about according to laws different from those which normally pertain.

Another central point [...] is the way in which the text shifts 'off-course', so to speak, at line [15]. From about line [10] to the end of the text no new headwords or modifiers are introduced. The same features recur but in different combinations resulting initially in something of a loss of identity of the objects concerned. But from line [15] the collocations of modifier and headwords become increasingly random or even incompatible. So the connections in our 'inventory' between object and its attribute/classificatory label seemingly get more and more arbitrary and void.

The typographical 'arrangement' of the text means that at the end we are left in an unpunctuated, unending space of free floating connections where the mind perceiving these features in this 'stream-of-consciousness-like' progression is apparently as disconnected and 'off-course' as the objects themselves. What was previously an embodiment of a disorientation in gravity-free conditions has now become a more profound dislocation. Where for the most part the lines up to line [15] represent a clear and definite, even if constantly changing, categorisation of things, the remaining lines succeed only in embodying the sense of a world and/or mind shifting out of control.

COMPARATIVE TEXTOLOGY

Texts are usually compared on the basis of related or contrasting themes; and there is little doubt that particular features of a text are placed in sharper relief through a process of comparison. A further dimension can be added by comparing texts which are constructionally and formalistically related. A stylistic examination of a text can provide a systematic and principled basis for grading texts for comparison or for further analysis. These texts can then be progressively introduced to students on the basis of their linguistic accessibility.

Literary stylistic work can be enhanced by such comparison as can be seen from a comparison of 'Off Course' with texts which have finite verbs deleted and/or exist as strings of nominal groups. Among the most interesting 'juxtapositions' are: Louis MacNeice, 'Morning Song'; George Herbert, 'Prayer'; Theodore Roethke, 'Child on Top of a Greenhouse'; Ezra Pound, 'In a Station of the Metro' [see unit C3 – P.S.]. Prose passages organised in this way include the opening to Dickens's *Bleak House* [see unit B3 – P.S.] and the opening to Isherwood's *Goodbye to Berlin*. We should explore here the similar and different effects produced in different literary contexts by the same linguistic procedures. [. . .]

Comparative textology moves the focus more centrally on to the essentially literary nature of the text (though the underpinning is consistently by linguistic means) and allows questions concerning differences between prose and poetry, between writers from the same period writing in similar ways, about literary movements, etc., and allows these questions to be generated at an appropriate level of abstractness. One seminal insight students should derive is that the same linguistic forms can function in different ways to produce different meanings according to context and according to the nature of the overlay of effects at other levels of language organisation. As we shall see in the next section, interpreting such 'meanings' is no simple matter of one-for-one correlation between form and function.

STUDYING THE 'NATURE' OF LITERARINESS

[. . .]

Two basic questions are: what is it in the organisation of the language of a text which makes it a literary text? how and why does it differ from other discourse types? Comparative textological investigation is going to be primary here and in its relation to the poem 'Off Course' we should want to return here to such features of the text as the way punctuation is used, the nature and function of the repetitions and parallelisms, the role of the title and of typography, the way it displays its own language, the interpenetration or convergence of different linguistic levels in the creation or constitution of meanings. This may lead to further exploration of plurality of meaning in literary discourse (the hyperactivity of the signifier), of how different literary discourses and kinds of reading are socially constituted and of how different cultures can impose different kinds of 'reading'. [...]

Issues to consider

Carter sets considerable store by the notion of 'literariness' as a concept in and for stylistic investigation. Although not attempting to distinguish literature from non-literature on purely linguistic grounds, Carter, like Jakobson (see B1 and C1), argues for the existence of a type of linguistic praxis which links and underpins various creative uses of language, of which literature is (uncontroversially) a preeminent example. This model of 'literariness', and the stylistic theory which informs it, is fleshed out in the second chapter of Carter and Nash (1990) and this makes for useful follow-up reading.

Carter flags up many other areas for further study throughout his article. In particular, or additionally, consider the following suggestions:

❑ With respect to Carter's call for a 'comparative textology', the structures which make up the poem 'Off Course' are like a number of the 'verb-less' patterns observed across this unit which might be classed as *minor clauses* (A3). That is not to say that the stylistic effect of these patterns will always be the same, nor will they share the same interpretative outcomes. Think of other literary texts which display dominant minor clause patterns. Worth chasing up are some of the texts which Carter himself suggests: Louis MacNeice's 'Morning Song', George Herbert's 'Prayer', Theodore Roethke's 'Child on Top of a Greenhouse' and the opening of Christopher Isherwood's novel *Goodbye to Berlin*.

❑ Think of text-types other than literature where features like minor clauses tend to congregate. Then assess the stylistic impact of the same grammatical structure in these different discourse contexts. (Newspaper headings and subheadings would be a good place to start.)

❑ Related to the previous task, consider the following online posting on a UK sports website (3/03/2013):

Chelsea lining up Mourinho

In grammatical terms, what does this sequence have in common with the passage from Dickens examined in B3? Do grammatical similarities invite the same type of interpretation across different discourse contexts? In other words, can we say that the newspaper text is 'Dickensian' in feel? Or is it that the Dickens text is newspaper-like in feel?

SOUND, STYLE AND ONOMATOPOEIA

The principal focus of attention across this strand has been on the stylistic significance of patterns of sound. The sound system of language offers numerous resources for linguistic creativity in style, with metrical and rhythmic structure on the one hand, and phonetic and phonological patterning on the other. In B4, a distinction was drawn, echoing Attridge (2004), between *lexical* and *nonlexical* onomatopoeia, and that unit went on to explore the way the former category can function in poetry. The reading that follows, which concentrates on the second type of onomatopoeia, is an extract from the same ground-breaking study by Attridge. Nonlexical onomatopoeia is perhaps the most direct form of verbal imitative art insofar as patterns of sound are crafted to represent the real world without the intercession of grammatical or lexical structures. Attridge's is a slightly irreverent yet hugely entertaining account of this principle at work in a passage from James Joyce's *Ulysses*.

'Fff! Oo!': nonlexical onomatopoeia

Derek Attridge (reprinted from: Derek Attridge, *Peculiar Language: Literature as Difference from the Renaissance to James Joyce* London: Routledge 2004: p.136–47)

Derek Attridge

Joyce's dexterity in handling the sounds and patterns of English is evident on every page of his published work, but one episode of *Ulysses* is explicitly concerned with music and imitative sound, the chapter known from the Odyssean scheme as 'Sirens'. We can expect to find here not only Joyce's customary linguistic agility and ingenuity but also some consideration – if only by example – of the whole question of language's capacity to imitate directly the world of the senses. In the well-known closing passage of the chapter, we find a very rudimentary type of onomatopoeia: the use of the phonetic characteristics of the language to imitate a sound without attempting to produce recognisable verbal structures, even those of traditional 'onomatopoeic' words. I shall call this type *nonlexical onomatopoeia*. Indeed, the device is perhaps too simple to be called 'onomatopoeia,' which means in Greek 'word-making' and usually implies reliance on the imitative potential of the accepted lexicon. In its naked ambition to mimic the sounds of the real world, however, nonlexical onomatopoeia exposes sharply some important but easily overlooked features of more sophisticated imitative figures.

Leopold Bloom, having imbibed a glass of burgundy at lunch and a bottle of cider at four o'clock, is walking along the Liffey quay uncomfortably aware that the aftereffects of this indulgence will be embarrassing for him should they be heard by any passer-by. In particular, he wants to avoid being noticed by an approaching prostitute, and he therefore gazes strategically into a shop window that happens to contain a print of Robert Emmet together with Emmet's famous last words on Irish nationhood. Just at that moment a tram passes, providing an acoustic cover under which he can achieve the desired release without fear of detection:

Derek Attridge

Seabloom, greaseabloom viewed last words. Softly. *When my country takes her place among.*

Prrprr.

Must be the bur.

Fff! Oo. Rrpr.

Nations of the earth. No-one behind. She's passed. *Then and not till then.* Tram kran kran kran. Good oppor. Coming. Krandlkrankran. I'm sure it's the burgund. Yes. One, two. *Let my epitaph be.* Kraaaaaa. *Written. I have.*

Pprrpffrrppffff.

Done.

(11.1284 [Numbers refer to the corrected text, ed. Hans Walter Gabler *et al.*, and indicate episode and line nos])

Several nonlexical onomatopoeic sequences occur here, proffering with a vivid and comic directness the sounds and sensations of tram and fart and contributing to the undoubted memorability of the writing:

Prrprr.
Fff! Oo. Rrpr
. . . kran kran kran.
Krandlkrankran.
Kraaaaaa.
Pprrpffrrppffff.

But how simple, obvious, or direct *is* the onomatopoeic imitation of sound here? Several factors complicate the picture, and I shall isolate eight of them. The first four are concerned with the assumption that onomatopoeia involves an unusually *direct* or *unmediated* link between language and its referent, the next four with the complementary assumption that onomatopoeia involves an unusually *precise* representation in language of the physical world.

(1) The most elementary question to be asked is how these black marks on the page represent sound at all, and the answer is, of course, that they rely as much on the reader's knowledge of the phonological system of spoken English and the graphological system of written English as does lexical onomatopoeia or, for that matter, any English text. Onomatopoeia does not lead us into a realm of direct and concrete significance, where many writers have dreamed of going; we remain firmly held within an already existing system of rules and conventions, and whatever mimetic capability the sequences have they owe entirely to this fact. Putting it another way, although these are not words and sentences, they mimic words and sentences – and it is this mimicry that permits us to pronounce them at all. In reading 'Fff! Oo. Rrpr,' for instance, we give a specific phonetic interpretation to the sequence exclamation mark (or full stop)/space/capital letter and treat it quite differently from the rhythmic repetitions of 'Tram kran kran kran,' with its absence of punctuation and its lower case, or the continuous 'Krandlkrankran,' which has the graphic form of a single word. Even if the normal phonological restrictions are breached, as in the climactic string of letters

('Pprrpffrrppffff'), the resulting articulatory awkwardness helps draw attention to the sounds themselves, an effect that is equally dependent on the reader's prior familiarity with rules of graphology and phonology. Elsewhere in *Ulysses* Joyce goes even further in the direction of unpronounceability within the conventions of English: the Blooms' cat goes 'Mkgnao!' 'Mrkgnao!', and 'Mrkrgnao!' (4.16, 25, 32), and in 'Circe' the 'dummymummy' produces the sound 'Bbbbblllllblblblblobschb!' as it falls into Dublin Bay (15.3381). The difficulty of pronunciation is obviously part of the comic point (when Bloom imitates the cat in reply he goes, conventionally, 'Miaow!' [4.462]).

(2) The sequences we are looking at do not constitute lexical items, but they do not function purely as phonetic chains either, without reference to the morphological system of the language and its semantic accompaniment. (It would be difficult to find a string of letters that had no semantic colouring, given a specific fictional setting and the eagerness of readers to find meanings in what they read.) The letter 'f' hints at the word 'fart,' and 'kran' is not very far from 'tram.' There are also links with words accepted in the lexicon as representations of sound: 'Prr-' suggests 'purr' (another long-drawn-out sound made by the expulsion of air through a restricted passage), and 'kran' has elements of two of the words used elsewhere in the novel to represent the sound of trams, 'clang' (7.10) and 'crack' (15. 190). 'Krandl-' evokes phonetically related verbs of movement and noise such as 'trundle,' 'rumble,' 'grumble,' 'shamble,' 'scramble' – what has been called a 'phonesthetic constellation'' (Bolinger 1965: 191–239; see also Graham 1981 for further discussion of the 'phonestheme'). Mechanical associations, moreover, are evoked by its closeness to 'handle' and by the presence of '-krank-' later in the string. We might also note that the most salient word in the quotation from Emmet is 'epitaph'; its [p] and [f] echo the onomatopoeic fart, deflating the heroic gesture as it is made. This link is all the stronger because Joyce has implanted it in the reader's mind in the chapter's prelude, where it occurs in the initially uninterpretable 'My eppripfftaph' (11.6 1). The reader might also be induced to make a connection with another sign system, that of musical dynamics, where 'ppffff' would signal 'very soft' and 'very loud indeed.' (When Molly breaks wind in 'Penelope,' and also does her best to be quiet about it, she addresses the words 'piano' and 'pianissimo' to herself at the critical moment [18.907, 908].)

The onomatopoeic effect also relies on an *avoidance* of certain morphological associations where these would be irrelevant or distracting: this is one reason – we shall look at others in a moment – why the spelling *cran* with a *c*, though it would indicate exactly the same pronunciation as *kran* with a *k*, would seem less appropriate, as it would produce associations with cranberries or craniums or Stephen's erstwhile companion Cranly. And what if the tram went 'bramble' or 'gran, gran, gran . . .'?

(3) The passage relies on our knowledge not only of the conventions of graphology, phonology, and morphology, however, but also of those of the rhetorical device of onomatopoeia itself. To take one example, the convention that a repeated letter automatically represents a lengthened sound is not to be found among the rules of the English language; the spelling of *gaffer*, for instance, does not imply that the medial consonant is pronounced at greater length than that of *loafer*. The rules cannot handle a succession of *more* than two repeated letters at all. But we have no difficulty with Joyce's triple *Fff*, which we interpret as an indication of marked duration, and such

Derek Attridge

breaches of the graphological rules function, in fact, as strong indicators that we are in the presence of an onomatopoeic device.

The conventions of onomatopoeia relate not just to spelling, however, but also to the associations evoked by sounds and letters. Within the tradition of English poetry, the onomatopoeic associations of /s/ and /ʃ/ are more appealing than those of /f/, though there is nothing intrinsically beautiful about the former or ugly about the latter. [. . .]

More generally, to respond to onomatopoeia of any kind it is necessary to have learned how to do so, because it means overriding the normal procedures of language comprehension whereby the sound functions, in Saussure's vocabulary, entirely as a differential entity and not as a positive term. [. . .] In sum, onomatopoeia requires *interpretation* as much as any other system of signs does; it is a convention among conventions. [. . .]

(4) Although we have been discussing onomatopoeia as if it were a purely aural device, it is evident that the effect of these sequences is partly visual. [. . .] A mere glance at the passage, in fact, signals to the eye the presence of sequences of letters which go beyond the normal configurations of written English, and the visual patterns contribute to the mimetic impressions received by the reader – the short, visually contrasted segments of 'Fff! Oo. Rrpr'; the identical repetitions of 'kran kran kran'; the undifferentiated extension of 'Kraaaaaa,' with a run of letters all the same height; and the more varied continuities (and presumably sonorities) of 'Pprrpffrrppffff,' where the graphic shapes not only differ from one another but protrude above and below the line. (The reader familiar with musical scores might even respond subliminally to this up-and-down movement as a representation of pitch changes.) The unpronounce-able examples mentioned earlier rely even more on apprehension by means of the eye: they remain resolutely visual, rendering any attempt to convert them into sound arbitrary and inadequate. One does not have to go to *Finnegans Wake* to find a text in which neither eye nor ear is sufficient on its own; indeed, one does not even have to go to Joyce or to 'experimental' writing.

(5) Turning now to the common notion that onomatopoeia constitutes an unusually precise representation of the physical qualities of the external world, we may ask how successful we would be in identifying the sounds referred to by these strings of letters outside the specific context of this passage from *Ulysses*. Joyce in fact poses this question at the beginning of the chapter, as if to underline the point in advance. Among the brief fragments that open 'Sirens' are the following, without any accompanying explanation:

Fff! Oo! (11.58)

Rrrpr. Kraa. Kraandl. (11.60)

These enigmatic scraps, like all the items in the list, convey very little in terms of the fictional setting and can be interpreted only retrospectively. Appearing where they do, they highlight the dependence of linguistic formations – onomatopoeic and otherwise – on their immediate context. Thus our 'hearing' of the tram in the final passage of 'Sirens' depends entirely on a clue not given in the prelude, the word 'tram' itself,

Derek
Attridge

without which we could make no sense of the onomatopoeic sequence. And the fart
has already been carefully prepared for earlier in the chapter, without, it is true,
anything so gross as the word 'fart' crossing Bloom's mind or the text's surface. (Molly,
in a similar predicament at the end of the book, is not so squeamish.) Several
intimations of flatulence have appeared at intervals on the preceding pages:

> Rrr. (11.1155)
> Rrrrrrrsss. (11.1162)
> . . . bloom felt wind wound round inside.
> Gassy thing that cider: binding too. Wait. (11.1178)
> . . . then all of a soft sudden wee little wee little pipy wind.
> Pwee! A wee little wind piped eeee. In Bloom's little wee. (11.1201)
> Rrrrrr.
> I feel I want . . . (11.1216)
> Wish I could. Wait. (11.1224)
> I must really. Fff. Now if I did that at a banquet. (11. 1247)
> Must be the cider or perhaps the burgund. (11. 1268)

The final release is therefore the culmination of a little private drama, a kind of interior
dialogue, and we are left in no doubt as to the sound represented by the letters on the
page before us. (Though some readers of refined sensibilities may have taken the
problem to be the less embarrassing one of an urge to belch: the text seems to offer
this possibility in its references to the gassiness of the cider and to the Persian custom
of burping at banquets, and in the apparent, if deceptive, hint in 'Must be the bur.'
Such an uncertainty as to oral and anal alternatives would be entirely in keeping
with the rest of the episode [. . .].) The same letters can in fact perform very
different onomatopoeic tasks: in *Ulysses* a sequence of *es* stands not only for a release
of wind, as in 'A wee little wind piped eeee,' but for a stick trailing along a
path ('Steeeeeeeeeeeeephen!' [1.629]), a creaking door ('ee: cree' [7.50] and 'ee'
[11.965]), a turning doorhandle (['Theeee!' [15. 2694]), and a distant trainwhistle
('Frseeeeeeeeefronnnng' [18.595], 'Frseeeeeeeeeeeeeeeeeeeeefrong' [18.874], 'sweeeee
. . . eeeee' [18.908]). In the last example the context does not allow us to distinguish
that trainwhistle from Molly's own anal release.

(6) For onomatopoeia to work at all, however, it is not enough to know from the
context what sound is supposed to be represented; it is also necessary to have some
prior familiarity with that sound. [. . .] Bloom produces a sound with which we are all
familiar, but we are less likely to know what a 1904 Dublin tram sounded like and so
are less likely to be impressed by the imitative appropriateness of Joyce's phonetic
formulae. To take a more extreme example, readers who do not know the sound of a
badly adjusted gaslight (among whom I number myself) will not be able to find out
what it is from the letters given to represent the noise in the 'Circe' episode: 'Pooah!
Pfuiiiiiii!' (15.2280). (We might suspect, from the much more helpful lexical description
the gasjet wails whistling, that there is a Circean extravagance about this utterance
as about so many utterances in that chapter, but even if the representation were as
accurate as letters could make it, we would still be little the wiser.) Onomatopoeia

Derek Attridge

is not a means of gaining knowledge about the world; after all, we can praise a literary text for the precision of its descriptions only if we are already fully acquainted with what the text purports to be describing.

(7) Even when these two conditions, an unambiguous situating context and prior familiarity with the sound, are met, the imitative effects of onomatopoeia – even of this very direct type – remain extremely imprecise. What, for instance, are we to make of 'Oo'? Is this a voiced (or thought) exclamation of Bloom's? An accompanying burp? A noisy passage in the anal performance? (As every actor knows, the letter 'O' can represent a wide variety of speech sounds.) Are the 'rrr' sequences here and earlier to be taken as stomach rumbles, or as premonitory activity in the bowels? And what aspects of the tram's sound are represented? The other noises made by trams in the novel provide no help: earlier they are to be heard 'honking' (5.131) and 'clanging ringing' (7. 10), and in 'Circe' a sandstrewer bears down on Bloom, 'its trolley *hissing* on the wire,' while the motorman '*bangs* his footgong' and the brake '*cracks* violently' (15.186, 187, 190). One reader, at least, does not even hear a tram at the end of 'Sirens,' but something more euphonious: David Hayman, in a plot summary of *Ulysses*, refers to Bloom's 'carefully releasing a final fizzle of fart to the sound of band-music.' (Hayman 1981: 142; cf. 112–14, where Hayman takes Bloom's thoughts about a drummer in a military band as evidence that there is a real band on the Liffey quay). Most readers would no doubt regard this as a highly idiosyncratic interpretation, but it does testify to the lack of a wholly obvious sonic referent.

Only a few nonvocal sounds, in fact, can be imitated with any degree of closeness by the speech organs, and the significance (and pleasure) to be drawn from Bloom's fart lies partly in its exceptional character: it is unusually amenable to vocal imitation in being a sound produced by an orifice of the human body. This fact enables the sequence 'fff' to be appropriate in both the ways open to onomatopoeic imitation, in its articulatory processes and in its acoustic properties – it is both produced like and sounds like a fart. (Even then, we take little pleasure in accuracy of imitation for its own sake: a more precise rendition of a fart than 'Pprrpffrrppffff' would be 'Fffffffffffff.') Few of the sounds that we hear, and that writers attempt to convey, are as well qualified as this one is for imitative representation. We might even say that the only fully successful onomatopoeia occurs when the human voice is imitated, which is what written language, in a sense, does all the time – except, that is, when it is attempting nonlexical onomatopoeia.

(8) A further complication is most obvious in the case of nonlexical onomatopoeia, though it remains a possibility in all onomatopoeic devices. The reader who responds to these strings of letters as attempts at direct representation of familiar sounds is likely to go beyond the normal phonological rules of English in essaying an imitation (in the imagination if not in actual utterance) more accurate than language normally permits. Doing so amounts to treating the sequences as instructions to the reader: [*sound of fart*], [*sound of passing tram*]. If we look at it in this way, mimetic precision in the string of letters is completely unnecessary, and the reader is in fact likely to do a better job of imitating or imagining the sound required if he or she is unhindered by the writer's attempt to make it compatible with the normal phonological properties of the English language. Difficulty in pronunciation according to the normal rules of English may

Derek Attridge

also encourage the reader's inventiveness: strictly speaking, for example, it is impossible to give a plosive any degree of duration, but the doubling of *p* in the final onomatopoeic effusion of 'Sirens' may suggest a continuant very close to the sound represented. And most readers probably take the unpronounceability of 'Mrkrgnao!' as an invitation to imitate a cat's cry in a way less stylised than the conventional 'Miaow!'. In 'Circe' Joyce plays with the curious relationship between stage directions describing utterances and the utterances themselves, as in the gasjet's wailing whistle, and we might ask whether in 'Lestrygonians' Davy Byrne's yawn 'Iiiiiichaaaaaaach!' (8.970), which Hugh Kenner praises for its 'deftness of rhythmic imitation' (Kenner 1980: 85), would even be recognised without a prior announcement of what is coming. (When Byrne is assigned a similar string of letters in 'Circe' – 'Iiiiiiiiiaaaaaaach!' (15. 1697) – interpretation is again aided by the stage direction ['*yawning*'].) At the same time, the extraordinary sequence of letters clearly gives the reader more scope for a bravura performance and in so doing provides greater pleasure than would a mere 'Davy Byrne yawned loudly.'

It can be demonstrated, then, that any sense of appropriateness which an example of nonlexical onomatopoeia may produce is not primarily the result of an unusually close resemblance between the sounds of language and the sounds of the external world. This being the case, it is easier to understand how the experience can be accompanied by a heightened consciousness of the sounds of language themselves. Indeed, the inevitable incongruity of such devices frequently intrigues and amuses the reader, even while the letters successfully perform their referential duties. Jakobson's double emphasis seems justified, therefore, at least as far as nonlexical onomatopoeia is concerned: the series of linguistic sounds *and* their referents receive simultaneous, if separate, enhancement. But this pleasurable double foregrounding is achieved by something other than the art of imitation.

Issues to consider

An important point of theory to emerge from Attridge's study is his contention that the use even of nonlexical onomatopoeia, that most mimetic of stylistic devices, is not of itself sufficient to represent directly the object or activity it echoes. This is because recognition depends on a series of other in-text indicators, and even when two important conditions – an unambiguous situating context and prior familiarity with the sound – are met, the imitative potential remains imprecise. Attridge's point articulates a broad principle about stylistic analysis which was rehearsed in B4; namely, that linguistic structures do not embody textually aspects of the 'real world' but instead serve as gateways to the understanding and interpretation of those texts *vis-à-vis* their relationship to the real world.

Some suggestions follow.

❏   Although his focus is principally on the style of a single literary text, much of what Attridge says has general validity and his observations can therefore be translated to other textual practices – this is always the test of an insightful and far-reaching stylistic analysis. Developing this, reference was made in A4 to the importance of sound symbolism in the 'advertising jingle', and this is a type of discourse that lends itself well to the study of both lexical and nonlexical

Ronald
Carter

onomatopoeia. For example, a long-running British advertisement for a popular stomach and headache remedy displays the dropping of two effervescent tablets into a glass of water. In both its billboard and televisual versions, this activity is accompanied by the written logo 'Plink, plink, fizz'. Can you (i) identify the types of onomatopoeic devices at work in this jingle and (ii) think of other ads where similar stylistic techniques are used?

❏ Following from the previous suggestion, here is another advertising text (for a local bakery) which displays an interesting sound texture:

> This is the bread
> To greet any guest
> Because it's the bread
> That mother knows best.

Drawing on any of the relevant material offered across this thread, try to provide an account of sound patterning, including metrical structure, in this advertising jingle.

❏ English words which begin with 'sl' are often thought to be onomatopoeic because they frequently connote an unpleasant action or thing. Can you list five 'sl' words that have an unpleasant feel to them? Now, can you think of any words which begin with 'sl' but which do *not* have such connotations? If you succeed at the latter task, what does this say about the supposed unpleasantness of 'sl' words in English? Do the historical origins of the words (that is, whether they are Anglo-Saxon or Latinate in derivation, for example) have any bearing on their supposed onomatopoeic qualities?

D5   A TYPOLOGY OF NARRATIVE GAPS

This reading, by Donald Hardy, probes a very important aspect of narrative fiction, the *narrative gap*. While there is no doubt that stylistic research on the discourse of stories tends, understandably, to concentrate on events that are actually narrated, there are a number of key storytelling techniques that quite deliberately leave certain events 'un-narrated'. Prince's concept of *disnarration* refers to narrative events that did not happen but whose significance is such that we are told about them (Prince 1988, 2005). Disnarrated events are normally delivered through negative constructions (e.g. 'He did not see the knife coming towards him'). *Counterfactuals* by contrast are imagined, hypothetical narrative events, but which also do not come to pass in the story (e.g. 'She dreamt of an escape through the bathroom window'). Finally, a *narrative gap* is when a specific piece of information concerning a narrative event and / or participants(s) is noticeably absent or delayed. Following Hardy's model, although narrative gaps are 'non-narrated' events in the strict sense, they can be presupposed to have occurred and can be 'filled in' retrospectively because their absence from the story is marked in some way. Hardy focusses on the fiction of the southern American Catholic writer Flannery O'Connor. Hardy points out elsewhere that this writer, who frequently commented that her Christian rhetorical sights were set on her largely secular audience, was preoccupied with questions of epistemology and causality, and it is this preoccupation that helps explain in part both the motivation for, and the effect of, her narrative gaps (Hardy 2003 *passim*). Building from his close stylistic analyses of O'Connor's work, Hardy offers a comprehensive account of the function of the narrative gap in prose fiction.

In advance of reading Hardy's article, I would like to propose two short 'warm-up' exercises, the relevance of which will emerge in the course of Hardy's analysis. The first exercise involves sorting, without any context, the three jumbled pieces of text below into a coherent narrative order. In other words, arrange the sentences into a sequence that makes sense for you.

Activity ✪

The car turned over once and landed right-side-up in a gulch off the side of the road.

The children were thrown to the floor and their mother, clutching the baby, was thrown out the door onto the ground; the old lady was thrown into the front seat.

The instant the valise moved, the newspaper top she had over the basket under it rose with a snarl and Pitty Sing, the cat, sprang onto Bailey's shoulder.

The second warm-up exercise involves looking closely at the text below, which is derived from O'Connor's short story, 'A Good Man is Hard to Find'. Here, the main character Rayber becomes exasperated, in a barber's shop, by the racist discussion around him. Make a note of the ways in which each narrative event in the passage precipitates (and contextualises) the event that follows:

The blood began pounding up Rayber's neck just under his skin. He turned and pushed quickly through the men around him to the door. He was so angry that he had forgotten to remove the barber's bib or cleanse his face of the lather. Outside, the sun was suspending everything in a pool of heat and before he had turned the first corner, almost running, lather began to drip inside his collar and down the barber's bib, dangling to his knees.

Watch out for the (re)appearance of these texts in the reading that follows. The significance of the stylistic warm-up exercises here will become clear through Hardy's analysis and commentary on key narrative gaps in O'Connor's fiction.

Towards a typology of narrative gaps: knowledge gapping in Flannery O'Connor's fiction

Donald Hardy

Donald Hardy (reprinted from *Language and Literature*, 2005, 14, 4, 363–75)

I understand a 'narrative gap' to be a specific piece of information, either a participant in an event or an entire proposition (event plus participants), that is noticeably missing or delayed in the narrative discourse. There is another kind of missing element or elements that I will exclude from detailed consideration. This is the innumerable and relatively meaningless ellipses that one can, if forced, reconstruct for a text but which are either unannounced or practically unnoticeable because there is neither a 'significant lacuna in the chronology' nor a 'retrospective filling-in'. This is the second category covered by Prince's 'unnarratable'.

[. . .] Flannery O'Connor's 1947 MFA thesis story 'The Barber' [. . .] ends with the following paragraph:

> The blood began pounding up Rayber's neck just under his skin. He turned and pushed quickly through the men around him to the door. Outside, the sun was suspending everything in a pool of heat and before he had turned the first corner, almost running, lather began to drip inside his collar and down the barber's bib, dangling to his knees.
>
> (O'Connor 1988: 724)

There are at least two missing pieces of information in the paragraph, information that is provided by the reader's gestalt sense of good continuation. Rayber, who has just ignominiously lost an argument and his temper with the racist men of the barbershop, runs out of the shop half-shaved and still wearing his barber's bib. The first missing piece of information is that Rayber actually walks out the door of the barbershop, which I classify as an ellipsis. The second piece of missing information, a noticeable gap, is that he leaves the barbershop so hastily that he is half-shaved and still bibbed. That information is provided through the 'retrospective filling-in' of the narrator's description of the dripping lather and the dangling bib. This passage nicely illustrates the difficulty in deciding between noticeable gaps and unnoticeable ellipses. The recognition of a gap invites reading significance into the absence of information. Thus, it is difficult to imagine a significance to the elision of the action of walking out the barbershop door. However, the gapping of the information that Rayber did not take his bib off or wipe the lather from his face before he left the barbershop invites the reader to imagine his panicked and mindless rush to escape his embarrassment.

I will not attempt what is probably the impossible – the determination of a sharp dividing line between the ellipsis and the gap. I will instead pursue the question of whether there is a stylistics of gaps, that is whether one can identify in an individual author repetitive gapping patterns over the entire span of her work. [. . .]

In the case of the announced gap, it is clear that something has been left out. The reasons for the announced gap might be many (e.g. lack of interest), and what is gapped can be of many types, from description to core narrative events. Flannery O'Connor

**Donald
Hardy**

was modern in the sense in which she commented on the disappearance of the author 'in explaining and psychologizing'. [She continues]:

> By the time we get to James Joyce, the author is nowhere to be found in the book. The reader is on his own, floundering around in the thoughts of various unsavory characters.
>
> (O'Connor 1969: 74).

Mosher (1993) makes much the same point to explain the predominance of the narrative gap in Joyce's 'Dubliners'. The 'disappearance' of the author is responsible in part for the rarity of the announced gap in modern literature. O'Connor's statement is, however, a bit of an exaggeration. There is still narrational control in O'Connor's modern fiction, even control of the gap, although her most recognizable announced gap is attenuated to the indefinite pronoun **something**. In 'A Good Man is Hard to Find', the narrator does not give the exact words that Bailey utters when his mother seals her family's fate by blurting out that she recognizes The Misfit – the escaped convict who is to murder the entire family: 'Bailey turned his head sharply and said **something** to his mother that shocked even the children' (1988: 147) (bolding mine throughout). Even this relatively oblique but still lexically explicit (*something*) narrative gap is frequent in O'Connor's fiction, certainly to the point of making it stylistically marked in her fiction. Consider the following additional examples:

(1) He came back almost at once, plugging **something** into his ear. (1988: 386)

(2) He lifted the gun to his eye and leaned forward. Something slipped beneath him and he slid backward on his heels. (1988: 709)

In each of these examples, the indefinite pronoun gaps information that is not retrospectively filled in, although in each case the reader quite likely interpretively fills the gap. In (1), the focalizer Francis Tarwater of *The Violent Bear It Away* observes his uncle Rayber, who is partially deaf, plug 'something', almost certainly the earpiece of his hearing aid, into his ear. In (2), Old Dudley of 'The Geranium' falls when 'something', perhaps leaves or dirt or a fallen tree limb, slips beneath him as he is bird hunting. Wilson (2000: 197) points out 'Subtle shifts and overlaps between narrative voice and character focalization are often a source of narrative gaps, especially in modernist fiction'. Thus, focalized gapping helps produce a blend of narrative voices, minimally those of the narrator who represents the gap, the focalizer-character who reflects the gap, and the reader who interprets the gap.

The gaps in (1) and (2) are filled almost effortlessly by a reader's gestalt knowledge of the mechanics of hearing aids and the details of a hunting expedition. Some gaps, those for which the reader does not have a nearly omniscient perspective, leave a bit more ambiguity. Bell (1986: 88) argues that if the gaps of one consciousness 'be filled by recourse to another limited viewpoint, even then no absolute authority adjudicates between relativities'. Bell's point is particularly well illustrated when the reader might work in interpretively active ways on the gap, as in (3):

(3) **Something** forced Mr Head from behind the trash box and forward, but only at a creeping pace. (1988: 226)

Here, Mr Head of 'The Artificial Nigger' has tricked his grandson, Nelson, into thinking that he has abandoned him in the city. Nelson panics and collides on the sidewalk with an elderly woman. Mr Head is forced by 'something' to go forward. That something might be guilt, a sense of responsibility, or even the beginnings of the operation of O'Connor's famous exploration of grace. The multivoiced gap here is significant because it represents the lack of full and explicit knowledge on the part of all participants in the narrative act.

O'Connor uses *something* to announce not only gaps that are filled solely by the interpretive work of the reader, however effortless or effortful that work might be, but also those that are retrospectively filled by the narrator, as in the following [example]:

([4]) He took **something** small from his pocket and showed it to them. (1988: 249)

The overarching narratological significance of [this] example is the same as that of (1)–(3), the focalized presentation of gapped knowledge, all as a result of limited perception, whether that be on the part of the focalizers, the reader, the narrator, or some combination of the three. [. . .] In ([4]), Sally Virginia Cope, the almost comically consistent focalizer of 'A Circle in the Fire', watches as Powell, one of the three juvenile delinquents who invade the Cope farm for a weekend, pulls something out of his pocket. This 'something' turns out to be some of the matches that the boys use to set the woods on fire as the last in a series of destructive acts. It is in part because the child Sally Virginia serves so consistently as the focalizer for this story that ([4]) contains a true gap for the reader, one that cannot be filled simply by a cognitive gestalt; the first-time reader cannot know what Powell pulls out of his pocket until the boys start setting the woods on fire. As a rough indication of the stylistic markedness of *something* as an indicator of the gap in O'Connor, it occurs 12.61 times for every 10,000 words in O'Connor's fiction but only 7.74 times for every 10,000 words in the general fiction subcorpus of the Brown Corpus, a randomly collected sample of American fiction published in 1960–1 and therefore an excellent comparative corpus for O'Connor's fiction, which was published in the years from 1946 through 1965.

The gaps signalled by the use of *something* are not isolated narrative elements in O'Connor's fiction; there are related gapping techniques signalled in part through focalization of the same characters. The gaps, of whatever particular technique, help to represent general character traits such as emotional, or spiritual confusion or distraction. [. . .]

I turn in the remainder of this article to demonstrating that O'Connor's fiction has a gapping style in its use of recognizable repeated uses of unannounced narrative gaps.

The unannounced gap is one element, among many, that contributes to one of O'Connor's well-recognized stylistic habits at the thematic level – her celebrated questioning of human rationality (e.g. Desmond, 1987; Hardy, 2003; Keller, 1972; Marston, 1984; Shloss, 1980). O'Connor fundamentally distrusted the human intellect as the sole source of knowledge and thus of control. Given one of the primary patterns of the unannounced gap to be discussed below, and given her occasional comments about the unexpected, I believe that the gap is one way that O'Connor questioned the rationality of cause and effect. Thus, she repeatedly dramatized the operation of free will. In a long letter to Alfred Corn, O'Connor detailed her belief in the operation of free will in her literature. She writes of Rayber and Tarwater in *The Violent Bear It Away*:

> An absence of free will in these characters would mean an absence of conflict in them, whereas they spend all their time fighting within themselves, drive against drive.
>
> (1988: 1173)

It is the combination of free will within characters, conflicting wills among characters, and a lack of determinism that makes the gaps in O'Connor's fiction possible. She described the characters of modern Southern writing of the grotesque, a genre into which her fiction fits perfectly, as 'lean[ing] away from typical social patterns, toward mystery and the unexpected.' Furthermore, she says that a writer who is interested in mystery, as she certainly was, 'will be interested in possibility rather than in probability' (1988: 815–16). Thus, she repeatedly dramatized mystery, the unexpected, and possibility; one of the major narrative devices that she used for those dramatizations is the narrative gap.

The most common unannounced narrative gaps in O'Connor's fiction are produced within focalization, just as are the announced ones with *something*. These focalized gaps are produced in one of two ways. First, the character might be concentrating so hard on his or her wishes and desires that the actual narrative outcome – which is different from the character's wishes or desires – is read as a gap. Second, the character might simply be surprised by the narrative turn of events without especially planning or hoping for a different turn of events. One gap results from planning too hard for the future, the other from the unpredictability of human behavior and the circumstances that affect human behavior. In both cases, there is a gap between human cause and effect. *Wise Blood* is particularly rich in the type of focalized gap in which a character plans so intently on controlling events that he or she is surprised by the unexpected outcome. One of the primary uses of the gap in *Wise Blood* is comedy, as Enoch plans to not do a series of events and finds himself doing them anyway. On the day that he senses in his wise blood that he will have to do something 'to justify his daddy's blood', he 'decided not to get up'. The next paragraph reports, 'He was at the zoo by nine-thirty, only a half-hour later than he was supposed to be'. Consider the following concentrated series of gaps between Enoch's intentions and his actions as he contemplates buying a movie ticket:

> I ain't going in no picture show like that, he said. . . . I ain't got the money to buy a ticket, he said, taking out his purse again. I ain't even going to count thisyer change.
>
> It ain't but forty-three cent here, he said. . . . A sign said the price of a ticket for adults was forty-five cents, balcony, thirty-five. I ain't going to sit in no balcony, he said, buying a thirty-five cent ticket.
>
> I ain't going in, he said.

Two doors flew open and he found himself moving down a long red foyer. . . . I ain't
going to look at it, he said furiously. He didn't like any picture shows but colored musical
ones.

The first picture was about a scientist named The Eye. . . .

(1988: 78–9)

Clear indications or statements of Enoch's intentions occur before each of the gaps
in this passage. He isn't going to buy a ticket, he isn't going to count his money, he
isn't going to sit in a balcony, he isn't going to enter the movie theater, and he isn't
going to watch the movie. As the narrator says, 'Enoch's brain was divided into two
parts. The part in communication with his blood did the figuring but it never said
anything in words. The other part was stocked up with all kinds of words and phrases'
(1988: 49). It is the part with words and phrases that says he will not buy the ticket,
sit in a balcony, enter the theatre, or watch the movie; it is the part in communication with his wise blood that leads him to do what he does not intend to do. The divide
between the two halves produces the narrative gaps between his intentions and
actions. [. . .]

A second narrative gap category contains those gaps that are not due to one
character's focalization reflecting an unrealistic intention, as we have seen, for example,
in Enoch [. . .]. These gaps occur, rather, as a reflection of surprise on the part of the
character and/or the reader, as in the following from 'A Good Man Is Hard to Find',
which I [classify elsewhere] as an example of Prince's nonnarrated (Hardy, 2003: 165):

The instant the valise moved, the newspaper top she had over the basket under it rose
with a snarl and Pitty Sing, the cat, sprang onto Bailey's shoulder.

The children were thrown to the floor and their mother, clutching the baby, was thrown
out the door onto the ground; the old lady was thrown into the front seat. The car turned
over once and landed right-side-up in a gulch off the side of the road.

(1988: 144)

The paragraph break contains a gap in the narration of the actual car crash as the car
leaves the road. Gaps such as this focalize the categorically unexpected in that neither
the reader nor the focalized character could foresee the sequence of events. Frequently,
but not always, the gestalt interpretation of the gap is that the focalized character is
suffering from some sort of limited awareness, as is the case in the following passage
from 'Revelation'. Here, the self-satisfied Ruby Turpin thanks Jesus for making her who
she is and giving her what she has, including her husband Claud:

'Oh thank you, Jesus, Jesus, thank you!' she cried aloud.

The book struck her directly over her left eye. It struck almost at the same instant that
she realized the girl was about to hurl it.

(1988: 644)

The retrospective gap-filling of the narrator's information that the girl threw the book
is ambiguous about whether Ruby realizes, before or after it hit her, that Mary Grace

is about to throw the book. In any case, the gap registers surprise both to the reader and to Ruby and signifies many things, including the disjunct between what Ruby thinks of herself, what Jesus might think of her, and what we know Mary Grace thinks of her. [. . .]

This article has demonstrated distinctions between announced gaps, attenuated announced gaps, ellipses, indeterminacies, and unannounced narrative gaps. I have argued that the attenuated announced narrative gap and the unannounced narrative gap are stylistically indicative of O'Connor's prose from her earliest to her latest work, both in the particular forms that they take and in their functioning generally to encode concerns with the limitations and possibilities of human knowledge, a thematic concern of heavy significance throughout O'Connor's fiction. [. . .]

Issues to consider

Hardy's study of Flannery O'Connor develops a model of narrative gaps that can be applied more generally both to prose, and, as we shall see below, to film. Note also how Hardy sets his observations on the occurrence of *something* in O'Connor prose against a broader subcorpus of general fiction – and this means that he is able to stand over his generalisation about the frequency of this word in the texts studied (see further strand 12).

Some suggestions follow.

❏ Go back to the two 'warm-up' exercises that opened this unit. The purpose of such   **Activity**
exercises is to solicit in advance some impressions about basic 'well-formedness' in narrative structure, and this serves as a useful point of contrast with the techniques O'Connor *actually* uses. How did your own predicted configuration of events in the excerpt from 'A Good Man is Hard to Find' compare with the actual text? And in the fragment from 'The Barber', how did the additional sentence of explanation in the exercise text compare with the way in which O'Connor herself narrates Rayber's abrupt departure from the barber's shop?

❏ Re-acquaint yourself with these terms as defined in Hardy's article:

the *announced* narrative gap,
the *attenuated announced* gap
the *unannounced* narrative gap

Now look at the following three passages and try to identify which of Hardy's three categories best describes the type of narrative gap exhibited by each. The first is from David Mitchell's novel *Cloud Atlas*, where the elderly narrator, Timothy Cavendish, takes issue with the dropping of litter by three teenage girls on the streets of London:

> Tim Cavendish the Disgusted Citizen exclaimed to the offenders: 'You know, you should pick those up.'
> A snorted 'Whatchyoo gonna do'bou'it?' glanced off my back.
> Ruddy she-apes. 'I have no intention of doing anything about it,' I remarked over my shoulder, 'I merely said that you –'

Donald Hardy

> My knees buckled and the pavement cracked my cheek, shaking loose an early memory of a tricycle accident before pain erased everything but pain. A sharp knee squashed my face into leaf mould. I tasted blood. My sixtysomething wrist was winched back . . . before my muggers could filch my wallet.
>
> (Mitchell 2004: 147)

The second extract is from Henry Fielding's *Tom Jones* (1749). Here the narrator explains how Captain Blifil appears to have reached a rather dubious reconciliation with Mr Allworthy on the matter of his marriage to Allworthy's sister:

> THE Reader, from what hath been said, may imagine that the Reconciliation (if indeed it could be so called) was only Matter of Form; we shall therefore pass it over, and hasten to what must surely be thought Matter of Substance.
>
> (Fielding 1970: 55).

The third passage is from another of Flannery O'Connor's short stories. Here Bevel, of 'The River', is run over by a pig that the Connin boys have tricked him into releasing:

> Something snorted over him and charged back again, rolling him over and pushing him up from behind and then sending him forward; screaming through the yellow field, while it bounded behind.
>
> (O'Connor 1988: 159)

❏ Hardy's reading probes narrative gaps in prose fiction, but there is enormous potential for the study of gaps in film narrative. Just as prose writers do, film directors make use of the technique of ellipsis to skip obvious narrative progressions that can be easily inferred by viewers. For instance, if a character is seen outside the door of a room and then shown sitting in a chair inside that room, the progressions that connect the two scenes (opening the door, going inside and so on) need not be relayed – not least because it wastes valuable screen time. This is often referred to by directors as 'cutting the shoe leather' in the sense that it trims unnecessary material around the edges.

However, many directors make strategic use of the unannounced gap for a number of reasons, and an interesting topic for study would be locating and analysing these gaps (and their effects) in contemporary film. This study could also be supplemented by the material on narrative comprehension that was developed and discussed in unit B10. Hardy describes the numerous functions of the narrative gap as suggesting 'possibility', dramatising 'mystery', creating 'the unexpected', or in signalling 'limited awareness'. These functions are as true to narrative gaps in film as they are to those in prose.

Without being too programmatic here, an interesting film for such exploration is the Coen brothers' adaptation of *No Country for Old Men*. The film's central character Llewelyn Moss (Josh Brolin) stumbles upon a drug deal gone wrong and makes off with two million dollars, pursued by a cold-blooded contract killer.

The bulk of the film's running time is devoted to the peril of Moss's attempt to escape, but an important stylistic question to ask is: how is the final demise of the main character narrated? Consider also Stanley Kubrick's *Full Metal Jacket*. What sort of transition is there in this film between the oppressive boot camp opening and the later scenes of conflict from the Vietnam War? Quentin Tarantino's *Reservoir Dogs* is a film based around a heist – but in narrative terms, where is the heist? Consider John Ford's *The Searchers*, where the Civil War veteran Ethan Edwards (John Wayne) leads a party in search of a young niece captured by Native Americans. But how does the viewer come to learn how long the eponymous searchers have been away from home? Finally, in Tomas Alfredson's *Let the Right One In*, Oskar is a neglected and bullied young boy. At one point, his bullies attempt to drown him in a swimming pool, but the viewer comes to discover that he is assisted by the arrival of the vampire, Eli. How is this discovery narrated?

Donald
Hardy

TRANSITIVITY AT WORK: A FEMINIST-STYLISTIC APPLICATION

D6

Activity ✪

This reading is a famous feminist-stylistic application of the model of transitivity where Deirdre Burton uses the framework to explore relationships of power in a passage from Sylvia Plath's semi-autobiographical novel *The Bell Jar*. Burton argues provocatively for a political dimension in textual interpretation and suggests that links between literary analysis and political standpoint can be articulated clearly through systematic and principled methods of analysis – precisely the sorts of methods that are offered by stylistics. Before you read Burton's article, you should refamiliarise yourself with the basic model of transitivity as outlined in A6.

One further note of contextualisation is necessary on the reading that follows. When Burton wrote her paper, the transitivity framework was to some extent in its infancy and in the intervening years the model has undergone various revisions and refinements, a natural progression which has been reflected in subsequent work in stylistics. One important revision was the addition of 'behavioural processes', a category which, as noted in A6, sits at the interface between material and mental processes. Although this type of process does not feature in the version of the model used by Burton, its absence is compensated for to some degree by an expanded interpretation of material processes. This expanded category draws a primary distinction between *event* processes, where the Actor is inanimate (as in 'The lake shimmered'), and *action* processes, which are performed by an animate Actor. Action processes may themselves be further subdivided into *intention* processes, where the Actor performs the process of doing voluntarily and *supervention* processes, where the process of doing just happens. Thus, while a process like 'Mary kissed Clare' is clearly material-action-intention, a process like 'The boy coughed loudly' is (arguably) accidental and would therefore be coded as material-action-supervention. Figure D6.1 is a network which

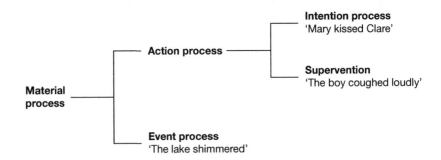

Figure D6.1 Subdivision of material processes in Burton's study

explains the way material processes are subdivided in Burton's study. Of course, the problem with a classification that relies on judgments about 'intention' is that in the absence of full contextualisation we can never really know whether or not a particular action was done accidentally or deliberately. For this reason, these subdivisions for material processes dropped out of later versions of the transitivity model, just as the category of behavioural processes came progressively more to the fore.

Although I have not attempted to alter to the newer framework any of the original classifications in Burton's study, it is important to bear in mind that her study draws on just one version of a theoretical model that has proved popular in stylistics. Indeed, her study is a good exemplum of the 'three Rs' at work because it is *rigorous*, its methods are *retrievable* and its analysis can be *replicated* using different versions of the same analytic model.

Through glass darkly: through dark glasses. On stylistics and political commitment – via a study of a passage from Sylvia Plath's *The Bell Jar*

Deirdre Burton

Deirdre Burton (reprinted from Ronald Carter (ed) *Language and Literature: An Introductory Reader in Stylistics* London: George Allen and Unwin, 1982: 195–214)

[. . .] The piece of prose fiction I am going to consider in some detail is a short passage from Sylvia Plath's autobiographical novel *The Bell Jar*. It is a passage which details her experience of electric-shock treatment as a 'remedy' for severe depression. Readers may care to look ahead at this point, to where the text is given, in order to contextualise general points made here. Essentially, I will be analysing aspects of clause construction and, in a preliminary reading of the passage, readers may find it useful to pay specific attention to the simple question 'who does what to whom?'.

Here, then, I want to consider two issues as preliminaries to that analysis. First, I want to map out a model of some relevant features of clause construction in general, against which any text can be charted, and our Plath text will be charted. Secondly, I want to discuss why this type of analysis is particularly relevant to the issues raised in the introduction, and similarly why this specific text was chosen for analysis.

D6

Deirdre
Burton

The model of processes and participants in the structure of clauses that I shall draw here is adapted from ideas in the work of Halliday (1970, 1973, 1978). Let me quickly try to explain why processes and participants are a strong place to begin analysis [...]. If the analyst is interested in 'making strange' the power relationships that obtain in the socially constructed world – be it the 'real' world of public and private social relationships or the spoken and written texts that we create, hear, read, and that ultimately construct us in that 'real' world – then, crucially, it is the realisation of *processes* and *participants* (both the actors and the acted upon) in those processes that should concern us. Ultimately, I want to suggest, with Sapir (1956), Whorf (1956) and Volosinov (1973 [1930]), that the 'world' is linguistically constructed. But rather than a crude Whorfian view, which might lead us to believe that we are trapped and constrained by that linguistic construction, I want to suggest a far more optimistic line of thought. Simply, once it is clear to people that there are alternative ways of expressing 'reality', then people can make decisions about how to express 'reality'; both for others and themselves. By this means, we can both deconstruct and reconstruct our realities to an enabling degree.

And this brings me to an explanation of why the Plath text seemed peculiarly appropriate to a feminist-linguistic polemic.

Where the topic of 'women and literature' is concerned, there are three immediate areas of thought and study that are being researched:

(1) Images of women in literature written by males – particularly in relation to details of social history. This is, of course, work that draws upon, and contributes to, a 'new' feminist version of that history. (See Rowbotham, 1973a, 1973b.)
(2) Images of women in literature written by feminist women. This may well involve finding them in the first place. (See Showalter 1977; Rich 1977)
(3) Images of women in literature by women who were not/are not feminists – either by 'free' choice, or because they were unaware that that choice was available to them.

Sylvia Plath's work and life can clearly be seen in relation to the third point here. Reading her prose, poems and letters, and reading about her, in the context of the raised consciousness and women's support groups of the 1970s and 1980s, is a moving, and disturbing, experience. It is so easy for us to locate her contradictions, dilemmas and pressures as they are expressed by her texts. It is so easy to see her writing herself *into* a concept of helpless victim, and eventually, perhaps, into suicide itself. Her texts abound in disenabling metaphors, disenabling lexis, and – I wish to demonstrate here – disenabling syntactic structures.

[...] I want to assert the importance of perceiving those sorts of forces, pervasive in the language around us, and would maintain that both individuals and social institutions require analytical access to knowledge about the intricacies of the relationship between linguistic structures and reality, such that, with that knowledge, reality might be reconstructed in less damaging ways – and again, I would emphasise, with regard to both individuals and social institutions.

Deirdre
Burton

I do not, by any means, wish to suggest that only women 'are' victims, or construct themselves as such. If this were a text written by a man (and there are, of course, similar texts), then it would be open to similar sympathetic analysis and discussion. However, that seems to me to be a job for somebody else to do, given that life is short and we must follow our immediate priorities. My general message is: stylistic analysis is *not* just a question of discussing 'effects' in language and text, but a powerful method for understanding the ways in which all sorts of 'realities' are constructed through language. For feminists who believe that 'the personal is political' there is a burning issue which has to be investigated immediately, and in various triangulated ways. We want to understand the relationships between severe and crippling depression that many women experience and the contradictory and disenabling images of self available for women in models of literature, the media, education, folk notions of the family, motherhood, daughterhood, work, and so on. [. . .] Any reader with any other radical political commitment should see what follows as a model to appropriate and to be made relevant to his or her own convictions. [. . .]

On reading the passage, readers repeatedly formulate the following sorts of responses:

(1) the persona seems quite helpless;
(2) the persona seems 'at a distance', 'outside herself', 'watching herself', 'detached to being with – and then just a victim';
(3) the medical staff seem more interested in getting the job done than caring.

In order to understand something of what is happening in the language of this passage, that gives rise to such responses, the following instructions enable us to get a firmer grasp of the persona's 'reality' as constructed in the clause-by-clause make-up of the text as a whole:

(1) isolate the processes *per se*, and find which participant (who or what) is 'doing' each process;
(2) find what sorts of process they are, and which participant is engaged in which type of process;
(3) find who or what is affected by each of these processes.

First, then, here is the text with sentences numbered for ease of reference, and processes isolated and italicised.

THE TEXT

(1) The wall-eyed nurse *came* back. (2) She *unclasped* my watch and *dropped* it in her pocket. (3) Then she *started tweaking* the hairpins from my hair.

(4) Doctor Gordon *was unlocking* the closet. (5) He *dragged out* a table on wheels with a machine on it and *rolled* it behind the head of the bed. (6) The nurse *started swabbing* my temples with a smelly grease.

Deirdre
Burton

(7) As she *leaned over to reach* the side of my head nearest the wall, her fat breast *muffled* my face like a cloud or a pillow. (8) A vague, medicinal stench *emanated* from her flesh.

(9) 'Don't worry,' the nurse *grinned* down at me. (10) 'Their first time everybody's scared to death.'

(11) I *tried to smile*, but my skin *had gone stiff*, like parchment.

(12) Doctor Gordon *was fitting* two metal plates on either side of my head. (13) He *buckled* them into place with a strap that dented my forehead, and *gave me a wire to bite*.

(14) I *shut* my eyes.

(15) There *was* a brief silence, like an indrawn breath.

(16) Then something *bent down* and *took hold* of me and *shook* me like the end of the world. (17) Whee-ee-ee-ee-ee, it *shrilled*, through an air crackling with blue light, and with each flash a great jolt *drubbed* me till I *thought* my bones *would break* and the sap *fly out* of me like a split plant.

(18) I *wondered* what terrible thing it *was* that I *had done*.

(Plath 1986 [1963]: 151–2)

Given this simple skeleton analysis, we can abstract out the Actors in each process, and spell out the lexical realisation of each of the processes associated with them:

Sentence No.	Actor	Process
1	nurse	came back
2a	nurse	unclasped
b	nurse	dropped
3	nurse	started tweaking
4	doctor	was unlocking
5a	doctor	dragged out
b	doctor	rolled
6	nurse	started swabbing
7a	nurse	leaned over to reach
b	nurse's body part	muffled
8	nurse's body contingency	emanated
9a	n.a.	n.a.
b	nurse	grinned
10	n.a.	n.a.
11a	persona	tried to smile
b	persona's body part	had gone stiff
12	doctor	was fitting
13a	doctor	buckled
b	doctor's equipment	dented
c	doctor	gave . . . to bite
14	persona	shut
15	–	was
16a	something (electricity)	bent down and took hold

b	something (electricity)	shook
17a	something (electricity)	shrilled
b	electricity part	drubbed
c	persona	thought
d	persona body part	would break
e	persona body part	fly out
18a	persona	wondered
b	–	was
c	persona	had done

The analysis is simple, but the resultant table above gives access to a clear, general picture of who is doing what and when in the persona's description of the 'world' around her. The first half of the text gives the Nurse and Doctor performing all actions (1–10). We have a brief mention of the persona as Actor (11), and then the Doctor and his equipment dominate the action (12, 13). We have another brief mention of a negative persona as Actor (14), the electricity as Actor in a very positive sense (16–17) and finally the persona as Actor – in a hypothetical sense at least. We shall be able to say more about the types of process below. A simple counting of Actors and their actions shows us very little:

> nurse (including body parts) as Actor: 8
> doctor (including his equipment) as Actor: 7
> electricity as Actor: 4
> persona (including body parts) as Actor: 7

This is interesting in view of the often expressed pre-analytic response, 'the persona doesn't *do* anything'. Clearly, we can see what readers 'mean' when they say that, but we have to pursue the analysis further, and rephrase the response to capture the 'reality' of the text. What this analysis does lay bare is the *succession* of Actors in the scene. The Nurse, for example, drops out after sentence 9, although she has certainly played the major part in the action till then (eight clauses out of eleven), and has been the focus of the persona's (and therefore our) attention. The Doctor, his equipment and the persona interact together, then he drops out and is superseded by a succession of clauses where the 'something' takes over very forcefully. Finally the persona is left acting alone.

Charting through the *types* of processes involved allows us much more room for discussion:

1	nurse came back = material-action-intention
2a	nurse unclasped = material-action-intention
b	nurse dropped = material-action-intention
3	nurse started tweaking = material-action-intention
4	doctor was unlocking = material-action-intention
5a	doctor dragged out = material-action-intention
b	doctor rolled = material-action-intention
6	nurse started swabbing = material-action-intention

7a	nurse leaned over to reach	= material-action-intention
b	nurse's body part muffled	= material-action-supervention
8	nurse's body contingency emanated	= material-event
9a	n.a.	
b	nurse grinned	= material-action-intention
10	n.a.	
11a	persona tried to smile	= material-action-intention
b	persona's body part had gone stiff	= material-event
12	doctor was fitting	= material-action-intention
13a	doctor buckled	= material-action-intention
b	doctor's equipment dented	= material-action-supervention
c	doctor gave . . . to bite	= material-action-intention
14	persona shut	= material-action-intention
15	- was	= relational
16a	something took hold	= material-action-intention
b	something shook	= material-action-intention
17a	something shrilled	= material-action-intention
b	something drubbed	= material-action-intention
c	persona thought	= mental-cognition
d	persona's body part would break	= material-action-supervention
e	persona's body part fly out	= material-action-supervention
18a	persona wondered	= mental-cognition
b	- was	= relational
c	persona had done	= material-action-intention

Deirdre
Burton

Here, the overwhelming fact revealed by the analysis is the definite preponderance of the selection of the option material-action-intention; twenty clauses out of thirty make this choice. A closer consideration brings out the following interesting features of the text. First, all the Nurse's actions are material-action-intention processes; though where the Nurse's body is the Actor we have supervention or event processes, so that the effect is of her deliberately carrying out determinate actions, in the persona's environment, while her body produces contingent, 'accidental', yet none the less substantial effects on her thought-world also. Similarly all of the Doctor's actions are material-action-intention processes, but, like the Nurse's body, his equipment produces effects on the environment tangentially, as it were. The electricity is also only represented in terms of material-action-intention processes. Thus, all three of these major Actor-participants are seen as overwhelmingly 'in control' of whatever events take place. They are presented and given as being in charge of the construction of the reality that the persona perceives and expresses.

But what of the patient herself? Her attempt at what is (technically) a material-action-intention process (11a) fails. Her related body-part action is similarly only an 'accidental' event, that is, beyond her control (11b). At sentence 14, she succeeds in a material-action-intention process but, whereas all the other actors are doing constructive, concrete tasks by that option, her contribution is to shut her eyes – to remove herself from the scene. At 17c and 18, she has the only mental-internalised-cognition processes in the passage – a fact which makes it absolutely clear that the piece

Deirdre Burton

is very much – and only – from her point of view. At 17d and e we are given two possible (but hypothetical) supervention processes for her body parts – so, again, material actions that are not part of the actual reality, but only subordinated possible outcomes of others' actions. And, finally (18c), her 'successful' material-action-intention process is located away in the past, in mysterious circumstances.

This further analysis, then, gives us a little more scope in the way of accounting for our understanding of the persona's conception of her world. The next analysis, which isolates who or what is affected by each process takes us a little further:

1	nurse affects ø by intention process
2a	nurse affects persona's possession by intention process
b	nurse affects persona's possession by intention process
3	nurse affects persona's possession by intention process
4	doctor affects equipment by intention process
5a	doctor affects equipment by intention process
b	doctor affects equipment by intention process
6	nurse affects persona's body part by intention process
7a	nurse affects persona's body part by intention process
b	nurse's body part affects persona's body part by intention process
8	nurse's body contingency affects ø by event process
9a	n.a.
b	nurse affects persona by intention process
10	n.a.
11a	persona affects ø by intention process
b	persona's body part affects ø by event process
12	doctor affects equipment by intention process
13a	doctor affects equipment by intention process
b	doctor affects persona and equipment by intention process
14	persona affects persona's body part by intention process
15	ø affects the environment by relational process
16a	something affects persona by intention process
b	something affects persona by intention process
17a	something affects ø by intention process
b	something affects persona by intention process
c	persona affects persona's body part by cognition process
d	persona's body part affects ø by supervention process
e	persona's body part affects ø by supervention process
18a	persona affects ø by cognition process
b	ø affects ø by relation process
c	persona affects ø by intention process (hypothetical)

Reading this skeleton gives us a firmer grasp of the abstract reality of the persona's world. Massively, it is the Nurse who affects both the persona's possessions and body parts (2a, 2b, 3, 6, 7, 8) and, in one instance, the whole of her (9b). The Doctor, on the other hand, uses his intention processes to affect equipment (4, 5a, 5b, 12, 13a,

Deirdre
Burton

13c) and, in one localised area, via the persona's body part (13a) and the equipment (13b), the persona herself (13c). At this point he disappears from her world view. The electricity, not surprisingly, continually affects the whole persona (16a, b, 17a, b).

And the patient herself? At 11a she affects nothing – despite her intentions. At 11b her body part affects nothing. At 14 she successfully affects her own body – but remember that this is her escapism clause. At 17c she again 'successfully' carries out a cognition process on her own body – but remember that the resultant effect is only hypothetical. At 17d and e, 18a and c, the remaining clauses which have the persona as Actor, the persona and her body parts still affect nothing at all.

This third analysis, then, gives us a much neater and more delicate way of addressing ourselves to readers' responses. Obviously we could discuss much more in this text, and I do not mean to suggest that this is a 'full analysis'. Nevertheless, by pursuing these important sets of related features in this way, we have begun to refine our understanding of the 'reality' presented by this text. [. . .]

To sum up let me offer the following programme of eight points, which I see the teacher of stylistics as pursuing. It assumes students with an interest in literature in general, but little or no linguistic knowledge. Points 1–4 are, I take it, uncontentious; points 5–8 are offered as a programme for radical stylistics.

(1) Stylistics can be part of a programme to enable students to handle competently a coherent and comprehensive descriptive grammar, which can then be used in either literature-oriented studies, or linguistics-oriented studies.
(2) It is always at least a 'way in' to a text.
(3) It can shift discussion to awareness of effects that are intuitively felt to be in a text in the process of reading it, and a contingent 'making strange' of those effects and feelings simultaneously. It is towards 'knowing how' as well as 'knowing that' (Ryle 1949).
(4) It can spell out a shared vocabulary for describing the language of any text – whether those effects are straightforward or ambiguous.
(5) Crucially, stylistics can point the way to understanding the ways in which the language of a given text constructs its own (fictional) reality.
(6) It should then point the way towards understanding the ways in which language constructs the 'reality' of everyday life – and an awareness that always *must* do so. So that, in a sense, everyday 'reality' can usefully be seen as a series of 'fictional' constructs – as texts open to analysis and interpretation in just the same way as texts marked out for literary study are.
(7) This would lead to an awareness of the importance of perceiving the constituent parts of the fictions we live *in* and *by*, if only to map them against alternative constructions of reality.
(8) Finally, this would lead to an understanding that the fictions (both large and small) that we live in and by can be rewritten. Both individually and collectively. As reform or revolution, whichever is more appropriate.

As for my title? See it as notes for a poem, on Sylvia Plath, Women, Feminism, Radical Stylistics, academic work in general. Optimistic notes.

Issues to consider

As with a number of the scholars whose work constitutes Section D, Burton raises many areas for further stylistic investigation in the course of her article. However, you might wish to consider additionally the following issues:

⭐ **Activity**

❏ Burton uses a version of the transitivity model that has been partly reworked in subsequent linguistic research. A useful exercise is to comb through the Plath text using the version of the analytic model presented in A6 and B6, concentrating in particular on Plath's use of *behavioural processes* (as they relate to the persona's actions) and on her use of *meronymic agency* (as it relates to her depiction of the nurse).

❏ Rewrite the paragraph from *The Bell Jar* from the point of view of either the Nurse or the Doctor, staying as close as possible to the words of the original text. What overall changes to the transitivity profile are brought about by your rewrites? What sorts of processes now dominate? Look again at these rewrites once you have completed unit 7, on point of view. To what extent do your rewrites involve a realignment in the visual perspective of each of the characters in the scene?

❏ Since Burton's study, certain critical theorists have suggested that feminism has given way to a so-called 'post-feminist' era. Using the transitivity model, you could evaluate this claim by looking at other texts by and/or about women. Are there any novels or short stories that you have read which portray women through what Burton calls 'disenabling' patterns of language, whether metaphorical, lexical or grammatical in design? Is Burton's feminist-stylistic polemic as viable today as it was on its publication in 1982?

D7 STYLE VARIATION AND POINT OF VIEW

Like many readings in this D section, Mick Short's essay achieves a number of useful goals. First of all, it demonstrates how a focussed analysis of patterns of language can open the way for the critique and interpretation of a challenging literary work. Second, it develops in more detail the particular aspect of stylistic organisation, point of view, which has been elaborated across this strand. And third, it illustrates how the stylistic analysis of prose fiction can – and should – make appeal to varied levels of language organisation and not just to one textual pattern in isolation.

More specifically, Short examines the use of graphological deviation as an indicator of viewpoint in Irvine Welsh's novel, *Marabou Stork Nightmares*. After providing an interpretative summary of its plot line (see unit A5), Short explores the narrative structure of Welsh's novel which, unusually, comprises three interwoven 'levels' of narration, all produced by the same narrator. Although graphological deviation is normally seen as the preserve of stylistic experimentation in poetry, Short's analysis, which is orientated principally towards the opening of the novel, demonstrates how prose fiction can draw on this level of language for stylistic effect. Short also develops in a theoretically more rigorous way some of the terms, such as *viewpoint*, *focaliser* and *reflector*, which have been used across this strand.

The work of Irvine Welsh featured in unit C2 where a passage from *Trainspotting* formed the principal focus of attention. This Scottish writer is renowned, indeed infamous, for his grimly realistic portrayals of criminal counter-cultures and of the social consequences of violence and drug addition. With its sociolinguistic code the lower status urban vernacular of Edinburgh, and its frequent mixing of levels and structures of language, Welsh's work is challenging, often disturbing and at times unsuitable, as it were, for the stylistically faint-hearted. Nevertheless, and as Short's analysis demonstrates, the writing of this novelist pays many useful dividends in stylistic terms.

Graphological deviation, style variation and point of view in *Marabou Stork Nightmares* by Irvine Welsh

Mick Short (reprinted from *Journal of Literary Studies/Tydskrif vir Literatuurwetenskap*, 1999, 15, 3/4, 305–23).

Mick Short

Introduction

In this article I want to provide an account of Irvine Welsh's *Marabou Stork Nightmares* (1995), based mainly on a representative stylistic analysis of the opening of the novel. I have chosen to concentrate on this rather bizarre and disturbing novel because, in spite of its horrific qualities, I think it has considerable intrinsic artistic merit (something which I hope my analysis will begin to show). [. . .]

[B]elow I will give an interpretative summary of the novel, to which I will then link a stylistic commentary of its opening. But for those who have not already read the novel, it will be helpful to experience how the novel begins [see Figure D7.1] without such explanation (I have numbered the sentences for ease of reference).

An interpretative summary of Marabou Stork Nightmares

Irvine Welsh is probably best-known for *Trainspotting*, a novel about the drugs culture in Britain which was also made into a highly successful film. In *Marabou Stork Nightmares*, drug-taking is a minor theme, but the subject-matter of the novel is also extremely distasteful. [. . .] The I-narrator is a young Edinburgh Scot who is lying in hospital in a coma, caused, as we discover towards the end of the novel (on p. 255 of a novel which ends on p. 264), by a failed suicide attempt. He had tried to kill himself – while watching a video of his favourite football team (the Edinburgh side, Hibernian FC, or 'Hibs') – using the pain-killer, paracetamol, and a plastic bag over the head, as recommended in a book he had read called *Final Exit: The Practicalities of Self-Deliverance and Assisted Suicide for the Dying*.

If the passage above was your first experience of *Marabou Stork Nightmares*, you may have found it initially difficult. This is because the events of the story are presented out of chronological sequence, and in an apparently piecemeal and disorganised fashion by an unconscious narrator who is in a vegetative state. At the outset of the novel he is fantasising about himself and an imaginary friend, Sandy Jamieson, who

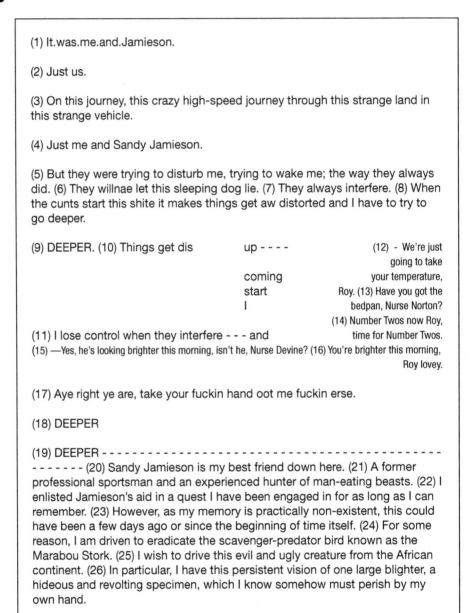

(1) It.was.me.and.Jamieson.

(2) Just us.

(3) On this journey, this crazy high-speed journey through this strange land in this strange vehicle.

(4) Just me and Sandy Jamieson.

(5) But they were trying to disturb me, trying to wake me; the way they always did. (6) They willnae let this sleeping dog lie. (7) They always interfere. (8) When the cunts start this shite it makes things get aw distorted and I have to try to go deeper.

(9) DEEPER. (10) Things get dis   up - - - -   (12) - We're just
going to take
coming   your temperature,
start   Roy. (13) Have you got the
I   bedpan, Nurse Norton?
(14) Number Twos now Roy,
(11) I lose control when they interfere - - - and   time for Number Twos.
(15) —Yes, he's looking brighter this morning, isn't he, Nurse Devine? (16) You're brighter this morning,
Roy lovey.

(17) Aye right ye are, take your fuckin hand oot me fuckin erse.

(18) DEEPER

(19) DEEPER - (20) Sandy Jamieson is my best friend down here. (21) A former professional sportsman and an experienced hunter of man-eating beasts. (22) I enlisted Jamieson's aid in a quest I have been engaged in for as long as I can remember. (23) However, as my memory is practically non-existent, this could have been a few days ago or since the beginning of time itself. (24) For some reason, I am driven to eradicate the scavenger-predator bird known as the Marabou Stork. (25) I wish to drive this evil and ugly creature from the African continent. (26) In particular, I have this persistent vision of one large blighter, a hideous and revolting specimen, which I know somehow must perish by my own hand.

Figure D7.1 Extract from *Marabou Stork Nightmares*: Irvine Welsh (1995: 3–4) are supposedly in South Africa on an extraordinary 'quest' to kill the Marabou Stork. To make matters even more difficult for the reader, there are three distinct 'levels' of narration in the novel, through which the I-narrator, Roy Strang, is continually shifting/being shifted by external intervention. The deepest level is the South African fantasy narration concerning his hunt for the Marabou Stork, and the highest is one where the narrator is aware of what is going on around him in the Edinburgh hospital as he drifts towards consciousness (something which is never fully achieved, but which he gets closer to as the novel proceeds). The middle level is a rather jumbled, and sometimes contradictory, account of Roy Strang's life leading up to his attempted suicide, his resulting vegetative state (which he has been in for two years) and his eventual death at the end of the novel.

It could be argued that the novel has three distinct narrations, where the same narrator tells three stories at the same time, but I prefer to call them three *levels* of narration because (a) they all have the same narrator and the same 'default' narratee (the reader), (b) as the novel proceeds, the narrative levels 'interact' and reflect one another more and more and (c) there is textual evidence (see below) to suggest that we are meant to see the three narrations as a series of connected levels. The top level and the middle level are, in any case, part of the same general fictional world (what Ryan 1991 would call the 'text-actual world'), the top level coinciding with what appears to be the narrator's coding time ('what is happening to the I-narrator in his fictional now') and the middle level being what happened to the I-narrator/what the I-narrator did in his fictional past. The deepest level of narration is distinct from the other two in that it is a fantasy (what Ryan 1991: 119 calls a 'fantasy-universe'). But the connections and correspondences between it and the two levels of the text-actual world are so many that they begin to interpenetrate, and become 'explanations of one another', as we will see below.

The movements from one level of narration to another, sometimes forced by external stimuli and sometimes by connections made within the mind of the narrator, are clearly meant to be representative of a mind drifting towards, and away from, consciousness. Our major tasks as readers, then, are (a) to work out when we are in which narrative level, and why, (b) to construct a characterisation and narrative structure for the text which explains how Roy Strang came to be in a coma and (c) to make sense of the connections which become apparent among the different levels of narration, many of which do not become clear until the last few pages of the novel. For example, on p. 255, when the suicide attempt is being described, the footballer on the video, who is gesticulating at the referee, is called Jimmy Sandison, allowing us to see that Sandy Jamieson, Roy's friend in the Marabou Stork fantasy, is an imaginative metathetic creation derived from the footballer's name, something we have been prepared for by the fact that on occasion the I-narrator 'mis-refers' to Sandy as 'Jimmy' (e.g. p. 169). In Ryan's terms, then, Roy Strang's fantasy universe is clearly prompted by the text-actual world in which he lives. [. . .]

When Roy is ten, the family emigrates to South Africa [. . .] [b]ut the dream of a new life for the family in South Africa is not realised. John Strang is jailed for attacking a taxi-driver when drunk, and the rest of the family returns to Edinburgh a year and a half after they had emigrated. For Roy, who [. . .] has his father's love for nature, and

D7

for wild animals in particular, the South African period was a very mixed experience. His uncle, a paedophile, secretly abuses him, forcing him into both oral and anal sex, but at the same time showers him with presents, including wonderful trips to safari parks to see the animals.

As a young man, Roy has a good job working for an insurance company as an IT specialist, but in his spare time he satisfies his now ingrained thirst for violence as a member of a 'casuals' football gang who fight other such gangs. It is this activity which results in his eventual downfall. He and his pals gang-rape a young woman called Kirsty, also forcing her to have anal and oral sex with them. These activities are reminiscent of what Roy's uncle forced him to do in South Africa, and, in his fantasy universe, (a) of what he 'sees' his girlfriend doing with his fantasy friend, Sandy Jamieson, near the beginning of the novel (p. 5) and (b) the various distasteful activities of a businessman in the fantasy called Lochart Dawson, a figure who resembles Roy's uncle Gordon in a number of ways. Ironically, it later transpires that, unbeknown to Roy, Kirsty was romantically attracted to him at the time he raped her.

The gang is arrested, but at their trial they are all acquitted through the adversarial skills of an experienced lawyer who, at the same time is clearly very unsympathetic to the young men. Roy's initial account of the rape depicts him as an unwilling participant, something which later appears not to be true, but which helps to suggest his growing sense of guilt. [. . .]

In the last few pages of the novel, Kirsty secretly visits Roy in hospital. Her experience of the rape and the humiliation of the trial make her want to take systematic revenge on those who raped her. She has already killed one of the gang, and now she proceeds to kill Roy by stabbing him with a pair of scissors, after first removing his eyelids, and then cutting of his genitalia and stuffing them into his mouth. This process parallels both her own rape and the other events referred to above, in the text-actual world and Roy's fantasy universe, which I have already said are reminiscent of that rape.

And what of the Marabou Stork? As the novel proceeds, the leader of the Marabou Storks which Roy is hunting in his fantasy universe accrues more and more connections with Roy himself in his remembered text-actual world. In that world, he sees Marabou Storks for the first time, with his father, when his uncle Gordon, who has already systematically abused Roy sexually, takes the family to the Kruger National Park. Roy sees the Storks destroy and eat some pink flamingos, and that night he has his 'first Marabou Stork nightmare' (p. 74). As a young boy, then, he is a victim, the equivalent of the flamingos, and uncle Gordon is the oppressor, the equivalent of the Marabou Stork. But when Roy describes Kirsty immediately after the rape (p. 190), he does so in terms which resembles the damaged flamingos, and by extension he has also changed status from flamingo to Marabou Stork. After the rape he has more nightmares in which he clearly associates Kirsty with the flamingos, and himself and his friends with the Storks (pp. 221, 233). Roy's pursuit of his personal Marabou Stork in his fantasy universe thus appears to be a subconscious attempt to come to terms with, and defeat, his own evil. But he never destroys the Stork, never really catches up with it. And indeed, at the moment of his death, when his fantasy universe and the text-actual world finally coincide on the last page of the novel (p. 264), he clearly sees himself as the Marabou

Stork: 'Captain Beaky, they used to call me at school . . . I spread my large black wings
. . .' This coincidence of narrative levels means that he dies at the same time in both
his fantasy universe and the text-actual world. This is indicated by the fact that people
and objects from the fantasy universe and the text-actual world are now represented
as if they are in the same textual world. He is both stabbed by Kirsty in the Edinburgh
hospital and shot by his erstwhile fantasy friend in 'South Africa', and his nurse can
do nothing to help:

> I can move my lidless eyes, I can see my cock dangling from my mouth and I can see the
> scissors sticking out from my neck. . . . Patricia runs to get help but she's too late because
> Jamieson's facing me and he's pointing the gun and I hear it going off and it's all just one
> big
>
> # Z.

The novel thus ends with a final marked graphological device using a letter which is
conventionally associated with sleep, and hence, by extension, death. However, the
normal comfortable associations for sleep are minimised here as a consequence of the
fact that in the previous twenty-three pages (i.e. from p. 241 onwards) graphologically
marked forms of this letter have systematically been associated with the 'Z' of the posters
in the Zero Tolerance campaign against rape and sexual oppression. In real life, this
campaign has had a considerable impact in Edinburgh in recent years and, in the
fictional world of the novel, Roy's exposure to the posters is partly responsible for his
increasing feelings of guilt. Whether, as the blurb on the back cover of the paperback
suggests, these feelings of guilt and Kirsty's final treatment of him amount to a final
'redemption' is, however, not so clear. [. . .]

A stylistic commentary on the opening passage in relation to the rest of the novel

It will be apparent from the discussion above that *Marabou Stork Nightmares* has an
extremely distasteful subject matter, which could deter some from reading it. But it is
also an extremely interesting novel. In particular, it is sophisticated narratologically,
and this complex narratological structuring has well-worked-out interpretative
consequences. This narratological innovation is, in turn, signalled/controlled through
considerable linguistic invention, which we can now explore through a detailed
examination of the novel's opening.

The novel opens with what in the 20th century has become a fairly standard *in
medias res* device, presenting what must be new information to the reader as if it were
given information, to draw the reader into seeing events from the narrator's viewpoint
and with his ideological assumptions. However, the technique is taken to quite an
extreme here. In the first four sentences we are not told who the narrating 'I' is,
who Sandy Jamieson is, where the characters are, or what exactly they are doing.
And in spite of the repeated use of the quasi-deictic natural spoken narrative use of
'this' in sentence (3), we do not know what journey they are on, or why it is crazy,
which land they are in, or why it is strange, and what vehicle they are in, and why that

vehicle is strange. These matters become a bit more clear in sentences (20)–(26), but Africa is not narrowed to South Africa until p. 13 of the novel, when it can be deduced from a small child offering sexual services 'for rand.' We are thus made to struggle hard for coherence. The issue of the identity of the vehicle mentioned in (3) is even more problematic. It is referred to as a jeep on p. 2, and this assumption holds for a while, but by p. 8 it has apparently become some sort of aircraft, probably a helicopter. It is this sort of changing and contradictory characterisation which leads the reader to assume that we are being presented with some sort of fantasy universe.

In addition to the oddities of the given-new structure, the first few sentences of the text are characterised by syntactic and graphological oddity. Sentences (2)–(4) are minor sentences grammatically and are also separated from one another by line-spaces. Sentence (1) is grammatically complete, and has the standard narrative past tense, which leads us to assume this tense as a background default for the next three minor sentences. But sentence (1) is also very deviant orthographically, full stops separating the words instead of spaces. Indeed, this oddity caused a problem for me when I numbered the sentences for ease of presentation. Should what I have labelled as sentence (1) really be represented as five separate sentences? I decided not to do this because the first five words form a grammatically normal English sentence and only the sentence-initial word and the final word, a proper name, begin with upper case letters.

These features need explanation, although it would be impossible for a reader to find a satisfactory one from the first few sentences alone. In content terms, they are, of course, sentences describing the narrator's fantasy universe which I outlined above, and once we have deduced that the narrator must be in a coma, we can relate the minor sentence construction, the stops among the words in the first sentence and the line spaces among the other sentences as indicative of a mind having some difficulty in getting going at the beginning of the narration: they thus represent mental disjunctions, which, like the deviant given-new information structure, can be put down to a mind struggling to cope.

GRAPHOLOGICAL DEVIATION AND STYLE VARIATION

In spite of the minor sentence syntax, the first four sentences would appear to be reasonably characterised as Standard English. However, there is a switch in sentences (6)–(8), within the first orthographically normal paragraph, to the representation of a non-standard Scots dialect. Later on in the novel, when we know where the narrator comes from, we will be able to characterise this dialect as working class Edinburgh Scots. The orthographic indicators of a Scots dialect are 'willnae' for 'won't', 'shite' for 'shit' and 'aw' for 'all' [see C2 – P.S.]. This indication of a pronunciation change also corresponds with the introduction of a rude scatological vocabulary ('shite', 'cunts').

This marked style shift also needs explanation, of course. What appears to happen is that the real Roy Strang, as yet un-named, begins to appear in these sentences, where, note, the tense has also changed from past to present. When Roy 'speaks' in his fantasy narration, however, he uses a Standard English which is at the same time marked as belonging to a kind of upper class between-the-wars RAF Biggles-speak, which is parodic of what might be called the 'English of Empire'. The only clear indicators of this style in the passage quoted in 1 above are the narrator's reference to his friend by last name only, and the word 'blighter' in sentence (26). But in the following page of text the word 'blighter' appears again, along with 'Wizard!' (meaning 'great!'), 'Yuk!', 'yukky' and 'a cunning but somewhat morally deficient native fellow'. This pattern of 'Biggles-speak' for the fantasy universe narration and Edinburgh Scots for the text-actual world narrations is used consistently throughout the novel and helps to contrast brutal reality with a wish-world (see Ryan 1991: 117–18) which the narrator appears to be struggling towards but does not properly achieve mentally, let alone physically.

So far I have studiously avoided discussion of sentence (5), which begins the paragraph I have been discussing. Its tense is consistent with that of the first four sentences, and there are no orthographic indications of Edinburgh Scots. But it is orthographically connected to the Edinburgh Scots narration, and the unanchored, given-information use of 'they' also coheres better with the 'they' of sentences (6)–(7) and 'the cunts' of (8) than with sentences (1)–(4). Indeed, in the fantasy universe narration, sentences (1)–(2) appear to rule out the possibility of reference to individuals other than the narrator and Jamieson. Sentence (5) thus appears to be a transition sentence which moves the reader from one level of narration to the next. It also indicates something which is true throughout the novel, namely that it is not possible to associate particular tenses exactly with particular levels of narration. Although the text-actual world in the narrator's 'coding-time fictional present' is usually accorded the present tense, and the fantasy universe narration and the narration of the text-actual world in the narrator's past are mainly in the past tense, there are 'janus-faced' sentences like (5) from time to time, and there are also some other textually strategic tense shifts within the default tense for a particular narrative level.

GRAPHOLOGICAL DEVIATION AND VISUALLY SYMBOLIC EFFECTS

The narrator's response to what he sees as interference by the as yet non-specific outsiders is to 'try to go deeper'. This phraseology is then used as the trigger for the first of a series of 'graphology-symbolic' representations which can be found throughout the novel, and which provide textual evidence for the notion, which I introduced above, that the different narrations are best seen as levels of the same narration. As I said, the narrator represents the unfolding of his fantasy universe as the deepest level of narration, and that of his presently experienced coding time as the highest. In the opening to the novel which I am concentrating on, there is no clear representative of the middle level, the narrator's past in the text-actual world (although, interestingly, the narratorially ambivalent sentence (5) could be seen as relating to this middle level as well as to the other two). A clear characterisation of this middle level in relation to the other two can be seen on pp. 48–9, for example.

The first 'graphology-symbolic' movement between the narratorial levels of the novel (sentences (9)–(19) of the passage) is complex, as a result of the fact that it contains an upward movement embedded inside a downward one. Elsewhere, in more simple cases, when the narrator moves down a level, this is usually represented symbolically by the word 'DEEPER' in capitals repeated on three successive lines. A series of dashes of varying length occur after the final 'DEEPER', apparently representing the size of the mental pause between the effort to go deeper and the resumption of the lower (in this case fantasy universe) narration. Sometimes, as here, the instances of 'DEEPER' are directly under one another. On other occasions they are 'raked' rightwards down across the page as in:

DEEPER

        DEEPER

                DEEPER

Although the normal representation involves a three-fold repetition of the word, larger or smaller repetitive sequences sometimes occur, appearing to indicate the amount of effort needed to move between levels. For example, the narrator needs a sequence of nine raked repetitions of 'DEEPER' on p. 40 to stop thinking about the attractive Nurse Devine (a play on 'divine') and get back to his fantasy.

Not surprisingly, when the narrator moves upwards between narrative levels, the words go up the page, sometimes vertically, as in the passage we are discussing, and sometimes raked from left to right. In the passage under discussion the reader needs to go down five lines from the uncompleted word 'dis' to 'I lose control . . .' in order to read up and then down again through the block of nurse-talk on the right-hand side of the page. Note also here the effect of sentence (10) ending in the middle of a word as Roy struggles unsuccessfully to stay in his fantasy universe. In context it would appear that the uncompleted word is 'disturbed' or 'disrupted', and so 'dis' is itself graphology-symbolic (note the lack of a final hyphen – as in 'din-', which would normally be used in writing to indicate an interrupted item).

A further graphology-symbolic effect that can be seen in (9)–(19) relates to font and type-size. Sentences (12)–(16) are in a different and considerably smaller type face than those surrounding them. These sentences, with their stereotypical euphemisms and friendly vocatives, clearly represent a conversation between two nurses, Nurse Norton and Nurse Devine who also 'interact' with Roy as they care for him. This conversation is important for us in beginning to make sense of the movements among narrative levels in the novel, and we also glean the name of the narrator from their conversation. The change in type size is thus an appropriate foregrounding device for the reader. But it also appears that the particular size (smaller than the surrounding type) can be seen as representative of Roy's viewpoint relation to what they say. They interrupt his fantasy universe thoughts, causing him to rise up through the narrative levels, but at the same time they appear to be less important or less vivid for him than what he 'hears' inside his head. This symbolic use of type size and related features like capitalisation is a feature to be found throughout the novel. For example, on p. 15, when his parents are leaving after a visit, their farewells ('CHEERIO SON! CHEERIO ROY!') are in capitalised small print to represent an increase in volume and pitch variation compared to the rest of their speech (cf. also the exclamation marks). But the fact that even the capitalised words are still in the smaller type size indicates their lack of interest from Roy's perspective.

In the novel's opening passage, Roy 'responds' to what the nurses say with his most dialectally marked sentence in the passage ((17) 'Aye right ye are, take your fuckin hand oot me fuckin erse.'). Six of the twelve words are non-standard in some way, and three of them are also taboo words. When Roy uses 'fucking' in his fantasy universe it is spelled normally, but here the spelling indicating a dialect pronunciation omits the final 'g' and does not even signal its omission by the conventional apostrophe. But in spite of the anger of Roy's response, there is no indication that the nurses hear him. There is no indication that those in the hospital hear him anywhere else in the novel either, so we must assume that (17), and sentences like it, must be Direct Thought, not Direct Speech (see Short 1996: Ch. 10).

Elsewhere in the novel, graphological foregrounding devices like capitalisation, italicisation, unusual spellings and so on are also often used within this Direct Thought mode to indicate simultaneously Roy's dialect and the strength of his attitude:

– Awright son!
AW FUCK! *THIR* HERE.

(p. 10)

In this section, although my analysis has not been exhaustive by any means, I hope to have shown that graphological deviation and patterning and style variation are important factors in how viewpoint shifts, and in particular how movements among the levels of narration are controlled in the opening to *Marabou Stork Nightmares*. Indeed, the use of graphological deviation to signal viewpoint occurs in a number of his works, and so can be seen as part of Irvine's overall style. Moreover, the features seen in the opening passage of *Marabou Stork Nightmares* are representative of, and also explained by, what happens in the rest of the novel. Perhaps one final point to note is that sentence (23) ('However, as my memory is practically non-existent, this could have been a few days ago or since the beginning of time itself.') is one of a number of clear indications in the novel, both in its direct statement and the accompanying hyperbole, that the narrator is unreliable. This correlates with the extraordinary movements we have seen in the rest of the passage, and with the fact that the narrator does not always face reality direct in the rest of the novel. For example, as I have already pointed out, he first characterises his role in the rape of Kirsty as less bad than it really is, and nowhere in the novel does he appear to be able to confront his own evil directly, having to resort instead to the symbolic quest to kill the Marabou Stork in his fantasy universe.

[...]

Marabou Stork Nightmares is an extraordinary novel. Its extremely distasteful subject-matter and the attitudes of the characters portrayed will be enough to dissuade many from reading it at all. But I hope to have shown that it also has considerable artistic interest in general narratological terms, in its linguistic detail and the inter-relations between this linguistic detail and the larger-scale narratological structuring. [...]

Issues to consider

It is important to reiterate that the scope of Mick Short's article is wide-ranging and that it makes many general points of interest for narrative stylistics. In this respect it ties in directly with the issues covered both in this strand and in strand 5 on narrative structure.

Some suggestions follow.

❒ **Activity** ❏ On the basis of Short's analysis, to what extent can you align the various narrative techniques he uncovers in Welsh with the six-part model of narrative proposed in A5? Are all the features he uncovers readily positioned in the model or are further categories or expansions to the model warranted?

❏ Graphological effects are more commonly associated with poetry than with prose fiction, although Laurence Sterne's *Tristram Shandy*, published in the eighteenth century, is the first novel in English to make extensive use of symbolic graphological representation. If you have read the novel, to what extent are the techniques of analysis developed by Short applicable to Sterne's narrative? What other works of prose fiction do you know of that employ graphological deviation and to what sort of stylistic effect?

❏ 'Orientational metaphors' are used to express emotional states through physical direction, as in GOOD IS UP, BAD IS DOWN and so on (see further thread 11). To what extent can the graphologically symbolic patterns in Welsh be considered orientational metaphors? In terms of the narrator's orientation, which narrative level – the higher, middle or lower – is the positive preference? For example, does 'up' necessarily equate with 'good' in the discourse world of *Marabou Stork Nightmares?*

THE EFFECTS OF FREE INDIRECT DISCOURSE

The focus of this reading, by Joe Bray, is on techniques of speech and thought presentation in fiction and as such it complements well the themes explored across this strand. The reading is also a good example of a practice common in modern stylistics: the use of classroom activities and reading tasks as a support to analysis and interpretation. Asking others for their reactions to a particular piece of text can often be illuminating and both in this instance and in unit C8 across the strand, the speech and thought categories are explored by groups of undergraduate students. While Bray's tests are admittedly informal in design, they nonetheless help consolidate the sorts of conclusions drawn from the stylistic analysis.

Bray's main interest is in the stylistic effects of that intriguing mode of speech and thought presentation, Free Indirect Discourse. As we saw in unit B8, FID is an important term that subsumes the two categories of Free Indirect Speech and Free Indirect Thought. It is generally assumed that the speech variant of this mode (FIS) often imbues the discourse with a sense of irony because the intervention of the narrator marks a shift away from the immediacy of the character's directly reported speech. By contrast, the thought variant (FIT) is often believed to engender a feeling of empathy in the reader because it moves him or her closer to the assumed workings of a dynamic and functioning mind (see, for example, McHale 1978: 275; Leech and Short 1981: 334). In the context of the historical development of the novel, the 'norm' for the presentation of a character's thought processes had been Indirect Thought. This was because the portrayal of the inner thoughts of a fictional character demands, after all, a great deal of artistic licence (see A8). Against this framework, then, the narrative transition into the more free-flowing FIT mode signals immediacy, proximity and, arguably, empathy. Bray's focus in this piece is on this issue of empathy in FID, and his analysis is supplemented by a small-scale reading test based on passages from Fanny Burney's *Camilla* (1796) and Tom Wolfe's *I am Charlotte Simmons* (2004).

The Effects of Free Indirect Discourse

Joe Bray (reprinted from 'The Effects of Free Indirect Discourse: Empathy Revisited'. In Lambrou, M. and Stockwell, P. (eds) *Contemporary Stylistics* London: Continuum, 2007: 56–66)

Joe Bray

This chapter argues that, in the context of free indirect discourse, empathy [. . .] needs to be considered as, at least in part, a construction of the reader, rather than as an intrinsic feature of the text. After some consideration of critical approaches to the term itself, I discuss a small-scale reading task designed to investigate whether FID does evoke empathy in readers. Originally from the German 'einfühlung', 'empathy' is defined by the *OED* as 'the power of projecting one's personality into (and so fully comprehending) the object of contemplation'. The term began to be used with this sense of 'projection' in German aesthetics at the turn of the century (see Lipps 1900), and soon spread into psychology, where it became linked to the concept of 'identification' (see Zillmann 1994: 34–5, 39–40). As Kuno puts it, 'Empathy is the speaker's identification, which may vary in degree, with a person/thing that participates in the event or state that he describes in a sentence' (Kuno 1987: 206). Yet recent critics have been sceptical about the possibility of 'identification' in the reception of art. In his discussion of empathetic responses to film, Tan notes that 'identification in a literal sense is characterized by the viewers' experience of the very same emotion that the character is imagined to have' (Tan 1994: 24). He then describes some problems with this notion:

> The viewers' presumed sharing of concerns is the difficult part of the identification concept. For viewers to share completely the concerns of the character in his or her situation would mean that they do not understand or imagine those concerns, but have them – an obviously impossible situation. Incomplete sharing of concerns makes it doubtful whether viewers can have emotions similar to the imaginary ones of the character.
>
> (Tan 1994: 24–5)

Tan concludes that 'we can, at best, assume that it is possible for viewers to imagine actually having a concern, which in turn results in an experience that parallels the

Joe
Bray

character's "emotion" as closely as possible', and that 'all in all, it seems doubtful whether there is any use at all for the concept of identification in describing film viewing and concomitant emotion' (1994: 25). He proposes an alternative model of empathy, according to which 'the viewers are led to imagine themselves an *invisible witness* in the fictional world', and claims that 'the witnesses' situation is completely analogous to that of the observer in the real world, who is neither called upon to intervene nor physically able to react' (1994: 16–17). Thus an 'empathic emotion', for Tan, is simply one in which the viewers 'relate to' the character's experience of the fictional world. This brings 'empathy' closer to its related term 'sympathy'; Tan claims that 'most, though not all, empathic emotions are sympathetic, that is, they depend on a basic sympathy concern' (1994: 23). In fact the terms have often been used interchangeably, as Oatley observes, 'under the heading of sympathy, empathic processes have received much attention and have been scrutinized by numerous scholars' (1994: 39). 'Sympathy' has usually been defined as fellow feeling rather than 'einfühlung'; one of the senses in the *OED* is 'the quality or state of being affected by the condition of another with a feeling similar or corresponding to that of the other' (*OED*, 3b). Philosophers of 'sympathy' have often emphasized the ways in which it differs from 'identification'. For Adam Smith in *The Theory of Moral Sentiments*, for example, the crucial point about our sympathy with others is that it can never give us direct access to their feelings. He argues that:

> as we have no immediate experience of what other men feel, we can form no idea of the manner in which they are affected, but by conceiving what we ourselves should feel in the like situation. Though our brother is upon the rack, as long as we ourselves are at ease, our senses will never inform us of what he suffers. They never did, and never can, carry us beyond our own person.
>
> (Smith 1976: 9)

As Griswold observes of Smith's theory, 'sympathy does not dissolve the sense of separateness of either party' as 'in no case of sympathy [. . .] do we simply identify with the other' (1999: 88).

It is clear then that the term 'empathy' can involve a range of meanings; from 'identification' at one end of the continuum to 'sympathy' at the other. The relationship between these three feelings, and the ways in which they are generated by literary texts, have rarely been investigated empirically, as [Kuiken *et al.*] observe, 'although narrative feelings are most frequently discussed by object-relations theorists [. . .], the effects of empathy, identification, and their associated narrative feelings have not been systematically examined in empirical studies' (2004: 175) [. . .]

The task focuses specifically on the representation of thought since, as noted above, FIT is more commonly associated with empathy than FIS. Extracts from two novels were chosen: Frances Burney's *Camilla* (1796) and Tom Wolfe's *I Am Charlotte Simmons* (2004) (hereafter *Charlotte*). The task therefore also tests whether there is a difference in the response of readers to a relatively early example of the style, when it was just beginning to enter into the English novel in extended form, and to a contemporary example over 200 years later, by which time FIT has become an omnipresent feature of the novel. Despite the historical difference, there are similarities between the two texts. *Camilla* is often cited as an example of the 'novel of manners', a genre in which the leading character (usually female) enters into society and is forced to negotiate its complexities, frequently stumbling into embarrassing situations along the way [. . .]. Charlotte Simmons is similarly plunged into a new and bewildering social world as she starts life at Dupont University, a fictional American college. Like Camilla, she is forced to learn how to deal with being pursued aggressively by a series of unsuitable men.

The passages chosen for the task from the two novels both involve the heroine reflecting on an awkward recent experience with the opposite sex in which she feels she has compromised herself beyond all hope of repair. Below are the passages as they were given to the subjects (with some brief context in square brackets). I have numbered the sentences for ease of reference.

Extract 1A

[Camilla's admirer, Sir Sedley Clarendel, has given her a gift of £200, in order to help her penniless brother Lionel. Her first thought was to return the money at once, but Lionel has seized the cheque and she now fears she is in Sir Sedley's debt]

(1) Camilla was too much confounded either to laugh or explain, and hastily wishing them good-night, retired to her chamber.

(2) Here, in the extremest perturbation, she saw the full extent of her difficulties, without perceiving any means of extrication. (3) She had no hope of recovering the draft from Lionel, whom she had every reason to conclude already journeying from Tunbridge. (4) What could she say the next day to Sir Sedley? (5) How account for so sudden, so gross an acceptance of pecuniary obligation? (6) What inference might he not draw? (7) And how could she undeceive him, while retaining so improper a mark of his dependence upon her favour? (8) The displeasure she felt that he should venture to suppose she would owe to him such a debt, rendered but still more palpable the species of expectation it might authorise.

Extract 2A

[Charlotte Simmons, a fresher at Dupont University, has been to her first fraternity party the night before, at which one of the coolest students on campus, Hoyt Thorpe, spent much of the evening with his arm around her]

(1) Well past ten o'clock the next morning, Charlotte was still in bed, lying flat on her back, eyes shut . . . eyes open . . . long enough to gaze idly at the brilliant lines of light where the shades didn't quite meet the windowsill . . . eyes shut . . . listening for sounds of Beverly, who occasionally sighed or moaned faintly in her sleep . . . eyes open, eyes shut, running the night before through her mind over and over to determine just how much of a fool she had made of herself. (2) She was at her most vulnerable, her most anxious, during this interlude between waking and getting up and facing the world . . . which she knew, but that didn't make the feeling any less real . . . how could she have let

him keep *touching* her that way? (3) Right in front of everybody! (4) Right in front of Bettina and Mimi! (5) She had fled the Saint Ray house without even trying to look for them . . . walked back to Little Yard through monstrous shadows in the dead of the night. (6) How could she ever look them in the eye?

There are significant differences between the type of FIT in each passage, perhaps reflecting the development of the style in the centuries that separate the two. In the first example the proximal deictic 'Here' in sentence 2 is the first sign that Camilla's point of view is about to enter into the narrative, though this sentence otherwise remains the narrator's report. In sentence 3, 'She had no hope of recovering the draft from Lionel' appears to be the character's opinion, though 'whom she had every reason to conclude already journeying from Tunbridge' reintroduces the narrator's perspective (a free indirect version would be 'who was surely already journeying from Tunbridge'). The next four questions (sentences 4–7) are clearer examples of FIT, coming from Camilla's point of view while retaining the third person and past tense of the modal verbs ('could', 'might'). Yet in sentence 4 the deictic expression 'the next day' suggests the narrator's perspective rather than the character's, indicating that free indirect thought has not fully emerged from narratorial control (a 'freer' version would be 'What could she say tomorrow to Sir Sedley?'). The lingering presence of the narrator is also indicated by the formal lexis ('so gross an acceptance of pecuniary obligation'). Sentence 8 appears to return to indirect thought. Throughout the passage then the character's and narrator's perspectives are hard to untangle, perhaps reflecting the fact that the style is still in its early stages of development in the late eighteenth-century novel, and not yet being commonly used for the extended representation of a character's thoughts.

In the example from *Charlotte* (Extract 2A), on the other hand, FIT seems freer from narratorial control. Sentence 1 starts from an external perspective, until the ellipses take us inside Charlotte's barely conscious thought processes. Her perception is implied in 'the brilliant lines of light where the shades didn't quite meet the windowsill', and it is clearly her opinion that she has 'made a fool of herself'. Sentence 2 seems to start as narratorial comment, yet the ellipsis again marks a transition to Charlotte's perspective. It is her judgement that the feeling is 'real', and the following question is clearly FIT, with the italics emphasising her mortification at what she sees as the most incriminating aspect of the evening. The lack of verbs in the following exclamations (sentences 3 and 4) suggests direct thought, as the passage slips into interior monologue. In sentence 5 ellipsis is again used to suggest a transition to Charlotte's perspective, with 'monstrous shadows in the dead of the night' indicating her overheated Gothic imagination. Sentence 6 returns to unambiguous FIT. In comparison with the example from Camilla then, this extract contains more sophisticated techniques for representing the character's thought processes, and less narratorial intrusion, giving the impression that Charlotte's thoughts and feelings are being represented with more directness.

Half the subjects in the reading task received the passages 1A and 2A given above. The other half read the following versions, in which instances of FIT were rewritten as indirect thought (IT) (subjects were supplied with the same context in square brackets):

Joe
Bray

Extract 1B

(1) Camilla was too much confounded either to laugh or explain, and hastily wishing them good-night, retired to her chamber.

(2) Here, in the extremest perturbation, she saw the full extent of her difficulties, without perceiving any means of extrication. (3) She realized that she had no hope of recovering the draft from Lionel, whom she had every reason to conclude already journeying from Tunbridge. (4) She wondered what she could say the next day to Sir Sedley. (5) She was unsure how she would account for so sudden, so gross an acceptance of pecuniary obligation, and was concerned about the inference he might draw. (6) In addition she did not know how she could undeceive him, while retaining so improper a mark of his dependence upon her favour. (7) The displeasure she felt that he should venture to suppose she would owe to him such a debt, rendered but still more palpable the species of expectation it might authorize.

Extract 2B

(1) Well past ten o'clock the next morning, Charlotte was still in bed, lying flat on her back, intermittently opening her eyes long enough to gaze idly at the brilliant lines of light where the shades didn't quite meet the windowsill, and listening for sounds of Beverly, who occasionally sighed or moaned faintly in her sleep. (2) As she continued to doze she ran the night before through her mind over and over to determine just how much of a fool she had made of herself. (3) She knew that she was at her most vulnerable, her most anxious, during this interlude between waking and getting up and facing the world, but that didn't make the feeling any less real. (4) She was incredulous and mortified that she had let him keep touching her inappropriately, right in front of everybody, especially Bettina and Mimi. (5) She had fled the Saint Ray house without even trying to look for them, and walked back to Little Yard through monstrous shadows in the dead of the night. (6) She wondered how she would ever be able to look them in the eye again.

It should first be noted that in keeping with the relative absence of the narrator in the passage 2A, the transposing of lA into 1B was easier than 2A into 2B. For example, 'What could she say the next day to Sir Sedley?' can be rendered relatively unproblematically in IT as 'She wondered what she could say the next day to Sir Sedley', whereas 'How could she have let him keep *touching* her that way? Right in front of everybody! Right in front of Bettina and Mimi!' requires more invention to convey the strength of feeling. I eventually decided on two adjectives ('incredulous and mortified'), though other indirect versions are of course possible and equally valid.

Twenty-four subjects completed the task. All were second or third-year under-graduates at the University of Sheffield, and native speakers of English. Fourteen were reading English Literature and ten English Language and Literature. All were female; it was supposed that male readers might experience a different (not necessarily lesser) degree of empathy to the heroines in these examples. A future experiment testing the responses of male readers to the same passages could obviously yield interesting comparisons. All subjects were asked if they had read either novel; none had. Twelve were given passage 1A and twelve 1B. In a different combination twelve read 2A and

Joe
Bray

twelve 2B. All subjects therefore read one passage from *Camilla* and one from *Charlotte.* Below each passage the subjects were asked the following:

> Rank on a scale of 1–10 how close you felt to the character Camilla/Charlotte while reading this passage (10 = I felt I was in her position, 1 = I couldn't understand why she was making such a fuss).

> Comment below on the features of the language of the passage that led you to your ranking.

I decided to ask the subjects about their 'closeness' to the character rather than use the more specific term 'empathy' for three reasons. I was worried that the latter might confuse subjects who were not sure of its meaning, or, worse, lead them to ask me for an exact definition. Second, I was interested in whether, unprompted, they would use the term (or related terms such as 'sympathy' or 'identification') in their comments. Finally, as some of the subjects would have come across specific discussion of free indirect discourse and its effects on their course, I feared that the term 'empathy' might trigger a recognition of free indirect discourse and lead to a more self-conscious response than would otherwise have been the case. In fact only one subject mentioned FIT in her comments, and this did not seem to affect her perception of her closeness to the character (see below). Though it is of course true that 'closeness' is not synonymous with 'empathy', the use of a scale of 'closeness' from 1 to 10 (with 1 representing a complete lack of 'sympathy' and 10 the traditional definition of 'identification') does reflect the range of the term 'empathy' in the critical literature.

Based on most criticism of FID, my hypothesis was that the passages from the two novels containing FIT (1A and 2A) would evoke more feelings of closeness than those without FIT (2A and 2B). I also predicted that the difference between responses to 2A and 2B would be greater than that between 1A and 1B, since, as discussed above, 1A is a less 'free' form of FIT than 2A and contains more signs of the narrator's presence. Finally, given that the subjects were all university students and may have encountered similar experiences to Charlotte it was supposed that overall the empathy for Charlotte would be greater than that for Camilla, whose predicament seems more particular to that of an eighteenth-century heroine and less obviously relatable to student experience.

The subjects were given up to ten minutes to make their rankings and comment on the two passages. The average ranking for each passage was as follows:

Camilla	1A:	5.96
	1B:	4.75
Charlotte	2A:	7.08
	2B:	6.5

First it is not surprising that more empathy was experienced as a whole for Charlotte than for Camilla; the indirect version from *Charlotte* evoked more empathy than the FIT version from *Camilla.* Also as expected was that in the case of both novels the passages containing FIT generated more empathy than those without, though in both cases the difference is quite small. If empathy is the predominant effect of FIT, one would have expected the differences between the rankings for passages A and B in both cases to have been greater. It was also surprising that the gap was greater for the *Camilla* examples than the *Charlotte* ones (1.21 vs 0.58), given that, as discussed above, passage 2A seems a 'freer' form of FIT. Some possible explanations for these unexpected results are discussed below.

The subjects' comments in response to the second part of the task turned out to be as, if not more, revealing than their rankings. Four responses included the word 'empathy' or 'empathise', with another five referring to 'sympathy' and its derivatives and two to 'pathos'. The difficulty of experiencing these feelings was a recurring theme, however. In particular, ten subjects cited the high register of the *Camilla* passages as a barrier to empathy. For example, in response to passage lA one subject wrote, 'Use of fairly high register – Latinate words – perturbation, extrication, pecuniary – distanced me harder to read and respond/empathise'. Five of those who read passage lB commented on the use of the third person rather than the first as affecting their response, with one writing for example that [it] 'is written in 3rd person so doesn't feel like a 1st-hand experience/personal experience'. However, this reader nevertheless ranked her 'closeness' to Camilla as 6, and another who described the 'measured and logical' style of the narrator as 'slightly distancing' added that 'the feelings do seem believable so I felt quite a lot of empathy', and also gave a ranking of 6. Somewhat paradoxically, a subject who commented on the combination of the third person in passage lA with the questions which provide 'a sense of her feelings' ranked her 'closeness' as 3, and the subject who noted the use of free indirect thought added that there are 'no real comments about her feelings', and gave a ranking of 5. The recognition of the presence of both narrator's and character's perspectives in passage IA, in other words, does not seem to result automatically in a higher degree of empathy.

Similarly, of those who read passage 2A, few commented on the relatively direct way in which the character's thoughts were represented. One subject, who ranked her 'closeness' to Charlotte as 8, did observe that the passage was 'more like stream of consciousness, exclamation marks and "..." help to add to tension and bring the situation alive', while another, who gave a ranking of 7, noted that 'writer logs her thoughts, e.g. "Right in front of everybody!" – makes the reader feel closer to the character as are able to enter character's thoughts'. In general though, observations on the language of 2A tended to be accompanied by a comment on its relevance to student experience. Thus one subject wrote that 'the fractured language represents her thoughts and the fact that this piece is relevant to student life makes it more accessible'. Five subjects said they could 'relate' more to Charlotte, either because of her 'age' or 'the situation', with one commenting that the passage represents a 'frequent female experience'. Similarly, several responses to lA and lB mentioned the unfamiliarity of Camilla's situation; one subject, who gave a ranking of 5, wrote that 'Gender, social conditions influence the relationship with the character', while another, who gave a ranking of 3, simply noted 'Never been in that situation'.

In other words, despite the instruction to focus on 'features of language', the amount of empathy that subjects felt for the two characters often seemed to depend, from the evidence of their comments, on non-linguistic factors. Even when the language was thought to evoke empathy, rankings could be swayed by other influences. Thus a subject who noted of passage lB that 'use of omniscient narrator rather than 1st person made it more difficult to empathise', gave a ranking of 7 on the basis that 'her situation definitely arouses pity'. The same subject then ranked her 'closeness' to Charlotte in 2A as 5, revealingly commenting that:

> The language makes it easier to empathise as more dramatic words like 'vulnerable' are used, and the more colloquial style allows the reader to identify with her more (perhaps because it is more modern), but the situation is not as serious.

This reading task represents a preliminary investigation only of the effects of FID, and clearly much more empirical work is required. Its findings do suggest, however, that though 'empathy' may indeed be an effect of FIT, it may not be as pervasive and as defining a feature of the style as critics have tended to assume. The degree to which readers feel 'close' to characters in literary texts may, at least on the evidence of the responses given here, depend less on the language of a particular passage than on a reader's assessment of the 'seriousness' of 'the situation', and its relevance to his/her own life. Most criticism of the effects of FID is based on the textual interaction of narrator and character that results from its supposed 'dual voice'. This task suggests, however, that the way readers respond to FIT is more complex than has been supposed, and that empathy is not generated automatically. In particular, it seems that formal features may be overridden by non-linguistic considerations, including the extent to which the reader can 'relate' to the character represented.

Issues to consider

In keeping with the principles adopted in the present book, Bray's study of style makes use of transposition as a way of conceiving how a literary text might otherwise have been wrought. And in probing informants' reactions to the original and to the 'tweaked' texts, his study asks as many questions as it answers. For instance, in spite of the prevailing orthodoxy in narrative stylistics about the effects of FID and the attribution to FIT of empathy, Bray's reading tests suggest that readers may feel 'close' to characters on the basis of their assessment of the 'seriousness' of the situation in which the characters find themselves. The technique of FIT may therefore be only one determinant of empathetic responses to fictional characterisation.

Some suggestions follow.

 ❏ In view of the outcomes of Bray's reading tests, think about how you might develop a similar experiment to probe the assumed *ironic* effects of free indirect speech. There are of course very many writers who use FIS in stylistically innovative ways, but consider as a starting point the following passage from Nabokov's *Lolita*:

> Hardly had the Farlows gone than a blue-chinned cleric called – and I tried to make the interview as brief as was consistent with neither hurting his feelings nor arousing his doubts. Yes, I would devote all my life to the child's welfare. Here, incidentally, was a little cross that Charlotte Becker had given me when we were both young.

> I had a female cousin, a respectable spinster in New York. There we would find a
> good private school for Dolly. Oh, what a crafty Humbert!
>
> (Nabokov 1986 [1955]: 99–100)

This passage, which incidentally is analysed in Leech and Short (1981: 329), clearly contains, in between its first and last sentences, a sequence of reported speech. Transpose this speech into the DS mode, adding in reporting clauses ('I said', 'I added' and so on) where appropriate. You should now have two versions of the text, which differ in stylistically interesting ways. If you decide to conduct a reading test with the two passages, make sure that any questions you ask avoid the term 'irony' – just as Bray avoided the expression 'empathy' in his tests. You could probe the extent to which readers felt that the first person narrator, Humbert Humbert, was being sincere, serious or honest in his interaction with the 'blue-chinned cleric'. Any descriptions of the FIS version as 'ironic' will therefore be unprompted by your questions. By the way, what would you do in your transposition with the final sentence of this extract?

❏ In the context both of the preceding exercise and of the ironic and sometimes comic effects of FIS, examine the techniques of speech presentation used in the opening paragraph of unit B12 in this book.

❏ Bray's article also touches on the differences between first-person narration and 'omniscient' third-person narration. This raises wider issues to do with the way speech and thought is presented in these two narrative modes. Consider the following extract from a novel by Roddy Doyle, where the first-person narrator, Paula Spencer, delivers a seemingly unambiguous affirmation of love and commitment to her husband Charlo:

> I had nothing going for me. I was only Paula Spencer because of him. It was the only
> thing I was. People knew me because of him. We had the house because of him. I
> was there because he looked at me and proved it. One nice look could wipe out
> everything. I loved him with all my heart. I could never leave him. He needed me.
>
> (Doyle 1998: 211)

On the face of it, this seems like a straightforward narrative report, by Paula, of her thoughts and feelings about her husband. However, look now at the last line of this same paragraph where the full import of Paula's pronouncement becomes fully clear:

> He told me so, again and again. I was everything to him.
>
> (Doyle 1998: 211)

This final sequence confirms that the narrative 'voice' of the paragraph has not been Paula's, but that of her violent and abusive husband. Can you identify what mode of speech has been in use in the first extract? And can you transpose it into a FDS version, where the utterances of the speaker are presented in an unmediated way by the first-person narrator?

Joe
Bray

The novel from which these fragments have been taken is Doyle's *The Woman who Walked into Doors* – a bleak portrayal of domestic abuse and isolation. On the basis of your analysis, is there a case for arguing that Charlo's brutalisation of Paula even extends to the colonisation of the very voice of his wife? (See Simpson [2010: 297–8] for a short analysis of this text.)

D9

MULTIMODAL ANALYSIS AND THE STYLISTICS OF DRAMA

This is another reading which opens up the potential of stylistic analysis in different ways. With its focus on the discourse of drama dialogue, McIntyre's article very obviously complements the themes developed in the units across this strand. However, McIntyre's study also adopts a *multimodal* approach, which means that the more familiar stylistic analysis of verbal text is supplemented by a parallel analysis of the other features of discourse that surround it. The importance of multimodal analysis, not just for stylistics but for language study generally, is that it covers the totality of a text's meaning-making structures as opposed to its linguistic organisation only (see Kress and van Leeuwen 2001; Forceville 1996; Machin and Mayr 2012). Broadcast advertisements, for instance, are rarely composed solely of verbal text but are normally complemented by a visual storyline and, often, a musical score. Multimodal stylistics therefore approaches literary texts in a similar way, in terms (where relevant) of the texts' full range of compositional and organisational structures (see the applications in, for example, Busse 2010; Nørgaard 2010a; Page 2010).

In this article, McIntyre explores multimodal aspects of the soliloquy scene from Ian McKellen's film version of Shakespeare's *Richard III*. Where stylistics has traditionally focussed on the analysis of dramatic texts rather than dramatic performances, McIntyre's position is that no two performances of the same text are entirely alike, so accurate critical discussion is impossible unless everyone has seen the particular performance analysed. This problem is exacerbated when a particular performance of a play incorporates production elements that add substantially to the original play script and arguably guide our interpretation of the play. However, McIntyre's position is that in the case of plays that have been filmed, this methodological problem can be circumvented because the film version constitutes a permanent record of a particular production of the play in question. McIntyre bases his stylistic analysis on a transcript that incorporates linguistic and non-linguistic elements of the production. Importantly, he also covers *paralinguistic* features of communication, which include variations in voice quality (such as loudness, tempo or pitch) as well as non-vocal signals like the nodding or shaking of the head to signal assent or disagreement. McIntyre concludes that multimodal elements of the production contribute to our interpretation of the play as much as the linguistic elements of the dramatic text.

A little more context is necessary here on the range of models that McIntyre employs in his study. In addition to his analysis of the pragmatic and discoursal features of the play dialogue (of the sort undertaken across this strand), McIntyre also draws on concepts from film studies. He is particularly interested in *mise-en-scène*, which is the broad term for all the elements placed in front of the camera. Shadowing the categories in Bordwell and Thompson (2001: 156), McIntyre explores the following *mise-en-scène* techniques in the soliloquy: setting, costume, lighting and staging. This exploration is supplemented by recourse to work on the grammar of visual design, notably that of Kress and van Leeuwen on the structure of visual images (Kress and van Leeuwen 2006). Echoing the transitivity model set out in unit A6, the terms Actor and Goal are often employed in multimodal analysis when a visual 'proposition' has two participants. According to Kress and van Leeuwen (2006: 62), a visual proposition can be recognised by the existence of *vectors*. Vectors are lines which connect the participants and our understanding of the visual grammar of a scene is predicated upon our ability to determine these lines. While the idea of vectors is useful and is touched upon in the present reading, McIntyre and others have expressed significant reservations about the visual grammar model. These reservations centre on the model's lack of attention to the unfolding context of film narrative, to the dynamic and changing roles of participants in film, and to the sequential progression in which a frame or scene is embedded (see further McIntyre 2008: 316–17; Forceville 1999: 172).

Integrating multimodal analysis and the stylistics of drama: a multimodal perspective on Ian McKellen's *Richard III*

Dan McIntyre (reprinted from *Language and Literature*, 2008, 17, 4, 308–34)

Dan McIntyre

In order to demonstrate the feasibility of [a multimodal approach to drama], in this article I present an analysis of the famous soliloquy scene (beginning 'Now is the winter of our discontent . . .') from Ian McKellen's 1995 film version of Shakespeare's play, *Richard III*. I argue that the production and performance elements of the film are as integral to this particular version of the play as the dialogue, and that to account for a reasonable interpretation of this version of the play, it is necessary to consider the relationship between the linguistic and the non-linguistic elements of the production, what Elam (1980: 209) calls the 'complex of reciprocal constraints' that exist between dramatic texts and performances. In so doing, I also make some suggestions as to a method for integrating linguistic and non-linguistic elements in the stylistic analysis of drama.

[. . .] Bearing in mind the importance of context in analysing film, it is worth beginning with some background information concerning the film in general.

The 1995 film version of *Richard III* stars Ian McKellen as Richard and differs from more traditional productions of the play by setting the action in a fictionalised 1930s Britain where fascism is rife. This updating of the story is a powerful way of bringing to the fore the unsettling characteristics of Richard and the film received many positive reviews in the press at the time of its release. One of the most obvious differences between McKellen's film version and the traditional stage play is in the staging of the famous opening soliloquy. Rather than Richard performing this alone, in McKellen's version he addresses the soliloquy to an audience at a glamorous party held in a palace ballroom. The soliloquy comes immediately after the opening credits of the film, which appear over a variety of shots of partygoers dancing and laughing. Jazz music is playing and the party is in full flow. Having greeted several of the guests, Richard limps to the stage and signals for the band to stop playing. He then steps up to the microphone and begins his speech. At just 34 lines the soliloquy is shorter than that of the folio text but incorporates three lines from *Henry VI Part III* (in bold). The soliloquy as it appears in McKellen and Loncraine's (1996) screenplay is reproduced below (dialogue lines are numbered for ease of reference and screen directions are indicated in italics):

Scene 16

Int. Ballroom – The Palace – Night.

[. . .] The whole company turns toward Richard, as he clears his throat and scratches the mesh of the singer's microphone.

Richard

Now is the winter of our discontent   [1]
Made glorious summer by this son of York!

Richard toasts the smiling new King. King Edward regally acknowledges the laughter and applause of his family, friends and national leaders from politics and commerce.

Richard (*continuing*)

And all the clouds that loured upon our house
In the deep bosom of the ocean buried.
Now are our brows bound with victorious wreaths;   [5]
Our bruised arms hung up for monuments;
Our stern alarums changed to merry meetings,
Our dreadful marches to delightful measures.

Applause as Richard smiles. The popular war leader is working well in these civilian surroundings.

Hastings smiles, satisfied; the Archbishop looks benignly content.

The appreciative audience misses Richard's irony, with the exception of Buckingham, who listens intently and quizzically, puffing on his Havana and sipping his Napoleon 5-star.

Richard (*continuing*)

Grim-visaged war has smoothed his wrinkled front:
And now, instead of mounting barbed steeds,   [10]
To fight the souls of fearful adversaries
He. . .

Scene 17

Int. Washroom – The Palace – Night

Dan
McIntyre

*Richard flings open the door of the stately lavatory and makes for the WC cubicle, past the
ornate, carved mirrors above the deep washstands, with their gold taps and luxurious selection
of towels, brushes, soaps and lotions. In the distance, the Dance Band plays 'A Delightful
Measure'.*

Richard (*continuing*)
. . . capers nimbly in a lady's chamber,
To the lascivious pleasing of a lute.
But I, that am not shaped for sportive tricks,   [15]
Nor made to court an amorous looking-glass,
I, that am rudely stamped –
Deformed, unfinished, sent before my time
Into this breathing world, scarce half made up,
And that so lamely and unfashionable   [20]
That dogs bark at me, as I halt by them:

Richard pulls the chain and emerges to wash his hand.

Richard (*continuing*)
Why, I, in this weak piping time of peace,
Have no delight to pass away the time,
Unless to spy my shadow in the sun,
And descant on my own deformity.   [25]

*Richard looks in the mirror at his blasted, sagging, left profile, the Brylcreemed hair smooth
over his alopeciaed dome. He dries his right hand. . .*

Richard (*continuing; his lips scarcely move as he addresses both himself and the camera
through the mirror*)

Why, I can smile; and murder while I smile;
And wet my cheeks with artificial tears
And frame my face to all occasions!
And, therefore, since I cannot prove a lover,
I am determined to prove a villain   [30]
And hate the idle pleasures of these days.
Plots have I laid. . .

Scene 18
Int. Walkway – The Palace – Night
*As Richard returns to the celebrations he looks down from the cast-iron walkway that leads
back to the ballroom.*

Richard (*continuing to camera*)
To set my brothers, Clarence and the King,
In deadly hate, the one against the other.   [34]

(McKellen and Loncraine 1996: 59–65)

**Dan
McIntyre**

Appendix 1 (below, pp. 238–241) contains an audio-visual transcript detailing the main linguistic, paralinguistic and non-linguistic elements of the soliloquy scene. As can be seen from this transcript, one major difference between McKellen's version of the soliloquy and that of the folio text is that the former takes place in three different settings while the latter is performed by Richard alone in one location. Following line 12 in McKellen and Loncraine's (1996) screenplay, there is a cut from the palace ballroom to the interior of the men's bathroom in the palace, where Richard continues the soliloquy. In the screenplay, the final two lines of Richard's speech take place on a palace walkway, though in the film performance, this scene occurs outside, overlooking the landing stage where Clarence is being taken on board a military launch which will take him to the Tower of London.

The scene in the bathroom of the hotel is where Richard becomes aware of the implied presence of an audience, apparently noticing them in the bathroom mirror. This has the effect of changing the addressee of the soliloquy which, combined with a number of different camera techniques, has the consequent effect of enhancing Richard's deceitful and dangerous character. In the sections below I provide first a linguistic stylistic analysis of the soliloquy section of the screenplay and then an analysis of the multimodal aspects of it in McKellen's film. My aim here is to demonstrate that a solely text-based stylistic analysis does not capture the range of interpretative effects that the film version generates. [. . .]

If we concentrate solely on the linguistic aspects of the opening soliloquy, a stylistic analysis raises a number of interesting interpretative issues. Lines 1 and 2 comprise perhaps the play's most famous metaphor: 'Now is the winter of our discontent/Made glorious summer by this son of York'. Critical discussion of this line has often focused on who 'this son of York' actually is. Is Richard making a reference to himself, or does the phrase refer to one of his brothers? In the folio text, the fact that the soliloquy is intended to be performed by Richard while alone in a London street would seem to suggest that the reference is to himself. Support for this would be the fact that the demonstrative 'this' is a proximal deictic term which, when spoken by Richard, would suggest that the referent of the noun phrase is something close to Richard's deictic centre; in effect suggesting a third-person reference to himself. If we assume this to be the case then the logical conclusion we must come to is that Richard is responsible for the transformation of 'the winter of discontent' into 'glorious summer'. If this is the case, we must also assume that he has effected this purposefully and must consequently be pleased with the results. This, though, does not fit with Richard's later description of the situation as a 'weak, piping time of peace' (24). An alternative explanation is that 'this son of York' is a reference to either Edward or Clarence. This seems much more likely when we consider Richard's later behaviour in the play, since if we make this interpretation then Richard's attitude to the 'glorious summer' he describes becomes much more ambiguous. On the surface it would appear that he is happy about the change in fortunes for the York family, but when contrasted with his reference to a 'weak, piping time of peace', it seems that the reference to a 'glorious summer' is instead a sarcastic remark. This has the effect of characterising Richard as scornful and sardonic as opposed to the straightforward egotist that is suggested if we assume that 'this son of York' is a reference to himself and his own achievements. Hammond (1981) believes the pun on the homophone 'son' to be instrumental in defining who 'this son of York' refers to. He explains that this is likely to be Edward because 'Edward IV assumed the device of a sun as his emblem in consequence of the vision of three suns which appeared to him during the battle of Mortimer's Cross' (Hammond, 1981: 125). The two potential interpretations of line 2 give rise to different characterisations of Richard. As I have suggested above, one seems more probable than the other and this is likely to be brought out in a film (or stage) performance. ·

From line 14 onwards Richard explains his discontent with the peace that currently prevails. The contrastive 'but' of line 14 suggests that the personification of 'grim-visaged war' (9) cannot refer to Richard himself and is thus likely to refer to his brothers, Edward and/or Clarence. Spencer and Wilson, cited in Clemen (1957: 3), believe it to be Edward. The implicature deriving from the metaphor in line 9 is that Richard is not well disposed towards his brothers (assuming it is indeed Edward or Clarence who are responsible for the peace).

Richard's description of his physical appearance (lines 14 to 23) breaks the Maxim of Quantity (Grice, 1975) in that it provides more than enough information about how Richard looks. In terms of the discourse structure of the play-text (see Short, 1996; [and see unit A9 – P.S.]) this can be read as a flout at the level of playwright-to-reader, thereby acting as an intra-dialogic stage direction from which the actor and director can make a series of inferences about Richard's physical appearance. At the level of the character, however, this looks more like an infringement of the maxim. In a perform-ance, the audience would be well aware of Richard's looks, therefore the infringement of the Maxim of Quantity would seem to convey Richard's extreme bitterness about his appearance, as well as a narcissistic quality, thus revealing another aspect of his character. Further aspects of Richard's character and appearance are conveyed in the screen directions. For example, he 'flings' the lavatory door open, the verb suggesting an overly violent action and hence an outward display of extreme emotion. His physical appearance is described using negatively-charged evaluative adjectives (italicised): 'Richard looks in the mirror at his *blasted, sagging*, left profile, the Brylcreemed hair smooth over his *alopeciaed* dome.'

Finally, we can note that the status of lines 1 to 36 as a soliloquy give rise to certain expectations on the part of the reader. Culpeper and McIntyre (2006) suggest that:

> The main purpose of the soliloquy is to provide an outlet for self-expression on the part of the speaking character. This self-expression comes about partly because of the absence of other characters from the communicative act. The result of this is that characters are able to speak freely (without discounting effects), and this means that we can make a strong assumption that what characters say within a soliloquy is the truth as they believe it to be. In other words, most soliloquizers uphold Grice's (1975) maxim of quality.
>
> (Culpeper and McIntyre, 2006: 784)

For these reasons, we are to assume that in the folio text, all of what Richard says in the soliloquy is likely to be a true reflection of his feelings. As a multimodal analysis reveals, though, this is not necessarily the case in the McKellen version. [. . .]

**Dan
McIntyre**

The opening scenes of *Richard III* show Richard's car moving through London and arriving at the palace, and these non-linguistic contextual cues effectively act as visual world-building elements (Werth, 1999; [and see unit B10 – P.S.]) for our construction of the fictional world, which is a dystopian 1930s London. The time period is instantiated through aspects of *mise-en-scène* such as costume; the style of Richard's uniform is likely to trigger associations with Second World War Nazi uniforms. Such fascist connotations are further triggered by aspects of the setting. For example, as Richard approaches the palace we see banners draped on the outside of buildings that are reminiscent of Nazi flags (a black boar's head in a white circle on a red background).

The soliloquy in the film is unusual in that, initially, Richard is not alone as he recites it. Rather he makes the speech as an address to a crowd of party-goers in the plush palace ballroom. The scene is brightly lit and colourful, with an air of opulence. There are a number of elements of *mise-en-scène* that affect how we are likely to interpret the soliloquy, and these include setting, and staging. The syntactic structure of the shots is also important and I will consider this once I have discussed aspects of *mise-en-scène*.

To begin with the issue of staging, the opening soliloquy is instrumental in defining the complex character of Richard. I noted the ambiguity concerning who Richard is referring to when he mentions 'this son of York'. In the film performance this is made explicit. As Richard speaks the second line he extends his hand towards his brother, Edward (shot 4 in the transcript). There is then a shot of the crowd as they turn to look at Edward who smiles and acknowledges them as they applaud (shot 5). There is, then, irony in the fact that later on in the soliloquy Richard bemoans the 'glorious summer' that he initially appears to praise. Richard's later comments (line 12 onwards) reveal his opening lines to be a violation of the Maxim of Quality (Grice, 1975). For viewers already familiar with the play this will be apparent from the beginning of Richard's speech; for those unfamiliar with it, lines 12 to 36 are likely to cause them to re-evaluate their initial impression of Richard generated by his opening lines. What is clear is that Richard's opening speech does not have the same status as a traditional soliloquy, in that we cannot assume that Richard is observing the Maxim of Quality and telling the truth as he believes it to be.

The next unusual feature of the film version of the soliloquy is that as soon as Richard delivers the line, 'To fright the souls of fearful adversaries/He –' (shot 11), there is a sharp cut to a men's lavatory in the hotel (shots 11/12). Richard enters and picks up the soliloquy at the second word of line 12: 'capers nimbly in a lady's chamber'. From this point on until line 28 it appears that Richard is initially talking to himself, thereby restoring the status of the speech to that of a soliloquy. The upshot of this is that the viewer is now more likely to assume that this is self-expression on Richard's part and therefore the truth as he believes it to be. In effect, we have been cued to interpret the soliloquy in this way as a result of the zoom to an extreme close-up of Richard in shot 11, immediately prior to the cut to the bathroom. This camera movement towards Richard suggests an increase in our psychological closeness to Richard. The facial movements of McKellen are important here; the close-up allows us to see that his mouth is contorted into a grimace. Additionally, Richard's yellowing teeth, suggestive of decay, are likely to provoke negative feelings towards his character, suggesting that his true character is not the jovial speech-maker of the ballroom scene.

Dan
McIntyre

There is, of course, dramatic irony here in that the viewer is privy to Richard's private thoughts whereas the other characters in the film are not. By staging the soliloquy in this way, the film makes explicit the complex and devious nature of Richard in a way that would be difficult to effect on stage. What is also interesting stylistically about the soliloquy is that the cut from shot 11 to shot 12 supposes a temporal deictic shift (Galbraith 1995) and therefore implies an interpolation to the original text which we do not hear. This implied time-lapse foregrounds the difference in status of the speech in the ballroom and the remainder of the soliloquy in the bathroom. The difference in status of the two parts of the soliloquy is further emphasised by the contrast in settings. The dimly lit bathroom contrasts sharply with the brightly lit, colourful opulence of the palace ballroom.

If we now turn to the semiotic structure of the shots, here too we find elements that result in a different interpretation of the soliloquy to that which we would be likely to come up with on the basis of a textual analysis alone. A major difference in performance between the McKellen version and Shakespeare's original play text (and, indeed, other film productions) is that in this film Richard begins the soliloquy unaware of the viewing audience. He does not address his speech direct to camera until line 25, in the bathroom of the hotel. At this point, as he is staring into the bathroom mirror, he apparently notices his audience, as if seeing them in the reflection (shot 17). The change of gaze direction that follows results in both a change of address and a change in grammatical process. In the bathroom up to this point, Richard's address has been indirect. Applying Kress and van Leeuwen's (2006) terminology would lead us to define Richard as the Actor in a non-transactional process, since he appears until line 25 to be speaking simply to himself. The change in gaze direction at line 25 (shot 17) entails the creation of an eye-line vector between Richard and the camera (i.e. the viewing audience), thus altering Richard's status so that he is now a Reacter and the audience a Phenomenon in an interactive reactional structure (see stills 1 and 2 for this change in address). Richard's direct address also increases the salience of his character in the shot and consequently it may be argued that we attach a greater information value to his image. The salience of Richard's character in the shot is then increased as he advances towards the camera. The effect of this movement is to increase the sense of unease that Richard exudes. This is not something that is easily explained using either Kress and van Leeuwen's approach or tools from Film Studies, but Brown and Levinson's (1987) framework for the analysis of linguistic politeness can shed some light on what happens here. In Brown and Levinson's (1987) terms, Richard's movement towards the camera (shot 18), and the camera's consequent backing away from him, represents a paralinguistic threat to the viewer's negative face (i.e. his or her desire to be unimpeded). This is because the eye-line vector established between Richard and the camera suggests that Richard is now looking at the viewer (in effect, the camera creates the illusion that the viewer is somehow in the bathroom with Richard). Richard's movement closer to the camera impinges on what we perceive, as a result of what we know the camera to represent, to be our personal space. The position of the camera creates the illusion of there being a direct connection between the discourse world (Werth, 1999; [and see unit B10 – P.S.]) and the text world of which Richard is a part.

**Dan
McIntyre**

Still 1 Shot 17 from *Richard III*: Soliloquy

Still 2 Shot 17 from *Richard III*: Soliloquy – change of address via change in gaze
direction

Dan
McIntyre

The illusion of a paralinguistic threat to the audience's negative face further characterises Richard as a threatening and potentially dangerous character.

From this point on the camera continues to represent the viewing position of the audience with the consequent effect of our being treated as Richard's confidants. Indeed, he even motions to the camera to follow him as he leaves the bathroom, in order that he might explain his plans further (shot 20). This camera movement creates the effect of an increase in our physical proximity to Richard as he rushes to the dock where Clarence is being arrested. [. . .]

My aim in this article has been to explain how an analysis of performance is methodologically possible in the stylistic analysis of drama on film, and to show how such a multimodal analysis is necessary in order to account for the range of interpretative effects apparent in dramatic performance. In relation to Ian McKellen's film version of *Richard III*, my overall point is that a purely text-based stylistic analysis does not reveal the variety of interpretative effects that arise from watching the film version of the play. Consequently, a comprehensive stylistic analysis of the film must include a multimodal analysis. What also becomes apparent from the above multimodal analysis is that McKellen's version of the play constrains the interpretative possibilities. For instance, the ambiguity of the line 'this son of York' is removed in McKellen's performance.

I hope to have shown, then, that it is possible and profitable to incorporate the analysis of production and performance with a more tradition, text-based stylistic analysis of drama. Although my analysis has been of a filmed version of the play, assuming that a recording of a stage production is available, the same techniques might be employed in the analysis of a stage performance. One aspect of the methodological approach described in this article that is key is the practice of working from a transcript of the film, in addition to referring to the film directly. Only by doing this are we able to accurately describe overlapping elements of production and identify in detail specific stylistic effects. For example, the paralinguistic threat to negative face described [above] may not have been picked up on without recourse to a transcript of the linguistic and non-linguistic elements of the soliloquy scene.

The practice of this kind of multimodal stylistic analysis also demonstrates how stylistics might contribute to our understanding of film more generally (as opposed to simply concentrating on filmed versions of plays). Indeed, some steps have already been taken in this direction (e.g. Simpson and Montgomery 1995; Montoro 2006). As I mentioned earlier, however, in order to be of value it is important that the stylistic analysis of film contributes something over and above what Film Studies traditionally focuses on. In this respect, we might identify a number of objectives for a stylistics of film:

1   We should be able to describe the language used in screenplays (including both dialogue and screen directions) in order to account for its interpretative effects on the reader/film viewer. This linguistic analysis may involve, for example, pragmatic analysis of dialogue or computational analysis of electronic corpora of screenplays.

Appendix 1 Audio-visual transcript of linguistic, paralinguistic and non-linguistic performance features of the soliloquy from *Richard III* (1995)

Shot no.	Time (minutes and seconds into film)	Shot description	Linguistic audio (OS = out of shot)	Paralinguistic visual	Paralinguistic audio	Non-linguistic visual
1	8.38	Close-up of Richard's finger tapping a microphone.	—	—	Applause from audience.	—
2	8.40	Medium close-up on Richard at microphone.	—	—	Applause from audience.	—
3	8.42	Medium close-up on Duchess of York.	—	—	Applause from audience.	—
4	8.45	Medium close-up on Richard at microphone.	**Richard:** Now is the winter of our discontent made glorious summer by this	Richard extends his hand.	Applause dies down.	—
5	8.55	Long shot of Edward and Elizabeth.	**Richard:** (OS) son of York graciously.	Edward waves	Laughter from Edward and applause and laughter from audience.	—
6	8.59	Medium close-up on Richard at microphone.	**Richard:** And all the clouds that loured upon our house/In the deep bosom of the ocean buried./Now are our brows bound with victorious wreaths;	Richard shakes fist.	—	—

7	9.13	Long shot of Lord Hastings and Duchess of York.	—	Lord Hastings and Duchess of York smile.	Laughter from audience.	—
8	9.15	Medium close-up on Richard at microphone.	**Richard:** Our bruised arms hung up for monuments;/ Our stern alarums changed to merry meetings;	—	—	—
9	9.24	Long shot of Lord Rivers and others.	**Richard:** (OS) Our dreadful marches to delightful measures.	Lord Rivers flicks his lighter and the child on his knee blows out the flame.	—	—
10	9.29	Medium close-up on Duke of Buckingham.	—	—	Loud laughter and applause from Buckingham.	Buckingham smoking a cigar.
11	9.33	Close-up on Richard at microphone and zoom to extreme close-up on Richard's mouth.	**Richard:** Grim-visaged war hath smoothed his wrinkled front;/And now, instead of mounting barbed steeds/To fright the souls of fearful adversaries/He	—	—	Extreme-close-up on Richard's yellowing teeth.
—	—	—	—	—	—	Cut to next scene.
12	9.46	Long shot of Richard opening door and entering bathroom	**Richard:** capers nimbly in a lady's chamber	—	—	—
13	9.50	Tracking shot of Richard as he walks to urinal.	**Richard:** /To the lascivious pleasing of a lute.	—	—	—

Appendix 1 *(continued)*

Shot no.	Time (minutes and seconds into film)	Shot description	Linguistic audio (OS = out of shot)	Paralinguistic visual	Paralinguistic audio	Non-linguistic visual
14	9.56	Medium close-up on Richard at urinal with his back to camera.	**Richard:** But I, that am not shaped for sportive tricks/Nor made to court an amorous looking-glass;/I, that am rudely stamped,/Deformed, unfinished, sent before my time/Into this breathing world, scarce half made up,	—	—	Richard pulls chain-flush (10.12)
15	10.20	Tracking shot of Richard as he walks to washbasin.	**Richard:** And that so lamely and unfashionable/That dogs bark at me	—	—	Richard washes his hands at sink.
16	10.26	Medium close-up on Richard at washbasin (shot includes Richard's reflection in mirror above basin).	**Richard:** as I halt by them:/	—	—	—
17	10.29	Slow zoom in on Richard looking into mirror.	**Richard:** Why, I, in this weak piping time of peace,/Have no delight to pass away the time,/Unless to spy my shadow in the sun/And descant on mine own deformity:/ Why, I can smile, and murder while I smile,/Wet my cheeks with artificial tears,/ And frame my face to all occasions.	—	—	Richard dries his hand on a towel (10.30). Richard appears to notice audience in reflection (10.56). Richard turns

No.	Time	Shot description	Dialogue			
18	10.59	Extreme close-up on Richard. Camera pulls back.	**Richard:** And therefore, since I cannot prove a lover,/To entertain these fair well-spoken days,/I am determined to prove a villain/And hate the idle pleasures of these days.	Richard advances towards camera as it pulls back.	—	round to face camera (10.58).
19	11.10	Tracking shot of Richard moving to bathroom door.	—	—	—	—
20	11.12	Medium close-up on Richard.	**Richard:** Plots have I laid	—	Jazz music plays in background (11.12).	Richard opens door and turns to face camera. (11.13). Richard beckons with his finger and turn to exit (11.14).
—	—	—	—	—	—	Cut to next scene.
21	11.16	Long shot of a dock.	**Richard:** To set my brother Clarence and the king/In deadly hate the one against the other.	—	—	Richard moves into right of shot and faces camera (11.20). Looks towards dock and moves out of shot (10.23).

**Dan
McIntyre**

2   We should be able to account for how film performance can be inferred from the screenplay (see Short, 1981; 1998 for examples of how this can be achieved).

3   We should be able to account for the relationship between screenplays and film performances. By this I mean that we should attempt to answer such questions as (i) Are there equivalent effects in film performances/productions to the linguistic effects found in texts? (ii) In what ways do performance/production elements enhance the linguistic effects generated in a screenplay? (iii) Does watching a film require less cognitive effort than reading a text?

A multimodal stylistic analysis of film drama should attempt to take account of all of the objectives set out above (providing, of course, that these are relevant to the film performance/production and screenplay in question). [. . .]

Issues to consider

McIntyre's multimodal stylistic analysis offers some important insights into the general principles behind the adaptation of plays, novels and short stories into films. Such analysis enables us to think about why, for example, adaptations sometimes restructure the order of events in the original narrative, or why certain elements of plot are left out. McIntyre's paper also sets out an explicit and rigorous methodology for approaching film texts from a stylistic perspective, and it is worth noting that the organisational scheme he develops for film is also suitable for the analysis of, amongst other things, the discourse of broadcast advertisements.

Some suggestions follow.

Activity

❏   Look again at how McIntyre schematises the multimodal progression of the scene from *Richard III*. The categories along the top of his grid run thus: shot number, time into the film, shot description, linguistic audio, paralinguistic visual, paralinguistic audio, and non-linguistic visual. Is there anything you can think of that might usefully complement this set of features? You can now practice doing a multimodal analysis by picking a scene from a film that you have access to (either in DVD form or in some other electronic facility). This scene can be from anywhere in the film once the opening credits have finished, although it helps if the scene is a short one – less than two minutes long. Try to organise the scene into its constituent multimodal elements. What difficulties have you encountered? How long would it take you to do a comparable multimodal breakdown of the entire film's running time?

❏   McIntyre poses some intriguing questions towards the end of his article. Think particularly about any novels or plays you have read that have been made into films. How have the stylistic features of the written text been captured in the film version? How do directors encapsulate linguistic effects in elements of performance and production? Have you ever been disappointed by a film version because of what it 'loses in translation'? By contrast, have you ever encountered a film that actually improves and embellishes the source text from which it derives? And is it the case, *pace* McIntyre's exploratory question, that watching a film requires less cognitive effort than reading a literary text?

❏ McIntyre touches on the role of music in his reading, noting how jazz music plays in the background of the scene he analyses. The role of music in the architecture of film narrative is a crucial one, although it must be said that, with the very notable exception of van Leeuwen (1999), it has largely been overlooked in multimodal stylistics. Echoing the definitions offered in A7, the framing question for the initial analysis of a music track or theme is to ask whether it is *intradiegetic* or *extradiegetic*. Intradiegetic music forms part of the internal dynamic of the story being viewed – the music is, in other words, produced by participants *within* the narrative. However, most music in films (other than musicals, paradoxically) is extradiegetic because it emanates from *outside* the story. Extradiegetic scores may range from simple incidental music to major motif-framing compositions. Think about the variety of stylistic effects a musical accompaniment may impart to a film. Consider in particular films where the soundtrack intersects with key narrative themes. For instance, John Landis's *American Werewolf in London* (1981) has a delightfully ironic score, comprising songs such as 'Moondance' and 'Blue Moon', whose 'lunar' subject matter fits uncomfortably well with the events on screen. With respect to the intradiegetic / extradiegetic distinction, can you think of any films where the musical score cuts across these layers of narrative organisation? For instance, Mel Brooks's comedy western *Blazing Saddles* (1974) contains a startling transposition across the layers with the appearance in the desert of the Count Basie orchestra playing 'April in Paris'. Or consider Ennio Morricone's famous 'chimes' motif in the final gunfight scene of the spaghetti western *For a Few Dollars More* (1965). Finally, and returning to the scene from *Richard III*, the music here is being performed on a stage by a jazz band fronted by a female singer. Is this intradiegetic or extradiegetic? Furthermore, the lyrics to the song the band is playing include the line: 'come live with me and be my love'. Can you work out the rather erudite literary connection that is referenced in this line?

Dan McIntyre

CONCEPTUAL BLENDING AND STYLISTIC ANALYSIS

D10

This reading, by Barbara Dancygier, applies the cognitive framework of *conceptual blending theory* in the analysis of several travel narratives by the writer Jonathan Raban. Conceptual blending theory (or conceptual 'integration' theory as it is sometimes known) is based on the invocation and mapping of mental spaces. These spaces are defined by Fauconnier and Turner as small conceptual packets that are constructed, as we think and talk, for the purposes of local understanding and action (Fauconnier and Turner 2002: 40; see also Dancygier 2006: 5). As Fauconnier argues, thought and language depend among other things on our capacity to manipulate webs of mappings between mental spaces. He proposes that blending operates on two input mental spaces to yield a third space, the *blend*, adding that 'the blend inherits partial structure from the input spaces and has emergent structure of its own' (Fauconnier 1997: 149). An elegant and detailed account of the blending framework is provided early in Dancygier's reading.

The broad aim of Dancygier's article is to show how the analysis of blending strategies used in a text may help in the recognition of the specific features of a writer's narrative style. As with most of the readings in this D section, Dancygier's paper offers insights on a number of stylistics fronts, in this instance serving as a discussion of the relation between blending strategies and narrative viewpoint. It is argued that the concept of narrative viewpoint crucially relies on the structure of blending networks and that interpretation of viewpoint builds on the mechanism she terms *viewpoint compression.*

Blending and Narrative Viewpoint: Jonathan Raban's Travels through Mental Spaces

Barbara Dancygier

Barbara Dancygier (reprinted from *Language and Literature*, 2005, 14, 2, 99–127)

In this article, I apply some of the basic concepts of the blending approach to an analysis of a number of examples from various books by Jonathan Raban, a well-known author of travel literature, novels, and essays. Raban's narrative style is quite unusual in that it makes an exceptionally bold and broad use of images the writer constructs through various applications of the mechanisms of conceptual integration. At the same time, he exploits these mechanisms skilfully to establish or maintain narrative viewpoint. Raban's main story lines are interwoven with themes from his past and from the literature he reads in a way which maintains a uniform writer's perspective in the construction of the narrative. His style is thus an exceptionally clear example of the way in which the construction and manipulation of mental constructs influence the choice of linguistic form, not only within a phrase or sentence, but also in the structure of the narrative. At the same time, more traditional tools of stylistic analysis would not be able to clarify the cognitive underpinnings of Raban's style with the level of specificity possible within the blending framework.

The blending framework relies to a large degree on earlier work in mental spaces theory (Fauconnier 1994 [1985], 1997). A 'mental space' is described as a cognitive construct which is set up, mainly through the use of language expressions, as a temporary framework allowing meaning construction to take place. In the simplest case, mental spaces may be set up by temporal or spatial expressions, thereby allowing the speaker and the hearer to make mental construal of situations which can be remote from the current discourse context. Mental spaces can also be marked with modal, epistemic, or emotional attitudes and can represent fictional, counterfactual, or otherwise imagined situations. [. . .]

Selecting blending as the primary framework of the analysis has been motivated in several ways. First, blending seems to be ideally suited to clarifying the specific stylistic features of Raban's text. Second, it has recently been successfully applied to phenomena which would traditionally belong to different fields of the humanities – linguistics, literature, anthropology, musicology and art (Hougaard and Lund 2002). In fact, blending seems to offer us a more disciplined and accurate, but also much broader, understanding of human imagination and creative thought. [. . .]

Barbara
Dancygier

Conceptual integration (or blending) theory was introduced by Fauconnier and Turner in a number of papers [. . .] and given its final form in their book, *The Way We Think* (2002). It postulates that numerous cognitive mechanisms responsible for construction of meaning rely on interwoven configurations of mental spaces. Such configurations, called *blending networks*, allow us to construe situations in complex and more communicatively efficient ways. One (now classic) example (Fauconnier and Turner, 2002) of an integration network is known as the Debate-with-Kant blend. When a contemporary philosopher lectures about Kant, he may, among other things, propose his own views as well. If he comments on one of his statements by saying *Kant disagrees with me on this*, he has to construct a mental space in which he (our contemporary, a speaker of English, who knows Kant's views from reading) is sharing a spatial and temporal space with Kant (now dead, speaking and writing in German, who never knew our philosopher's views) and is exchanging opinions with him. This mental construct is a blend – a new cognitive structure which is created by projecting structure from other spaces and which allows new lines of reasoning not possible in any of the initial spaces.

The most typical integration network involves four related spaces. The *generic* space contains schematic information which is shared by other spaces in the network and provides a background against which the new projections are possible. The crucial information content comes from two *input* spaces. Each of the input spaces may represent a different situation, but there is enough shared structure between them for it to be possible to consider certain elements of the spaces as counterparts. When the two spaces are integrated into one, *blended*, space, their content is partially mapped into the new space. The mapping is partial, because only some elements of the input spaces are projected into the blend, even though the blend preserves the essential topology of the inputs. At the same time, by creating a new configuration of elements, the blended space contains a new *emergent* structure, which allows for the construction of meanings that would not have been possible in any of the input spaces alone.

The construction of the blend crucially relies on the mechanism of *compression*, whereby relations among elements in the input spaces are contracted to the point where elements which were independent in the inputs will be seen as one in the blended space. In most cases, the compressions rely on metonymic connections among elements. For example, a visitor in a museum who points to a portrait and says 'This is King Philip' compresses the relation between a person and the person's pictorial representation, and refers to the representation using the name of the person. Compression has been found to be essential to the construction of blended concepts, especially to the expression of relations among concepts and entities contributing to the structure of mental spaces. The relation of Representation mentioned here is one of a number of such relations. They are termed Vital Relations by Fauconnier and Turner, and include concepts such as Time, Space, Change, Cause and Effect, Analogy, Disanalogy, and Identity. However, the reversal of compression, called (not surprisingly) *decompression*,

**Barbara
Dancygier**

whereby a unified mental construct may be decomposed into parts, is an equally powerful mechanism, and, as the examples below will show, is particularly useful in the establishment of narrative viewpoint.

The vital relation which is perhaps most saliently subject to numerous compressions and decompressions is Identity. Every person's sense of a unique identity is in fact a result of various types of blends. Conceptual integration can explain how we maintain a coherent sense of self in spite of a number of changes in appearance, social and family role, behavioural patterns, and beliefs which everyone goes through as time passes. Compressing various images of ourselves along the dimensions of Time, Change, Cause-Effect, or Representation allows us to recognize the same person in a photograph of a five-year-old, in a valentine card written by a teenager to his sweetheart, and in a résumé attached to a job application.

However, the unique sense of self can easily be suspended. In fact, there are linguistic expressions which seem to be particularly useful in signalling that one's identity is viewed as 'split'. For instance, as Lakoff (1996) observes, reflexive pronouns are commonly used for such purposes, as in *I am at war with myself about the contract.* Counterfactual sentences such as *If I were you I would hire me* (see Fauconnier, 1997) signal a split in which the speaker imagines herself to simultaneously play the role of an employer and an applicant. In terms of conceptual integration theory, the expressions suggesting such split selves require decompressing the standard (blended) concept of the self. Similarly, saying *I am not the same person I was when we first met* or *I'm a lousy chessplayer, but I'm a pretty good cook* can only be interpreted if that unique self is decompressed along the dimension of Time or Role. In fact, common usage (especially the use of personal pronouns and proper names [Dancygier 2004 and 2008]) suggests that the concept of identity is particularly open to the processes of decompression, in colloquial and literary usage alike.

Let me now illustrate the concepts summarized above with an example from Raban's book, *Coasting* (2003 [1987]; hereafter *CO*). While sailing his boat around the British Isles, the author takes the reader back to his childhood days:

(1) For days I had been dreading the arrival of the brown envelope with the Worcester postmark. [. . .] The boy described in it was lazy. He showed no house spirit, no team spirit, [. . .].

(*CO*: 20)

In the passage, Raban talks about a past situation, when he was still a boy, negatively evaluated by his school. In the first sentence quoted he refers to himself in the first person (*I had been dreading . . .*), while in the second part of the quote the third-person forms are used (*the boy, he*). The shift into the third person suggests that the writer reminiscing about his past feelings and the boy described in the letter cannot be viewed as two aspects of a coherent identity, which calls for different descriptive expressions to be used. The *I* of the passage is the adult, the author writing his story, as he recollects his childhood worries. The persona represented by *I* is not in fact decompressed, as it includes both the writer's current sense of self and the memory of his childhood thoughts. In other words, the writer's adult, present understanding

Barbara
Dancygier

of his childhood is projected into the past space. At the same time, the first-person pronoun anchors the writer (and the narrative viewpoint) deictically to the 'present' of the narrative, since the *I* belongs to the main narrative space of the story. The expression *the boy*, on the other hand, refers to the writer's counterpart from over 30 years earlier, but only as he was seen by the school, not as the writer would have described himself then or now. He is, in a way, a different person, known to the school, but not coherent with the youngster's (or the adult's) perception of himself. One could imagine *I* being used to refer to both of them (as in *I was described in the letter as lazy*). Such usage would agree with the standard, compressed, view of identity, but it would prevent Raban from making his point – that the boy so negatively described in the letter is viewed entirely from the point of view of the school, and that the *I* of the passage (the writer's persona) would have offered an evaluation based on different criteria.

As in many other fragments of the text, the choice of referring expressions signals identity decompressions. In the case of (1), the mental space configuration includes the present narrative space, the past space, where the letter from the school is being read by the boy's father at the breakfast table, and the 'letter' space, representing the negative evaluation of the boy. The decompression of the 'Raban-child' persona is necessary so that the two viewpoints can be anchored to two different spaces.

Raban then describes his father. The first part of the description is given from the point of view of the present narrative space, that of the *I* of the passage. The past tense suggests that the writer is talking about the past space of his childhood, but the *I* continues to anchor the viewpoint to the present narrative. In the second part, introduced with *now*, a blended space is set up, where the writer's *now* and the past breakfast scene are integrated in a way that allows Raban to look at his father in a different way.

(2) At thirteen I was easily fooled by clothes, and this aged cassock made my father himself seem like a very old man to me, [.]. He was thirty-six. Sitting now in another dusty room, its air thickened with pipe smoke of the same brand, I find myself staring back, puzzledly, at a man much younger than myself. [. . .] His hair is black and thick, his skin unlined. His preposterously old clothes only serve to underline his youth as he returns my gaze – astonished to find himself the father to this bulky balding fellow in his forties.

(*CO* 21)

The blend (represented in Figure [D10.1]) in which Raban's father (as a young man) and his son (as an adult narrator) are described as sharing the same space is constructed against the background of a generic space, containing a standard scenario of two people looking at each other. The first input space is the past space (introduced with the past tense form *was*), containing the 36-year-old father and Raban-child. The second input space (the present one, marked with *now*) is the one portraying Raban as an adult sitting in a room, smoking his pipe. The sentences which follow belong to the blended space, in which both men are looking at each other. The integrated image preserves the features of the men as they were originally introduced in the input spaces: the father

D10

**Barbara
Dancygier**

is quite young, black-haired, unfashionably dressed, while Raban is in his forties. The emergent structure in the blend puts both men in the same compressed time, so they can look at each other, while at the same time preserving the actual time gap between the two input spaces, so that Raban can stare back (a very subtle contribution of a metaphorical understanding of time in terms of space, with the future located forward and the past behind). The emergent structure exists only in the blended space, and cannot be traced back to any of the input spaces alone.

The use of tenses in the passage marks not only the temporal anchoring of the two input spaces, but also shifts of viewpoint from one of the spaces to the other. With the use of the present tense to describe the content of the blended space the writer shifts to his present, 'adult', viewpoint. The blended temporal space is talked about as 'present', because the situation is described from the point of view of the adult writer now, not from the viewpoint of the child then.

In the blended space there are in fact three characters: the writer, describing the scene, the writer as a boy, who remains only in the background in (2), and the writer's father, who can now also see his son, as an adult, and acknowledge his presence (in

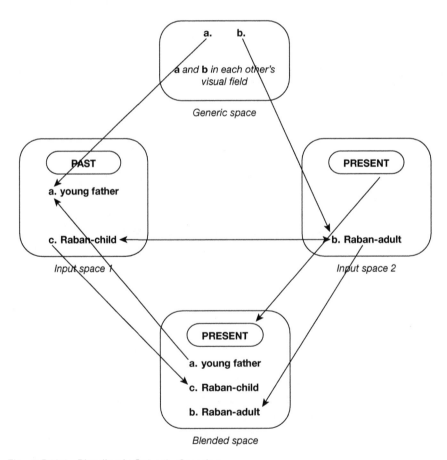

Figure D10.1 Blending in Raban's *Coasting*

Barbara
Dancygier

Figure [D10.1]), all the cross-space links among the three participants are represented by arrows). At the same time, the blend has the effect of both putting the two men in the same visual context and maintaining the distance of over 30 years between them. Consequently, the construction of the blend opens the passage to an interpretation whereby, after years of resentment, Raban is coming to an understanding of who his father was. The passage which follows elaborates that interpretation, while maintaining and developing all the spaces set up earlier.

(3) What I saw across the breakfast table – and saw with the pitiless egotism of the thwarted child – was not my father, it was England. [. . .] there sat the Conservative Party in person, the Army in person, the Church in person [. . .].

Seeing him now through different eyes, I find myself watching a sorrowful, lean and angular young man, hopelessly lost for words. [. . .] He searches the face of his child for a clue as to how to go on [. . .].

The child is blind to all this. He is putting on the finishing touches to his Bored Aristocrat face. [. . .]

(CO 22–3)

This passage again starts with the past tense. The situation is that of the past input space (with the boy and the father), with the adult writer offering an explanation of the child's behaviour as it is now seen by his adult counterpart (the boy would surely have formulated his thought differently).

The second part (with the present tense), returns to the blend, where the Raban-adult writer is observing his father in a conversation with Raban-child, revising the perception of the situation described earlier in the 'past' space. It is worth noting that the blend (as elaborated in [2] and [3]) achieves its goal largely through its implicit reliance on the KNOWING IS SEEING conceptual metaphor, typically found in expressions such as *I see*, which signal understanding rather than visual perception. The point of the passage is reaching a new understanding of the father, but it is presented through putting the father in the same time and location as the adult son, so that visual perception is possible. Each of the fragments in (2) and (3) refers to vision in some way. First, the adult is looking at a young man from his past (and he returns the gaze). Then, the adult's (*I*'s) memory of the childhood perception of the father is talked about as 'seeing' serious and potentially demanding institutions in his place. Finally, the adult is looking at the father *through different eyes* (through adult eyes, with an adult understanding of the situation). Meanwhile, the child recruited into the blend from the past space is *blind to all this*, and is thus not capable of thinking of the father in adult terms.

The visual framing of the blend goes beyond the thoughts of Raban-adult in an interesting way. In (2), the father returns his gaze, looking at his adult son in astonishment. This behaviour is not recruited into the blend from the past input space, but is possible only as a result of the emergent structure of the blend itself. As in other examples of blends discussed by Fauconnier and Turner, the 'running' of the blend (allowing it to mentally play itself out) creates meanings which could not arise in any of the input spaces alone. At the same time, the new structure inherent to the blend can reflect back on the meaning of the inputs. The 'returning of the gaze' seems to be a perfect example of how the blend may contribute to the understanding of the inputs. If the adult son can see his young father in the blend, then the father can see him too. Raban builds on that to suggest that the father's past behaviour indicated his lack of realization that when children grow up, their adult lives may be astonishingly different from what could have been predicted when they were children. Since the father looks back at Raban-adult only in the blend, there is no implication that in any aspect of the present he actually begins to perceive his son differently or that he had such thoughts in the past input space. All the blend does is allow Raban to reflect on how his father would feel over 30 years earlier if he could think of his son as a potential adult, not just as a disappointing child. [. . .]

In another book, *Old Glory (OG)*, Raban is travelling down the Mississippi in a small boat. His departure is recorded by local TV. He watches the coverage in a hotel room and describes it as follows:

([4]) The TV news went local. An Englishman had left Minneapolis that day in a small motor boat [. . .]. In the picture on the screen his face had a cheesy pallor. [. . .] He looked to me like a clowning greenhorn.

(OG 60)

The narrative looks as though Raban were talking about another man. First, he quotes (in free indirect style) the expressions used by the newscaster (clearly, the expression 'an Englishman' could not be used in this way by Raban himself). Then he talks about the traveller, using third-person pronouns. Everything (except the content of the news, of course) suggests that the TV station is talking about someone else. It is only at the end of the paragraph that Raban acknowledges that the man on the screen represents him:

([5])[. . .] rueful to see myself so travestied by this foolish character.

(OG 60)

Blending of an object and its representation (as in the *King Philip* example earlier) is a common phenomenon in discourse. In this case the person and his representation are decompressed into independent entities, so that the representation on the TV screen is talked about as if it were linked to a person other than the writer himself. The reason is Raban's dissatisfaction with the image on the screen. It simply does not 'feel' like him, so, for the purposes of the narrative, it is not him. At the same time, the 'Englishman' is seen as he would be by any viewer watching the news, thus Raban's viewpoint is here that of a man watching TV, not of a traveller seeing himself on the screen. As in the other cases, Raban's style maintains visual viewpoint as the primary narrative perspective.

In a fragment from *Hunting Mister Heartbreak (HMH)* quoted in ([6]), decompressions at the service of narrative viewpoint take an extreme form: they are given different proper names. In the town of Guntersville the writer refers to himself as *Jonathan Raban* when his own viewpoint is being represented, and *John Rayburn* when the narrative presents him through the eyes of the people of Guntersville. Raban and Rayburn exist in the same time and place, and they do look very much alike, but their beliefs, behavioural patterns; lifestyles, and friendships are different, seen from two different perspectives.

> ([6]) 'Hey, John, you look real good!' sang out a passing salesclerk as I stood in front of
>   a tarnished mirror, inspecting Rayburn in his new Guntersville uniform.
>
>   (*HMH*: 196)

In ([6]), the decompression of Raban and Rayburn goes even further. Raban is looking at his reflection in a department store mirror, but, partly because of the attire he is wearing, he looks more aligned with the character known to the Guntersville folk than with his old self. [T]he object and its representation have been partly decompressed, but the representation is viewed through the eyes of people other than the man actually standing in front of the mirror. [. . .]

Decompressions of identity apply not only to people. Whenever there are two possible perspectives, they can be presented as two different realities. Examples ([7]) and ([8]) illustrate this with respect to places. ([7]) is Raban's reflection on his own experience of going down the Mississippi by boat as markedly different from the perspective of a visitor seeking the charm of the olden days, while ([8]) describes his impression upon arrival in Cairo after a long travel through much more exotic countries of Arabia.

> ([7]) The Mississippi was two rivers. They lay right beside each other, but flowed in
>   opposite directions. The steam boats, the fancy Golden Age hotels, the scenic bluffs
>   and gift shops were all going one way, while the river on the charts, with its tows,
>   grain elevators, [. . .] was going quite another. I had done my share of travelling on
>   the first river, but it was a cute irrelevance compared with the deep, dangerous, epic
>   power of the real Mississippi.
>
>   (*OG* 229)

> ([8]) My fellow-diners and I had come at Cairo from different angles, and we'd arrived
>   at different places. They'd flown from Gatwick to the land of the Pharaohs, while I
>   had made a homecoming of sorts from Sana'a.
>
>   (*Arabia* 267)

The Mississippi river and the city of Cairo are each presented as existing in two independent mental spaces, structured by two different viewpoints. Where the tourists find traces of history and signs of grandeur, the people who look beyond the glamour of advertising brochures will find different realities that are not exotic at all, but perhaps more true instead. Consequently, even though the restaurant in Cairo is a shared location for Raban and other diners, they are not sharing the same experience of the city. In his own way Raban is telling the reader that what he himself found in

**Barbara
Dancygier**

those places is a reality which has nothing in common with the tourist perception. As in the other cases, his personal viewpoint is in sharp contrast to the experience of others – to the point where he presents himself as a traveller in a different land.

The decompressed perceptions are marked not only with different viewpoints, but also with contrasting features. Raban talks about the two rivers flowing in opposite directions – the image that clearly suggests that there is no way to blend them and (mentally) have the Delta Queen and a tow travelling on the Mississippi together. In the case of Cairo, Raban's perception is also built on the idea of going in opposite directions. Contrary to those flying in *from* Europe, he sees his arrival in the city as a return *to* Europe, because in comparison to other cities of Arabia that he has visited Cairo feels almost like home. The spatial differentiation of the two perceptions adds an interesting dimension to the construction of viewpoint. The realities experienced by different people are incoherent partly because their spatial vantage point is presented as different – they 'see' different places, if only metaphorically. [. . .]

The examples discussed throughout this article pose interesting questions about the ability of mental space networks, and especially blended networks, to represent viewpoint. Much has been said about how mental spaces which serve as viewpoint spaces (those from the perspective of which other spaces are set up and developed) project their temporal, spatial, or epistemic viewpoint (along with the accompanying grammatical forms) to the spaces lower in the network (Cutrer, 1994; Sanders and Redeker, 1996; Sweetser, 1996; Dancygier, 2002; Dancygier and Sweetser 2009). Looking at the narrative data suggests that, in the cases of rich spaces, especially those containing a sentient observer as an actual participant in the situation portrayed, other kinds of viewpoint, such as emotional, ideological or evaluative (cf. Simpson, 1993; Harding, [2004, 2007]), can also be attributed to the mental space structure. For example, in the case of the first-person narrative, the story will typically be told from the point of view of the main narrative space, marked with its temporal or spatial features, but also with all the viewpoint dimensions that the narrator brings into the story. Furthermore, the type of narrative termed *mind style*, recently described in cognitive terms by Semino (2002; [and see unit C7 – P.S.]), seems to be a particularly salient example of the narrative where the focaliser is also the sole source of viewpoint in the narrative.

The questions that Raban's blending strategies pose, however, are of a more specific nature, as we need to see how blending is exploited for the representation of viewpoint and find the blending mechanism whereby viewpoint is allocated to one of the spaces in the network. Even though all the networks discussed above include a space which can be identified as the main narrative space (which is also the locus of the narrative viewpoint), the viewpoint does not always remain in that space once the blend is set up. The examples discussed above seem to fall into two main categories, with the main narrative space contributing to the network in different ways.

In a large number of cases the main narrative space is simply one of the two input spaces, so it contributes to the construction of the blend along with the other input space [. . .]. In other cases, the main narrative space serves as the starting point from which decompressed spaces will be set up, typically as loci of new perspectives. This is the case for examples like (1), where the 'letter' space is added to the main story line to offer the school's evaluation of the boy. Also in the cases of the 'Mississippi' and

Barbara
Dancygier

'Cairo' examples [7 and 8 – P.S.], the decompression starts from the main narrative space, in which the writer gives his account of the story. Such decompressions, as I have tried to show, construct new spaces which offer a new point of view (of the school, in the case of [1] [. . .]).

Interestingly enough, even though the blended or decompressed spaces are often set up to make new viewpoints available, the main narrative space remains in the network as an available locus of viewpoint, even if the blend is set up to temporarily alter it. I will account for such possibilities of simultaneous viewpoint maintenance and shift in the network by postulating a blending mechanism which I term *viewpoint compression*. I will discuss three cases of viewpoint compression, using some of the examples discussed above.

The most common configuration among the examples discussed throughout this article relies on the set-up where the main narrative space is one of the inputs. Once the blend is set up, the narrative viewpoint moves to the blend, but it retains its global narrative function. In other words, the viewpoints of the main narrative space and the blended space are compressed. This seems to be the case in the fragments in (2) and (3) discussed above. When the blended space is set up, there are potentially two viewpoints in the network – that of the main narrative space (with writer-narrator), and that of the blend, with an observer who is present in the past scene (box A in Figure [D10.2]). But in fact the part of the story told from the viewpoint of the blend (v-l) also represents the viewpoint of the narrator (v-0). As a result (see box B), the main narrative viewpoint and the blend viewpoint are now the same, and the story is told from the joint viewpoint of the narrator in the main narrative space and the observer in the blended space. The two viewpoints have been compressed, although the reader maintains the independent understanding of Raban as the narrator and Raban as the silent observer of the scene in the blend. [. . .] This kind of viewpoint compression seems to be the most common in Raban's style. He sets up a blended space to represent a new understanding of the situation and then temporarily treats it as the main narrative space – hence the impression that he tells his stories exactly as he himself perceives them. At the same time this might explain why many of his blends evoke the visual perspective – accepting the visual viewpoint as the narrative viewpoint seems to happen through the same kind of viewpoint compression.

In the cases in which an aspect of the structure of the main narrative space undergoes decompression the potential for the newly set-up spaces to be the locus of viewpoint can be exploited in two ways. In the first case, one of the decompressed spaces offers a new viewpoint which is then compressed with the main narrative viewpoint. In ([4]), for example, the narrator is split into two 'personas', each with his own viewpoint (see box A in Figure [D10.3]). There is not just one narrator there, but the 'TV-viewer' and the 'sailor'. For the duration of the discussion of the TV show, the narrator's viewpoint is identified with that of the 'viewer', while the 'sailor' space temporarily disappears from the story (box B in Figure [10.3]). What seems to be happening in the integration network is that the decompression of the narrator's identity allows for two different viewpoints to be set up, but then one of them is selected to take over the narrative viewpoint for the duration of the blend's operation in the text. I would argue, then, that after the initial decompression of a crucial aspect of the structure of the main

Barbara
Dancygier

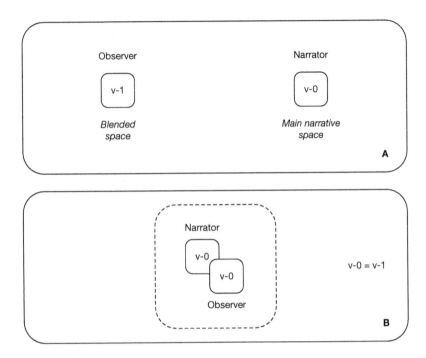

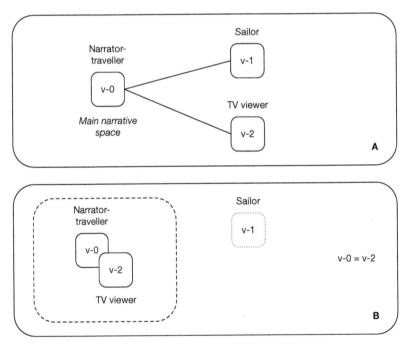

Figure D10.2   Viewpoint compression type 1

Figure D10.3   Viewpoint compression type 2

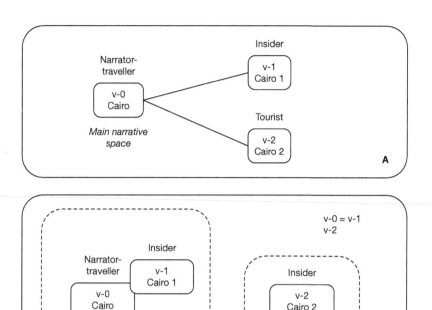

Figure D10.4 Viewpoint compression type 3

narrative space, the narrative space and the selected decompressed space have their viewpoints compressed. Such a viewpoint compression allows a temporary shift of viewpoint without the loss of continuity in the narrative.

The second case of new viewpoint allocation after decompression is represented by the examples where two independent viewpoints need to be maintained in the fragment. This is the case, for instance, in ([7]) and ([8]). The decompression of the Mississippi and Cairo into 'two different places' is performed for the specific purpose of contrasting two different viewpoints; in fact, the establishment of the two viewpoints seems to be the very point of the fragment. The main narrative space is decompressed into two – one representing the 'tourist' viewpoint, the other presenting the 'insider' viewpoint in contrast to the other one (see box A in [D10.4)]). But the narrator himself is the participant who represents the 'insider' viewpoint (he is not just a traveller now, but a traveller who sees the 'true' nature of things). His perception of the situation is thus contrasted with a competing perspective – perhaps a more common one, and thus worth showing in the specific context. For the purposes of the fragment, the compressed 'narrator-as-insider' viewpoint and the 'tourist' viewpoint are simultaneously maintained (see box B in Figure [D10.4]). Other examples of such treatment of viewpoint can be found in [example 6] where Raban-narrator is contrasted with 'Rayburn', seen in the mirror through the eyes of Guntersville folk.

Raban's style is probably unusual in the pervasiveness of the blending and decompression strategies he employs. In his writings, conceptual integration is a powerful stylistic tool, allowing the writer to create complex images and invoke numerous levels of interpretation with precision, but also unquestionable aesthetic value. His prose clearly illustrates the nature of the close correlation between the mental space structure used and the perspectivizing strategy intended. But we can expect to find similar phenomena in other examples of narrative prose. [. . .]

Issues to consider

As there was not the space to reproduce it all here, readers interested in pursuing the topic of conceptual blending further should consult the original, substantial article from which this reading is taken (Dancygier 2005). Another important resource is the special issue of the journal *Language and Literature* (2006, Volume 15, Issue 1) which, under the guest editorship of Barbara Dancygier, offers seven articles exploring the potential of conceptual blending theory for stylistic analysis. Other important work in the same broad area includes Emmott (2002) who probes the idea of the 'split self' (touched upon in Dancygier's reading above) in narrative fiction. Emmott's article also looks at the same phenomenon in 'medical life stories'. These stories are autobiographical accounts of the aftermath of illness or injury, and Emmott uses a cognitive stylistic framework to assess whether the loss of bodily function or mental faculty leads to a corresponding loss of 'self'.

Some suggestions follow.

❑   Elsewhere, Dancygier (2006: 9–11) has discussed the effects of conceptual blending in film, making particular reference to Woody Allen's *Annie Hall* (1977). She focusses on an episode where Alvin Singer, the film's central character, reminisces, direct to camera, about his childhood, after which he voices over scenes from that childhood. Alvin (the adult) says 'In 1942 I had already discovered girls' while on screen, in a classroom, young Alvy kisses a girl. Everyone is outraged and Alvy is called to the front of the class. The scene continues thus:

(1) Camera pans back to Alvy's desk where the adult Alvin is now sitting.
(2) Adult Alvin: 'I was expressing a healthy sexual curiosity'.
(3) Teacher (with young Alvy beside her): 'Six-year-old boys don't have girls on their minds'.
(4) Alvin, direct to camera: 'I did'.
(5) Teacher expresses a wish that all pupils should be good like Donald.
(6) Alvy (the child) to Donald: 'What are you today Donald?'
(7) Donald and other children carefully explain their adult lives direct to camera.
(8) One of the children: 'I used to be a heroin addict, now I'm a methadone addict'.

Consider the following questions in relation to this scene:

(a) What is the principle conceptual blend in this scene and how would you describe its emergent structure?
(b) What elements are projected into the scene from the past?
(c) What elements are projected from the movie's present?
(d) What type of 'Vital Relation' (refer to the reading above) is involved in the construction of the blended concepts?

(e) What is the time reference of 'today' in (6)?

(f) To whom is the utterance in (4) directed? (i.e. the teacher, the viewer, or both?)

(g) If Alvin were positioned at the front of the class alongside the teacher, to what extent would the classroom 'schema' be disrupted (or, perhaps more appropriately, put back in place)?

(h) Cross-check your responses here with the analysis in Dancygier (2006).

Barbara Dancygier

❑ In the reading experiment touched upon in B10, Canning and Simpson (2012) elicited responses to a missing word in a line of poetry ('I have known the inexorable sadness of _____'). The missing word was the (utterly unpredictable) entry 'pencils'. In the experiment, participants were then given this missing word before being asked to make further predictions for each subsequent line of the text, all of which had a blanked out item. After each prediction the 'correct' word was provided. Remarkably, by the third line of the poem ('All the _____ of manila folders and mucilage'), a number of participants were able accurately to predict that the word 'misery' had been blanked out.

Is there any way in which conceptual blending theory can explain this pattern of prediction? For example, what two input spaces are involved in the anomalous pattern in the first line (and for that matter in the third line, quoted above)? What emergent structure follows from this blend? If you described your pencils to a friend as sad, or your favourite manila folder as miserable, what reaction might you expect from them? So how is it that the participants in the reading test experienced no difficulty with these conceptual anomalies, even predicting them in some cases? (The concept of 'running the blend' might help here . . .).

COGNITIVE STYLISTICS AND THE THEORY OF METAPHOR

D11

Peter Stockwell's article explores, challenges and ultimately rejects an important and widely accepted theory of metaphor comprehension. This theory, known as the *Invariance Hypothesis*, postulates that our understanding of a metaphor works in one direction only. Whereas our conceptualisation of the *target* domain of the metaphor (see unit A11) is affected and altered by the use of the metaphor, our conceptualisation of its source domain (that is, the concept we draw upon to develop the metaphor), remains unaffected. Thus, in the metaphor WAR IS CLEANING, which was discussed in A11, the thing we are trying to describe (our conception of war) is configured into a new way of thinking, although in the process we do not revise our mental schema of the source domain (our conception of cleaning).

More specifically, Stockwell draws on the concept of the Idealised Cognitive Model (see unit A10) in order to explore the Invariance Hypothesis as it relates to the processing of metaphor. According to Stockwell, the Invariance Hypothesis places a constraint on the ways in which ICMs are used to understand new experiences in a metaphorical mapping, allowing only the receiver's knowledge about the target domain of the metaphor to be altered. Using some examples from literature to support his case, he demonstrates that *both* domains are altered in a metaphorical mapping, an observation which suggests that the basic assumption of asymmetry in metaphorical mapping is ill-founded. Stockwell therefore rejects the Invariance Hypothesis as it relates to the reading of literature and in its place suggests an alternative source for a solution to the problems which the Invariance Hypothesis was invented to solve.

The inflexibility of invariance

Peter Stockwell

Peter Stockwell (reprinted from *Language and Literature*, 1999, 8, 2, 125–42).

[. . .] In general, cognitive linguistics has attempted to demonstrate how all representations of reality are based on metaphorical habits, conventionalised into domains of knowledge labelled *Idealised Cognitive Models* (or ICMs) (Lakoff 1987; [see also unit A10–P.S.]). These are presented as dynamic, radial structures that are altered by experience. They are *dynamic* in the sense that the categories of knowledge they represent can alter during on-going discourse in the world. They are *radial* in the sense that the arrangement of items in the structure displays prototype effects, such that there are central and peripheral examples of the category. Put most simply for illustration, 'apples' and 'oranges' are good, central examples of the 'fruit' category, whereas 'mangoes' and 'tomatoes' are not so central. Categories are thus seen not as absolutes but as culturally-determined and potentially fluid continua of knowledge. A 'potato' isn't simply 'not-a-fruit'; rather it is just a very bad example of a 'fruit'.

[. . .] underlying metaphorical mappings of ICMs are so ingrained in our usage that we barely perceive their metaphorical force at all: in the context of a popular romantic novel, 'She surrendered to his advances' is a realisation of the LOVE IS WAR metaphorical mapping of ICMs. The dozens of other realisations of this metaphor, and associated isomorphisms such as ARGUMENT IS WAR, POLITICS IS WAR, SPORT IS WAR and so on, all point to the habituated and accustomed nature of much of the evidence from everyday language on which cognitive linguistics rests.

[. . .] The simplest version [of the Invariance Hypothesis] is as follows:

> *The Invariance Hypothesis: Metaphorical mappings preserve the cognitive typology (this is, the image-schema structure) of the source domain.*
>
> (Lakoff 1990: 54)

The need for a restriction on the information which is mapped between ICMs is apparent when counter-intuitive anomalies are thrown up. Turner [. . .] gives the LIFE IS A JOURNEY metaphor as an example, where JOURNEY is the source domain and LIFE is the target. Life is structured and understood in terms of a journey, in the expressions, 'He's getting nowhere in life, She's on the right track, and, He arrived at a new stage in life' (from Turner 1990: 248). In this example, the Invariance

Peter
Stockwell

Hypothesis constrains us from saying, 'First I was getting somewhere in life and then I got off to a good start' (Turner 1990: 249), since the physical order of passing points on the path in a journey cannot be violated by the metaphorical mapping. It is the Invariance Hypothesis that explains here the anomalous meaning which 'disturbs us badly' (Turner 1990: 249).

[. . .] The central point is the *unidirectionality* of the isomorphism. Our idea of LIFE is structured by our familiar idea of a JOURNEY, but we do not conversely revise our idea of JOURNEYS on the basis of metaphors in which they are equated with LIFE. The cognitive typology of the source domain, JOURNEY, remains inviolable in this mapping. Turner (1990: 253–4) goes on to demonstrate that, when in life we might make a decision (understood as taking a fork in the path on the journey), then we cannot un-make that decision, though we could, on a journey, certainly retrace our steps and take the other fork. If the Invariance Hypothesis were not applied here, then the LIFE IS A JOURNEY metaphor would also allow us forks in paths that irrevocably disappear once we have chosen one way to go!

[. . .] As mentioned above, there is an assumption associated with the Invariance Hypothesis that there is a unidirectionality in the mapping of items and structure in conceptual metaphor. It would seem on first glance that this is the case with the TIME IS SPACE metaphor discussed by Lakoff (1990: 57). The fact that SPACE is the base (source) ICM in this example seems obvious, since

> we have detectors for motion and detectors for objects/locations. We do not have detectors for time (whatever that could mean). Thus, it makes good biological sense that time should be understood in terms of things and motion.
>
> (Lakoff 1990: 57)

TIME is thus the target ICM. We understand it in terms of our familiar idea of three-dimensional space. Indeed, H.G. Wells' (1895) time traveller explains 'time' to his dinner guests in precisely these terms, as an extension into 'four-dimensional' space at right angles to our familiar world, just before he literalises the metaphor by sweeping off into the future.

Lakoff (1990: 57) goes on to point out contradictory vectors in the TIME IS SPACE conceptual metaphor: 'The time has passed' and 'He passed the time'. For each, he argues that these simply illustrate that there are different correspondences of the metaphor. But this means that a single conceptual metaphor can be manifested and realised by a variety of utterances which reframe the detail in the mapping of ICMs slightly in the process. This conclusion would mean that cognitive linguistic methodology can produce more 'openness' in possible interpretation than it has been accused of [. . .].

More importantly, I would argue that examples such as 'The time has passed' or 'He passed the time', compared with 'Liverpool is three days' sailing from here', show a reversal of the conceptual metaphor: TIME IS SPACE and SPACE IS TIME. Each concept is understood in terms of our conventional understanding, by now well established, of the other. There is a consistency here in the mathematical logic that the two sides of an equational expression can be reversed without any change in meaning or value.

Peter
Stockwell

The Invariance Hypothesis seeks to restrict such a reversal, acting (to apply another ICM mapping) like a conceptual non-return valve.

In any case, it is not true to say that we don't have detectors for time: we have watches, clocks and a calendar (where progress through space represents time). These are indexes of time rather than detectors, strictly, but our tools have always and increasingly become extensions of our biology in ways that must affect our language, if the root of metaphor is the everyday and habitualised that Lakoff and Johnson (1980) claim it is. Rather than being unidirectional, it would seem that conceptual metaphor, even in the TIME IS SPACE example, might be *interanimating*. [. . .]

Let me give a couple of examples to illustrate this. The first is a phrase from a Paul Simon song, 'Diamonds on the Soles of His Shoes', in which a poor boy is walking down the street, 'empty as a pocket'. Here the ICMs of the boy's EMPTY LIFE and the general notion of POCKETS are mapped together. However, what results from this phrase is two ideas: the boy's life is like a pocket (a small insignificant container personal to him), but the type of pocket that is evoked by this mapping with the poor boy is an empty one. *Both* domains of the mapping have been altered (or specified) in the mapping.

The second example is of a different sort, and demonstrates what I have elsewhere (Stockwell 1996: 13) called 'flashpoint reference'. This is when a noun phrase invokes a referent but the utterance (usually through the predicate or a negation particle) immediately revokes or cancels the referent from active memory (see Stockwell (1994, 1996) for a fuller account of this). This happens in T.S. Eliot's poem *The Waste Land*:

> Sweet Thames, run softly, till I end my song.
> The river bears no empty bottles, sandwich papers,
> Silk handkerchiefs, cardboard boxes, cigarette ends
> Or other testimony of summer nights. The nymphs are
>   departed.
> And their friends, the loitering heirs of City directors;
> Departed, have left no addresses.
>   (Eliot 1963: 70)

Here, the 16th century Elizabethan River Thames is invoked, firstly by the quotation of the coda to each stanza of Spenser's *Prothalamion* (1596), and then by the description of the river in its pre-industrial pre-urbanised state, clean and unpolluted by social rubbish. Of course, in describing the non-existence of the litter, the poem simultaneously invokes the image of the modern, dirty, degraded river as well, even in the act of denying it all. The two image-schemas of Elizabethan river and 20th century river are mapped together dialectically to suggest a comment on the degradation of the modern world; and the movement from the high art of the Elizabethan Renaissance to the rather tawdry and sleazy mundane concerns of modern times is further suggested. The mapping itself, in other words, can be *thematised*, in this literary context, and this action involves moving *beyond* the simple mapped restructuring of image-schemas.

When discussing 'image metaphors', Lakoff (1990: 66) cites several poetic examples as 'one-shot metaphors', in which both image-schemas are conventional, but the

**Peter
Stockwell**

mapping is novel or striking [. . .]. Lakoff cites the surrealist writer André Breton's line: 'My wife . . . whose waist is an hourglass', to argue that such 'part-whole' mappings can be explained using the Invariance Hypothesis. He suggests it provides an answer to the question of which parts of the source domain are mapped to the target (and which parts of image-schematic structure are left behind). In this example, the curvy shape of the hourglass is mapped onto the poet's wife's body, but presumably the flowing sand inside, the glass coldness and perhaps the notion of time running out (literalised and dramatised in the hourglass) are not mapped. It is from such literary examples that Lakoff and Turner generalise the Invariance Hypothesis.

Let's look at the Breton example in detail. The line is most commonly found in English in the translation by Edouard Roditi of Breton's poem 'Freedom of Love'. [. . .] It begins:

> My wife with the hair of a wood fire
> With the thoughts of heat lightning
> With the waist of an hourglass
> With the waist of an otter in the teeth of a tiger
> My wife with the lips of a cockade and of a bunch of stars of the last
>   magnitude
> With the teeth of tracks of white mice on the white earth
> With the tongue of rubbed amber and glass
> My wife with the tongue of a stabbed host
> With the tongue of a doll that opens and closes its eyes
> With the tongue of an unbelievable stone [. . .]
>   (Breton/Roditi in Germain 1978: 69)

This is a poem generated by surrealism. A multi-media art movement flourishing in Europe in the 1920s and '30s, surrealism had as one of its main objectives the destruction of rationalist and bourgeois thought by unusual juxtaposition. This collage technique manifested itself in verbal art mainly in the form of highly striking and deviant metaphor, of which the Breton passage above provides several good examples. [. . .]

Verbal art in surrealism is founded on isomorphism, but it is a very different conception from that posed within cognitive linguistics through the Invariance Hypothesis. Here is a perception of language that is transcendental and uses metaphor to go beyond everyday meaning, in order to reframe fundamentally our view of the world and ourselves. In other terms, here is a perception of language that is dialectical and uses metaphor to go beyond the familiar understandings of ICMs, in order to recast all our ICMs and retroactively alter our perceptions of base *and* target in our conceptual experience. This is metaphor as interanimation, in which the process of 'metaphoring' encourages us to see the familiar world in a new light as a synthesis of base and target mapping.

Let me demonstrate this by returning to the opening of Breton's poem quoted above. Each line contains a single metaphorical mapping, except the fifth which maps the wife's lips with two bases (a 'cockade' and 'stars'). Her 'waist' is mapped with two ICMs, and

Peter
Stockwell

lines 7–10 map her 'tongue' with four different things. Applying the Invariance Hypothesis to a reading of this would predict only incoherence, as Turner points out (Turner 1990: 248) [. . .]. On first inspection the Breton passage is not exactly like this: in the line, 'My wife with the lips of a cockade and of a bunch of stars of the last magnitude', two distinct sources are mapped onto one target; and in the last four lines of the quoted passage, four distinct sources ('rubbed amber and glass', 'a stabbed host', 'a doll' and 'an unbelievable stone') are mapped onto one target ('tongue'). However, if the whole poem is read as a general conceptual mapping in which the poet's wife is the target ICM, then there are possibly 75 distinct components of very diverse ICMs, and there are 11 source ICMs even just in the passage from the beginning of the poem I quoted above. All of these map, sometimes severally, onto particular components of the 'wife'. If the passage is to be read as surrealism, then simple incoherence does not seem an adequate account of this poem.

This paper began by noting that ICMs are radial structures that display prototype effects. They are built up by accumulated experience and are constantly being revised and altered to a greater or lesser degree. Those ICMs that are revised the least constitute the individual's relatively stable view of the world and the things in it. Those that are revised the most encompass new experiences, unfamiliar things, items of debate or uncertainty, or perhaps areas of which the person does not have a strong opinion and has been swayed by the arguments in various incoming bits of language.

The aspect of cognitive linguistics that is essential here is the notion of prototype effects: categories are not absolutes but are fluid continua of knowledge. Together with the notion of radiality, this means that ICMs have central, secondary and peripheral elements in their structures. The central problem which the Invariance Hypothesis was invented to solve is a consequence of the question of how to decide which elements are mapped and which are left behind. This question can be answered directly, without any need for Invariance.

The key idea here is *salience*. This involves a judgment of match between the incoming text and the individual's expectations and propensities. In other words, it is a readerly notion as well as a text-based one. Let me outline the process of encountering a metaphorical structure-mapping, as follows, by recalling again the example from Breton that Lakoff (1990) suggested: 'My wife . . . with the waist of an hourglass'. In the discussion above, I suggested that the curvy shape of the hourglass was mapped, but presumably not the flowing sand inside, nor the glass coldness and perhaps not the notion of time running out. But why not? And why 'presumably'? Certainly this seems intuitively right. So how do we decide that the line is not about the poet's wife's similarity to these other things?

It seems that the notion of the *shape* of the hourglass is the most salient feature. Maybe this has become conventionalised (and thus comes to mind most readily) in the phrase 'hourglass figure'. It is plausible to suggest that the centrally prototypical feature of the 'hourglass' ICM is its distinctive shape. In any case, what seems to happen is that once this feature has been mapped onto the target ('wife'), then that is satisfactory enough to carry on with the reading of the poem. This was enough for me on my first reading. The flowing sand inside is a relatively secondary feature, and one that I only began to consider when I re-read the line in the article by Lakoff. But I can see no

Peter Stockwell

salience in this feature for my reading of the poem, so I don't think it is mapped to my image-schema of the 'wife'. [. . .]

Unfamiliar ICMs are only unfamiliar once, and after several practices of the mapping the pattern becomes conventionalised. It then becomes difficult to see which is source and which target [. . .]. [I]t is plausible to suppose that we become accustomed to approaching novel metaphors using the same interpretative strategies: that is, we look for the most salient features – on the basis of their prototypical ordering – that will produce a satisfactory reading for the context in hand. I have tried to demonstrate how changing contexts and reading purposes can account for different interpretations, within this model.

The key ideas outlined in this paper include the notion that image-schematic structure-mappings are *interanimating* rather than unidirectional, and this allows meaning and interpretation to be *dialectical* and *exponential* to the surface realisation of the proposition. The notion that ICMs are *radial* and display *prototype effects* allows an account of which features are mapped and which left behind, subject to *salience*. This notion, related to the pragmatic description of relevance, centres on the purpose of reading a particular text, joined to a recognition that genres encourage readers to interpret in particular ways. And finally, it is a key idea that ICM-construction is not treated as a completed process prior to the reading experience, but that reading itself serves to refine and revise the features, structures and domains of knowledge. [. . .]

My main interest is in cognitive poetics, which I believe is able to provide a coherent, valid and workable theory of literature (as argued clearly by M. Freeman (2000)). The Invariance Hypothesis curtails the perception of metaphor as creative. It limits our understanding, condemning us to see things only in the way that we have always seen them. It would prevent us from seeing how we could possibly genuinely perceive anything new or challenging. It cannot explain the capacity of language for reference to a new sense beyond source and target, that is embodied in surrealist poetry, science fiction, and all imaginative works of art. Such limitations are counter to the larger, more fundamental claims of cognitive linguistics concerning the linguistic basis and embodiment of culture and perception. Here, I have sought to preserve the general value of cognitive linguistics, while escaping the inflexibility of invariance.

Issues to consider

Stockwell's paper illustrates well how stylistics can be used to rethink ideas about language and linguistics. Indeed, it addresses a question posed at the very start of this book, in A1, which asks 'What can stylistics tell us about language?'. Specifically, Stockwell orientates his analysis of examples from literature towards the Invariance Hypothesis as conceived in cognitive linguistics, which then allows him to challenge the theory and suggest an alternative solution. In the light of Stockwell's solution, it is worth revisiting the passage from Jeanette Winterson provided in unit C11. A key question to ask of the passage is whether it is only one side of the metaphorical expression, our understanding of misery, which is altered in the mapping, or is our perception of the numerous source domains altered also? Similarly, look again at the four examples from Irish poetry that also formed the basis of an exercise in unit C11. To what extent are the image schemata ('dairy farming', 'an ancient burial

**Peter
Stockwell**

ground' and so on) that contributed to the source domains in these metaphors left *unaltered* conceptually by these novel metaphorical mappings? In general, are metaphors *interanimating* in the sense described by Stockwell? And by the same token, is the Invariance Hypothesis really the 'conceptual non-return valve' that Stockwell describes?

More suggestions follow:

❑ Take an anthology of poetry and write down every metaphor you can find across any five pages of print. Consider what mappings between source and target domain are involved, which elements are mapped and whether the metaphorical mapping is 'novel' in the sense described across this strand.

❑ Using the selection of metaphors provided in C11 as a starting point, develop a comparative analysis of the sorts of metaphors you typically find in specific discourse contexts. What sorts of metaphors, for example, do you commonly find in advertising? Or in tourist information, popular science, cook books and so on?

D12   CORPUS STYLISTICS

This reading, by Michaela Mahlberg and Catherine Smith, presents a computer-assisted approach to the study of character discourse in Dickens. It focusses on the concept of the *suspended quotation*, which can be defined broadly as the interruption of a character's speech by at least five words of narrator text. Very much in keeping with the corpus-stylistic method, Mahlberg and Smith use quantitative techniques to compare selected parts of a novel with the patterns found across the whole text and beyond, although they also offer a qualitative analysis of the particular suspensions they isolate. They draw on a new corpus tool, CLiC, to assist their investigation of interruptions in the speech of Mrs Sparsit in *Hard Times*. In keeping with the broader stylistic rationale for all corpus-assisted stylistics, they link their analysis to important literary themes and motifs.

Dickens, the suspended quotation and the corpus

**Mahlberg
and Smith**

Michaela Mahlberg and Catherine Smith (reprinted from *Language and Literature* 2012, 21, 1, 51–65)

The 'suspended quotation', that is, an interruption of a character's words by the narrator, has been extensively discussed by Lambert (1981), who draws both on quantitative and qualitative methods. Although he uses his data to make some rather provocative claims that we do not want to follow up in our study, his observations also suggest interesting questions from a corpus stylistic point of view. The computer-assisted study of literary texts can make an important contribution to the study of linguistic devices by increasing the scale at which they are analyzed. In this way, the study of the suspended quotation provides insights into the presentation of character information as well as the organization of character discourse. Although we raise some questions about the way in which Lambert approaches suspensions we also want to show that the concept is a useful one to include in the stylistician's checklist. [. . .]

Lambert (1981: 6) defines the 'suspended quotation' as a 'protracted interruption by the narrator of a character's speech. And here, "protracted" means containing at least five words.' Lambert (1981: 6ff.) explains that the criterion of five words is based on an intuitive judgement: an interruption of five words seems to be intrusive while a shorter one mostly does not. One of his examples is the following with the suspended quotation in italics.

(1) 'I am proud to see,' said Mr. Carker, *with a servile stooping of his neck, which the revelations making by his eyes and teeth proclaim to be a lie,* 'I am proud to see that my humble offering is graced by Mrs. Dombey's hand . . .'

(Dombey and Son)

Lambert (1981: 41) points out that the suspension is 'a handy place to put information, gestures, facial contortions' and other details that he subsumes under the heading of 'suprasegmentals'. He points out that suprasegmentals play an important role for the representation of life-like dialogue, but are difficult to capture because of the linearity of the text (Lambert 1981: 42). Suspensions thus are useful places to create an impression that comes close to synchronicity of presentation. Korte (1997: 97) makes a similar observation when she discusses ways in which body language accompanies fictional speech. Korte (1997: 97) points out that the two devices that are most frequently used to suggest that body language and speech occur simultaneously are '(a) the interruption of the character's speech by a description of the body language, and (b) the syntactical subordination of the body language to the character's speech'. While Lambert (1981) acknowledges that the description of suprasegmentals is one of the functions of suspensions, he sees the main reason for the frequency of the phenomenon elsewhere. In his discussion of example (1), he points out that the information in the suspension is 'distinctly unflattering', which he takes as evidence for his provocative explanation of suspensions in terms of Dickens's aggressiveness towards his characters (Lambert 1981: 59). Lambert (1981: 35) claims that suspended quotations in Dickens's early novels occur more frequently than in his late novels, because 'the heavy Dickensian use of suspended quotation seems to be fundamentally a sort of aggression' – even if the content of the suspensions is not overtly aggressive. He views the suspended quotation as a device employed by a jealous author who expresses hostility towards the characters he created. As this hostility stems from Dickens's resentment of the characters' attractiveness to the audience, Lambert claims, the use of suspended quotations decreases in Dickens's later novels. For him the division into early and late novels is between *David Copperfield* and *Bleak House*. He argues that with the start of the public readings in 1853, the year *Bleak House* was completed, Dickens found another way of seeking contact with his audience. Thus the indirect audience contact that was enabled through the suspended quotation became less relevant (Lambert 1981: 140). The claims that Lambert makes about Dickens's intentions when using suspended quotations cannot be tested by a linguistic analysis of Dickens's novels. However, claims about frequencies and functions of suspensions can be scrutinized in more detail. A methodological point that is crucial to Lambert's (1981) approach is the deliberate focus on striking cases when aiming to explain the prevalence of suspensions. He suggests: 'when trying to make sense of an uncommon pattern of usage, we may begin with those examples of the pattern which are the strangest of the strange and hope those oddest cases and most bizarre subvarieties will suggest something about the less startling examples' (Lambert 1981: 44). What Lambert spells out is a way of approaching linguistic examples that is not uncommon but usually not made explicit. However, developments in corpus linguistics raise questions about what is to be regarded as 'uncommon patterns of usage', because it is the common patterns that are far less noticeable than the uncommon ones. This point also comes into play in Carter's (2004) approach to the concept of literariness. Instead of making a distinction between literary and non-literary language, Carter suggests a 'cline of literariness', which makes it possible amongst other things to account for literary language in everyday conversations. The notion of the cline plays an important role in the description of linguistic patterns, especially when those patterns are observed on the basis of corpus data. Sinclair's (1991: 100) observation that '[t]he language looks rather different when you look at a lot of it at once' still holds true for the analysis of literary texts. [. . .]

While Lambert's (1981) approach is based on manual counting, corpus linguistic methods enable us to build on his study by scaling it up to look at the full texts of the novels rather than just a few sections from each book. In order to be able to count all of the suspensions in a text they need to be annotated with XML. The text files for the corpus are taken from *Project Gutenberg* (see 'Issues to consider' below – P.S.) and the annotation process for our corpus is fully automated using a set of Python scripts. Key to the automated annotation is the use of regular expressions. These are essentially complex patterns of characters that specify certain features of the text and can be used to find matching strings in the text, in this case they are used to find sentences and text in quotes. In a first pass through the text files, chapters and paragraphs are identified using the graphological conventions present in the base text. Sentences are then annotated using a sentence tokenizer, which is based on regular expressions. The regular expression defines a graphological pattern equivalent to a sentence. Every time a section of text is found that matches the pattern, that section of text is taken to be a sentence and is annotated as such. In a third pass regular expressions are used again to identify passages of text between quotation marks. These sections are marked as quotes using milestone elements, which are empty XML elements containing no text, as they overlap with the sentence hierarchy. An example of the resulting XML is given in Figure [D12.1]: <qs/> is the milestone element for the start of a quotation and <qe/> the milestone element for the end of a quotation.

The suspension annotation is based on the XML structure shown in the figure. We take as our definition of suspensions any text of five or more words which occurs between a <qe/> tag and a <qs/> tag within a single paragraph. Based on this definition another pass through the corpus annotates the suspensions with more milestone

```
<p type="speech" id="BH.c6.p114">
        <s id="BH.c6.s340'>
                <qs/>
                    "My dear Miss Summerson,"
                <qe/>
                said Richard in a whisper,
                <qs/>
                    "I have ten pounds that I received from Mr. Kenge.
        </s>
        <s id="BH.c6.s341'>
                        "I must try what that will do."
                <qe/>
        </s>
</p>
```

Figure D12.1 Example of annotation

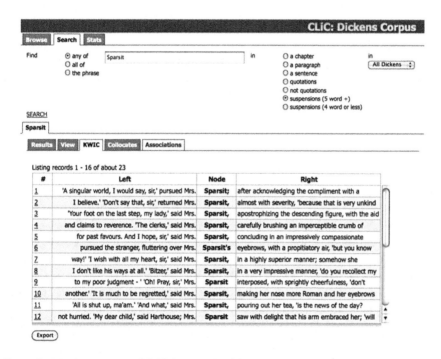

Figure D12.2 Screen shot of CLiC for search of *Sparsit* in suspensions

```
1    world, I would say, sir,' pursued Mrs. Sparsit; after acknowledging the compliment wit
2    .' 'Don't say that, sir,' returned Mrs. Sparsit, almost with severity, 'because that is
3     on the last step, my lady,' said Mrs. Sparsit, apostrophizing the descending figure,
4      to reverence. 'The clerks,' said Mrs. Sparsit, carefully brushing an imperceptible
5    st favours. And I hope, sir,' said Mrs. Sparsit, concluding in an impressively compassi
6    sued the stranger, fluttering over Mrs. Sparsit's eyebrows, with a propitiatory air,
7    wish with all my heart, sir,' said Mrs. Sparsit, in a highly superior manner; somehow s
8    e his ways at all.' 'Bitzer,' said Mrs. Sparsit, in a very impressive manner, 'do you r
9    poor judgment - ' 'Oh! Pray, sir,' Mrs. Sparsit interposed, with sprightly cheerfulness,
10   It is much to be regretted,' said Mrs. Sparsit, making her nose more Roman and her
11   shut up, ma'am.' 'And what,' said Mrs. Sparsit, pouring out her tea, 'is the news of
12    'My dear child,' said Harthouse; Mrs. Sparsit saw with delight that his arm embraced
13   Gradgrind's daughter?' 'Yes,' said Mrs. Sparsit, suddenly compressing her mouth, 'he ha
14   ss all the morning. 'Bitzer,' said Mrs. Sparsit that afternoon, when her patron was
15   dence! Come out, ma'am!' then said Mrs. Sparsit, to some one inside, 'come out, or
16   , 'but it is my duty to remember,' Mrs. Sparsit was fond of observing with a lofty
17   you.' 'I certainly, sir,' returned Mrs. Sparsit, with a dignity serenely mournful, 'was
18   luxury.' 'I do not, sir,' returned Mrs. Sparsit with a shake of her head, 'deny it.' Mr.
19   urables.' 'I trust, sir,' rejoined Mrs. Sparsit, with decent resignation, 'it is not
20   consider, I cannot consider,' said Mrs. Sparsit, with a most extensive stock on hand of
21    to understand these things,' said Mrs. Sparsit, with dignity, 'my lot having been
22   heard in Dutch clocks. Not,' said Mrs. Sparsit, with a lofty sense of giving strict
23   ur feelings?' 'Yes, sir,' returned Mrs. Sparsit, with a meek shake of her head, 'he
```

Figure D12.3 The 23 occurrences of *Sparsit* in suspensions in *Hard Times*

elements. It is important to point out that at this stage, the annotation does not distinguish whether the text between quotation marks is speech or thought, but this is not crucial to points we aim to make in this article [. . .] In order to investigate our XML annotated corpus, the web interface CLiC (Corpus Linguistics in Cheshire) has been developed. CLiC has been created on top of Cheshire 3, an open source search retrieval engine for XML data (cheshire3.org, no date). It allows searches to be carried out in different sections of the corpus. In particular, CLiC makes it possible to search for words and phrases in suspensions – as illustrated in Figure [D12.2] with a search for the name *Sparsit*. The example of Mrs Sparsit in *Hard Times* serves to illustrate some of the characteristics of suspensions and the opportunities that CLiC offers.

There are 23 suspensions in the Dickens Corpus that contain the name *Sparsit*. All of them come from the novel *Hard Times*. As the screen shot in Figure [D12.2] only shows part of the examples, Figure [D12.3] focuses just on the concordance with all 23 suspensions. Of those 23 examples, 21 interrupt the speech of Mrs Sparsit and the suspensions contribute to revealing character information. Among the repeated patterns visible in the concordance are non-finite clauses and prepositional phrases that contain circumstantial information, as in examples (2) and (3) which correspond to concordance lines 11 and 17 respectively.

(2) 'And what,' *said Mrs. Sparsit, pouring out her tea,* 'is the news of the day? Anything?'

(3) 'I certainly, sir,' returned Mrs. Sparsit, with a dignity serenely mournful, 'was familiar with the Italian Opera at a very early age.'

Both -*ing* clauses and prepositional phrases support the effect of synchronicity between the speech and the body language in those examples. In example (2), Mrs Sparsit accompanies her words with practical action body language: she pours out her tea. In example (3), there is no explicit description of body language, but the narrator provides an interpretation of Mrs Sparsit's body language: she speaks 'with a dignity serenely mournful'. In other examples where the narrator interprets body language, reference is also made to Mrs Sparsit's manner of saying something (the noun *manner* appears in concordance lines 7 and 8, as well as 5, which is not visible in the amount of context included in Figure [D12.2] though).

The picture that is presented through the suspensions in Figure [D12.3] depicts Mrs Sparsit as having a lofty way of behaving. The adjective *lofty* occurs twice (lines 16 and 22), but there are also examples referring to her impressive or superior manner (lines 5, 7, 8) and the dignity and severity with which she behaves (lines 2, 17, 19, 21). All these examples reflect that Mrs Sparsit acts as if she were better than other people. She now is Bounderby's housekeeper, but she 'had not only seen different days, but was highly connected' (*Hard Times*, Chapter 7). When she is introduced in Chapter 7, her nose and her eyebrows are two features that are highlighted:

(4)   And here she was now, in her elderly days, with the Coriolanian style of nose and
      the dense black eyebrows . . .

The references to her 'Coriolanian' or 'Roman' nose then recur as external features of her lofty manner. The suspension in concordance line 10, corresponding to example (5) here, also refers to Mrs Sparsit's nose. It shows how her nose and her eyebrows are signs of her severity – this severity being part of her loftiness, as highlighted by the patterns in the concordance.

(5)   'It is much to be regretted,' *said Mrs. Sparsit, making her nose more Roman and her
      eyebrows more Coriolanian in the strength of her severity*, 'that the united masters allow
      of any such class-combinations.'

These examples show how the information in the suspensions relates to similar information in other descriptions of Mrs Sparsit. The suspensions do not introduce a new view of her, but by repetition enforce features typical of this character.

The function of suspensions as places to describe habitual behaviour or typical character features is not limited to the example of Mrs Sparsit but also found with other characters [. . .]. Suspensions seem to be a useful place for such information. When presented as circumstantial information, character information that has already been mentioned appears less strikingly repetitive. If a character has a typical manner of saying something it appears almost natural that the same body language occurs again. In this sense, suspensions also help to show what behaviour is to be regarded as character information in contrast to behaviour that may be untypical and a reaction triggered by a specific situation. Behaviour that is due to a particular situation would have to be discounted in the assessment of what constitutes character information,

**Mahlberg
and Smith**

as Culpeper (2001) also explains in his discussion of characterization. [. . .] Lambert finds further evidence for his claim that Dickens is jealous of his characters in the use of suspensions to handle pauses in character speech. Even without interpreting them as a sign of authorial jealousy, pauses in character speech can be seen as techniques of an intrusive narrator. Lambert (1981: 67ff.) describes the use of an 'artificial sequence' as an effective device to make the reader feel to some extent similar discomfort to that experienced by the characters throughout the pause. One of Lambert's 1981 examples is example ([6]) below – from *Hard Times*. Here the narrator only refers to a silence once the character started speaking again. This way the character's speech is interrupted to refer to a pause at a point where – in the story – no pause actually occurs in the character's speech. With regard to example ([6]), Lambert (1981: 68) describes the effect of presenting two narrated pauses in the form of artificial sequences as recreating for the reader 'the painfulness' of the silences.

> ([6])'Mrs. Bounderby,' said Harthouse, *after a short silence*, 'may there be a better confidence between yourself and me? Tom has borrowed a considerable sum of you?'
>
> 'You will understand, Mr. Harthouse,' she returned, *after some indecision*: she had been more or less uncertain, and troubled throughout the conversation, and yet had in the main preserved her self-contained manner; 'you will understand [. . .]'
> [our italics]

Claims about the way in which pauses are actually perceived by readers can ultimately only be verified by experiments involving participants. However, corpus methods can contribute to formulating hypotheses about potential effects. Corpus evidence seems to suggest that pauses described in suspensions may not necessarily be perceived as such striking interruptions of character speech as Lambert claims. The effect that the narrating of a pause in the form of a suspension will have depends not only on the presence of a suspension but also on textual patterns around it, as well as on the patterns that are found repeatedly in suspensions. To see links between pauses and other patterns in suspensions, example ([7]), which corresponds to concordance line 1, in Figure [D12.3], might be helpful. The example also illustrates how the order of presentation departs from the order of the narrated activities. We have pointed out earlier that suspensions can be seen as devices to suggest synchronicity between speech and body language. Example ([7]), in effect, explicitly sequences the speech and body language, but employs an order of presentation that does not match the order of the speech and body language. However, as the body language is presented as circumstantial information, the reversal of the actual order of speech and body language does not seem to be highlighted. Similarly, the prepositional phrase *after a short silence*, in example ([6]), might make the narration of the pause less striking than Lambert (1981) wants to argue.

> ([7])'A singular world, I would say, sir,' pursued Mrs. Sparsit; *after acknowledging the compliment with a drooping of her dark eyebrows . . .*

Mahlberg
and Smith

While individual examples raise some interesting points, we can get a better picture of options for presenting pauses in character speech, if we look at a larger number of instances. Patterns of the word *pause* can serve as a useful starting point. The word occurs altogether 418 times in the Dickens corpus [of 4.5 million words – P.S.], of which 83 occurrences appear in suspensions, which means 335 occurrences appear in text outside of suspensions. Of the occurrences of pause that do not appear in suspensions, not all refer to a silence, some are forms of verbs or refer to the meaning of 'break', as in 'We made a pause at the toy shop in Fleet Street . . .' (*David Copperfield*). In suspensions, *pause* always refers to a silence. Of the 83 occurrences 78 appear in a prepositional phrase with *after*. Table [D12.1] shows the most frequent patterns of these prepositional phrases and compares them to the numbers of the respective patterns outside suspensions. [. . .]

Table D12.1   Patterns of pause in suspensions compared to text outside suspensions

	Text without suspensions	Suspensions	LL
pause	335	83	242.53
after a pause	47	20	75.76
after a short pause	16	15	82.08
after a moment's pause	7	13	75.47

For all three patterns, the numbers refer only to cases where the pattern constitutes the whole prepositional phrase, in other words there is no postmodification as in example ([8]). For each of the patterns most of the suspensions in which they occur have the form 'reporting verb + subject (or subject + reporting verb, in the case of a pronominal subject) + Adverbial, as in examples ([9]) and ([10]).

([8]) 'And when,' asked my guardian, *rising after a pause, during which Mr. Kenge had rattled his money and Mr. Vholes had picked his pimples,* 'when is next term?'
(*Bleak House*)

([9]) 'Still, it is a triumph to me to know that he is so true to himself, and to his name of Dombey; although, of course, I always knew he would be. I only hope,' *said Mrs Chick, after a pause,* 'that she may be worthy of the name too'.
(*Dombey and Son*)

([10]) 'That's all I say. And I suppose,' *added the lofty young man, after a moment's pause,* 'that visitor will . . .'
(*Little Dorrit*)

The point that Table [D12.1] makes is that the word *pause* tends to occur in suspensions and typically in the three patterns shown. Corpus linguistic findings emphasize that the patterns that are frequent are not necessarily the same patterns that are easily noticeable. The *after . . . pause* patterns may also fall into this category. In examples ([9]) and ([10], the emphasis is less on the pause as such, but the patterns support the organization of the character discourse. In both examples, the sentences that are interrupted add another thought to what is said before and the interruption follows the prefaces *I only hope* and *And I suppose*. The description of pauses in examples such as ([9]) and ([10]) is different from examples where the description of the pause receives more emphasis as in ([11]) and ([12]). Here the discourse between characters is interrupted, but the interruption does not appear within a turn of a character, but between turns. Also the pause is not presented in the form of an adverbial, but in more prominent grammatical structures.

> ([11]) There was a *pause*. The countenance of Nicholas fell, and he gazed ruefully at the fire.
>
> > (*Nicholas Nickleby*)

> ([12]) A *pause* ensued, in which the schoolmaster looked very awkward.
>
> > (*Our Mutual Friend*)

[. . .] Suspensions analyzed in the form of concordances can be useful places to study character information. The example of *pause* [. . .] points to similarities between the presentation of body language that accompanies speech and pauses in character speech. While they can be highlighted in the text, common patterns in suspensions describe pauses in the form of circumstantial information so that the pause as such might receive less attention. However, assumptions about what readers do and do not notice will ultimately need to be verified by psycholinguistic experiments. The definition of suspensions as consisting of at least five words thus also requires further study. While our examples are specific to Dickens and only provide some initial insights into the range of functions of suspensions, it is clear that the more general approach illustrated in this article has far-ranging potential.

Issues to consider

It is important to note that Mahlberg and Smith, throughout their essay, frame their corpus-assisted analysis in the context of the critical observations of Lambert (1981) on Dickens's prose. This underscores the position taken across this book that stylistic analysis (whether corpus-assisted or not) should *not* take as its starting point an out-of-hand rejection of a literary-critical reading (if one exists) of the same text or writer. Instead, as Mahlberg and Smith have done, it is better to think through the issues the critical reading raises before developing an evidence-based description of style which may or not run counter to the critical commentary. Admittedly, the technical aspects of corpus stylistics are challenging and require access to electronic data and knowledge of how to process that data through applications like XML (eXtensible Mark-up Language). Moreover, the CLiC model used in the present reading is, at the time of writing, a prototype and is not yet freely accessible, although updates on this and other developments will be posted on the web material that accompany this book. Nonetheless, even a rudimentary exploration of a digitized text, with basic search terms and keywords, can reveal much about a writer's use of particular or recurring types of vocabulary, structure and phrasing.

Mahlberg and Smith

Some suggestions along these lines follow.

Activity ✪

❑   It was noted in unit B11 that many of our common sayings and figures of speech originated from (what were once) novel metaphors in literature. Corpus tools offer an excellent resource for exploring this aspect of creativity in language and, indeed, for verifying and checking the authenticity of academic claims against assumed textual sources. Unit B11 offered some examples of everyday expressions commonly believed to originate in the plays of William Shakespeare. Here is a fuller set of such expressions:

> cold comfort
> a tower of strength
> play fast and loose
> to the manner born
> a foregone conclusion
> the mind's eye
> it was Greek to me
> cruel only to be kind

There are a number of websites which have gathered together the complete works of Shakespeare, the most useful of which is: www.opensourceshakespeare.org. Using this website, try to trace each of the expressions above, checking whether or not they are genuine 'Shakespeareanisms' and, if they are, from which act and scene of which play they originate. How much time did it take you to complete this exercise? Without the corpus search, how long would it have taken you to complete such a task? A complaint against the use of corpus-assisted methods of analysis is that it de-sensitizes readers to the subtle and nuanced patterns that are embedded in the fabric of literary texts. These patterns, it is argued, can only be genuinely understood and appreciated when one reads a text slowly, carefully and intimately. Is this a valid criticism of the corpus method?

❑   Related to the previous suggestion, here is an activity based on James Joyce's novel *Ulysses*, whose word-formation techniques were touched upon briefly in unit C12. A *hapax legomonon* refers to a word or expression that is found only once in a literary work; the example given earlier was Joyce's lexical compound 'brightwindbridled'. The *Project Gutenberg* website (drawn upon by Mahlberg and Smith) is a freely accessible digitised archive of material that includes many classical literary works (www.gutenberg.org). These texts are out of copyright and therefore downloadable, so they make for an invaluable resource for training and practice in corpus-assisted work. Returning to Joyce, it is astonishing how so many of his words are used only once in a novel that is well over a quarter of a million words long. Moreover, very many of these hapax legomena tend to cluster in key episodes in the book, such as in the 'Proteus' episode where Stephen Dedalus walks along the beach at Sandymount Strand. Using the relevant part of the *Project Gutenberg* website, look for the following three compounds in *Ulysses*: 'seaspawn',

**Mahlberg
and Smith**

'snotgreen' and 'seawrack. Find out where they occur and if they appear anywhere else in Joyce's novel. In other words, which, if any, are hapax legomena? When you locate these words in the novel, look at the textual material around them to within a span of fifty words on either side. How many other words in this co-text might also lay claim to being comparably innovative? Finally, on reading *Ulysses* for the first time many years ago (and, alas, in the days before computers were invented), I came away with the sense that Joyce, in a characteristically arcane pattern of allusion, makes reference to a mid-fourteenth-century Kentish text called *Agenbite of Inwit.* The title literally means 'again-biting of inner knowledge' in the sense of the pricking of one's conscience. My impression was that this curious motif appeared in different places in the novel, though I was hard put to recall exactly where, or in association with what character (Leopold Bloom or Stephen Dedalus), or even whether the phrase had been subjected to some Joycean grammatical twist or alteration in its different representations in the text. To what extent could a corpus-assisted exploration of the novel help clarify these impressions?

❏ The methods developed in this reading can of course be replicated in studies of other prose, and the *Gutenberg* website, as noted, offers instant access to many classical works of prose fiction. Think, for example, of how the suspended quotation is developed by Jane Austen in her novel *Pride and Prejudice* (1813). A rudimentary search phrase to begin such a study would be to track the occurrence of the expression 'said Mrs. Bennet'. Other reporting verbs could then be filtered in, as in 'cried [Darcy]', 'observed [Miss Bingley]', '[he] continued' and so on. Additionally or alternatively, look out for key abstract nouns in Austen's novel, such as the lemmas of *civil,* or, for an interesting contrast to the discussion of (Mahlberg's work on) Dickens in B12, explore textual references to body parts, especially *eyes.* Rather conveniently, Mahlberg and Smith (2010) is an article which uses corpus tools to explore all of these features and more in Austen's novel, and, after the preliminary investigation suggested here, readers are directed to this very useful explication of the corpus stylistic methodology.

FURTHER READING

What is stylistics?

❏ Lecercle's attack on stylistics, entitled 'The Current State of Stylistics', was published as Lecercle (1993). Wales (1993a) is a riposte to Lecercle, which appeared in a subsequent issue of the same journal.

❏ Here are some representative samples of the sorts of studies alluded to across this opening unit. For work in feminist stylistics, cognitive stylistics and discourse stylistics see, respectively, Mills (1995), Semino and Culpeper (2002) and Carter and Simpson (1989). An overview of the aims and scope of 'pedagogical stylistics' is Clark and Zyngier (2003) and useful recent collections of essays on this topic include Watson and Zyngier (2007) and Burke et al. (2012). Wales's dictionary of stylistics, now in its third edition, offers compact definitions of the key terms and topics in the field (Wales 2011), while Nørgaard et al. (2010) is a guide to the central concepts and the major practitioners in the discipline. Valuable 'readers' in stylistics, comprising reprints of selected influential papers, are Carter and Stockwell (2008) and Weber (1996).

❏ Literary criticism and stylistics are of course united by a shared emphasis on the close reading of literary texts, although it must be said that the aims and scope of stylistics have not always been represented accurately within literary-critical work (see Simpson 1997a: 2–7). Barry (2002) contains a useful chapter on stylistics written from the perspective of critical theory. A useful exercise would be to compare the angle taken on stylistics in Barry's description with that taken in this book.

❏ As noted in A1, most major academic publishers have now produced significant texts in stylistics. There are many excellent collections, handbooks and companions appearing on the market, including Lambrou and Stockwell (2007), McIntyre and Busse (2010), Stockwell and Whiteley (2014), Burke (2014) and Sotirova (forthcoming). Not only do these collections offer wide coverage but the individual contributions are written by international stylisticians on the particular topics in which they specialise. At the risk of talking up the opposition, there are a number of textbooks, in addition to this one, which pitch the subject at an accessible, introductory level: see (if you must!) Verdonk (2002), Gregoriou (2008) and Jeffries and McIntyre (2010). Alongside these publications are numerous specialist monographs on different aspects of language and style, but these will be referenced across this book in the places most appropriate to their area of coverage.

Grammar and style

❏   A useful introduction to grammar and vocabulary, which offers a much fuller treatment than can be accommodated within a single unit like this, is Jackson's textbook in the RELI series (Jackson 2001). Young (1984) remains an excellent introductory guide to the grammar of English.

Rhythm and metre

❏   Attridge (1982) is an important book on the rhythms of verse, while Leech (1969) remains an authoritative account of this and other features of the language of poetry. Scholarly articles by Cureton (1994) and Fabb (2002) offer more advanced treatments of metre. Winn and Idsardi (2008) is an interesting article exploring the connections between music and metre. An excellent and accessible broad overview of the 'meaning' of metre is Carper and Attridge (2003).
❏   Brazil's paper on the intonation patterns of reading aloud makes some illuminating observations on how people can read a piece of poetry in different ways (Brazil 1992). His study shows how metrical emphasis in verse is open to a variety of interpretations.

Narrative stylistics

❏   A version of the six-part model proposed here is used by Simpson and Montgomery (1995) in an extended stylistic analysis of Bernard MacLaverty's novel *Cal* (and see further C6).
❏   The definitive stylistic introduction to narrative is Toolan (2001) while Leech and Short (1981) offer a comprehensive introduction to the stylistic techniques of prose fiction. Specialist monograph-length treatments of narrative from a stylistic perspective include Toolan (2009) and Shen (forthcoming).

Style as choice

❏   The authoritative account of the transitivity model can be found in Halliday's functional grammar (1994: 106–75; and see the extended version in the third edition of that grammar, Halliday and Matthiesson 2004). Other detailed summaries of the model may also be found in Eggins (1994: 220–70) and Thompson (1996: 76–116).

Style and point of view

❏ Fuller treatments of point of view in fiction can be found in books by Fowler (1996) and Simpson (1993), while useful scholarly articles on the topic include Sasaki (1994) and Chapman (2002).

❏ The terms homodiegetic and heterodiegetic come from Genette's study of narrative discourse (Genette 1980), although a useful introductory summary can be found in Rimmon-Kenan (1983).

Representing speech and thought

❏ Full and authoritative accounts of speech and thought presentation can be found in Leech and Short (1981) and Short (1996). The categories proposed in this unit are based largely on those accounts.

❏ Important monographs by Fludernik (1993, 1996) cover many core areas in narratology and explore a number of the stylistic issues covered in this unit, and in units A4 and A6. Sotirova (2013) explores the presentation of consciousness in modernist fiction and draws on some of the stylistic frameworks covered in this and related units on aspects of narrative style.

Dialogue and discourse

❏ A more comprehensive survey of the areas covered in this unit can be found in Simpson (1997a: 129–78), while Simpson and Hall (2002) offers an overview of more recent developments in the field of discourse stylistics. A useful collection of papers on the stylistic analysis of dialogue (including film dialogue) is Culpeper *et al.* (1998), while Herman (1996) is a monograph-length study of dramatic discourse from a stylistic perspective.

❏ The authoritative study of politeness phenomena, of which stylisticians have made extensive use over the years and from which a number of the categories in A9 are derived, is Brown and Levinson (1987). Underpinning much work in discourse stylistics is Austin's seminal book on speech acts and illocutionary force (Austin 1962) and Grice's development of a model of conversational implicature (Grice 1975). Black (2006) is a useful overview of a number of pragmatic theories and of their usefulness to the interpretation of literary texts. Culpeper's work on impoliteness (2011) supplements and extends politeness theory in interesting ways, as does Bousfield (2008) and Bousfield and Locher (2008).

❏ The linguistic analysis of fictional dialogue has continued to be an important area of research in stylistics and related fields of study (see for example Jobert 2013). A number of more recent monographs have sustained this tradition and have built and developed from the earlier publications that were reviewed in units A9 and B9. Richardson (2010) explores from a sociolinguistic perspective the particular kind of 'artificial talk' that we recognise as dialogue on television, while Mandala (2007) continues the strong tradition of research in discourse stylistics in her analysis of four modern plays. Mandala also pitches her analyses, polemically, against the ways in which drama critics have dealt with the language of the same plays. Canning (2012) has a broad focus on styles of Renaissance writing and includes analysis of dialogue in the plays of Shakespeare (see also unit D9).

Cognitive stylistics

❑ Two key publications in this area are related textbooks by Stockwell (2002) and Gavins and Steen (2003). The former is a general introduction to the field, covering its history, development and methods, and the latter a collection of readings offering practical advice and exercises for cognitive stylistic exploration. A collection of more advanced papers is Semino and Culpeper (2002). Important monographs in the field are Gavins (2013) on the absurd in narrative fiction, Stockwell (2009), which is a cognitive–aesthetic account of the concept of 'texture' in literary discourse, and Dancygier (2012), which explores the conceptual and linguistic mechanisms we employ when we read stories. Sanford and Emmott (2012) is a groundbreaking study of the intersection between narrative style and the psychological mechanisms of language comprehension we use to understand and respond to stories.

❑ Cognitive stylistic research often draws upon and assimilates work by psychologists on textual processing and interpretation, as in key publications by Gerrig (1993), Gibbs (1994) or Oatley (2003).

❑ The idea of an Idealised Cognitive Model was first developed by Lakoff (1987; and see also reading D11). Other influential studies in cognitive linguistics and artificial intelligence, which have shaped the development of cognitive poetics, are Lakoff and Johnson (1998); Fauconnier (1994); Fauconnier and Turner (2002) and Schank and Abelson (1977; and see further B10).

Metaphor and metonymy

❑ Good introductions to metaphor include Goatly (1997), Knowles and Moon (2006), Kövecses (2002), Semino (2008), and chapter 8 of Stockwell (2002) is also very useful. Two of the more 'classic' books on metaphor are Brooke-Rose (1958) and Ortony (1979) while seminal publications in cognitive linguistics which focus on metaphor are Lakoff and Johnson (1980), Lakoff (1987) and Lakoff and Turner (1989). The stylistician Gerard Steen has written extensively on metaphor over the years, of which a representative sample of his work includes: Steen (1994, 1999a, 2002a and 2002b). Also relevant is a co-edited collection of papers, Gibbs and Steen (1999). A key academic journal in the field, edited by Lynne Cameron and Graham Low, is *Metaphor and the Social World*.

Stylistics: corpus approaches

❑ Useful core publications in the rapidly developing field of corpus linguistics, the techniques of which underpin the kinds of stylistic applications surveyed in this unit, include (and this is a short representative sample only): Biber *et al.* (1998), Stubbs (2001), McCarthy and O'Keeffe (2010), Baker (2006), Zyngier *et al.* (2008) and McEnery and Hardie (2011).

❏ Important monographs and collections in corpus stylistics include Mahlberg (2013), which is explored further in unit B12. Creating his own machine-readable versions of the two texts concerned, Ho (2011) examines key stylistic differences between the first and second editions of John Fowles's novel *The Magus*. Archer's collection of essays (2009) probes keyword patterns across a range of historical texts. Hoover (1999) uses corpus-assisted methods in an examination of William Golding's *The Inheritors*. Hoover has also carried out research in 'attributional stylistics' (2001, 2003), a practice which uses corpus methods to determine authorship in cases where the text under scrutiny is of disputed, contested or unknown origin.

❏ The website for Early English Books online can be found at: http://eebo. chadwyck.com/home. Webcorp, which is a database specifically tailored for linguists, can be found at: http://www.webcorp.org.uk/live/. Generally speaking, the remaining corpora referred to across this strand can be accessed easily online, and even the website's abbreviation (e.g. BNC, COCA) is normally sufficient to yield a link.

Developments in stylistics

❏ Leech (2008) is a book-length treatment of the interface between style and foregrounding. The stylistician Willie van Peer has also written extensively on foregrounding theory, two representative samples of which are van Peer (1986) and (1993). Cook (1994) contains an excellent overview of both the Russian Formalist and Prague School movements, while Durant and Fabb (1990: 32–4) includes a useful chronological map showing how these movements developed in the context of related developments in critical theory.

❏ Wales's study of Philip Larkin's poem 'Church Going' makes for an interesting synthesis of the techniques of rhetoric with the methods of stylistics (Wales 1993b). Burke (2010) explores the persuasive qualities of rhetoric, while Cockcroft and Cockcroft (2005) remains the authoritative introduction to the field of rhetoric studies.

Levels of language at work: an example from poetry

❏ Traugott and Pratt (1980) is a generally informative book in stylistics that also contains a short analysis of the same e e cummings poem explored in this unit. Their analysis draws on a very different model of language to the one adopted here, so the two studies should make for an interesting point of comparison. The fact that it is possible for different scholars to approach the same text with different models of analysis illustrates well the point made in A1 on the importance of stylistic method being replicable.

❏ Other stylistic work focussed specifically on e e cummings includes Simpson (1997a: 44ff) and van Peer (1987). Using a variety of stylistic approaches, Burke (2007) offers an analysis of cummings's poem 'the hours rise up'.

Sentence styles: development and illustration

❏ Leech and Short (1981) contains a number of detailed analyses of prose fiction which pay particular attention to patterns of grammar. A number of the papers collected in both Carter (1982) and Verdonk (1993a) also offer accessible explorations of style and grammar.

Interpreting patterns of sound

❏ Attridge (2004) has a chapter which explores in depth many of the issues raised in this unit, while Nash (1986) is an article which looks at the problems involved in teaching sound symbolism in a stylistic context. Montgomery *et al.* (1992: 86–9) contains a useful short section on the problems associated with interpreting sound patterns in poetry.

Developments in structural narratology

❏ Toolan has applied Propp's categories to a passage from Joyce's short story 'Eveline' (2001: 17–22), and this analysis, along with his general development of this model of narrative structure, is accessible and informative. See also Durant and Fabb (1990: 182–6) for a useful explication of Propp's model.

Style and transitivity

❏ Simpson (1993: 86–118) contains an application of an admittedly older version of the model of transitivity, along with a more detailed review of the Fish-Halliday debate than has been attempted here. In Simpson and Canning's study (2014), all of the categories of the model are introduced and illustrated with (real) examples from prose fiction, before the discussion is widened to consider transitivity in the context of negation, presupposition and counterfactuals. Toolan (1998: 75–104) provides a useful outline of the transitivity model and offers for analysis an intriguing passage from J. M. Coetzee's (1983) novel *Life & Times of Michael K.*

❏ Halliday's and Fish's papers have been usefully gathered together in two collections of articles in stylistics, D. Freeman (1981) and Weber (1996). A subsequent stylistic investigation of Golding's *The Inheritors* is Hoover (1999). O'Halloran (2007), Shen (1988) and Toolan (1990) are three of many good ripostes to Fish that have been written by stylisticians over the years.

Approaches to point of view

❏ The four-way account of point of view is from Uspensky (1973) with summaries and adaptations in Fowler (1996).

Techniques of speech and thought presentation

❏ Again, full surveys of speech and thought presentation can be found in Leech and Short (1981) and Short (1996). Fludernik (1993) is a more advanced monograph-length study which includes substantial treatment of speech and thought presentation. Article length publications include a lively debate on the topic played out between Simpson (1997b) and Short *et al.* (1997).

Dialogue in drama

❏ Simpson (1998) develops in more detail the idea of incongruity as a feature of the absurd in drama. This essay also connects incongruity to theories of humour (see the special web unit on style and humour). Tan (1998) offers advice on how to write a stylistic analysis of drama dialogue. In no way a definitive guide to the writing of essays in stylistics, Tan's paper nonetheless contains a number of useful suggestions about how to organise a response to a passage of play dialogue. Another version of Burton's structural model of discourse, with a more pedagogical-stylistic emphasis, can be found in Burton (1982b).

Developments in cognitive stylistics

❏ In addition to the references posted throughout this unit, useful theoretical context for cognitive stylistics is provided by Steen and Gavins (2003), Stockwell (2000, 2003) and by the editors' foreword in Semino and Culpeper (2002).
❏ Another important cognitive-stylistic model, which complements usefully those outlined here, is provided in Semino's study of 'world creation' in poetry and other texts (Semino 1997). Jeffries (2001) and Semino (2001) form two sides of a provocative and entertaining debate about the usefulness for stylistic analysis of schema theory and related concepts in cognitive linguistics.
❏ Important individual papers in cognitive stylistics, which offer excellent illustrations of how different kinds of theoretical model can be used, include McIntyre's study (2007a) of deictic shift theory and point of view in Seamus Heaney's poem 'Mossbawn'. Lugea (2013) draws on text world theory in her analysis of the narrative architecture of Christopher Nolan's film *Inception* (2010). Whiteley (2011) examines psychological projection in an extract from Kazuo Ishiguro's *The Remains of the Day* and her analysis is shrewdly supplemented by evidence from a group of non-academic readers discussing the same novel.

Styles of metaphor

❏   A special issue of the journal *Language and Literature* (2002, 11, 1), edited by
    Gerard Steen, is devoted to metaphor identification, and readers will find in that
    issue many useful suggestions about how to identify and track metaphors in
    literature. M. Freeman (2002) explores the 'body' of a poetic text, making a
    number of connections between the visual form of a poem and its cognitive
    import. This paper is therefore a good follow-up to the sorts of issues raised in
    this unit about the connection between metaphor and graphological experimen-
    tation (and see also M. Freeman 1995, 2000). McRae's (1998) study of the language
    of poetry, which is a generally valuable stylistic survey of poetic technique, contains
    a short exercise based around the McGough poem and other visually striking
    poems.

Developments in corpus stylistics

❏   Corpus stylistics is a rapidly developing area and coverage in the units across this
    strand has of necessity been only a partial overview of the contemporary field. Of
    a number of important article-length publications in corpus stylistics, two in
    particular merit serious attention. Stubbs (2005) examines individual words and
    recurrent phraseology in Joseph Conrad's novella *Heart of Darkness*, and he
    uncovers a number of significant features that appear to have bypassed literary-
    critical readings of the same story. Consciously building on some of the methods
    and insights offered in Stubbs's paper, O'Halloran (2007) investigates James
    Joyce's short story 'Eveline'. O'Halloran's corpus analysis reveals a number of subtle
    'subconscious intimations' throughout the story that suggest that its central
    character, contrary to explicit plot signals, will not leave her home after all.

Is there a 'literary language'?

❏   The 'literary language' issue has been addressed in various stylistics publications,
    but the treatments in Fowler (1996) and Carter and Nash (1990) are especially
    useful. Tambling (1988) approaches the issue from a range of perspectives in his
    useful book on the subject. Finally, the problems involved in modelling a stylistic
    description of literature are addressed in van Peer (1991) and Steen (1999b). Many
    years ago, the critic F.W. Bateson became embroiled with stylistician Roger Fowler
    in a controversy over the usefulness of stylistics as a critical tool for studying
    literature. The essence of the 'Fowler-Bateson controversy', as it became known,
    is distilled in Fowler (1971).

Style, register and dialect

❏   Hess (1996) is an insightful exploration of code-switching in literature. Two
    articles on the representation of dialect in literature are Toolan (1992) and (2000),

while Cooper (1994) is a study of dialect in the novels of Thomas Hardy. A special issue of the journal *Language and Literature* (2001, 10, 2) is devoted to dialect analysis, specifically to the representation of African-American varieties of English in the work of Mark Twain and Harriet Beecher Stowe. Antilanguages in literature are the principal focus of attention in both Tsen (1997) and in a chapter of Fowler (1981).

❑ Follow-up reading to the practical activity set up in this unit includes Corbett (1997), which offers an excellent general overview of the language of Scottish literature. Mick Short's essay in D7 explores another of Irvine Welsh's novels, *Marabou Stork Nightmares*, and further relevant background reading is embedded in this essay.

Grammar and genre: a short study in imagism

❑ There are numerous literary-critical treatments of Imagism and of the life and work of Ezra Pound, although it should be noted that rarely does this work engage in any rigour with stylistic issues associated with Imagist poetry. On the other hand, Crisp (1996) is a scholarly article in stylistics which is devoted to the significance of the 'image metaphor' in the work of Pound and other poets. Although quite advanced theoretically, Crisp's article, which includes a commentary on 'In a station of the Metro' makes for rewarding reading.

Styles in a single poem: an exploration

❑ Brearton and Simpson (2001) is an article on the poetry of Michael Longley which balances literary critical methods and the methods of stylistics. Brearton (2006) is a book-length study of the same poet's work.

❑ Verdonk (1993b) offers an analysis of a range of levels of language in Seamus Heaney's poem 'Punishment', paying particular attention to patterns of deixis (see A2).

A sociolinguistic model of narrative

❑ Burton (1980) is an important stylistic exploration of drama dialogue which contains a full chapter on Ionesco's *The Bald Prima Donna*. Black (2006: 39–44), Simpson (1997a: 101–27) and Toolan (2001: 143–77) contain overviews of the Labov model, along with a number of suggested stylistic applications.

Transitivity, characterisation and literary genre

❑ Nash (1990) is an engaging general account of the language of popular fiction, which probes narrative techniques beyond those covered in this unit. More recently, Montoro (2012) has looked at the genre of 'Chick Lit' fiction from a stylistic perspective, and her study embraces a range of relevant models in narrative stylistics.

❑ Mills (1995: 143–9) examines transitivity from a feminist perspective, while Wareing, in two articles in which the transitivity model features, explores popular fiction written for women (Wareing 1990; 1994).

Exploring point of view in narrative fiction

❑ This unit is based on a (dangerously) simplified version of a framework set out in Simpson (1993), and readers are urged to consult the fuller model for further detail and illustration. Other books which cover point of view are Rimmon-Kenan's textbook (1983) and, of course, Genette's influential study (1980). Interesting articles on point of view include Sasaki (1994) and Chapman (2002).

Exploring dialogue

❑ As recorded earlier, Herman and Mandala offer extensive accounts of the way principles of social interaction can be brought to bear in the interpretation of play dialogue (Herman 1996, Mandala 2007). Birch (1991) is a generally interesting study of drama which balances critical theory with some insights from stylistics. Simpson (2000) includes a study, with an emphasis on discourse structure, of patterns of comic dialogue in the popular Irish sitcom *Father Ted*.
❑ With regard to dialogue in film, Bousfield and McIntyre (2011) examine the creation of emotion and empathy in the 'funny guy' scene from Martin Scorsese's film *Goodfellas*, while the collection in which their article appears, Piazza *et al.* (2011), contains generally a number of interesting accounts of the language of film and television.

Cognitive stylistics at work

❑ Gavins and Steen's collection (2003) contains applications to text, by different stylisticians, of a variety of models in cognitive stylistics. Most closely reflecting the interests of this unit are individual papers in the collection by Gavins, who explores a Donald Barthelme novel using text world theory and by Emmott, who examines 'twists in the tale' in fiction from a cognitive-discourse perspective.
❑ Wales (1992) is a book-length treatment of the style of James Joyce. Further reading (or exercises) built around the work of Joyce can be found in units D4 and D12.

Exploring metaphors in different kinds of texts

❑ With reference to the exploration of metaphor in text, each of the chapters in Kövecses' book on the subject is accompanied by helpful practical activities (Kövecses 2002), while useful exercises are distributed throughout Goatly's book on metaphor (Goatly 1997). Articles on metaphor with a text-based or practical orientation include Crisp (2003) and Heywood *et al.* (2002).
❑ Semino (2008) is a study of metaphor in a variety of types of discourse, including writing from science, education, politics and medicine. However, many of her

examples are taken from literature and among these stylistic applications is an elegant analysis of metaphor in Ian McEwan's novel *Atonement*. Readers interested in consulting Semino's analysis might want to think through a contextualising exercise first. If you suffer from (or have a friend who suffers from) migraine headaches, write a sentence (or get your friend to write a sentence) describing what a migraine headache *is like*. The simile-like description that results from the exercise will, trust me, make for an excellent point of entry to the McEwan text analysed by Semino (2008: 36–42).

Using corpora in stylistic analysis

❏ Archer (2007) and McIntyre (2007b) are useful general surveys of computer-assisted literary studies, while McIntyre (2012) offers a programme for developing corpus stylistics in the language classroom. Other articles which have particular practical relevance to language teaching can be found in a dedicated section on corpus stylistics in Watson and Zyngier's collection of essays (2007). Elsewhere, Watson (2006) uses corpus methods in an entertaining study of the lyrics of blues songs, with particular reference to the work of the early female artists in this genre. Semino and Short (2004) and Semino *et al.* (1997) use corpora to explore techniques of speech and thought presentation. Walker (2010) explores narrative perspective in Julian Barnes's novel *Talking it Over* (1991). Using the corpus-analysis tool Wmatrix developed by Rayson (2008), Walker extends the notion of key words into the concept of 'key semantic categories', using this revision to discover sophisticated variations in the voices of the novel's three main narrators.

REFERENCES

Andres Morrissey, F. (2008) 'Liverpool to Louisiana in one lyrical line: Style choice in British rock, pop and folk singing'. In Locher, M. and Strässler, J. (eds) *Standards and Norms in the English Language* Berlin: Mouton de Gruyter, 195–218.

Archer, D. (2007) 'Computer-assisted literary stylistics: The state of the field'. In Lambrou, M. and Stockwell, P. (eds) *Contemporary Stylistics* London: Continuum, 244–56.

Archer, D. (2009) *What's in Word List? Investigating Word Frequency and Keyword Extraction* Farnham: Ashgate.

Attridge, D. (1982) *The Rhythms of English Poetry* Harlow: Longman.

Attridge, D. (2004) *Peculiar Language: Literature as Difference from the Renaissance to James Joyce* London: Routledge.

Austin, J. L. (1962) *How to do Things with Words* London: Clarendon Press.

Baker, P. (2006) *Using Corpora in Discourse Analysis* London: Continuum.

Bakhtin, M. M. (1986) *Speech Genres and other Late Essays* Austin: University of Texas Press.

Ball, M. J. and Rahilly, J. (1999) *Phonetics: The Science of Speech* London: Edward Arnold.

Barry, P. (2002) *Beginning Theory: An Introduction to Literary and Cultural Theory* 2nd edition. Manchester: University of Manchester Press.

Barton, M. (1965) *Roles* London: Tavistock Publications.

Bateson, F.W. (1966) 'Editorial Postscript', *Essays in Criticism* 16, 4, 464–5.

Bell, M. (1986) 'Narrative Gaps/Narrative Meaning', *Raritan* 6, 1, 84–102.

Beal, J. C. (2009) '"You're not from New York City, You're from Rotherham": Dialect and identity in British Indie music', *Journal of English Linguistics* 37, 3, 223–40.

Bex, A., Burke, M. and Stockwell, P. (eds) (2000) *Contextualized Stylistics* Amsterdam/Atlanta, GA: Rodopi.

Biber, D., Conrad, S. and Reppen, R. (1998) *Corpus Linguistics: Investigating Language Structure and Use* Cambridge: Cambridge University Press.

Birch, D. (1991) *The Language of Drama* Basingstoke: Macmillan.

Black, E. (2006) *Pragmatic Stylistics* Edinburgh: Edinburgh University Press.

Blamires, H. (1988) [1966] *The New Bloomsday Book* London: Routledge.

Bolinger, D. (1965) 'Pitch accents and sentence rhythm'. In Abe, I. and Kanekiyo, T. (eds) *Forms of English: Accent, Morpheme, Order* Cambridge: Harvard University Press, 139–80.

Bordwell, D. and Thompson, K. (2001) *Film Art: An Introduction* 6th edition. New York: McGraw-Hill.

Bousfield, D. (2008) *Impoliteness in Interaction* Amsterdam: John Benjamins.

Bousfield, D. and Locher, M. (eds) (2008) *Impoliteness in Language: Studies on its Interplay with Power in Theory and Practice* Berlin: Mouton de Gruyter.

Bousfield, D. and McIntyre, D. (2011) 'Emotion and empathy in Martin Scorsese's *Goodfellas*: A case study of the "funny guy" scene'. In Piazza, R., Bednarek, M. and Rossi, F. (eds.) *Telecinematic Discourse: Approaches to the Language of Films and Television Series* Amsterdam: John Benjamins, 105–23.

Brazil. D. (1992) 'Listening to people reading'. In Coulthard, M. (ed.) *Advances in Spoken Discourse Analysis* London: Routledge, 209–41.

Brearton, F. (2006) *Reading Michael Longley* Newcastle upon Tyne: Bloodaxe.

Brearton, F. and Simpson, P. (2001) '"Deciphering otter prints": language, form and memory in the poetry of Michael Longley', *The Honest Ulsterman: Special Feature on Michael Longley*, 110, 17–31.

Breton, A. (1969) *Manifestoes of Surrealism* (trans. R. Seaver and H. R. Lane) Ann Arbor, MI: University of Michigan Press.

Brooke-Rose, C. (1958) *A Grammar of Metaphor* London: Secker and Warburg.

Brown, P. and Levinson, S. (1987) *Politeness* Cambridge: Cambridge University Press.

Burke, M. (2007) '"Progress is a comfortable disease": Cognition in a stylistic analysis of e e cummings'. In Lambrou, M. and Stockwell, P. (eds) *Contemporary Stylistics* London: Continuum, 144–55.

Burke, M. (2010) 'Rhetoric and persuasion'. In Hogan, P. (ed) *The Cambridge Encyclopedia of the Language Sciences* Cambridge: Cambridge University Press, 715–17.

Burke, M. (ed) (2014) *The Routledge Handbook of Stylistics* Abingdon: Routledge.

Burke, M., Csabi, S. Week, L. and Zerkowitz, J. (eds) (2012) *Pedagogical Stylistics: Current Trends in Language, Literature and ELT* London: Bloomsbury Continuum.

Burton, D. (1980) *Dialogue and Discourse: A Sociolinguistic Approach to Modern Drama Dialogue and Naturally Occurring Conversation* London: Routledge and Kegan Paul.

Burton, D. (1982a) 'Through glass darkly: through dark glasses'. In Carter, R. and Burton, D. (eds) (1982) *Literary Text and Language Study* London: Edward Arnold, 195–214.

Burton, D. (1982b) 'Conversation pieces'. In Carter, R. and Burton, D. (eds) (1982) *Literary Text and Language Study* London: Edward Arnold, 86–115.

Busse, B. (2010) 'Non-literary language: A stylistic investigation of the cover pages of British satirical magazine *Private Eye*'. In McIntyre, D. and Busse, B. (eds) *Language and Style* Basingstoke: Palgrave Macmillan, 468–96.

Canning, P. (2012) *Style in the Renaissance* London: Continuum.

Canning, P. and Simpson, P. (2012) 'Chicken and egg stylistics: From lexical semantics to Conceptual Integration Theory'. In Burke, M., Csabi, S., Week, L. and Zerkowitz, J. (eds) *Pedagogical Stylistics: Current Trends in Language, Literature and ELT* London: Continuum Press, 22–44.

Carper, T. and Attridge, D. (2003) *Meter and Meaning: An Introduction to Rhythm in Poetry* London: Routledge.

Carter, R. (ed.) (1982) *Language and Literature: An Introductory Reader in Stylistics* London: George Allen and Unwin.

Carter, R. and Burton, D. (eds) (1982) *Literary Text and Language Study* London: Edward Arnold.

Carter, R. and Nash, W. (1990) *Seeing through Language: A Guide to Styles of English Writing* Oxford: Blackwell.

Carter, R. (2004) 'Language and Creativity: The Art of Common Talk'. London: Routledge.

Carter, R. and Simpson, P. (eds) (1989) *Language, Discourse and Literature: An Introductory Reader in Discourse Stylistics* London: Unwin Hyman.

Carter, R. and Stockwell, P. (eds) (2008) *The Language and Literature Reader* Abingdon: Routledge.

Chapman, S. (2002) '"From their point of view": voice and speech in George Moore's *Esther Waters*', *Language and Literature* 11, 4, 307–23.

Clark, U. and Zyngier, S. (2003) 'Towards a pedagogical stylistics', *Language and Literature* 12, 4, 339–51.

Clemen, W. (1957) *A Commentary on Shakespeare's* Richard III London: Methuen.

Cockcroft, R. and Cockcroft, S. (2005) *Persuading People: An Introduction to Rhetoric* 2nd edition. Basingstoke: Palgrave Macmillan.

Cook, G. (1994) *Discourse and Literature* Oxford: Oxford University Press.

Cooper, A. (1994) '"Folk speech" and "book English": re-presentations of dialect in Hardy's novels', *Language and Literature* 3, 1, 21–42.

Corbett, J. (1997) *Language and Scottish Literature* Edinburgh: Edinburgh University Press.

Coupland, N. (2011) 'Voice, place and genre in popular song performance', *Journal of Sociolinguistics* 15, 5, 573–602.

Crisp, P. (1996) 'Imagism's metaphors – a test case', *Language and Literature* 5, 2, 79–92.

Crisp, P. (2003) 'Conceptual metaphor and its expressions'. In Gavins, J. and Steen, G. (eds) *Cognitive Poetics in Practice* London: Routledge, 99–113.

Crisp, P. (2005) 'Allegory and symbol', *Language and Literature* 14, 4, 323–38.

Crystal, D. (1998) *Language Play* Harmondsworth: Penguin.

Culpeper, J. (2001) *Language and Characterisation: People in Plays and Other Texts* Harlow: Longman.

Culpeper, J. (2011) *Impoliteness* Cambridge: Cambridge University Press.

Culpeper, J., Short, M. and Verdonk, P. (eds) (1998) *Exploring the Language of Drama: From Text to Context* London: Routledge.

Culpeper, J. and McIntyre, D. (2006) 'Drama: stylistic aspects'. In Brown, K. (ed.) *Encyclopedia of Language and Linguistics* 2nd edition, vol. 3. Oxford: Elsevier, 772–85.

Cureton, R. (1994) 'Rhythm and verse study', *Language and Literature* 3, 2, 105–24.

Cutrer, M. (1994) 'Time and Tense in Narratives and Everyday Language', PhD dissertation, University of California, San Diego, CA.

Dancygier, B. (2002) 'Mental Space Embeddings, Counterfactuality, and the Use of *Unless*', *English Language and Linguistics* 6, 2, 347–77.

Dancygier, B. (2004) 'Identity and Perspective: the Jekyll-and-Hyde Effect in Narrative Discourse'. In Achard, M. and Kemmer, S. (eds) *Language, Culture, and Mind* Stanford, CA: CSLI Publications, 363–76.

Dancygier, B. (2005) 'Blending and narrative viewpoint: Jonathan Raban's travels through mental spaces', *Language and Literature* 14, 2, 99–127.

Dancygier, B. (2006) 'What can blending do for you?', *Language and Literature* 15, 1, 5–15.

Dancygier, B. (2008) 'Personal pronouns, blending, and narrative viewpoint.' In Tyler, A., Kim, Y. and Takada, M. (eds). *Language in the Context of Use: Discourse and Cognitive Approaches to Language* (Cognitive Linguistics Research 37) Berlin and New York: Mouton de Gruyter, 167–82.

Dancygier, B. (2012) *The Language of Stories: A Cognitive Approach* Cambridge: Cambridge University Press.

Dancygier, B. and Sweetser, E. (2009) *Mental Spaces in Grammar: Conditional Constructions* Cambridge: Cambridge University Press.

Desmond, J. F. (1987) *Risen Sons: Flannery O'Connor's Vision of History* Athens: University of Georgia Press.

Durant, A. and Fabb, N. (1990) *Literary Studies in Action* London: Routledge.

Eagleton, T. (2007) *How to Read a Poem* Oxford: Wiley-Blackwell.

Eggins, S. (1994) *An Introduction to Systemic-Functional Linguistics* London: Pinter.

Elam, K. (1980) *The Semiotics of Theatre and Drama.* London: Methuen.

Emmott, C. (1997) *Narrative Comprehension* Oxford: Clarendon Press.

Emmott, C. (2002) '"Split-selves" in fiction and medical "life stories"'. In Semino, E. and Culpeper, J. (eds) *Cognitive Stylistics* Philadelphia: John Benjamins, 153–82.

Fabb, N. (2002) 'The metres of "Dover Beach"', *Language and Literature* 11, 2, 99–117.

Fauconnier, G. (1994) *Mental Spaces: Aspects of Meaning Construction in Natural Language* Cambridge: Cambridge University Press.

Fauconnier, G. (1997) *Mappings in Thought and Language* Cambridge: Cambridge University Press.

Fauconnier, G. and Turner, M. (2002) *The Way We Think: Conceptual Blending and the Mind's Hidden Complexities* New York: Basic Books.

Filardo, L. (forthcoming) 'From universal to de-contextualised text worlds', *Language and Literature.*

Fish, S. (1981) 'What is stylistics and why are they saying such terrible things about it?'. In Freeman, D. (ed.) (1981) *Essays in Modern Stylistics* London: Methuen, 53–78.

Fludernik, M. (1993) *The Fictions of Language and the Languages of Fiction* London: Routledge.

Fludernik, M. (1996) *Towards a Natural Narratology* London: Routledge.

Forceville, C. (1996) *Pictorial Metaphor in Advertising* London: Routledge.

Forceville, C. (1999) 'Educating the Eye? Kress and van Leeuwen's *Reading Images: The Grammar of Visual Design* (1996)', *Language and Literature* 8, 2, 163–78.

Foucault, M. (1986) 'What is an author?' In Adams, H. and Searle, L. (eds) *Critical Theory Since 1965* Gainesville: University Presses of Florida, 138–48.

Fowler, R. (ed.) (1966) *Essays on Style and Language* London: Routledge and Kegan Paul.

Fowler, R. (ed.) (1971) *The Languages of Literature* London: Routledge and Kegan Paul.

Fowler, R. (1977) *Linguistics and the Novel* London: Methuen.

Fowler, R. (1981) *Literature as Social Discourse* London: Batsford.

Fowler, R. (1996) [1986] *Linguistic Criticism* 2nd edition. Oxford: Oxford University Press.

Fraser, G. S. (1970) *Metre, Rhyme and Free Verse* London: Methuen.

Freeman, D. (ed.) (1981) *Essays in Modern Stylistics* London: Methuen.

Freeman, M. (1995) 'Metaphor making meaning: Emily Dickinson's conceptual universe', *Journal of Pragmatics* 24, 643–66.

Freeman, M. (2000) 'Poetry and the scope of metaphor: Toward a cognitive theory of metaphor'. In Barcelona, A. (ed.) *Metaphor and Metonymy at the Crossroads* Berlin: de Gruyter, 253–81.

Freeman, M. (2002) 'The body in the word: A cognitive approach to the shape of a poetic text'. In Semino, E. and Culpeper, J. (eds) *Cognitive Stylistics* Amsterdam: John Benjamins, 23–47.

Galbraith, M. (1995) 'Deictic Shift Theory and the poetics of involvement in narrative'. In Duchan, J. F., Bruder, G. A. and L. E. Hewitt (eds) *Deixis in Narrative: A Cognitive Science Perspective* Hillsdale: Lawrence Erlbaum Associates Inc, 19–59.

Garland, N. (1988) 'Political cartooning'. In Durant, J. and Miller, J. (eds) *Laughing Matters: A Serious Look at Humour* Harlow: Longman Scientific and Technical, 75–89.

Gavins, J. (2005) 'Text-world approach to narrative'. In Herman, D., Jahn, M. and Ryan, M-L. (eds) *The Routledge Encyclopedia of Narrative Theory* New York: Routledge, 596–7.

Gavins, J. (2007) *Text World Theory: An Introduction* Edinburgh: Edinburgh University Press.

Gavins, J. (2013) *Reading the Absurd* Edinburgh: Edinburgh University Press.

Gavins, J. and Steen, G. (eds) (2003) *Cognitive Poetics in Practice* London: Routledge.

Genette, G. (1980) *Narrative Discourse* New York: Cornell University Press.

Gerrig, R. (1993) *Experiencing Narrative Worlds* New Haven: Yale University Press.

Germain, E. B. (ed.) (1978) *Surrealist Poetry in English* Harmondsworth: Penguin.

Gibbs, R. W. jr. (1994) *The Poetics of Mind* Cambridge: Cambridge University Press.

Gibbs, R. W. jr. and Steen, G. (eds) (1999) *Metaphor in Cognitive Linguistics* Amsterdam: John Benjamins.

Goatly, A. (1997) *The Language of Metaphors* London: Routledge.

Graham, J. (1981) 'Flip, flap, flop: linguistics as semiotics', *Diacritics* 11, 1, 143–68.

Gregoriou, C. (2008) *English Literary Stylistics* Basingstoke: Palgrave Macmillan.

Green, K. (1992) 'Deixis and the poetic persona', *Language and Literature* 1, 2, 121–34.

Grice, H. P. (1975) 'Logic and Conversation'. In Cole, P. and Morgan, J. (1975) *Syntax and Semantics III: Speech Acts* New York: Academic Press, 41–58.

Griswold, C. L. (1999) *Adam Smith and the Virtues of Enlightenment* Cambridge: Cambridge University Press.

Hall, G. (2014) 'Stylistics and literary criticism'. In Stockwell, P. and Whiteley, S. (eds) *The Cambridge Handbook of Stylistics* Cambridge: Cambridge University Press.

Halliday, M. A. K. (1970) 'Language structure and language function'. In Lyons, J. (ed.) *New Horizons in Linguistics*, Harmondsworth: Penguin, 140–65.

Halliday, M. A. K. (1971) 'Linguistic function and literary style: an inquiry into the language of William Golding's The Inheritors'. In Chatman, S. (ed.) *Literary Style: A Symposium* New York: Oxford University Press, 330–68. [Reprinted in Freeman, D. (ed.) (1981) *Essays in Modern Stylistics* London: Methuen 325–60].

Halliday, M. A. K. (1973*) Explorations in the Functions of Language* London: Edward Arnold.

Halliday, M. A. K. (1978) *Language as Social Semiotic* London: Edward Arnold.

Halliday, M. A. K. (1994) *An Introduction to Functional Grammar* 2nd edition. London: Edward Arnold.

Halliday M. A. K. and Matthiesson, C. M. I. M. (2004) *An Introduction to Functional Grammar* 3rd edition. London: Edward Arnold.

Hammond, A. (ed.) (1981) *King Richard III* London: Methuen.

Hardy, D. (2003) *Narrating Knowledge in Flannery O'Connor's Fiction*. Columbia: University of South Carolina Press.

Hardy, D. (2005) 'Towards a typology of narrative gaps: knowledge gapping in Flannery O'Connor's fiction', *Language and Literature* 14, 4, 363–75.

Harding, J. Riddle (2004) 'Simple Regrets: Counterfactuals and the Dialogic Mind', PhD dissertation, University of Maryland.

Harding, J. Riddle (2007) 'Evaluative stance and counterfactuals in language and literature' *Language and Literature* 16, 3, 263–80.

Hayman, D. (1981) *Ulysses: The Mechanics of Meaning* 2nd edition. Madison: University of Wisconsin Press.

Herman, D., Jahn, M. and Ryan. M-L. (eds) (2005) *The Routledge Encyclopaedia of Narrative Theory* New York: Routledge.

Herman, V. (1996) *Dramatic Discourse: Dialogue as Interaction in Plays* London: Routledge.

Hess, N. (1996) 'Code switching and style switching as markers of liminality in literature', *Language and Literature* 5, 1, 5–18.

Heywood, J., Semino, E. and Short, M. (2002) 'Linguistic metaphor identification in two extracts from novels', *Language and Literature* 11, 1, 35–54.

Ho, Y. (2011) *Corpus Stylistics in Principle and Practice* London: Continuum.

Hoover, D. L. (1999) *Language and Style in* The Inheritors Lanham, MD: University Press of America.

Hoover, D. (2001) 'Statistical stylistics and authorship attribution: An empirical investigation', *Literary and Linguistic Computing* 16, 4, 421–44.

Hoover, D. (2003) 'Multivariate analysis and the study of style variation', *Literary and Linguistic Computing* 18, 4, 341–60.

Hougaard, A. and Lund, S. (eds) (2002) *The Way We Think*, 3 vols. Odense Working Papers in Language and Communication 23. Odense: University of Southern Denmark.

Hymes, D. (1972) 'On communicative competence'. In Pride, J. B. and Holmes, J. (eds) *Sociolinguistics* Harmondsworth: Penguin, 269–93.

Jackson, H. (2001) *Grammar and Vocabulary* London: Routledge.

Jakobson, R. (1960) 'Closing statement: linguistics and poetics'. In Sebeok, T. A. (ed) *Style in Language* Cambridge: The MIT Press, 350–77.

Jeffries, L. (2001) 'Schema affirmation and White Asparagus: Cultural multilingualism among readers of texts', *Language and Literature* 10, 4, 325–43.

Jeffries, L. and McIntyre, D. (2010) *Stylistics* Cambridge: Cambridge University Press.

Jobert, M. (2013) 'The art of fictional conversation: paralinguistic vocal features in Edith Wharton's "The Last Asset"', *Proceedings of the Poetics and Linguistics Association conference*, Roosevelt Academy, 2009. Available online at: www.pala.ac.uk/resources/proceedings/2009/jobert2009.pdf (last accessed 13 April 2013).

Keller, J. C. (1972) 'The figures of the empiricist and the rationalist in the fiction of Flannery O'Connor', *Arizona Quarterly* 28, 263–73.

Kennedy, C. (1982) 'Systemic grammar and its use in literary analysis'. In Carter, R. (ed) (1982) *Language and Literature: An Introductory Reader in Stylistics* London: George Allen and Unwin, 82–99.

Kenner, H. (1980) *Ulysses*, Unwin Critical Library. London: George Allen and Unwin.

Knowles, M. and Moon, R. (2006) *Introducing Metaphor* London: Routledge.

Korte, B. (1997) *Body Language in Literature* Toronto: University of Toronto Press.

Kövecses, Z. (2002) *Metaphor: A Practical Introduction* New York: Oxford University Press.

Kress, G. and Van Leeuwen, T. (2001) *Multimodal Discourse: The Modes and Media of Contemporary Communication*. London: Arnold.

Kress, G. and van Leeuwen, T. (2006) *Reading Images: The Grammar of Visual Design* 2nd edition. London: Routledge.

Kuiken, D., Miall, D. S. and Sikora, S. (2004) 'Forms of self-implication in literary reading', *Poetics Today* 25, 2, 171–203.

Kuno, S. (1987) *Functional Syntax: Anaphora, Discourse and Empathy* Chicago: Chicago University Press.

Labov, W. (1972) *Language in the Inner City* Philadelphia: University of Pennsylvania Press.

Lakoff, G. (1987) *Women, Fire, and Dangerous Things: What Categories Reveal about the Mind* Chicago and London: University of Chicago Press.

Lakoff, G. (1990) 'The Invariance Hypothesis: Is abstract reason based on image-schemas?', *Cognitive Linguistics* 1, 1, 39–74.

Lakoff, G. (1993) 'The contemporary theory of metaphor'. In Ortony, A. (ed) *Metaphor and Thought* Cambridge and New York: Cambridge University Press, 202–51.

Lakoff, G. (1996) '"Sorry, I'm Not Myself Today": The Metaphor System for Conceptualizing the Self'. In G. Fauconnier and E. Sweetser (eds) *Spaces, Worlds, and Grammars* Chicago: Chicago University Press, 91–123.

Lakoff, G. and Johnson, M. (1980) *Metaphors We Live By* Chicago, IL: University of Chicago Press.

Lakoff, G., and Johnson, M. (1998) *Philosophy in the Flesh* Chicago and London: University of Chicago Press.

Lakoff, G. and Turner, M. (1989) *More than Cool Reason: A Field Guide to Poetic Metaphor* Chicago, IL: University of Chicago Press.

Lambert, M. (1981) *Dickens and the Suspended Quotation* New Haven, CT and London: Yale University Press.

Lambrou, M. and Stockwell, P. (eds.) (2007) *Contemporary Stylistics* London: Bloomsbury Continuum.

Langacker, R. W. (1987) *Foundations of Cognitive Grammar* (vol. 1) Stanford: Stanford University Press.

Langacker, R. W. (1991) *Concept, Image, and Symbol: The Cognitive Basis of Grammar* Berlin and New York: Mouton de Gruyter.

Lecercle, J-J. (1993). 'The current state of stylistics', *The European English Messenger* 2, 1, 14–18.

Leech, G. N. (1969) *A Linguistic Guide to English Poetry* Harlow: Longman.

Leech, G. N. (2008) *Language in Literature: Style and Foregrounding* London: Pearson/Longman.

Leech, G. and Short, M. (1981) *Style in Fiction* Harlow: Longman.

Levin, S. R. (1962) *Linguistic Structures in Poetry* The Hague: Mouton.

Lipps, T. (1900) 'Aesthetische Einfühlung', *Zietschrift für Psychologie*, 22, 415–50.

Louw, W. (1993) 'Irony in the text or insincerity in the writer? The diagnostic potential of semantic prosodies'. In Baker, M., Francis, G. and Tognini-Bonelli, E. (eds) *Text and Technology: In Honour of John Sinclair* Amsterdam: John Benjamins, 157–76.

Louw, W. (2000) 'Contextual prosodic theory: Bringing semantic prosodies to life'. In Heffer, C. and Sauntson, H. (eds) *Words in Context* Birmingham: ELR, 48–94.

Louw, W. (2007) 'Truth, literary worlds and devices as collocation'. In Hidalgo, E., Quereda, L. and Santana, J. (eds.) *Corpora in the Foreign Language Classroom* Amsterdam and New York: Rodopi.

Louw, W. (2011) 'Philosophical and literary concerns in corpus linguistics'. In Viana, V., Zyngier, S. and Barnbrook, G. (eds) *Perspectives on Corpus Linguistics* Amsterdam: John Benjamins, 171–96.

Louw, W. and Milojkovic, M. (2013) 'Semantic prosody'. In Stockwell, P. and Whiteley, S. (eds) *The Cambridge Handbook of Stylistics* Cambridge: Cambridge University Press.

Lugea, J. (2013) 'Embedded dialogue and dreams: the worlds and accessibility relations of *Inception*', *Language and Literature* 22, 2, 133–53.

Machin, D. and Mayr, A. (2012) *How to Do Critical Discourse Analysis: A Multimodal Introduction* London: Sage.

Mahlberg, M. (2011) 'Corpus linguistic methods'. In McCabe, A. (ed) *An Introduction to Linguistics and Language Studies* London: Equinox, 351–4.

Mahlberg, M. (2013) *Corpus Stylistics and Dickens's Fiction* Abingdon: Routledge.

Mahlberg, M. and Smith, C. (2010) 'Corpus approaches to prose fiction: Civility and body language in Pride and Prejudice.' In McIntyre, D. and Busse, B. (eds.) *Language and Style* Basingstoke: Palgrave Macmillan, 449–67.

Mandala, S. (2007) *Twentieth-Century Drama Dialogue as Ordinary Talk: Speaking Between the Lines* Farnham: Ashgate.

Marston, J. (1984) 'Epistemology and the solipsistic consciousness in Flannery O'Connor's "Greenleaf"', *Studies in Short Fiction* 21, 4, 375–82.

McCarthy, M. and O'Keeffe, A. (eds) (2010) *The Routledge Handbook of Corpus Linguistics* Abingdon: Routledge.

McCawley, J. D. (1981) *Everything that Linguists have Always Wanted to Know about Logic (But were Ashamed to Ask)* Chicago, IL: The University of Chicago Press.

McEnery, T. and Hardie, A. (2011) *Corpus Linguistics: Method, Theory and Practice* Cambridge: Cambridge University Press.

McHale, B. (1978) 'Free indirect discourse: A survey of recent accounts', *Poetics and Theory of Literature* 3, 235–87.

McHale, B. (1987) *Postmodernist Fiction* New York: Methuen.

McIntyre, D. (2007a) 'Deixis, cognition and the construction of viewpoint'. In Lambrou, M. and Stockwell, P. (eds) *Contemporary Stylistics* London: Continuum, 118–30.

McIntyre, D. (2007b) 'Trusting the text: corpus linguistics and stylistics', *International Journal of Corpus Linguistics* 12, 4, 565–77.

McIntyre, D. (2008) 'Integrating multimodal analysis and the stylistics of drama: a multimodal perspective on Ian McKellen's *Richard III*', *Language and Literature* 17, 4, 308–34.

McIntyre, D. (2012) 'Corpus stylistics in the classroom'. In M. Burke, S. Csabi, L. Week and J. Zerkowitz (eds) *Pedagogical Stylistics: Current Trends in Language, Literature and ELT* London: Continuum Press, 113–25.

McIntyre, D. and Busse, B. (eds.) (2010) *Language and Style* Basingstoke: Palgrave Macmillan.

McRae, J. (1998) *The Language of Poetry* London: Routledge.

Merleau-Ponty, M. (1962) *Phenomenology of Perception* (trans. C. Smith.) London: Routledge and Kegan Paul.

Mills, S. (1995) *Feminist Stylistics* London: Routledge.

Montgomery, M., Durant, A., Fabb, N., Furniss, T. and Mills, S. (1992) *Ways of Reading: Advanced Reading Skills for Students of English Literature* London: Routledge.

Montoro, R. (2006) 'Analysing literature through films'. In Watson, G. and Zyngier, S. (eds) *Literature and Stylistics for Language Learners: Theory and Practice* Basingstoke: Palgrave Macmillan, 48–59

Montoro, R. (2012) *Chick Lit: The Stylistics of Cappuccino Fiction* London: Bloomsbury Continuum.

Mosher, H.F., Jr (1993) 'The narrated and its negatives: The nonnarrated and the disnarrated in Joyce's *Dubliners*', *Style* 27, 407–27.

Nash, W. (1986) 'Sound and the pattern of poetic meaning'. In D'Haen, T. (ed.) *Linguistics and the Study of Literature.* Dutch Quarterly Review, Studies in Literature 1. Amsterdam: Rodopi, 128–51.

Nash, W. (1990) *Language in Popular Fiction* London: Routledge.

Nørgaard, N. (2010a) 'Multimodality: extending the stylistic toolkit'. In McIntyre, D. and B. Busse (eds.) *Language and Style* Basingstoke: Palgrave Macmillan, 433–48.

Nørgaard, N. (2010b) 'Multimodality and the literary text: Making sense of Safran Foer's *Extremely Loud and Incredibly Close*'. In Page, R. (ed) *New Perspectives on Narrative and Multimodality* Abingdon: Routledge, 115–26.

Nørgaard, N., Busse, B. and Montoro, R. (2010) *Key Terms in Stylistics* London: Bloomsbury Continuum.

O'Halloran, K. (2007) 'The subconscious in James Joyce's "Eveline": A corpus stylistic analysis that chews on the "Fish hook"'. *Language and Literature* 16, 3, 227–44.

Oatley, K. (2003) Writingandreading: The future of cognitive poetics'. In Steen, G. and Gavins, J. (eds) *Cognitive Poetics in Practice* London: Routledge, 161–73.

Ortony, A. (ed) (1979) *Metaphor and Thought* Cambridge: Cambridge University Press.

Page, R. (2010) *New Perspectives on Narrative and Multimodality* Abingdon: Routledge.

Piazza, R., Bednarek, M. and Rossi, F. (eds.) (2011) *Telecinematic Discourse: Approaches to the Language of Films and Television Series* Amsterdam: John Benjamins.

Pope, R. (1995) *Textual Intervention* London: Routledge.

Pratt, M. L. (1977) *Toward a Speech Act Theory of Literary Discourse* Bloomington, Indiana: Indiana University Press.

Pratt, M. L. (1993) '"Yo soy la Malinche": Chicana writers and the poetics of ethno-nationalism'. In Verdonk, P. (ed) *Twentieth Century Poetry: From Text to Context* London: Routledge, 171–87.

Prince, G. (1988) 'The Disnarrated', *Style* 22: 1–8.

Prince, G. (2005) 'The disnarrated'. In Herman, D., Jahn, M. and Ryan, M-L. (eds) *The Routledge Encyclopedia of Narrative Theory* New York: Routledge, 118.

Propp, V. (1966) [1928] *The Morphology of the Folktale* Austin: University of Texas Press.

Rayson, P. (2008) *Wmatrix: A Web-based Corpus Processing Environment* Lancaster University. Available online at: www.comp.lancs.ac.uk/ucrel/wmatrix/ (last accessed 12 December 2010).

Reinhart, T. and Reuland, E. (1993) 'Reflexivity', *Linguistic Inquiry* 24, 4, 657–720.

Rich, A. (1977) *Of Woman Born: Motherhood as Experience and Institution* London: Virago.

Richardson, K. (2010) *Television Dramatic Dialogue: A Sociolinguistic Study* Oxford: Oxford University Press.

Rimmon-Kenan, S. (1983) *Narrative Fiction: Contemporary Poetics* London: Methuen.

Rowbotham, S. (1973a) *Woman's Consciousness: Man's World* Harmondsworth: Penguin.

Rowbotham, S. (1973b) *Hidden from History* London: Pluto Press.

Ryan, M-L. (1991) *Possible Worlds, Artificial Intelligence, and Narrative Theory* Bloomington and Indianapolis: Indiana University Press.

Ryle, G. (1949) *The Concept of Mind* London: Hutchinson.

Sanders, J. and Redeker, G. (1996) 'Perspective and the representation of speech and thought in narrative discourse'. In Fauconnier, G. and Sweetser, E. (eds) *Spaces, Worlds, and Grammars* Chicago, IL: Chicago University Press, 290–317.

Sanford, A. J. and Emmott, C. (2012) *Mind, Brain and Narrative* Cambridge: Cambridge University Press.

Sapir, E. (1956) *Culture, Language and Personality* Berkeley, California: University of California Press.

Sasaki, T. (1994) 'Towards a systematic description of narrative "point of view": an examination of Chatman's theory with an analysis of "The Blind Man" by D. H. Lawrence', *Language and Literature* 3, 2, 125–38.

Schank, R. C. and Abelson, R. P. (1977) *Scripts, Plans, Goals and Understanding* Hillsdale, NJ: Lawrence Erlbaum Associates.

Scott, M. (1999) *WordSmith Tools* Oxford: Oxford University Press.

Searle, J. R. (1969) *Speech Acts: An Essay in the Philosophy of Language* Cambridge: Cambridge University Press.

Semino, E. (1997) *Language and World Creation in Poems and other Texts* Harlow: Longman.

Semino, E. (2001) 'On readings, literariness and schema theory: a reply to Jeffries', *Language and Literature* 10, 4, 345–55.

Semino, E. (2002) 'A cognitive stylistic approach to mind style in narrative fiction'. In Semino, E. and Culpeper, J. (eds) *Cognitive Stylistics: Language and Cognition in Text Analysis* Amsterdam: John Benjamins, 95–122

Semino, E. (2007) 'Mind style twenty-five years on', *Style* 41, 2, 1–26.

Semino, E. (2008) *Metaphor in Discourse* Cambridge: Cambridge University Press.

Semino, E. and Culpeper, J. (eds) (2002) *Cognitive Stylistics* Amsterdam: John Benjamins.

Semino, E. and Short, M. (2004) *Corpus Stylistics: Speech, Writing and Thought Presentation in a Corpus of English Writing* London: Routledge.

Semino, E., Short, M. and Culpeper, J. (1997) 'Using a corpus to test a model of speech and thought presentation', *Poetics* 25, 17–43.

Shen, D. (1988) 'Stylistics, objectivity and convention', *Poetics* 17, 3, 221–38.

Shen, D. (forthcoming) *Style and Rhetoric of Short Narrative Fiction: Covert Progressions Behind Overt Plots* Abingdon: Routledge.

shire3.org (n.d.) Cheshire 3 Information Framework. Available at: http://cheshire3.org (accessed 31 December 2011).

Shloss, C. (1980) *Flannery O'Connor's Dark Comedies: The Limits of Inference* Baton Rouge: Louisiana State University Press.

Short, M. (1981) 'Discourse Analysis and the Analysis of Drama', *Applied Linguistics* 11, 2, 180–202.

Short, M. (1989) 'Discourse analysis and the analysis of drama'. In Carter, R. and Simpson, P. (eds) (1989) *Language, Discourse and Literature: An Introductory Reader in Discourse Stylistics* London: Unwin Hyman, 138–68.

Short, M. (1996) *Exploring the Language of Poems, Plays and Prose* Harlow: Longman.

Short, M. (1998) 'From Dramatic Text to Dramatic Performance'. In Culpeper, J., Short, M. and Verdonk, P. (eds) *Exploring the Language of Drama: From Text to Context* London: Routledge, 6–18.

Short, M., Semino, E. and Wynne, M. (1997) 'A (free direct) reply to Paul Simpson's discourse', *Journal of Literary Semantics* 26, 3, 219–28.

Showalter, E. (1977) *A Literature of Their Own: British Women Novelists from Brontë to Lessing* Princeton, NJ: Princeton University Press.

Simpson, P. (1989) 'Politeness phenomena in Ionesco's *The Lesson*'. In Carter, R. and Simpson, P. (eds) (1989) *Language, Discourse and Literature: An Introductory Reader in Discourse Stylistics* London: Unwin Hyman, 170–93.

Simpson, P. (1992a) 'Teaching stylistics: analysing cohesion and narrative structure in a short story by Ernest Hemingway', *Language and Literature* 1, 1, 47–67.

Simpson, P. (1992b) 'The pragmatics of nonsense: towards a stylistics of *Private Eye's* "Colemanballs"'. In Toolan, M. (ed.) *Language, Text and Context* London: Routledge, 281–305.

Simpson, P. (1993) *Language, Ideology and Point of View* London: Routledge.

Simpson, P. (1997a) *Language through Literature* London: Routledge.

Simpson, P. (1997b) 'A quadrant model for the study of speech and thought presentation', *Journal of Literary Semantics* 26, 3, 211–18.

Simpson, P. (1998) 'Odd talk: studying discourses of incongruity'. In Culpeper, J., Short, M. and Verdonk, P. (eds) (1998) *Exploring the Language of Drama: From Text to Context* London: Routledge, 34–53.

Simpson, P. (1999) 'Language, culture and identity: with (another) look at accents in pop and rock singing', *Multilingua* 18, 4, 343–65.

Simpson, P. (2000) 'Satirical humour and cultural context: with a note on the curious case of Father Todd Unctuous'. In Bex, A., Burke, M. and Stockwell, P. (eds) (2000) *Contextualized Stylistics* Amsterdam/Atlanta, GA: Rodopi, 243–66.

Simpson, P. (2003) *On the Discourse of Satire: Towards a Stylistic Model of Satirical Humour* Amsterdam: John Benjamins.

Simpson, P. (2010) 'Point of view'. In McIntyre, D. and Busse, B. (eds) *Language and Style* Basingstoke: Palgrave Macmillan, 293–310.

Simpson, P. (2011) '"That's not ironic, that's just stupid!": Towards an eclectic account of the discourse of irony'. In Dynel, M. (ed) *The Pragmatics of Humour across Discourse Domains* Amsterdam: John Benjamins, 33–50.

Simpson, P. (2012) 'Twenty years of *Language and Literature*: A reflection'. *Language and Literature* 21, 1, 12–17.

Simpson, P. and Canning, P. (2014) 'Action and Event'. In Stockwell, P. and Whiteley, S. (eds) *The Cambridge Handbook of Stylistics* Cambridge: Cambridge University Press, 281–99.

Simpson, P. and Hall, G. (2002) 'Discourse analysis and stylistics', *Annual Review of Applied Linguistics* 22, New York: Cambridge University Press, 136–49.

Simpson, P. and Montgomery, M. (1995) 'Language, literature and film: the stylistics of Bernard MacLaverty's *Cal*'. In Verdonk, P. and Weber, J. J. (eds) *Twentieth Century Fiction: From Text to Context* London: Routledge, 138–64.

Sinclair, J. (1991) *Corpus, Concordance, Collocation* Oxford: Oxford University Press.

Sinclair, J. (1996) 'The search for units of meaning', *Textus* IX, 75–106.

Smith, A. (1976) *The Theory of Moral Sentiments* (eds. Raphael, D. D and Macfie, A. L.) Oxford: Clarendon Press [original 1759 and 1790].

Sotirova, V. (2013) *Consciousness in Modernist Fiction* London: Palgrave.

Sotirova, V. (ed) (forthcoming) *The Companion to Stylistics* London: Continuum.

Steen, G. (1994) *Understanding Metaphor in Literature* Harlow: Longman.

Steen, G. (1999a) 'From linguistic to conceptual metaphor in five steps'. In Gibbs, R. W. jr. and Steen, G. (eds) (1999) *Metaphor in Cognitive Linguistics* Amsterdam: John Benjamins, 57–78.

Steen, G. (1999b) 'Genres of discourse and the definition of literature', *Discourse Processes* 28, 2, 109–20.

Steen, G. (2002a) 'Metaphor in Bob Dylan's "Hurricane": Genre, language, and style', In Semino, E. and Culpeper, J. (eds) (2002) *Cognitive Stylistics* Amsterdam: John Benjamins, 183–210.

Steen, G. (2002b) 'Towards a procedure for metaphor identification', *Language and Literature: Special Issue on Metaphor Identification* 11, 1, 17–33.

Steen, G. (2005) 'Metaphor'. In Herman, D., Jahn, M. and Ryan, M-L. (eds) *The Routledge Encyclopedia of Narrative Theory* New York: Routledge, 305–7.

Steen, G. and Gavins, J. (2003) 'Contextualising cognitive poetics'. In Gavins, J. and Steen, G. (eds) (2003) *Cognitive Poetics in Practice* London: Routledge, 1–12.

Stockwell, P. (1994) 'How to create universes with words: Referentiality and science fictionality', *Journal of Literary Semantics* 23, 3, 159–87.

Stockwell, P. (1996) 'New wor(l)ds', *UCE Papers in Language and Literature – Special Issue: Science Fiction* 3, 1–18.

Stockwell, P. (2000) *The Poetics of Science Fiction* Harlow: Longman.

Stockwell, P. (2002) *Cognitive Poetics* London: Routledge.

Stockwell, P. (2003) 'Schema poetics and speculative cosmology', *Language and Literature* 12, 3, 252–71.

Stockwell, P. (2009) *Texture* Edinburgh: Edinburgh University Press.

Stockwell, P. and Whiteley, S. (eds) (2014) *The Cambridge Handbook of Stylistics*, Cambridge: Cambridge University Press.

Stubbs, M. (1996) *Text and Corpus Analysis* Oxford: Blackwell.

Stubbs, M. (2001) *Words and Phrases: Corpus Studies of Lexical Semantics* Oxford: Blackwell.

Stubbs, M. (2005) 'Conrad in the computer: examples of quantitative stylistic methods', *Language and Literature* 16, 3, 227–44.

Sweetser, E. (1996) 'Mental spaces and the grammar of conditional constructions'. In Fauconnier, G. and Sweetser, E. *Spaces, Worlds, and Grammar* Chicago: University of Chicago Press, 318–33.

Tambling, J. (1988) *What is Literary Language?* Bucks: Open University Press.

Tan, E. S-H. (1994) 'Film-induced affect as a witness emotion', *Poetics* 23, 7–32.

Tan, P. (1998) 'Advice on doing your stylistics essay on a dramatic text: an example from Alan Ayckbourn's *The Revengers' Comedies*'. In Culpeper, J., Short, M. and Verdonk, P. (eds) *Exploring the Language of Drama: From Text to Context* London: Routledge, 161–71.

Taylor, J. R. (1989) *Linguistic Categorization: Prototypes in Linguistic Theory* Oxford: Clarendon Press.

Thompson, G. (1996) *Introducing Functional Grammar* London: Edward Arnold.

Thorne, J. P. (1965) 'Stylistics and generative grammars', *Journal of Linguistics* 1, 49–59.

Toolan, M. (1990) *The Stylistics of Fiction: A Literary-linguistic Approach* London: Routledge.

Toolan, M. (1992) 'The significations of representing dialect in writing', *Language and Literature* 1, 1, 29–46.

Toolan, M. (1998) *Language in Literature* London: Edward Arnold.

Toolan, M. (2000) 'Quasi-transcriptional speech: A compensatory spokenness in Anglo-Irish literary fiction'. In Bex, A., Burke, M. and Stockwell, P. (eds) *Contextualized Stylistics* Amsterdam/Atlanta, GA: Rodopi, 153–72.

Toolan, M. (2001) [1988] *Narrative: A Critical Linguistic Introduction* 2nd edition. London: Routledge.

Toolan, M. (2009) *Narrative Progression in the Short Story: A Corpus Stylistic Approach* Amsterdam: John Benjamins.

Traugott, E. C. and Pratt, M. L. (1980) *Linguistics for Students of Literature* New York: Harcourt Brace Jovanovich.

Trudgill, P. (1983) 'Acts of conflicting identity: the sociolinguistics of British pop- song pronunciation'. In Trudgill, P. *On Dialect* Oxford: Blackwell, 141–60.

Tsen, M. (1997) 'Symbolic discourse: mystical writing as anti-language', *Language and Literature* 6, 3, 181–95.

Turner, M. (1990) 'Aspects of the Invariance Hypothesis', *Cognitive Linguistics* 1, 2, 247–55.

Uspensky, B. (1973) *A Poetics of Composition* (trans. V. Zavarin and S. Wittig) Berkeley: University of California Press.

van Leeuwen, T. (1999) *Speech, Music, Sound* London: Palgrave Macmillan.

van Peer, W. (1986) *Stylistics and Psychology: Investigations of Foregrounding* London: Croom Helm.

van Peer, W. (1987) 'Top-down and bottom-up: interpretative strategies in reading e e cummings', *New Literary History* 18, 3, 597–609.

van Peer, W. (1991) 'But what is literature? Towards a descriptive definition of literature'. In Sell, R. (ed) *Literary Pragmatics* London: Routledge, 127–41.

van Peer, W. (1993) 'Typographic foregrounding', *Language and Literature* 2, 1, 49–61.

Verdonk, P. (ed) (1993a) *Twentieth Century Poetry: From Text to Context* London: Routledge.

Verdonk, P. (1993b) 'Poetry and public life: A contextualised reading of Seamus Heaney's "Punishment"'. In Verdonk 1993a, 112–33.

Verdonk, P. (2002) *Stylistics* Oxford: Oxford University Press.

Volosinov, V. M. (1973) [1930] *Marxism and the Philosophy of Language* (trans. L. Matejka and I. R. Titunik) New York: Seminar Press.

Wales, K. (1992) *The Language of James Joyce* Basingstoke: Macmillan.

Wales, K. (1993a) 'On the stylistics of Jean-Jacques Lecercle', *The European English Messenger* 2, 2, 30–1.

Wales, K. (1993b) 'Teach yourself rhetoric: an analysis of Philip Larkin's "Church Going"'. In Verdonk, P. (2002) *Stylistics* Oxford: Oxford University Press, 87–99.

Wales, K. (2011) *A Dictionary of Stylistics* 3rd edition. London: Longman.

Walker, B. (2010) 'Wmatrix, key concepts and the narrators in Julian Barnes's *Talking it Over*'. In McIntyre, D. and Busse, B. (eds) *Language and Style* Basingstoke: Palgrave Macmillan, 364–87.

Wareing, S. (1990) 'Women in fiction: stylistic modes of reclamation', *Parlance* 2, 2, 72–85.

Wareing, S. (1994) '"And then he kissed her": the reclamation of female characters to submissive roles in contemporary fiction'. In Wales, K. (ed.) *Feminist Linguistics in Literary Criticism* Woodbridge: Boydell and Brewer, 117–36.

Watson, G. (2006) 'The bedroom blues: love and lust in the lyrics of early female blues artists', *Language and Literature* 15, 4, 331–56.

Watson, G. and Zyngier, S. (eds) (2007) *Literature and Stylistics for Language Learners: Theory and Practice* Basingstoke: Palgrave Macmillan.

Weber, J. J. (ed.) (1996) *The Stylistics Reader* London: Edward Arnold.

Wellek, R. and Warren, A. (1949) *Theory of Literature* New York: Harcourt Brace.

Werth, P. (1999) *Text Worlds: Representing Conceptual Space in Discourse* London: Longman.

Whiteley, S. (2011) 'Text World Theory, real readers and emotional responses to *The Remains of the Day*', *Language and Literature* 20, 1, 23–42.

Whorf, B. L. (1956) *Language, Thought and Reality* (ed. J. B. Carroll) Cambridge, MA: MIT Press.

Widdowson, H. G. (1975) *Stylistics and the Teaching of Literature* Harlow: Longman.

Wilson, P. (2000) *Mind the Gap: Ellipsis and Stylistic Variation in Spoken and Written English* London: Pearson.

Winn, M. B. and Idsardi, W. J. (2008) 'Musical evidence regarding trochaic inversion', *Language and Literature* 17, 4, 335–49.

Young, D. (1984) *Introducing English Grammar* London: Routledge.

Zyngier, S., Bortolussi, M., Chesnokova, A. and Auracher, J. (eds) (2008) *Directions in Empirical Literary Studies* Amsterdam: John Benjamins.

Zillmann, D. (1994) 'Mechanisms of emotional involvement with drama', *Poetics* 23, 33–51.

PRIMARY SOURCES

This bibliography lists the primary sources for the texts used in the four sections of the book. Sources for shorter citations and illustrations of a line or two have not been included. Original dates of publication are given, where relevant, in square brackets.

Atwood, Margaret (1996) *Power Politics* Toronto: House of Anansi.

Banks, Iain (1993) *The Crow Road* London: Abacus.

Berkoff, Steven (1983) *Greek*. In *Decadence and Greek* London: Calder.

Conrad, Joseph (1995) [1912] *The Secret Sharer* Harmondsworth: Penguin.

cummings, e e (1954) [1939] 'love is more thicker', *Poems, 1923–1954* New York: Harcourt Brace Jovanovich Inc.

Dickens, Charles (1986) [1853] *Bleak House* Harmondsworth: Penguin.

Dickinson, Emily (1963) [1890] *The Poems of Emily Dickinson* (ed. T. H. Johnson) Cambridge, MA: The Belknap Press of Harvard University Press.

Doyle, Roddy (1998) *The Woman who Walked into Doors* London: Vintage.

Eliot, T.S. (1963) [various] *Collected Poems* London: Faber and Faber.

Faulkner, William (1980) [1931] *The Sound and the Fury* Harmondsworth: Penguin.

Fielding, Henry (1970) [1749] *Tom Jones* London: Pan Books Ltd.

Fitzgerald, F. Scott (1994) [1925] *The Great Gatsby* Harmondsworth: Penguin.

Fitzgerald, F. Scott (1986) [1934] *Tender is the Night* Harmondsworth: Penguin.

Hemingway, Ernest (1925) *In Our Time* New York: Charles Schribner's Sons.

Hemingway, Ernest (1960) [1952] *The Old Man and the Sea* London: Triad/Panther Books.

Hopkins, G. M. (1995) [1877] *God's Grandeur and other Poems* New York: Dover Thrift Editions

Ionesco, Eugene (1963) [1958] *The Bald Prima Donna*. In *Plays Volume 1* [Translated by Donald Watson] London: Calder.

Ionesco, Eugene (1964) 'My critics and I'. In *Notes and Counternotes* [Translated by Donald Watson] London: Calder.

James, Henry (2001) [1903] *The Ambassadors* Harmondsworth: Penguin.

Jerome, Jerome K. (1986) [1889] *Three Men in a Boat* London: Dent.

Joyce, James (1980) [1922] *Ulysses* Harmondsworth: Penguin.

Kafka, Franz (1985) [1925] *The Trial* Harmondsworth: Penguin.

Kelman, James (1998) *How Late it Was, How Late* London: Vintage Books.

Longley, Michael (1995) 'The Ghost Orchid'. In *The Ghost Orchid* London: Jonathan Cape.

Longley, Michael (2000) 'The Comber'. In *The Weather in Japan* London: Jonathan Cape.

Lowry, Malcolm (1984) [1947] *Under the Volcano* Harmondsworth: Penguin.

MacLaverty, Bernard (1984) *Cal* Harmondsworth: Penguin.

McEwan, Ian (1998) *Amsterdam* London: Vintage Books.

McEwan, Ian (2001) *Atonement* London: Vintage Books.

McGough, Roger (1971) '40-Love'. In *After the Mersey Sound* Harmondsworth: Penguin.

McKellen, I. and Loncraine, R. (1996) *William Shakespeare's King Richard III* London: Doubleday.

Monty Python's Flying Circus (1971) BBC Television/Kettledrum Lownes Productions Ltd.

Mitchell, David (2004) *Cloud Atlas* London: Sceptre Books.

Morgan, Edwin (1966) 'Off Course'. In *Poems of Thirty Years* London: Carcanet Press Ltd.

Morrison, Toni (1987) *Beloved* London: Vintage Books.

Nabokov, Vladimir (1986) [1955] *Lolita* Harmondsworth: Penguin.

O'Connor, Flannery (1969) *Mystery and Manners: Occasional Prose*, ed. S. Fitzgerald and R. Fitzgerald. New York: Farrar, Straus, and Giroux.

O'Connor, Flannery (1988) *Collected Works* New York: The Library of America.

Parker, Dorothy (1956) [1926] 'One Perfect Rose'. From *The Portable Dorothy Parker* New York: Penguin Books USA.

Pinter, Harold (1960) *The Dumb Waiter* London: Faber and Faber.

Plath, Sylvia (1986) [1963] *The Bell Jar* London: Faber and Faber.

Poe, Edgar Allan (1986) [1839] 'The Fall of the House of Usher'. In *The Fall of the House of Usher and other Writings* (ed. D. Galloway) Harmondsworth: Penguin.

Pound, Ezra (1969) [1912] 'In a station of the metro'. In *A Map of Modern English Verse* (ed. J. Press) Oxford: Oxford University Press.

Raban, Jonathan (1990) *Hunting Mister Heartbreak* New York: HarperCollins.

Raban, Jonathan (1998) *Old Glory* New York: Vintage Books.

Raban, Jonathan (2003) [1987] *Coasting* London: Simon & Schuster Adult Publishing Group.

Raine, Craig (2000) [1979] 'An Enquiry into Two Inches of Ivory', *Collected Poems 1978–1998* London: Picador.

Simpson, N. F. (1960) *One Way Pendulum* London: Faber and Faber.

Steinbeck, John (2000) [1945] *Cannery Row* Harmondsworth: Penguin Modern Classics.

Sterne, Laurence (2010) [1749] *The Life and Opinions of Tristram Shandy* London: Harper Collins.

Stoker, Bram (1998) [1897] *Dracula* Oxford: Oxford University Press.

Welsh, Irvine (1993) *Trainspotting* London: Minerva.

Welsh, Irvine (1995) *Marabou Stork Nightmares* London: Minerva.

Winterson, Jeanette (1993) *Written on the Body* London: Vintage Books.

Woolf, Virginia (1998) [1928] *Orlando* Oxford: Oxford University Press

Wolfe, Tom (2004) *I am Charlotte Simmons* London: Vintage Books.

GLOSSARIAL INDEX

Where the page reference for a keyword is highlighted in **bold**, this indicates that a definition is provided or that the term is used in a context which makes its meaning clear. Other page references for keywords are to significant places in the book where the term or concept is used.